1

Written by:
Regina Bradley, Barret Hendricks

Edited by:
Emily Ramsower, Laura Lundberg

Cover Design:
Peter Licalzi

Printed in the United States of America

Table of Contents

Introduction

Congratulations on your excellent decision to join the United States military! The choice to dedicate yourself to serving your country is admirable, and we want to help you do your absolute best. So what is your first step?
– Getting your AFQT score.

Reviewing the material isn't always enough – we want you to be able to face your examination with complete confidence, and that includes knowing what to expect from the test itself. In this introduction, we'll give you a detailed overview of the exam and how it works, while answering any questions you may have about what the AFQT score and ASVAB test are. We'll also provide some tips as to what you will need to do to prepare for this testing process.

What is the ASVAB?
The ASVAB stands for Armed Services Vocational Aptitude Battery. It is the test you will take to determine if you are eligible to enter the military.

Then what's the AFQT? Are They The Same?
The score you are given is called your AFQT score (Armed Forces Qualification Test). The acronyms can get rather confusing, but in short: you take the ASVAB and get an AFQT score. The AFQT is not a separate exam, just the name of the score you earn.

Breaking Down the ASVAB Test
The ASVAB has nine sections – but only the first four are used to calculate your AFQT score. The other sections are used as indicators of any extra skills you might have that would make you a strong candidate for certain specialized positions; but don't worry. They don't have any bearing on whether or not you are qualified to enlist.

The Nine Sections of the ASVAB:
General Science (GS)
Auto and Shop Information (AS)
Electrical Information (EI)
Mechanical Comprehension (MC)
Assembling Objects (AO)
Word Knowledge (WK)
Paragraph Comprehension (PC)
Arithmetic Reasoning (AR)
Mathematics Knowledge (MK)

The Four Sections that Make Up Your AFQT Score:
Word Knowledge (WK)
Paragraph Comprehension (PC)
Arithmetic Reasoning (AR)
Mathematics Knowledge (MK)

AFQT scores range from 0 – 99, but that score does not represent how many questions you got right or wrong. Instead, it is a percentile score of how well you did compared to a group of standardized ASVAB test takers. So, for example, a score of 60 means that you scored higher than 60% of that standardized group, but 40% of them did better than you. All potential enlisted personnel are tested against each other, regardless of which branch you want to enter.

The U.S. Congress has a legal minimum score of 9 to qualify for the military. If you don't make at least a 9, then you cannot legally enter. However, beyond that bare minimum requirement, each branch has its own minimum standards. These are:

> AIR FORCE: 50
> US ARMY: 31
> MARINE CORP: 32
> NAVY: 50
> COAST GUARD: 36

Let's use an example:

> You score a 34. While you would be eligible for the Army and Marines, you would not be able to enlist to the Navy; Air Force; or Coast Guard.

Keep in mind that these values do change from time to time – so it's a good idea to check with your recruiter what scores are required in your desired branch.

So why does the military care about your math, arithmetic, word, and paragraph skills? Once in the military, you won't necessarily need to solve math equations or demonstrate perfect paragraph comprehension (although these skills are certainly useful!).

Instead, a high AFQT score shows the military that you learned and remembered skills taught to you in high school. Their thought is: if you were teachable in high school, then you will be teachable in the military. The military has a lot to teach you, so they want to make sure you are up to the challenge beforehand. That way you aren't wasting your time, and they're not wasting their time.

Getting to Know the ASVAB – Format
The ASVAB is officially called the ASVAB-CAT (though when people refer to it, they just call it "ASVAB" for short). "CAT" means Computer Adaptive Test.

The ASVAB used to be administered as a paper-and-pencil exam, but, like many things, it has become computer based. Some people believe that the new computer-based test is the same as the old pencil-and-paper version, but that isn't true!

On the old test, there were no points taken away for wrong answers, so test-takers were encouraged to guess blindly if they didn't know an answer. The new test is called the ASVAB-CAT – and the word "Adaptive" in "CAT" means that the test is customized for each person as they take the exam.

Getting to Know the ASVAB – Adaptive Tests
On the ASVAB-CAT, everyone starts off with a question of medium-level difficulty. If you get it right, then your next question will be harder. It will also be worth more points.

If, however, you get questions wrong, you will be given easier questions. That may sound nice, but the easier questions are worth fewer points.

Here is a breakdown of how this works:

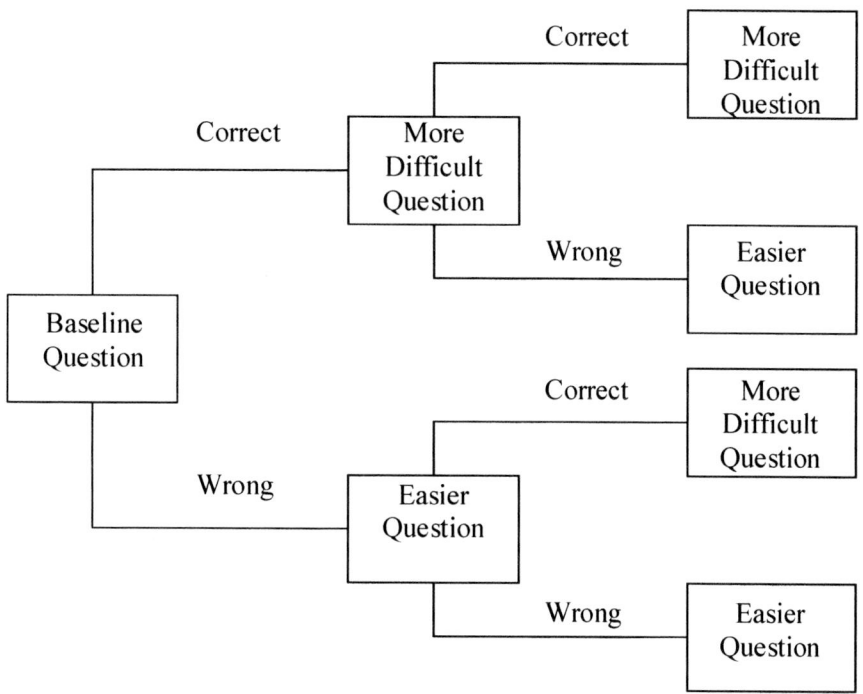

This process helps test officials score everyone more quickly and accurately – if someone misses a lot of easy questions, then they are less likely to qualify for the military.

Because of this new system, there is one HUGE difference between the ASVAB-CAT and the old test: never, ever guess! You run the risk of getting the answer incorrect, which will decrease your chances of getting more point-worthy questions.

Of course, there will be times when a question might be too difficult, and you just don't know the answer. What then? You should also know that you cannot skip questions on the ASVAB test. That doesn't mean you're stuck! If you can't figure out the answer to that question, then you need to guess.

However, this should be an *educated* guess – don't just wildly pick an answer at random. Instead, you need to do your best to narrow down your answer choices. Try to eliminate at least one or two choices; that will increase your odds of guessing correctly.

Obviously, you want to do your best on the ASVAB so that you can get a high AFQT score. Using this book is a great way to get started. It doesn't matter if you barely passed high school, or got poor grades; it doesn't matter if you feel like it's been too long since you've learned the material. This book will help you prepare. By studying efficiently for the ASVAB, you can receive a qualifying AFQT score.

Getting a good AFQT score isn't easy for everyone, but if you put your determination, dedication, and hard work into overcoming the challenges of studying, you will see amazing results.

Again, congratulations on your decision to join the military. We wish you the best in your new career, starting with a great AFQT score!

Chapter 1: General Science

The ASVAB General Science test measures your knowledge of the life sciences (plant and animal biology, human physiology), the earth and space sciences (geology, meteorology, oceanography, astronomy), and the physical sciences (physics and chemistry). You'll be asked 16 questions with an 8-minute time limit. Don't panic! You only need to know those basics learned through the 11th grade. Of course, you aren't going to be able to cover eleven years of schooling in one book – but this chapter will refresh your memory on those fundamental principles of science required, ensuring that you do well. Here's a breakdown of this chapter:

General Biology

This section covers the basics of biology, from the building blocks of life, to the fundamentals of biological chemistry and the classification of organisms.

BASICS OF LIFE

We began learning the difference between living (**animate**) beings and nonliving (**inanimate**) objects from an early age. Living organisms and inanimate objects are all composed of **atoms** from elements. Those atoms are arranged into groups called **molecules**, which serve as the building blocks of everything in existence (as we know it). Molecular interactions are what determine whether something is classified as animate or inanimate. The following is a list of the most commonly-found elements found in the molecules of animate beings:

1. Oxygen
2. Chlorine
3. Carbon
4. Nitrogen
5. Sodium
6. Calcium
7. Magnesium
8. Phosphorous
9. Iodine
10. Iron
11. Sulfur
12. Hydrogen
13. Potassium

Another way to describe living and nonliving things is through the terms **organic** and **inorganic.**

- **Organic molecules** are from living organisms. Organic molecules contain **carbon-hydrogen bonds.**

- **Inorganic molecules** come from non-living resources. They do not contain carbon-hydrogen bonds.

There are four major classes of organic molecules:

1. **Carbohydrates.**
2. **Lipids.**
3. **Proteins.**
4. **Nucleic acids**.

Carbohydrates consist of only hydrogen, oxygen, and carbon atoms. They are the most abundant single class of organic substances found in nature. Carbohydrate molecules provide many basic necessities such as: fiber, vitamins, and minerals; structural components for organisms, especially plants; and, perhaps most importantly, energy. Our bodies break down carbohydrates to make **glucose**: a sugar used to produce that energy which our bodies need in order to operate. Brain cells are exclusively dependent upon a constant source of glucose molecules.

There are two kinds of carbohydrates: simple and complex. **Simple carbohydrates** can be absorbed directly through the cell, and therefore enter the blood stream very quickly. We consume simple carbohydrates in dairy products, fruits, and other sugary foods.

Complex carbohydrates consist of a chain of simple sugars which, over time, our bodies break down into simple sugars (which are also referred to as stored energy.) **Glycogen** is the storage form of glucose in human and animal cells. Complex carbohydrates come from starches like cereal, bread, beans, potatoes, and starchy vegetables.

Lipids, commonly known as fats, are molecules with two functions:

1. They are stored as an energy reserve.

2. They provide a protective cushion for vital organs.

In addition to those two functions, lipids also combine with other molecules to form essential compounds, such as **phospholipids,** which form the membranes around cells. Lipids also combine with other molecules to create naturally-occurring **steroid** hormones, like the hormones estrogen and testosterone.

Proteins are large molecules which our bodies' cells need in order to function properly. Consisting of **amino acids,** proteins aid in maintaining and creating many aspects of our cells: cellular structure, function, and regulation, to name a few. Proteins also work as neurotransmitters and carriers of oxygen in the blood (hemoglobin).

Without protein, our tissues and organs could not exist. Our muscles bones, skin, and many other parts of the body contain significant amounts of protein. **Enzymes**, hormones, and antibodies are proteins.

Enzymes
When heat is applied, chemical reactions are typically sped up. However, the amount of heat required to speed up reactions could be potentially harmful (even fatal) to living organisms. Instead, our bodies use molecules called enzymes to bring reactants closer together, causing them to form a new compound. Thus, the whole reaction rate is increased without heat. Even better – the enzymes are not consumed during the reaction process, and can therefore be used reused. This makes them an important biochemical part of both photosynthesis and respiration.

Nucleic acids are large molecules made up of smaller molecules called **nucleotides. DNA** (deoxyribonucleic acid) transports and transmits genetic information. As you can tell from the name, DNA is a nucleic acid. Since nucleotides make up nucleic acids, they are considered the basis of reproduction and progression.

Practice Drill: Basics of Life

Let's test your knowledge over what you've learned so far!

1. Life depends upon:
    a) The bond energy in molecules.
    b) The energy of protons.
    c) The energy of electrons.
    d) The energy of neutrons.

2. Which of the following elements is **NOT** found in carbohydrates?
    a) Carbon.
    b) Hydrogen.
    c) Oxygen.
    d) Sulfur.

3. Which of the following is a carbohydrate molecule?
    a) Amino acid.
    b) Glycogen.
    c) Sugar.
    d) Lipid.

4. Lipids are commonly known as:
    a) Fat.
    b) Sugar.
    c) Enzymes.
    d) Protein.

5. Proteins are composed of:
    a) Nucleic acids.
    b) Amino acids.
    c) Hormones.
    d) Lipids.

Practice Drill: Basics of Life – Answers

1. **a)**
2. **d)**
3. **c)**
4. **a)**
5. **b)**

CELLULAR RESPIRATION

As you can imagine, there are a great deal of processes which require energy: breathing, blood circulation, body temperature control, muscle usage, digestion, brain and nerve functioning are all only a few examples. You can refer to all of the body's physical and chemical processes which convert or use energy as **metabolism**.

All living things in the world, including plants, require energy in order to maintain their metabolisms. Initially, that energy is consumed through food. That energy is processed in plants and animals through **photosynthesis** (for plants) and **respiration** (for animals). **Cellular respiration** produces the actual energy molecules known as **ATP** (Adenosine Tri-Phosphate) molecules.

Plants use ATP during **photosynthesis** for producing glucose, which is then broken down during cellular respiration. This cycle continuously repeats itself throughout the life of the plant.

Photosynthesis: Plants, as well as some Protists and Monerans, can use light energy to bind together small molecules from the environment. These newly-bound molecules are then used as fuel to make more energy. This process is called photosynthesis, and one of its byproducts is none other than oxygen. Most organisms, including plants, require oxygen to fuel the biochemical reactions of metabolism.

You can see in the following equation that plants use the energy taken from light to turn carbon dioxide and water – the small molecules from their environment – into glucose and oxygen.

The photosynthesis equation:

$$CO_2 + H_2O \xrightarrow{\text{Light}} C_6H_{12}O_6 + O_2$$

| Carbon Dioxide | Water | | Glucose (sugar) | Oxygen |

Chlorophyll
In order for photosynthesis to occur, however, plants require a specific molecule to capture sunlight. This molecule is called **chlorophyll**. When chlorophyll absorbs sunlight, one of its electrons is stimulated into a higher energy state. This higher-energy electron then passes that energy onto other electrons in other molecules, creating a chain that eventually results in glucose. Chlorophyll absorbs red and blue light, but not green; green light is reflected off of plants, which is why plants appear green to us. It's important to note that chlorophyll is absolutely necessary to the photosynthesis process in plants – if it photosynthesizes, it will have chlorophyll.

The really fascinating aspect of photosynthesis is that raw sunlight energy is a very nonliving thing; however, it is still absorbed by plants to form the chemical bonds between simple inanimate compounds. This produces organic sugar, which is the chemical basis for the formation of all living compounds. Isn't it amazing? Something nonliving is essential to the creation of all living things!

Respiration
Respiration is the metabolic opposite of photosynthesis. There are two types of respiration: **aerobic** (which uses oxygen) and **anaerobic** (which occurs without the use of oxygen).

You may be confused at thinking of the word "respiration" in this way, since many people use respiration to refer to the process of breathing. However, in biology, breathing is thought of as **inspiration** (inhaling) and **expiration** (exhalation); whereas **respiration** is the metabolic, chemical reaction supporting these processes. Both plants and animals produce carbon dioxide through respiration.

Aerobic respiration is the reaction which uses enzymes to combine oxygen with organic matter (food). This yields carbon dioxide, water, and energy.

The respiration equation looks like this:

$$\overset{\textbf{Enzymes}}{C6H12O6 + 6O2 \longrightarrow 7\ 6CO2 + 6H2O + \text{Energy}.}$$

If you look back the equation for photosynthesis, you will see that respiration is almost the same equation, only it goes in the opposite direction. (Photosynthesis uses carbon dioxide and water, with the help of energy, to create oxygen and glucose. Respiration uses oxygen and glucose, with the help of enzymes, to create carbon dioxide, water, and energy.)

Anaerobic respiration is respiration that occurs WITHOUT the use of oxygen. It produces less energy than aerobic respiration produces, yielding only two molecules of ATP per glucose molecule Aerobic respiration produces 38 ATP per glucose molecule.

So, plants convert energy into matter and release oxygen gas – animals then absorb this oxygen gas in order to run their own metabolic reaction and, in the process, release carbon dioxide. That carbon dioxide is then absorbed by plants in the photosynthetic conversion of energy into matter. Everything comes full circle! This is called a **metabolic cycle.**

Practice Drill: Cellular Respiration

1. Which of the following is **NOT** true of enzymes?
   a) Enzymes are lipid molecules.
   b) Enzymes are not consumed in a biochemical reaction.
   c) Enzymes are important in photosynthesis and respiration.
   d) Enzymes speed up reactions and make them more efficient.

2. Plants appear green because chlorophyll:
   a) Absorbs green light.
   b) Reflects red light.
   c) Absorbs blue light.
   d) Reflects green light.

3. Photosynthesis is the opposite of:
   a) Enzymatic hydrolysis.
   b) Protein synthesis.
   c) Respiration.
   d) Reproduction.

4. The compound that absorbs light energy during photosynthesis is:
   a) Chloroform.
   b) Chlorofluorocarbon.
   c) Chlorinated biphenyls.
   d) Chlorophyll.

5. What is the name of the sugar molecule produced during photosynthesis?
   a) Chlorophyll
   b) Glycogen
   c) Glucose
   d) Fructose

Practice Drill: Cellular Respiration – Answers

1. **a)**
2. **d)**
3. **c)**
4. **d)**
5. **c)**

CLASSIFICATION OF ORGANISMS

All of Earth's organisms have characteristics which distinguish them from one another. Scientists have developed systems to organize and classify all of Earth's organisms based on those characteristics.

Kingdoms

Through the process of evolution, organisms on Earth have developed into many diverse forms, which have complex relationships. Scientists have organized life into five large groups called **kingdoms**. Each kingdom contains those organisms that share significant characteristics distinguishing them from organisms in other kingdoms. These five kingdoms are named as follows:

1. **Animalia**
2. **Plantae**
3. **Fungi**
4. **Protista**
5. **Monera**

Kingdom Animalia

This kingdom contains multicellular organisms multicellular, or those known as complex organisms. These organisms are generically called **heterotrophs**, which means that they must eat preexisting organic matter (either plants or other animals) in order to sustain themselves.

Those heterotrophs which eat only plants are called **herbivores** (from "herbo," meaning "herb" or "plant"); those that kill and eat other animals for food are called **carnivores** (from "carno," meaning "flesh" or "meat"); and still other animals eat both plants *and* other animals – they are called **omnivores** (from "omnis," which means "all").

Those organisms in the Animal Kingdom have nervous tissue which has developed into nervous systems and brains; they are also able to move from place to place using muscular systems. The Animal Kingdom is divided into two groups: **vertebrates** (with backbones) and **invertebrates** (without backbones).

Kingdom Plantae

As you can guess from its name, the Plant Kingdom contains all plant-based life. Plants are multicellular organisms that use chlorophyll, which is held in specialized cellular structures called **chloroplasts,** to capture sunlight energy. Remember: photosynthesis! They then convert that sunlight energy into organic matter: their food. Because of this, most plants are referred to as **autotrophs** (self-feeders). There are a few organisms included in the Plant Kingdom which are not multicellular – certain types of algae which, while not multicellular, have cells with a nucleus. These algae also contain chlorophyll.

Except for algae, most plants are divided into one of two groups: **vascular plants** (most crops, trees, and flowering plants) and **nonvascular plants** (mosses). Vascular plants have specialized tissue that allows them to transport water and nutrients from their roots, to their leaves, and back again – even when the plant is several hundred feet tall. Nonvascular plants cannot do this, and therefore remain very small in size. Vascular plants are able to grow in both wet and dry environments; whereas nonvascular plants, since they are unable to transport water, are usually found only in wet, marshy areas.

Kingdom Fungi

The Fungi Kingdom contains organisms that share some similarities with plants, but also have other characteristics that make them more animal-like. For example, they resemble animals in that they lack chlorophyll – so they can't perform photosynthesis. This means that they don't produce their own food and are therefore heterotrophs. However, they resemble plants in that they reproduce by spores; they also resemble plants in appearance. The bodies of fungi are made of filaments called **hyphae**, which in turn create the tissue **mycelium.** The most well-known examples of organisms in this Kingdom are mushrooms, yeasts, and molds. Fungi are very common and benefit other organisms, including humans.

Kingdom Protista
This kingdom includes single-celled organisms that contain a nucleus as part of their structure. They are considered a simple cell, but still contain multiple structures and accomplish many functions. This Kingdom includes organisms such as paramecium, amoeba, and slime molds. They often move around using hair-like structures called *cilia* or *flagellums.*

Kingdom Monera
This kingdom contains only bacteria. All of these organisms are single-celled and do not have a nucleus. They have only one chromosome, which is used to transfer genetic information. Sometimes they can also transmit genetic information using small structures called **plasmids.** Like organisms in the Protista Kingdom, they use flagella to move. Bacteria usually reproduce asexually.

There are more forms of bacteria than any other organism on Earth. Some bacteria are beneficial to us, like the ones found in yogurt; others can cause us to get sick such as the bacteria *E. coli.*

KINGDOM	DESCRIPTION	EXAMPLES
Animalia	Multi-celled; parasites; prey; consumers; can be herbivorous, carnivorous, or omnivorous.	Sponges, worms, insects, fish, mammals, reptiles, birds, humans.
Plantae	Multi-celled; autotrophs; mostly producers.	Ferns, angiosperms, gymnosperms, mosses.
Fungi	Can be single or multi-celled; decomposers; parasites; absorb food; asexual; consumers.	Mushrooms, mildew, molds, yeast.
Protista	Single or multi-celled; absorb food; both producers and consumers.	Plankton, algae, amoeba, protozoans.
Monera	Single-celled or a colony of single-cells; decomposers and parasites; move in water; are both producers and consumers.	Bacteria, blue-green algae.

Levels of Classification
Kingdom groupings are not very specific. They contain organisms defined by broad characteristics, and which may not seem similar at all. For example, worms belong in Kingdom Animalia – but then, so do birds. These two organisms are very different, despite sharing the necessary traits to make it into the animal kingdom. Therefore, to further distinguish different organisms, we have multiple levels of classification, which gradually become more specific until we finally reach the actual organism.

We generally start out by grouping organisms into the appropriate kingdom. Within each kingdom, we have other subdivisions: **Phylum, Class, Order, Family, Genus, and Species.** (In some cases, "Species" can be further narrowed down into "Sub-Species.")

As we move down the chain, characteristics become more specific, and the number of organisms in each group decreases. For an example, let's try to classify a grizzly bear. The chart would go as follows:

Kingdom - Insect, fish, bird, pig, dog, bear

Phylum - Fish, bird, pig, dog, bear

Class - Pig, dog, bear

Order - Dog, bear

Family - Panda, brown, grizzly

Genus -
Brown, grizzly

Species -
Grizzly

Here is an easy way to remember the order of terms used in this classification scheme:

Kings **P**lay **C**ards **O**n **F**riday, **G**enerally **S**peaking.
Kingdom, **P**hylum, **C**lass, **O**rder, **F**amily, **G**enus, **S**pecies

Binomial Nomenclature
Organisms can be positively identified by two Latin words. Therefore, the organism naming system is referred to as a binomial nomenclature ("binomial" referring to the number two, and "nomenclature" referring to a title or name). Previously-used words help illustrate where the organism fits into the whole scheme, but it is only the last two, the genus and species, that specifically name an organism. Both are written in italics. The genus is always capitalized, but the species name is written lowercase.

Grizzly bears fall underneath the genus *Ursus*, species *arctos*, and sub-species *horribilis*. Therefore, the scientific name of the grizzly bear would be *Ursus arctos horribilis*. *Canis familiaris* is the scientific name for a common dog, *Felis domesticus* is a common cat, and humans are *Homo sapiens*.

Practice Drill: Classification of Organisms

1. Which feature distinguishes those organisms in Kingdom Monera from those in other kingdoms? Organisms in Kingdom Monera:
    a) Contain specialized organelles.
    b) Contain a nucleus.
    c) Contain chloroplasts.
    d) Lack a nucleus.

2. Which of the following has the classification levels in the correct order, from most general to most specific?
    a) Kingdom, Phylum, Class, Order, Family, Genus, Species.
    b) Order, Family, Genus, Species, Class, Phylum, Kingdom.
    c) Species, Genus, Family, Order, Class, Phylum, Kingdom.
    d) Kingdom, Phylum, Class, Species, Genus, Family, Order.

3. The _____ contains organisms with both plant-and-animal-like characteristics?
    a) Animal Kingdom.
    b) Plant Kingdom.
    c) Fungi Kingdom.
    d) Monera Kingdom.

4. Which of the following statements is true about the binomial nomenclature system of classification?
    a) The genus and species names describe a specific organism.
    b) The category of kingdom is very specific.
    c) The category of species is very broad.
    d) Three names are needed to correctly specify a particular organism.

5. Which of the following kingdom's members are multicellular AND autotrophic?
    a) Fungi.
    b) Animalia.
    c) Protista.
    d) Plantae.

6. Which of the following kingdom's members have tissue called hyphae?
    a) Fungi.
    b) Animalia.
    c) Protista.
    d) Plantae.

Practice Drill: Classification of Organisms – Answers

1. **d)**
2. **a)**
3. **c)**
4. **a)**
5. **d)**
6. **a)**

MICROORGANISMS

Microorganisms (microbes) are extremely small and cannot be seen with the naked eye. They can be detected using either a microscope or through various chemical tests. These organisms are everywhere, even in such extreme environments as very hot areas, very cold areas, dry areas, and deep in the ocean under tremendous pressure. Some of these organisms cause diseases in animals, plants, and humans. However, most are helpful to us and the Earth's ecosystems. In fact, we are totally dependent upon microbes for our quality of life. There are three types of microorganisms: **bacteria, protists, and fungi.**

Bacteria

Bacteria are microorganisms that do not have a true nucleus; their genetic material simply floats around in the cell. They are very small, simple, one-celled organisms. Bacteria are normally found in three variations: **bacilli** (rod-shaped), **cocci** (sphere-shaped), and **spirilla** (spiral-shaped). Bacteria are widespread in all environments and are important participants within all ecosystems. They are **decomposers**, because they break down dead organic matter into basic molecules.

Bacteria are also an important part of the food-chain, because they are eaten by other organisms. Still, bacteria remain the most numerous organisms on Earth. This is due to the fact that they are small, can live practically anywhere, and have great metabolic flexibility. But most importantly, bacteria have the ability to rapidly reproduce. In the right environment, any bacteria can reproduce every 20 or 30 minutes, each one doubling after each reproduction.

Benefits of Bacteria: Some bacteria are found in our intestinal tracts, where they help to digest our food and make vitamins.

To demonstrate the significance of bacteria, let's look at the cycle of nitrogen, which is used by organisms to make proteins. The cycle starts with dead plants being decomposed by bacteria. The nitrogen from the plant tissue is released into the atmosphere, where nitrifying bacteria convert that nitrogen into ammonia-type compounds. Other bacteria act upon these compounds to form nitrates for plants to absorb. When these new plants die, we are brought back again to the decomposing bacteria releasing the plant's nitrogen into the atmosphere.

Bacterial Diseases: Microorganisms, including bacteria, enter our bodies in a variety of ways: through the air we breathe, ingestion by mouth, or through the skin via a cut or injury. We can eliminate much of this threat by disinfecting utensils and thoroughly washing our hands. This destroys bacteria and other microorganisms which may cause disease.

Protists

Protists are very diversified and include organisms that range greatly in size – from single cells to considerably complex structures, some longer than 100 meters. Protists have a wide variety of reproductive and nutritional strategies, and their genetic material is enclosed within a nucleus. Even though protists are more simplistic than other organisms with cellular nuclei, they are not as primitive as bacteria. Some are autotrophic and contain chlorophyll; others are heterotrophic and consume other organisms to survive. Because protists obtain food in both of these ways, it is generally believed that early protists were both animal- and plant-like. Protists are important to food chains and ecosystems, although some protists do cause disease.

Fungi

Fungi are heterotrophic and can be either single-celled or multi-celled. They play an important decomposition role in an ecosystem, because they consume dead organic matter. This returns nutrients to the soil for eventual uptake by plants.

There are three types of fungi which obtain food: saprophytic, parasitic, and mycorrhizal-associated.

Saprophytic fungi consume dead organic matter; **parasitic** fungi attack living plants and animals; and **mycorrhizal-associated** fungi form close relationships (**symbiosis**) with trees, shrubs, and other plants, where each partner in the relationship mutually benefits. An organism called **lichen** is an example of a symbiotic union between a fungus and algae.

Fungi produce **spores** (reproductive structures) that are highly resistant to extreme temperatures and moisture levels. This gives them the ability to survive for a long time, even in aggressive environments. When their environments become more favorable, the spores **germinate** (sprout) and grow. Spores are able to travel to new areas, which spreads the organism. Fungi absorb food through **hyphae**. A large mass of joined, branched hyphae is called the **mycelium**, which constitutes the main body of the multicellular fungi. However, the mycelium is not usually seen, because it is hidden throughout the food source which is being consumed. The largest organism in the world is believed to be a soil fungus whose mycelium tissue extends for many acres!

What we do usually see of a fungus is the fungal fruiting body. A mushroom is a fruiting body filled with spores. The main body of the mushroom (the **mycelium**) is under the soil surface.

Practice Drill: Microorganisms

1. Fungi are decomposers, which is important for_____.
   a) Making nutrients available for recycling back into the soil.
   b) Producing oxygen by photosynthesizing.
   c) Producing oxygen by respiration.
   d) Living in mostly aquatic environments.

2. Which is the most numerous organism on Earth?
   a) Paramecium from the Protist Kingdom.
   b) Yeast from the Fungi Kingdom.
   c) Euglena from the Protist Kingdom.
   d) Bacteria from the Moneran Kingdom.

3. Which kingdom contains organisms that are able to convert atmospheric nitrogen to nitrate?
   a) Animalia.
   b) Plantae.
   c) Monera.
   d) Protista.

4. Why are spores produced?
   a) They are part of resistance.
   b) To reproduce.
   c) To photosynthesize.
   d) They are part of the support system.

5. Members of the Kingdom Monera are found in our digestive tracts and perform which of the following functions?
   a) Produce carbohydrates.
   b) Produce vitamins.
   c) Produce lipids.
   d) Produce proteins.

Practice Drill: Microorganisms – Answers

1. a)
2. d)
3. c)
4. b)
5. b)

ANIMALS

Animals are multi-celled and unable to produce their own food internally, just like plants. As mentioned previously, the Animal Kingdom is divided into two large groupings: the **invertebrates** and **vertebrates.**

Invertebrates are multicellular, have no back bone or cell walls, reproduce sexually, and are heterotrophic. They make up approximately 97% of the animal population.

Vertebrates, on the other hand, have well-developed internal skeletons, highly developed brains, an advanced nervous system, and an outer covering of protective cellular skin. They make up the remaining 3% of the animals.

What Is an Animal?

All animals, from sponges to human beings, share some fundamental characteristics. One such characteristic is cellular division. At the beginning of reproduction, an egg is fertilized and then undergoes several cell divisions (cleavages); this process quickly produces a cluster of cells. Cell division continues through many distinct stages before finally resulting in an embryo. The full, multi-celled organism then develops tissues and organ systems, eventually developing into its adult form.

All multicellular animals must come up with solutions to several basic problems:

- **Surface-area-to-volume issues**: Nutrients, air, and water must be able to enter an animal's body in order to sustain life; therefore, the surface area of an animal's body must be large enough to allow a sufficient amount of these elements to be consumed by the organism. In single-celled organisms, the cell size is limited to the amount of nutrients able to pass through the cell membrane to support the cell. In multi-celled organisms, specialized tissues and organ systems with very large surface areas bring in the necessary elements and then carry them to the cells. Those specialized tissues are found in the respiratory system, urinary system, excretory system, and the digestive system. These tissues and organs, along with the circulatory system, are able to support a large-sized body.

- **Body support and protection**: All animals have some form of support and protection in the form of their internal or external skeletal systems. These skeletal systems provide support for the animal's body and protect the internal organs from damage.

- **Mobility**: Animals are heterotrophs and must acquire food; this need, along with the need to mate and reproduce, requires the animal to move. Although plants move, they are considered stationary because they are rooted. Animals, on the other hand, move from place to place; this is called **locomotion.** Locomotion requires a muscular system. Muscles are found only in animals; they are not present in plants, fungi, or single-celled microorganisms.

- **Sensory integration**: Animals have many specialized sensory organs: eyes, ears, noses, etc. These organs make animals aware of the environment and give them the ability to respond to environmental stimuli. The integration and coordination of sense organs with other bodily functions requires an organized collection of specialized nervous tissue, known as a **central nervous system** (CNS).

A Few Animal Phyla

Phylum Porifera: Sponges.
Collections of individual cells with no tissues or organs, and no nervous system or skeleton.

Phylum Coelenterata: Jellyfish, sea anemones, and coral.
Bodies symmetrical in a circular fashion with rudimentary organs and systems, but no skeleton.

Phylum Echinodermata: Sea stars and sea urchins.
Bodies have circular symmetry with five body parts arranged around a central axis. They have calcium spines or plates just under the skin.

Phylum Mollusca: Snails, clams, and octopi.
These have a well-developed circulatory system, nervous system, and digestive system; octopuses have particularly well-developed brains.

Phylum Arthropoda: Crustaceans, spiders, and insects.
This phylum has more species than the other phyla. They have exoskeletons, and most undergo **metamorphosis** (a physical transformation that is a part of the growth process). They often have specialized body parts (antennae, pinchers, etc.), and they are well adapted to many environments.

Phylum Chordata: Amphibians, reptiles, fish, birds, and mammals (including humans).
All share four characteristics: a notochord that develops into the vertebral column in vertebrates, a nerve cord that runs along the spinal column, gill slits at some point in our development, and a tail or at least a vestigial tail (humans have the tailbone or coccyx).

Practice Drill: Animals

1. Multicellular animals have developed respiratory and excretory systems to overcome which of the following issues?
    a) Weight versus mass.
    b) Surface-area-to-volume.
    c) Height to weight.
    d) Mass to volume.

2. The two categories of animals are:
    a) Single-celled and multi-celled.
    b) Autotrophic and heterotrophic.
    c) Those that live in water and those that live on land.
    d) Vertebrate and invertebrate.

3. Jellyfish and coral are related to:
    a) Octopi.
    b) Sea anemones.
    c) Sea urchins.
    d) Sponges.

4. The Phylum Arthropoda contains which of the following animals?
    a) Spiders.
    b) Sea stars.
    c) Sponges.
    d) Seals.

5. Humans are classified under which of the following Phyla?
    a) Echinodermata.
    b) Chordata.
    c) Mollusca.
    d) Platyhelminthes.

Practice Drill: Animals – Answers

1. **b)**
2. **d)**
3. **b)**
4. **a)**
5. **b)**

PLANTS

Organisms within Kingdom Plantae are very diverse, but they usually share certain characteristics which make them recognizable as plants. Chlorophyll ensures that some, if not all, of a plants body will have a green color, and their root systems render plants incapable of locomotion. Remember photosynthesis? Plants are autotrophs; they create their own food through photosynthesis, which turns carbon dioxide and water into sugars and oxygen gas. This process takes place using chlorophyll in structures called **chloroplasts**. Plants also have hard cell walls made of the carbohydrate **cellulose**.

Diverse Environments and Plants

Plants are found in nearly every place on Earth. Since plants need light to photosynthesize, their ability to survive in different environments depends upon their access to sources of light. Water is also an important part of a plant's growth and development, partly because the water contained within a plant cells (by the cell wall) provide a plant with structure and support.

Land plants evolved from algae into two large groups: **bryophytes** (nonvascular plants) and **tracheophytes** (vascular plants).

Tracheophytes

These plants have tubes (vessels) which provide both support and a means of transporting water and nutrients throughout their bodies. This support enables them to grow much larger than bryophytes.

The tracheophyte group is further broken down into two types: **seedless** and **seeded** vascular plants.

Seedless vascular plants require moist environments, because they need water to reproduce. Millions of years ago, seedless plants dominated the Earth; you can see many of them still today, such as club mosses, horsetails, and ferns.

Seeded vascular plants have become dominant today because they have developed a reproductive system that includes pollen and seeds. In response to harsh and dangerous conditions, plants have developed **pollen** as a structure to protect sperm cells until they can safely reach the female part of a flower. Another structure which protects plants against the environment is a seed. **Seeds** contain and protect an immature plant in a state of dormancy until conditions are favorable. They then germinate and form a new plant.

Since plants cannot transport themselves (remember: no locomotion), they depend on dispersal systems to establish themselves in new areas. Many systems help distribute seeds, including wind, water, and animals.

Seeded vascular plants are divided into two groups: **gymnosperms** and **angiosperms**.

Gymnosperms are seeded vascular plants that do not flower. They include plants such as pines, spruce, and cypresses. Gymnosperms are adapted to cold dry areas. They have very thin, small leaves covered with a waterproof layer that keeps them from drying out; additionally, a biological antifreeze in their sap keeps them from freezing. Gymnosperms retain green leaves year-round and produce seeds in cones.

Angiosperms are seeded vascular plants that *do* form flowers. These plants have thrived. They dominate the Earth and are highly diverse, largely because they have developed flowers, fruits, and broad leaves.

Broad leaves capture more sunlight, and therefore produce more food than the narrow, thin leaves of the gymnosperms are able to produce.

Flowers are the place in plants where sperm and egg cells are produced – they contain both the male and female sexual parts. A flower is designed to attract animals, which is why their structures are so colorful and fragrant. Animals assist in the pollination process by carrying pollen and other seeds to diverse locations; the animal often receives a "reward" from the plant in the form of nectar or pollen. Bees, for example, receive nectar and pollen for food from flowering plants.

Fruits contain the fully developed seed of flowering seed plants. Animals are attracted to the plant, eat the fruit, and then disperse the seeds.

Bryophytes

Quite different from tracheophytes, bryophytes lack roots, leaves, and stems. Instead, structures called **rhizoids** (root-like hairs) absorb water and nutrients. Since they do not have a tubular system with which to move water throughout their bodies, bryophytes rely on diffusion to distribute water and nutrients. This process is slow, and not efficient enough to support large bodies, so bryophytes cannot grow very large. The largest types of bryophytes are liverworts and mosses.

Practice Drill: Plants

1. Which of the following characteristics is NOT a characteristic of plants?
   a) They are able to engage in locomotion by moving from place to place.
   b) They use chlorophyll contained in chloroplasts.
   c) They produce sugars and oxygen.
   d) They use carbon dioxide and water in photosynthesis.

2. Which of the following is a bryophyte?
   a) Horsetail.
   b) Fern.
   c) Liverwort.
   d) Spruce tree.

3. Which plant group currently dominates the Earth in terms of quantity over other plant groups?
   a) Gymnosperms.
   b) Bryophytes.
   c) Seedless vascular plants.
   d) Angiosperms.

4. "Tracheophytes" is another name for:
   a) Nonvascular plants.
   b) Angiosperm plants.
   c) Gymnosperm plants.
   d) Vascular plants.

5. Which of the following strategies does an angiosperm plant NOT use to attract animals?
   a) It produces pollen.
   b) It produces nectar.
   c) It produces chloroplasts.
   d) It produces fruit.

6. Rhizoids are similar to _____ in vascular plants?
   a) Leaves
   b) Chloroplasts
   c) Roots
   d) Stems

Practice Drill: Plants – Answers

1. a)
2. c)
3. d)
4. d)
5. c)
6. c)

ECOLOGY

Biosphere and Biome
Life is possible due to the presence of air (**atmosphere**), water (**hydrosphere**), and soil (**lithosphere**). These factors interact with each other and the life on Earth to create an environment called a **biosphere**. The biosphere contains all of Earth's living organisms. Smaller living systems called **biomes** exist in large areas, both on land and in water; they are defined by the physical characteristics of the environment which they encompass, and by the organisms living within it.

Ecosystem
An ecosystem is a community of living and non-living things that work together. Ecosystems have no particular size; from large lakes and deserts, to small trees or puddles. Everything in the natural world – water, water temperature, plants, animals, air, light, soil, etc. – all form ecosystems.

The physical environment of an ecosystem includes soils, weather, climate, the topography (or shape) of the land, and many other factors. If there isn't enough light or water within an ecosystem, or if the soil doesn't have the right nutrients, plants will die. If plants die, the animals which depend on them will die. If the animals depending upon the plants die, any other animals depending upon those animals will also die. Regardless of the type of ecosystem they are in, all organisms – even microscopic ones – are affected by each other and their physical surroundings.

There are two components of an ecosystem. The **biotic** (biological) component includes the living organisms; nonliving factors – such as water, minerals, and sunlight – are collectively known as the **abiotic** (non-biological) component. While all ecosystems have different organisms and/or abiotic factors, they all have two primary features:

1. **Energy flows in one direction**. Beginning in the form of chemical bonds from photosynthetic organisms, like green plants or algae, energy flows first to the animals that eat the plants, then to other animals.

2. **Inorganic materials are recycled.** When taken up from the environment through living organisms, inorganic minerals are returned to the environment – mainly via decomposers such as bacteria and fungi. Other organisms called **detritivores** (such as pill bugs, sow bugs, millipedes, and earthworms), help break down large pieces of organic matter into smaller pieces that are handled then by the decomposers.

But since that's a lot of information to take in at once, here's a simple and complete definition of an ecosystem: a combination of biotic and abiotic components, through which energy flows and inorganic material is recycled.

An Organism's Niche
The area in which an organism lives – and therefore acquires the many things needed to sustain their lives – is called a **habitat.** An organism's role within its community, how it affects its habitat and how it is affected by its habitat, are the factors that define the organism's **niche**. A niche is like an organism's "location" and "occupation" within a community.

For example, birds and squirrels both live in a tree habitat; however, they eat different foods, have different living arrangements, and have different food-gathering abilities. Therefore, the do not occupy the same niche.

THE ECOLOGICALORDER OF LIFE

Biosphere - All ecosystems on the planet make up the biosphere.

Ecosystem – Large community of numerous communities, and the physical non-living environment.

Community - A group of populations in a given area.

Population - A group of organisms of the same species in a given area.

Organism - A living thing.

Organ Systems - A group of organs that perform certain functions to form an organism.

Organs - A group of tissues that perform a certain function to form organ systems.

Tissues - A group of cells that perform certain functions to form an organ.

Cells - The building blocks of life which form tissues.

Organelles - Small parts of cells that have specific functions.

Atoms and Molecules - the building blocks of everything in the universe as we know it

One of the most important relationships among organisms exists between predators and their prey. You may have heard of this relationship described through **food chains** and **food webs**.

Food Chains represent the flow of energy obtained from the chemical breakdown of food molecules. When one animal (the predator) consumes another (the prey), the chemical bonds making up the tissues of the prey's body are broken down by the predator's digestive system. This digestive process releases energy and smaller chemical molecules that the predator's body uses to make more tissue. Prior to being the consumed, the prey obtains energy from foods for its own life processes.

Here's a basic example of a food chain:

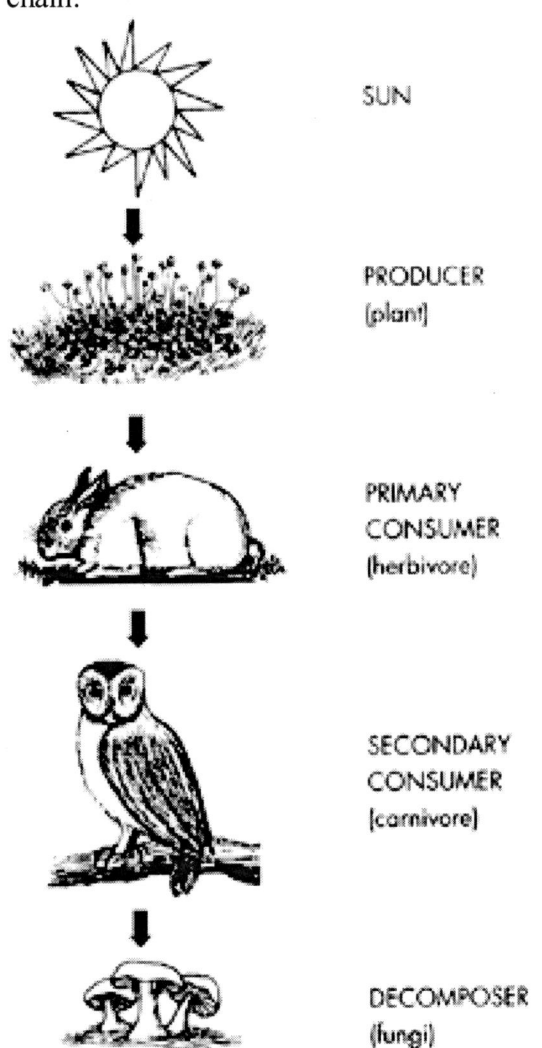

SUN

PRODUCER
(plant)

PRIMARY
CONSUMER
(herbivore)

SECONDARY
CONSUMER
(carnivore)

DECOMPOSER
(fungi)

Food chains are a part of **food webs**, which offer a more complex view of energy transfer. They include more organisms, taking into account more than one predator-prey relationship. Each step along a food chain, or within a food web, is called a **trophic** (or feeding) level. Organisms at that first trophic level are known as **primary producers**, and are always photosynthetic organisms, whether on land or in water.

At the second trophic level, herbivores (referred to as **primary consumers**) eat plants to produce the energy needed for their metabolism. Much of the energy that transfers from the first trophic level to the second level is not turned into tissue. Instead, it is used for the digestive process, locomotion, and is lost as heat. As you move from one trophic level to another, it is estimated that only 10% of the available energy gets turned into body tissue at the next level up.

---

[1] Graphic from: http://www.king.portlandschools.org

The following is an example of a food web:

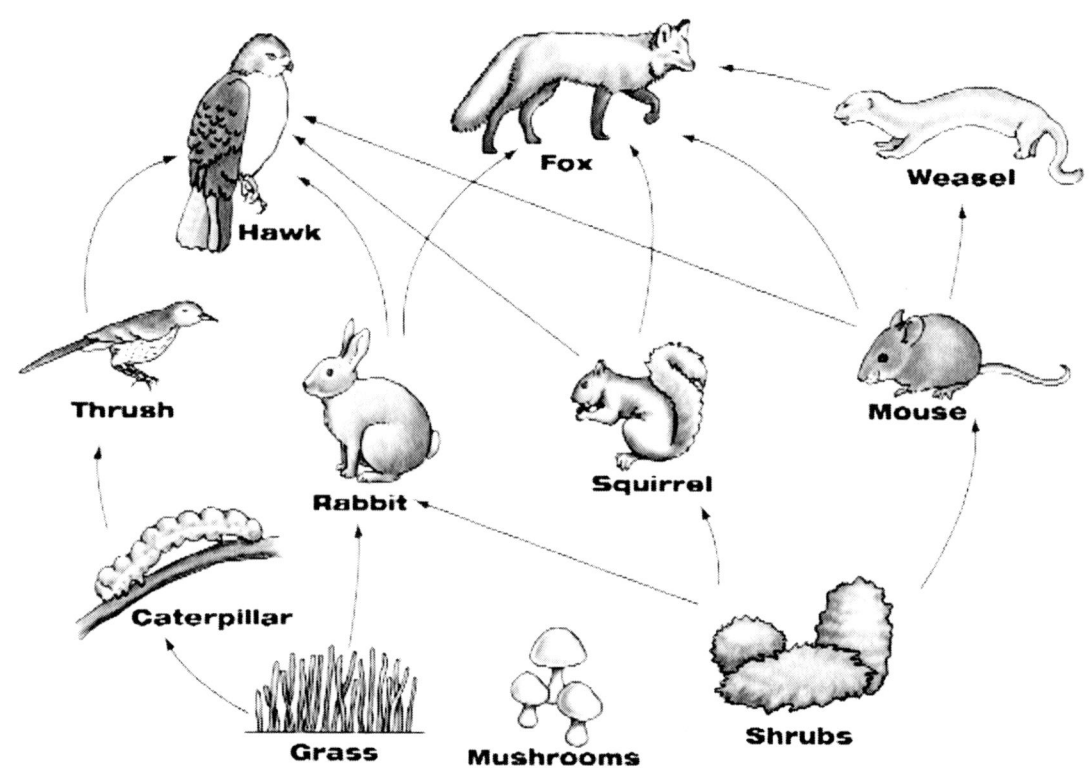

Practice Drill: Ecology

1. Ecology is the study of organisms interacting with:
   a) The physical environment only.
   b) The internal environment only.
   c) The physical environment and each other.
   d) Each other and the internal environment.

2. In terms of energy, an ecosystem is defined as:
   a) Moving energy back and forth between organisms.
   b) Moving energy in one direction from plants to animals.
   c) Not utilizing energy.
   d) Moving energy in one direction from animals to plants.

3. Decomposers are important because they:
   a) Recycle nutrients.
   b) Produce sugars.
   c) Produce oxygen.
   d) Engage in asexual reproduction.

---

[2] Graphic from: http://www.education.com

4. Which of the following best describes the concept of an organism's niche?
    a) It is the organism's function, or "occupation", within an ecosystem.
    b) It is the organism's location, or "address", within an ecosystem.
    c) It is both an organism's function and location in an ecosystem.
    d) It is the binomial classification of an organism in an ecosystem.

5. Pillbugs are also known as:
    a) Decomposers.
    b) Detritivores.
    c) Producers.
    d) Autotrophs.

6. The steps in a food chain or food web are called _____ and represent the _____ of an organism.
    a) biome levels; energy level
    b) trophic levels; energy level
    c) trophic levels; feeding level
    d) energy levels; feeding level

7. Another term for herbivores is:
    a) Plants.
    b) Secondary consumers.
    c) Primary consumers
    d) Third trophic-level organisms.

8. Several interacting food chains form a:
    a) Food pyramid.
    b) Food web.
    c) Food column.
    d) Food triangle.

9. Herbivores are at the second trophic level, so they are:
    a) Primary producers.
    b) Primary consumers.
    c) Secondary consumers.
    d) Secondary producers.

Practice Drill: Ecology – Answers

1. c)
2. b)
3. a)
4. c)
5. b)
6. c)
7. c)
8. b)
9. b)

General Physiology

The normal functioning of living organisms, and the activities by which life is maintained, are both studied in physiology. This study includes such things as cell activity, tissues, and organs; as well as processes such as muscle movement, nervous systems, nutrition, digestion, respiration, circulation, and reproduction.

One characteristic of living things is the performance of chemical reactions collectively called metabolism. Cells, the basic units of life, perform many metabolic reactions. In multi-celled organisms, cells group together and form tissues that enable the organisms' functions. Tissues group together and form organs, which in turn work together in an organ system.

CELLS, TISSUES, AND ORGANS

All organisms are composed of microscopic cells, although the type and number of cells may vary. A cell is the minimum amount of organized living matter that is complex enough to carry out the functions of life. This section will briefly review both animal and plant cells, noting their basic similarities and differences.

Cell Structure
Around the cell is the **cell membrane**, which separates the living cell from the rest of the environment and regulates the comings and goings of molecules within the cell. Because the cell membrane allows some molecules to pass through while blocking others, it is considered **semipermeable.** Each cell's membrane communicates and interacts with the membranes of other cells. In additional to a cell membrane, *plants* also have a **cell wall** which is necessary for structural support and protection. Animal cells do not contain a cell wall.

Organelle
Cells are filled with a gelatin-like substance called **protoplasm** which contains various structures called **organelles**; called so because they act like small versions of organs. The diagram on the next page illustrates the basic organelles of both a plant and an animal cell. Pay attention to the differences and similarities between the two.

PLANT CELL (A)

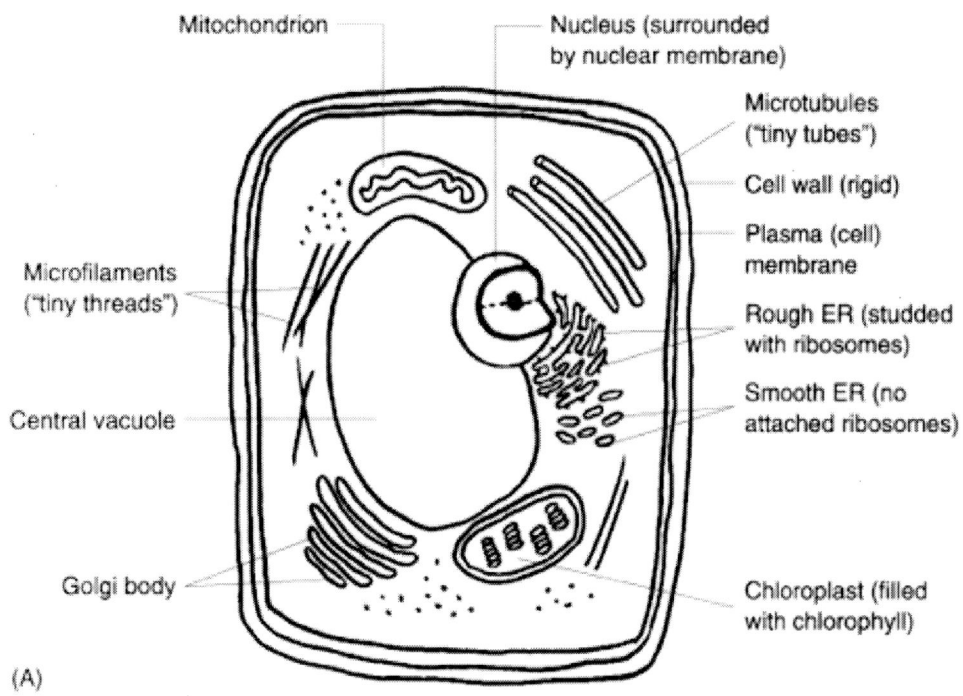

Mitochondrion

Nucleus (surrounded by nuclear membrane)

Microtubules ("tiny tubes")

Cell wall (rigid)

Plasma (cell) membrane

Rough ER (studded with ribosomes)

Smooth ER (no attached ribosomes)

Microfilaments ("tiny threads")

Central vacuole

Golgi body

Chloroplast (filled with chlorophyll)

(A)

ANIMAL CELL (B)

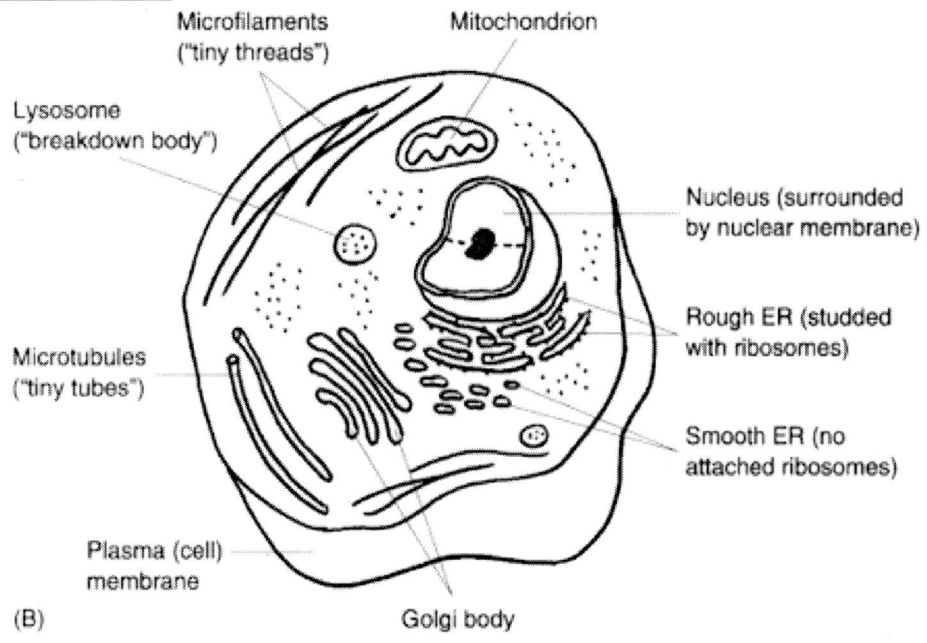

Microfilaments ("tiny threads")

Mitochondrion

Lysosome ("breakdown body")

Nucleus (surrounded by nuclear membrane)

Rough ER (studded with ribosomes)

Microtubules ("tiny tubes")

Smooth ER (no attached ribosomes)

Plasma (cell) membrane

Golgi body

(B)

[3] Graphics from: http://www.education.com

Mitochondria are spherical or rod-shaped organelles which carry out the reactions of aerobic respiration. They are the power generators of both plant and animal cells, because they convert oxygen and nutrients into ATP, the chemical energy that powers the cell's metabolic activities.

Ribosomes are extremely tiny spheres that make proteins. These proteins are used either as enzymes or as support for other cell functions.

The **Golgi Apparatus** is essential to the production of polysaccharides (carbohydrates), and made up of a layered stack of flattened sacs.

The **Endoplasmic Reticulum** is important in the synthesis and packaging of proteins. It is a complex system of internal membranes, and is called either rough (when ribosomes are attached), or smooth (no ribosomes attached).

Chloroplasts are only found in plants. They contain the chlorophyll molecule necessary for photosynthesis.

The **Nucleus** controls all of the cell's functions, and contains the all-important genetic information, or DNA, of a cell.

Cellular Differentiation

Single-celled organisms have only one cell to carry out all of their required biochemical and structural functions. On the other hand, multi-celled organisms – except for very primitive ones (i.e. sponges) – have various groups of cells called **tissues** that each perform specific functions (**differentiation**).

There are four main types of tissues: **epithelial**, **connective**, **muscular**, and **nervous**.

Epithelial tissue is made up groups of flattened cells which are grouped tightly together to form a solid surface. Those cells are arranged in one or many layer(s) to form an external or internal covering of the body or organs. Epithelial tissue protects the body from injury and allows for the exchange of gases in the lungs and bronchial tubes. There's even a form of epithelial tissue that produces eggs and sperm, an organism's sex cells.

Connective tissue is made of cells which are surrounded by non-cellular material. For example, bones contain some cells, but they are also surrounded by a considerable amount of non-cellular, extracellular material.

Muscular tissue has the ability to contract. There are three types:

1. **Cardiac** tissue, found in the heart.

2. **Smooth** tissue, located in the walls of hollow internal structures such as blood vessels, the stomach, intestines, and urinary bladder.

3. **Skeletal** (or striated) tissue, found in the muscles.

Nervous tissue consists of cells called **neurons.** Neurons specialize in making many connections with and transmitting electrical impulses to each other. The brain, spinal cord, and peripheral nerves are all made of nervous tissue.

Organs and Organ Systems

As living organisms go through their life cycle, they grow and/or develop. Single-celled organisms grow and develop very rapidly; whereas complex, multi-celled organisms take much longer to progress. All organisms go through changes as they age. These changes involve the development of more complex functions, which in turn require groups of tissues to form larger units called **organs.**

Examples of Organs

1. **The Heart**: Made of cardiac muscle and conjunctive tissue (conjunctive tissue makes up the valves), the heart pumps blood first to the lungs in order to pick up oxygen, then through the rest of the body to deliver the oxygen, and finally back to the lungs to start again.

2. **Roots**: A tree's are covered by an epidermis which is in turn made up of a protective tissue. They are also *composed* of tissue, which allows them to grow. The root organ also contains **conductive tissue** to absorb and transport water and nutrients to the rest of the plant.

Generally, in complex organisms like plants and animals, many organs are grouped together into **systems.** For example, many combinations of tissues make up the many organs which create the digestive system in animals. The organs in the digestive system consist of the mouth, the esophagus, the stomach, small and large intestines, the liver, the pancreas, and the gall bladder.

Practice Drill: Cells, Tissues, and Organs

1. Which statement is true about Earth's organisms?
   a) All organisms are based on the cell as the basic unit of life.
   b) Protists are an exception to the cell theory and are not based on cells.
   c) Only single-celled organisms are based on cells.
   d) All organisms are based on tissues as the basic unit of life.

2. What organelle produces the cell's energy source?
   a) Chloroplast.
   b) Nucleus.
   c) Mitochondrion.
   d) Endoplasmic reticulum.

3. The formation of tissue depends upon:
   a) Cell differentiation.
   b) Cell membranes.
   c) Cell death.
   d) Cell organelles.

4. Cardiac muscle is an example of what tissue?
   a) Smooth muscle.
   b) Nervous.
   c) Contractile.
   d) Connective.

5. Which organelle has two forms: rough and smooth?
   a) Mitochondrion.
   b) Golgi apparatus.
   c) Nucleus.
   d) Endoplasmic reticulum.

6. Which organelle is important in the production of polysaccharides (carbohydrates)?
   a) Mitochondrion.
   b) Golgi apparatus.
   c) Nucleus
   d) Endoplasmic reticulum.

Practice Drill: Cells, Tissues, and Organs – Answers

1. a)
2. c)
3. a)
4. c)
5. d)
6. b)

REPRODUCTION

Individual organisms have limited life spans; however, life continues due to reproduction. There are two types of reproduction. One requires the exchange of genetic material between two organisms (**sexual reproduction**), and the other does not (**asexual reproduction**).

Asexual Reproduction

All kingdoms have organisms that engage in asexual reproduction. Asexual reproduction very quickly produces large numbers of genetically identical (or **cloned**) offspring. Some organisms that engage in asexual reproduction can also engage in sexual reproduction at least part of the time.

	Asexual Reproduction	Sexual Reproduction
Number of Organisms Involved:	One.	Two.
Cell Division:	Mitosis.	Meiosis.
Variation in Offspring:	No.	Yes.
Advantages:	Quick. No need to search for mate.	Variation.
Disadvantages:	No variation.	Requires two organisms.

In single-celled organisms such as bacteria and protists, asexual reproduction occurs through a process known as **binary fission** (or **bipartition**). The cell first duplicates parts of itself before splitting into two separate, but identical, cells. Some organisms reproduce asexually using the process of **budding**, wherein an offshoot of their body grows into a complete organism.

Many multi-cellular invertebrates can also reproduce asexually by a process called **fragmentation**, where a portion of the organism's body is separated and then grows into a whole organism. This is similar to budding, except that the original body repairs itself as well, leaving behind two complete organisms.

Plants can reproduce asexually by budding or fragmentation, when they form tubers, rhizomes, bulbs, and other extensions of their bodies. Plants also have a major sexual phase of their life cycle, which is part of a process called **alternation of generations.**

Alternation of Generations

Although asexual reproduction allows plants to reproduce quickly, most plants engage in sexual reproduction, at least part of the time. Sexually reproducing plants cycle between two distinctly different body types. The first is called the **sporophyte**, and the second is called the **gametophyte.**

An adult sporophyte (the part of the plant we see) produces spores. The spores are transported to new areas by animals, wind, water, etc. If the conditions are suitable, those spores will sprout into a **gametophyte** form of the plant, which is not usually seen. This gametophyte produces the eggs and sperm that will join to form a new sporophyte. This change from sporophyte to gametophyte represents an alternation of generations. The gametophyte generation is small and dependent upon the sporophyte generation. An oak tree, for example, is really the sporophyte generation of the plant; the gametophyte generation is contained within its flowers.

Sexual Reproduction

Sexual reproduction is when genetic material from one parent is combined with the genetic material from another, producing offspring that are not identical to either parent. Each parent produces a specialized cell called a **gamete** that contains half of his or her genetic information.

Male animals produce the smaller, more mobile gamete known as a **sperm cell**. Females produce the larger, more sedentary gamete known as an **egg cell**. When these two gametes come into contact, they fuse and combine their genetic information in a process known as **fertilization**. This can happen either externally or internally.

An example of **external fertilization** would be **spawning,** where eggs and sperm are both released into water and must find each other. **Spawning** is dependent upon each gender's reproductive cycle matching the other. For some fish and amphibians, the male and female embrace to motivate the release of the gametes; however, internal fertilization does not take place.

Internal fertilization is dependent upon **copulation**: the process wherein a male deposits sperm cells directly into the reproductive tract of a female. Because a medium like water cannot be used to transport gametes on land, internal fertilization is critical to land-based organisms.

Practice Drill: Reproduction

1. The formation of tubers is an example of what kind of asexual reproduction?
   a) Budding.
   b) Binary fission.
   c) Bipartition.
   d) Root zone development.

2. Which of the following best describes alternation of generation?
   a) The sporophyte produces eggs and sperm that join and lead to the development of a gametophyte.
   b) The gametophyte produces eggs and sperm that join and lead to the development of a sporophyte.
   c) The gametophyte produces eggs and the sporophyte produces sperm that join to form a new plant.
   d) The sporophyte produces eggs and the gametophyte produces sperm that join to form a new plant.

3. In sexually reproducing organisms, gametes come from which parent?
   a) Only the male.
   b) Only the female.
   c) Both the male and female.
   d) Neither.

4. What is the main difference between asexual and sexual reproduction?
   a) Asexual reproduction is only for aquatic organisms.
   b) Asexual reproduction is practiced only by plants.
   c) Humans are the only organisms that utilize sexual reproduction.
   d) Asexual reproduction does not require a mate.

5. Which of the following is **NOT** a form of asexual reproduction?
   a) Fertilization.
   b) Cloning.
   c) Budding.
   d) Fragmentation.

Practice Drill: Reproduction – Answers

1. **a)**
2. **b)**
3. **c)**
4. **d)**
5. **a)**

HEREDITY

A duck's webbed feet, a tree whose leaves change color in the fall, and humans having backbones are all characteristics inherited from parent organisms. These inheritable characteristics are transmitted through **genes** and **chromosomes**. In sexual reproduction, each parent contributes half of his or her genes to the offspring.

Genes

Genes influence both what we look like on the outside and how we work on the inside. They contain the information that our bodies need to make the proteins in our bodies. Genes are made of DNA: a double helix (spiral) molecule that consists of two long, twisted strands of nucleic acids. Each of these strands are made of sugar and phosphate molecules, and are connected by pairs of chemicals called **nitrogenous bases** (just bases, for short). There are four types of bases:

1. **Adenine (A)**
2. **Thymine (T)**
3. **Guanine (G)**
4. **Cytosine (C)**

These bases link in a very specific way: **A** always pairs with **T**, and **C** always pairs with **G**.

A gene is a piece of DNA that codes for a specific protein. Each gene contains the information necessary to produce a single trait in an organism, and each gene is different from any other. For example, one gene will code for the protein insulin, and another will code for hair. For any trait, we inherit one gene from our father and one from our mother. Human beings have 20,000 to 25,000 genes, yet those genes only account for about 3% of our DNA.

Alternate forms of the same gene are called **alleles**. When the alleles are identical, the individual is **homozygous** for that trait. When the alleles are different, the individual is **heterozygous** for that trait. For example, a child may have red hair because she inherited two identical red color genes from each parent; that would make her homozygous for red hair. However, a second child may have brown hair because he inherited different hair color genes from each parent; this would make him heterozygous for brown hair. When genes exist in a heterozygous pairing, usually one is expressed over the other. The gene which is expressed is **dominant**. The unexpressed gene is called **recessive**.

If you took the DNA from all the cells in your body and lined it up, end to end, it would form a (very thin!) strand 6000 million miles long! DNA molecules, and their important genetic material, are tightly packed around proteins called **histones** to make structures called **chromosomes**. Human beings have 23 pairs of chromosomes in every cell, for 46 chromosomes in total. The sex chromosomes determine whether you are a boy (XY) or a girl (XX). The other chromosomes are called autosomes.

Patterns of Inheritance

Biologists refer to the genetic makeup of an organism as its **genotype**. However, the collection of physical characteristics that result from the action of genes is called an organism's **phenotype.** You can remember this differentiation by looking at the beginning of each word: *geno*type is *gen*etic, and *pheno*type is *phy*sical. Patterns of inheritance can produce surprising results, because the genotype determines the phenotype.

Practice Drill: Heredity

1. On paired chromosomes, two identical alleles are called:
    a) Heterozygous.
    b) Homozygous.
    c) Tetrad.
    d) Binomial.

2. The physical characteristics of an organism are known as its:
    a) Chromosomes.
    b) Genotype.
    c) DNA.
    d) Phenotype.

3. Which of the following is **NOT** a nucleotide found in DNA?
    a) Uracil.
    b) Guanine.
    c) Cytosine.
    d) Thymine.

4. The genotype describes an organism's:
    a) Appearance.
    b) Genetic code.
    c) Type of DNA.
    d) Eye color only.

5. The shape of the DNA molecule is a:
    a) Single spiral.
    b) Double spiral.
    c) Straight chain.
    d) Bent chain.

Practice Drill: Heredity – Answers

1. **b)**
2. **d)**
3. **a)**
4. **b)**
5. **b)**

THE RESPIRATORY SYSTEM

The human respiratory system is made up of a series of organs responsible for taking in oxygen and expelling carbon dioxide, and can be divided into two parts: **air conduction** and **gas exchange.** (We'll cover those in more detail soon.)

The respiratory system's primary organs are the lungs, which take in oxygen and expel carbon dioxide when we breathe. Breathing involves **inhalation** (the taking in of air) and **exhalation** (the releasing of air). Blood gathers oxygen from the lungs and transports it to cells throughout the body, where it exchanges the oxygen for carbon dioxide. The carbon dioxide is then transported back to the lungs, where it is exhaled.

Air Conduction
The **diaphragm**, a dome-shaped muscle located at the bottom of the lungs, controls breathing. When a breath is taken, the diaphragm flattens and pulls forward, making more space for the lungs. During exhalation, the diaphragm expands upwards to force air out.

Humans breathe through their noses or mouths, which causes air to enter the **pharynx** (upper part of the throat). The air then passes the **larynx** (the Adam's apple on the inside of the throat). The larynx is also known as the voice box because it changes shape to form sounds. Inhaled air passes into a tube in the center of the chest known as the **trachea**, (the windpipe) which filters the air.

The trachea branches into two **bronchi**, two tubes which carry air into the lungs. Once inside the lungs, each bronchus branches into smaller tubes called **bronchioles**. Bronchioles then lead to sac-like structures called **alveoli**, where the second function of the respiratory system – gas exchange – occurs.

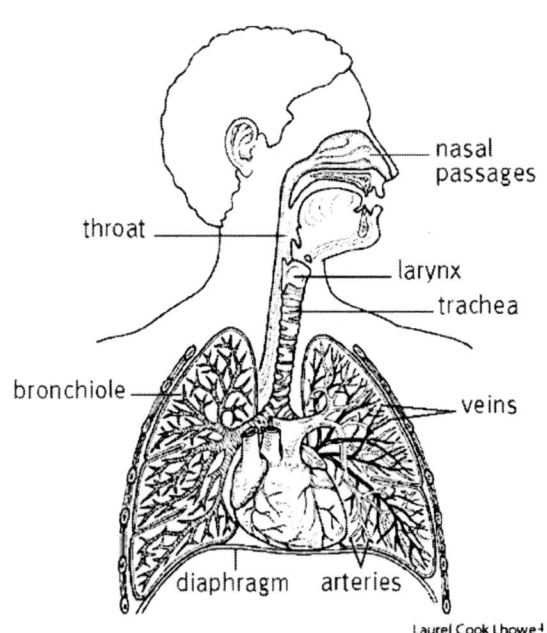

Laurel Cook Lhowe[4]

[4] The American Heritage® Science Dictionary Copyright © 2010 by Houghton Mifflin Harcourt Publishing Company. Published by Houghton Mifflin Harcourt Publishing Company.

Gas Exchange

Each lung contains over two million alveoli, which creates a large surface area for gas exchange: approximately 800 square feet!

The alveoli and the surrounding blood vessels have very thin walls, which allows for the diffusion of gases in either direction – specifically oxygen and carbon dioxide. Air entering the lungs from the atmosphere is high in oxygen and low in carbon dioxide. This means that the alveoli have a high concentration of oxygen and a low concentration of carbon dioxide.

The opposite is true for the blood within the alveoli's blood vessels. Blood entering the lungs is *low* in oxygen and *high* in carbon dioxide because of cellular respiration (metabolism).

Because the alveoli have a high concentration of oxygen and a low concentration of carbon dioxide, while their blood vessels have the opposite condition, the two gases flow in opposite directions (gas exchange).

Plants exchange gas as well. Single-celled plants, like their animal counterparts, simply exchange gases through the cell membranes. Multicellular plants use pores on the leaf surface, called **stomata**, to exchange gases with the atmosphere.

Practice Drill: The Respiratory System

1. The conduction of air through the respiratory system follows which of the following paths?
    a) Pharynx, larynx, alveoli, trachea, bronchus, bronchioles.
    b) Alveoli, bronchioles, bronchus, trachea, larynx, pharynx.
    c) Pharynx, larynx, trachea, bronchus, bronchioles, alveoli.
    d) Bronchus, bronchioles, alveoli, pharynx, larynx, trachea.

2. Each alveolus in the lungs is covered by tiny blood vessels to perform which of these functions?
    a) Excretion of fluids.
    b) Gas exchange.
    c) Blood production.
    d) Air intake.

3. The pores on a plant leaf that allow for gas exchange are called:
    a) Alveoli.
    b) Cell pores.
    c) Membrane gaps.
    d) Stomata.

4. Which of the following occurs during gas exchange in a cell?
    a) Oxygen is flowing from a low concentration inside the cell to a high concentration outside the cell.
    b) Oxygen is flowing from a high concentration in the red blood cells to a low concentration inside the body cell.
    c) Carbon dioxide is moving from the red blood cells into the body cells, while oxygen is moving from the body cells into the red blood cells.
    d) Carbon dioxide is flowing from a low concentration outside the cells to a high concentration inside the cells.

5. The lungs are very efficient at gas exchange because they have a:
    a) High mass.
    b) Low volume.
    c) High surface-area-to-volume ratio.
    d) Low surface-area-to-volume ratio.

Practice Drill: The Respiratory System – Answers

1. c)
2. b)
3. d)
4. b)
5. c)

THE SKELETAL SYSTEM

Skeletal systems provide structure, support, form, protection, and movement. Of course, muscles do the actual *moving* of an organism, but bones – a major component of the skeletal system –create the framework through which muscles and organs connect. The bone marrow in animal skeletal systems performs **hematopoiesis** (the manufacturing of both red blood cells and white blood cells).

Skeletal systems come in many different forms - those inside of the body are called **endoskeletons**, while those skeletal structures formed outside of the body are known as **exoskeletons**. Crabs and insects have hard shells made of **chitin** to protect their entire bodies. Some organisms, such as starfish, have skeletons made up of tubes filled with fluids running through their bodies. These fluid skeletal systems are called **hydrostatic**.

Joints are where two bones come together. **Connective tissues** at the joint prevent the bones from damaging each other. Joints can be freely movable (elbow or knee), slightly movable (vertebrae in the back), or immovable (skull).

Plants also have a need for support, shape, and protection. While nonvascular do not have a great need for support (remember, they don't grow very tall), vascular plants require a great deal of support. Remember cell walls (a semi-permeable, rigid structure that surrounds each cell outside the cell membrane)? The support and structure of plant cells are primarily derived from the cell wall. Additional support and structure is provided by the tubes used to move water and nutrients through the plant.

Practice Drill: The Skeletal System

1. Which of the following is NOT a function of the skeletal system in animals?
    a) Transport fluids.
    b) Produce oil.
    c) Placement of internal organs.
    d) Production of blood cells.

2. Which of the following is true of bones?
    a) They contain nerves.
    b) Some are unbreakable.
    c) They are present in vertebrates.
    d) They directly touch each other at a joint.

3. Which of the following animals does **NOT** have an exoskeleton?
    a) Insects.
    b) Crabs.
    c) Lobsters.
    d) Earthworms.

4. What type of tissue is found at joints and protects bones from rubbing against each other and becoming damaged?
    a) Contractile.
    b) Connective.
    c) Conductive.
    d) Catabolic.

5. Fluid skeletal systems are _____.
    a) Hydrostatic.
    b) Hydrolic.
    c) Hydrophobic.
    d) Hydroskeleton.

Practice Drill: The Skeletal System – Answers

1. **b)**
2. **c)**
3. **d)**
4. **b)**
5. **a)**

THE DIGESTIVE SYSTEM

Digestion involves mixing food with digestive juices, moving it through the digestive tract, and breaking down large molecules of food into smaller molecules. The digestive system is made up of the **digestive tract**: a series of hollow organs joined in a long, twisting tube that leads from the mouth to the anus. Several other organs that help the body break down and absorb food are a part of the digestive system as well.

The organs that make up the digestive tract are the **mouth, esophagus, stomach, small intestine, large intestine (colon), rectum,** and **anus**. These organs are covered with a lining called the **mucosa**. In the mouth, stomach, and small intestine, the mucosa contains tiny glands which produce juices to help break down food.

Two "solid" digestive organs, the **liver** and the **pancreas**, produce digestive juices that travel to the intestine through small tubes called **ducts**. The **gallbladder** stores the liver's digestive juices until they are needed in the intestine. The circulatory and nervous systems are also important to the digestive system.

Digestive pathway

The large, hollow organs of the digestive tract contain a layer of muscle that enables their walls to move. This movement propels food and liquid through the system and assists in mixing the contents within each organ. The movement of food molecules from one organ to the next, through *muscle action*, is called **peristalsis**.

The first major muscle movement occurs when food or liquid is swallowed. Although you are able to start swallowing by choice, once the swallow begins, it becomes involuntary (controlled by nerves).

Swallowed food is pushed into the esophagus, which connects the throat with the stomach. At the junction of the esophagus and stomach, there is a ring-like muscle (**lower esophageal sphincter**) that controls the passage between the two organs. As food approaches the closed sphincter, it relaxes and allows the food to pass through to the stomach.

The stomach has three mechanical tasks:

1. It stores the swallowed food and liquid.

2. It mixes the stored food and liquid with digestive juices produced by the stomach.

3. It empties its contents slowly into the small intestine.

Once in the stomach, the food is churned and bathed in a very strong acid (**gastric acid**). When food in the stomach is partly digested and mixed with stomach acids, it is called **chyme**. Several factors affect how long food molecules remain in the stomach, including the type of food, the degree of muscle action of the emptying stomach, and the breakdown of food occurring in the small intestine. Carbohydrates spend the least amount of time in the stomach, followed by proteins; fats remain in the stomach for the longest amount of time.

From the stomach food molecules enter the first part of the small intestine called the **duodenum**. They then enter the **jejunum**, and then the **ileum** (the final part of the small intestine). In the small intestine,

bile (produced in the liver and stored in the gall bladder), pancreatic enzymes, and other digestive enzymes produced in the small intestine help break down the food even further. Many accessory organs such as the liver, pancreas, and gall bladder contribute enzymes and buffering fluids to the mix inside of the small intestine; this also aids in the chemical break down of food molecules.

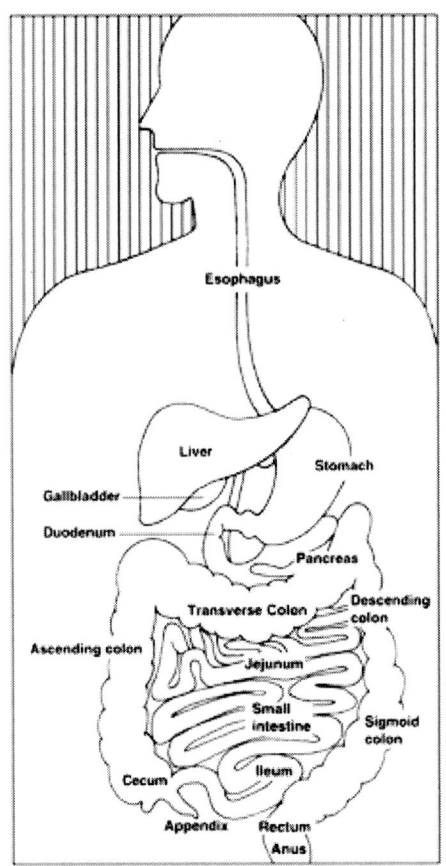

Food then passes into the large intestine, also known as the colon. The main function of the colon is to absorb water, which reduces the undigested matter into a solid waste called feces. Microbes in the large intestine help in the final digestion process. The first part of the large intestine is called the cecum (the appendix is connected to the cecum). Food then travels upward in the ascending colon. The food travels across the abdomen in the transverse colon, goes back down the other side of the body in the descending colon, and then through the sigmoid colon. Solid waste is then stored in the rectum until it is excreted.

---

[5] Graphic from: http://digestive.niddk.nih.gov

Practice Drill: The Digestive System

1. Food begins the digestive process in the:
   a) Esophagus.
   b) Stomach.
   c) Intestines.
   d) Mouth.

2. Chyme is:
   a) Water and completely broken down food molecules.
   b) Acids and completely broken down food molecules.
   c) Acids and partially broken down some food molecules.
   d) Water and partially broken down some food molecules.

3. Where is bile stored?
   a) In the pancreas.
   b) In the gallbladder.
   c) In the liver.
   d) In the small intestines.

4. Which of the following is NOT an accessory organ of the digestive system?
   a) Liver.
   b) Pancreas.
   c) Gall bladder.
   d) Urinary bladder.

5. The chief function of the colon is to:
   a) Absorb water from undigested waste.
   b) Produce sugars.
   c) Absorb protein from undigested waste.
   d) Produce carbohydrates.

Practice Drill: The Digestive System – Answers

1. **d)**
2. **c)**
3. **b)**
4. **d)**
5. **a)**

THE MUSCULAR SYSTEM

Muscles are often viewed as the "machines" of the body. They help move food from one organ to another, and carry out physical movement. There are three types of muscles in our body: cardiac, smooth, and skeletal. The nervous system controls all three types of muscle tissue, both consciously (controlled) and unconsciously (automatic).

Skeletal (or **striated**) muscle tissue is consciously controlled. The muscle is attached to bones, and when it contracts, the bones move. Skeletal tissue also forms visible muscles, as well as much of the body mass.

Smooth muscle is under automatic control and is generally found in the internal organs, especially in the intestinal tract and in the walls of blood vessels.

Cardiac muscle is found only in the heart. This type of muscle tissue is so automated that it will continue to contract even without stimulation from the nervous system. Isolated heart cells in a dish will continue to contract on their own until oxygen or nutrient sources are used up.

Muscle contraction begins when a nerve impulse causes the release of a chemical called a **neurotransmitter**. Muscle contraction is explained as the interaction between two necessary muscle proteins: thick bands of **myosin** and thin bands of **actin**. The thick myosin filaments have small knob-like projections that grab onto the thin actin filaments. As these knobs move slightly, they pull the actin filaments, which slide alongside the myosin filaments. This has the effect of shortening the muscle and thus causing a contraction.

Connective tissues known as **tendons** form a link between muscles and bones (whereas **ligaments** form a link between two bones). The contraction of a muscle causes an exertion of force upon the tendon, which then pulls its attached bone. This movement is synchronized by the central nervous system and results in movement.

Uni-cellular organisms, such as protists and sperm cells, have the ability to move as well. This kind of movement can be accomplished in three different ways. In the case of amoebas, which are one-celled formless blobs of protoplasm, movement is accomplished by extending a portion of the cell itself and then flowing into that portion. Other organisms use **cilia**, which are tiny hair-like projections from the cell membrane, or **flagellum**, which is a tail-like projection that whips around or spins to move.

Practice Drill: The Muscular System

1. What are the three types of muscle cells?
    a) Cardiac, synaptic, and skeletal.
    b) Cardiac, autonomic, and smooth.
    c) Skeletal, cardiac, and smooth.
    d) Smooth, cardiac, and spinal.

2. Which of the following is true about skeletal muscles?
    a) They all contract unconsciously.
    b) All muscle movement is consciously controlled.
    c) They connect directly to one another.
    d) They are also known as striated muscles.

3. What two protein molecules are needed for muscles to contract?
    a) Pepsin and insulin.
    b) Myosin and pepsin.
    c) Hemoglobin and insulin.
    d) Myosin and actin.

4. Flagellum and cilia:
    a) Work with an organism's muscles for movement.
    b) Are parts of all cells and are required for movement.
    c) Are used by organisms without muscular systems.
    d) None of the above.

5. Peristalsis is a process performed by which type of muscle tissue?
    a) Catabolic.
    b) Cardiac.
    c) Smooth.
    d) Skeletal.

Practice Drill: The Muscular System – Answers

1. c)
2. d)
3. d)
4. c)
5. c)

THE CARDIOVASCULAR SYSTEM (CIRCULATORY SYSTEM)

The cells in living organisms need to receive nutrients and have their waste products removed. Single-celled organisms are able to pass these substances to and from their environment directly through the cell membrane. However, in multi-celled organisms, these substances are transported by way of the circulatory system.

The cardiovascular system has three main parts: the heart (which is the pump in the system), the blood vessels providing a route for fluids in the system, and the blood which transports nutrients and oxygen and contains waste products.

Heart
The human heart has four chambers – right atrium, right ventricle, left atrium, and left ventricle – which separate fresh blood from the blood that is full of cellular waste.

When leaving the heart, blood travels through **arteries**. To remember this, imagine that the "a" in "arteries" stands for "away". *A*rteries carry blood *a*way from the heart. On its way to the heart, blood travels through **veins.**

The **superior vena cava** is the vein which brings blood from the body into the top right chamber of the heart. This top right chamber is called the **right atrium**. The right atrium is separated from the chamber below it by a valve, and separated from the chamber next to it by a wall of muscle tissue. The heart relaxes after each beat, which allows blood to flow from the right atrium, through the valve, and into the chamber below called the **right ventricle.**

The right ventricle sends blood through the **pulmonary arteries** to the lungs. Blood picks up oxygen in the lungs and then is moved through the **pulmonary veins** back to the upper part of the heart. But this time, it enters on the left side into the **left atrium.** Use that first-letter rule again to remember this: blood from the *l*ungs enters the *l*eft atrium.

The left atrium – like the right – is separated from the left ventricle below it by a valve. When this valve opens during the relaxed phase of the heart, blood flows into the left ventricle. This chamber has the largest and strongest muscular wall so that it can force blood into the **aorta**, which is the body's largest artery, pulling blood away from the heart to the rest of the body.

The Heart:

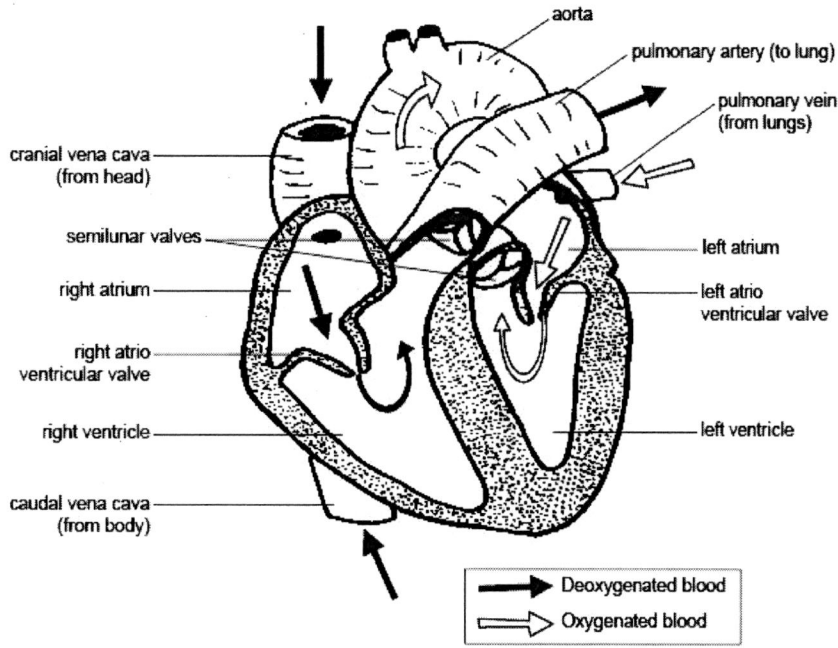

Labels on diagram: aorta, pulmonary artery (to lung), pulmonary vein (from lungs), cranial vena cava (from head), semilunar valves, right atrium, right atrio ventricular valve, right ventricle, caudal vena cava (from body), left atrium, left atrio ventricular valve, left ventricle. Legend: Deoxygenated blood, Oxygenated blood [6]

Arteries branch off from the aorta and travel to all parts of the body, continuing to branch and get smaller until they become **arterioles.** Arterioles lead to very small beds of tiny blood vessels called **capillaries.** Capillary beds are the site where the exchange of nutrients, gases, and wastes occurs. Blood that now contains wastes leaves the capillary beds, and enters small vessels called **venules.** These travel back through the body to the heart, becoming larger veins on the way, ending with the **large vena cava vein** that empties into the heart.

This begins the cycle all over again!

Things the Circulatory System Carries:
- Oxygen from the lungs to the body's cells.
- Carbon dioxide from the body's cells to the lungs.
- Nutrients from the digestive system to the cells.
- Waste products, other than carbon dioxide, to the liver and kidneys.
- Hormones and other messenger chemicals, from the glands and organs of their production to the body's cells.

Blood

Blood helps regulate our internal environment and keeps us in a generally constant state known as **homeostasis.** Blood transports and mixes elements up, making it possible for all the organs to contribute to maintaining homeostasis.

Blood is not a liquid; it is a **suspension** (fluids containing particles suspended inside them). Blood has two components: **plasma**, the liquid part, and the solid **blood cells** suspended throughout. There are three major types of cells: **red blood cells**, **white blood cells**, and cellular fragments called **platelets.**

---

[6] Graphic from: http://www.en.wikibooks.org

Plasma is mostly water, in which some substances such as proteins, hormones, and nutrients (glucose sugar, vitamins, amino acids, and fats) are dissolved. Gases (carbon dioxide and oxygen), salts (of calcium, chloride, and potassium), and wastes other than carbon dioxide are also dissolved in blood.

Red blood cells contain a protein molecule called **hemoglobin**, which holds an atom of iron. The hemoglobin molecule binds with oxygen and carbon dioxide, thus providing the mechanism by which the red blood cells can carry these gases around the body.

White blood cells come in many specialized forms and are used in the immune system to fight off invading organisms and keep us from getting diseases.

Platelets release substances at the site of a wound that start the blood-clotting reaction.

Plants
In plants, the transport system is based on the special properties of water.

The cells that make up the vascular tissue of plants form a continuous system of tubes running from the roots, through the stems, and to the leaves. Water and nutrients flow to the leaves through a vascular tissue called **xylem**, where they are used in the process of photosynthesis. Following that process, the products of photosynthesis then flow through a vascular tissue called **phloem** back down to the roots.

Practice Drill: The Cardiovascular System

1. Which of the following is NOT one of the chambers in the four-chambered vertebrate heart?
     a) Right atrium.
     b) Right ventricle.
     c) Left alveolar.
     d) Left ventricle.

2. Which of the following is true about blood flow in the four-chambered vertebrate heart circulatory system?
     a) Blood in the pulmonary vein is oxygenated.
     b) Blood in the pulmonary artery is oxygenated.
     c) Blood in the aorta is not oxygenated.
     d) Blood in the vena cava is oxygenated.

3. Which of the following are the major components of blood?
     a) Proteins and lipids.
     b) Plasma and cells.
     c) Proteins and platelets.
     d) Dells and lipids.

4. Platelets perform which of the following functions?
     a) Blood clotting.
     b) Carrying oxygen.
     c) Carrying carbon dioxide.
     d) Disease protection.

5. Capillary beds occur between:
   a) Arteries and veins.
   b) Aortas and vena cavas.
   c) Arterioles and venules.
   d) Atria and ventricles.

6. Red blood cells perform which of the following functions?
   a) Blood clotting.
   b) Carrying oxygen and carbon dioxide.
   c) Disease protection.
   d) Wound healing.

7. Xylem and phloem are plant tissues that:
   a) Produce sugar molecules and oxygen.
   b) Transport water and nutrients throughout the plant.
   c) Contain chloroplasts.
   d) Produce seeds.

8. The products of photosynthesis in the leaves flow to the roots through vascular tissue called:
   a) Phloem.
   b) Xylem.
   c) Meristem.
   d) Angiosperm.

Practice Drill: The Cardiovascular System – Answers

1. c)
2. a)
3. b)
4. a)
5. c)
6. b)
7. b)
8. a)

THE RENAL SYSTEM (FILTRATION/EXCRETION SYSTEM)

Single-celled organisms excrete toxic substances; either by diffusion through their cell membranes, or through specialized organelles called **vacuoles.** Likewise, metabolic chemical reactions occurring within the cells of organisms produce potentially harmful wastes which must be excreted. Multicellular organisms require special organ systems – specifically the circulatory and excretory systems, in humans – to eliminate wastes.

Organisms must be able to respond to changes in their external environment while still maintaining a relatively constant internal environment. **Homeostasis** – the physical and chemical processes that work to maintain that internal balance of water, temperature, salt concentration, etc. – is maintained by the cooperation of both the circulatory and renal systems

Remember digestion: Food is broken down, absorbed as very small molecules, and carried to the cells by blood. Cells need these broken-down molecules to perform the life-sustaining biochemical reactions of metabolism, which produce wastes.

For example: Aerobic respiration produces water and **carbon dioxide**; anaerobic respiration produces **lactic acid** and carbon dioxide; dehydration synthesis produces water; protein metabolism produces **nitrogenous wastes**, (i.e. **ammonia**); and other metabolic processes can produce salts, oils, etc.

Toxic wastes are disposed of according to their molecular make-up. For example, blood carries gaseous wastes like carbon dioxide to the lungs for exhalation. Other wastes need to first be filtered out of the blood before excretion. Nitrogenous wastes are the result of excess amino acids broken down during cellular respiration. The toxicity (harmfulness) of those nitrogenous wastes varies from: **Extremely Toxic** (Ammonia); **Less Toxic** (Urea); **Non-Toxic** (Uric Acid). **Non-toxic** wastes can be retained, released, or recycled through other reactions.

The Kidneys

Toxic wastes are carried by blood to the liver, where they are converted into **urea.** The blood then carries the urea to the **kidneys** (bean-shaped, fist-sized organs), where it will be converted from urea into **urine**. Urine is able to mix with water and be excreted from the body; the amount of water that is used in this process is regulated by the kidneys in order to prevent body dehydration. The kidneys are complex filtering systems which maintain the proper levels of various life-supporting substances, including sodium; potassium; chloride; calcium; glucose sugar; and amino acids. These life-supporting substances are absorbed by the kidneys from urine before it I expelled. The kidneys also help maintain blood pressure and the acidity (pH) level of the blood.

Each kidney contains at least a million individual units called **nephrons.** Nephrons perform similar functions as the alveoli do in the lungs; but whereas the alveoli function as areas of gas exchange, the kidney nephrons are structured to function as areas of *fluid* interchange. Each nephron contains a bed of capillaries. Those capillaries which are bringing in blood are surrounded by a **Bowman's capsule**.

Bowman's capsules are important parts of the filtration system. They separate the blood into two components: a cleaned blood product, and a filtrate which is moved through the nephron. As the filtrate travels through the nephron, more impurities are removed; and the filtrate concentrates into **urine**, which is then processed for elimination. The collected urine flows into the **ureters**, which take it to the **urinary bladder**. Urine will collect in the urinary bladder until the pressure causes an urge to expel it from the body through the **urethra**. Each of the hundreds of nephrons in the kidneys is attached to its own Bowman's capsule.

Kidneys are remarkably important structures; processing the body's blood about 20 times, each day! They also regulate the amount of water in the bloodstream. If the brain detects depleted levels of water, it increases the release of the **antidiuretic hormone** (**ADH**). ADH causes the kidneys to reabsorb water into the bloodstream, preserving water (and concentrating urine) in the body. The reason why you urinate more frequently when drinking alcohol is because alcohol inhibits the ADH signal from the brain.

The kidneys are truly a feat of natural engineering. In fact, despite the medical community's best efforts, it has so far been impossible to build a fully artificial kidney.

Practice Drill: The Renal System

1. The kidneys filter which of the following from blood?
   a) Undigested food.
   b) Metabolic wastes.
   c) Blood cells.
   d) Platelets.

2. Which of the following is **NOT** a function of the kidneys?
   a) Regulating pH (acidity) of blood.
   b) Regulating blood pressure.
   c) Assisting in the maintenance of homeostasis.
   d) Regulating hormone release.

3. The nephron is where _____ is produced.
   a) Urine.
   b) Ammonia.
   c) Nucleic acid.
   d) Amino acid.

4. Waste concentrated in the Bowman's capsule is called:
   a) Urine.
   b) Salts.
   c) Nucleic acids.
   d) Amino acids.

5. Alcohol consumption increases urination because it:
   a) Increases the amount of water in the body.
   b) Increases the action of antidiuretic hormone.
   c) Decreases the action of antidiuretic hormone.
   d) Stops water reabsorption.

Practice Drill: The Renal System – Answers

1. **b)**
2. **d)**
3. **a)**
4. **a)**
5. **c)**

THE NERVOUS SYSTEM

Irritability is a term used to describe an organism's response to changes, or **stimuli**, in its surroundings. All living organisms respond to environmental stimulus, usually by taking some sort of action: movement of a muscle, gland secretion, activating entire systems like digestion, etc.

Plants have cellular receptors that use chemical messengers to detect and respond to aspects of their environment such as light, gravity, and touch. For example, the orientation of a plant toward or away from light, called **phototropism** is mediated by hormones.

In multi-celled animals, a nervous system controls these responses.

The functioning unit of the nervous system is the **neuron**, a cell with structures capable of transmitting electrical impulses. A neuron must be able to first receive information from internal or external sources, before integrating the signal and sending it to another neuron, gland, or muscle. In multi-celled vertebrates, each neuron has four regions.

At one end of the neuron, there are branch-like extensions called **dendrites**, which receive signals from other neurons.

The **cell body** of the neuron is where the cellular functions take place and where signals are integrated.

The **axon** is an extension from the cell body which the nerve impulses travel along. Axons can be several feet in length, carrying signals from one end of the body to the other.

At the very end of the axon is the **synaptic terminal**, an area that contains chemical substances called **neurotransmitters.**

When an electrical nerve signal reaches the synaptic terminal, it causes neurotransmitters to be released. Neurotransmitters then move across the small space between the neuron and the next neuron (or gland or muscle). This small space is called the **synapse.** Once across the synapse, the neurotransmitter is received by the dendrites of another neuron (or the receptors on a gland or muscle) and then turned back into an electrical signal to be passed on.

The nervous system is divided into two main systems, the **central nervous system (CNS)** and the **peripheral nervous system (PNS)**.

CNS
The central nervous system consists of the brain and spinal cord (contained within the vertebral column or backbone). The brain integrates all the signals in the nervous system, and therefore is responsible for controlling every aspect of the body.

PNS
The peripheral nervous system consists of the nerves outside of the brain and spinal cord. The main function of the PNS is to connect the CNS to the limbs, organs, and **senses**. Unlike the CNS, the PNS is not protected by the bone of spine and skull. This leaves the PNS exposed to toxins and mechanical injuries. The peripheral nervous system is divided into the **somatic nervous system** and the **autonomic nervous system**.

The **somatic nervous system** deals with motor functions. Its nerves connect with skeletal muscle and control movement of all kinds, from fine motor skills to walking and running.

The **autonomic nervous system** works mostly without our conscious control. It is often responsible for critical life functions such as breathing and heart rate. The autonomic nervous system has two divisions.

> The **sympathetic division** is responsible for the fight-or-flight response; it prepares the body for high-energy, stressful situations.

> The **parasympathetic division** is responsible for rest and digestion functions, so it tends to slow down the body.

Nerves from each of these divisions usually make contact with the same organs, but they often have opposite effects.

The Endocrine System

Another important system in our body is the endocrine, or glandular, system. It controls growth rate, feelings of hunger, body temperature, and more. Many organs run the endocrine system: the **pituitary gland**, the **pancreas**, the **ovaries** (only in females) and **testes** (only in males), the **thyroid** gland, the **parathyroid** gland, the **adrenal** glands, etc.

Of all these, the pituitary gland is the most important endocrine gland in your body. About the size of a pea, the pituitary gland hangs down from the base of your brain and produces the hormone which controls growth.

Fun Fact: Humans grow faster at night because more hormones are released into your blood when you are sleeping.

Practice Drill: The Nervous System

1. _____ is the functional unit of the nervous system.
   a) The nephron
   b) The nucleus
   c) The neuron
   d) The neutrophil

2. Which of the following is a part of the CNS?
   a) Autonomic nerves.
   b) Sympathetic nerves.
   c) Peripheral nerves.
   d) Spinal cord nerves.

3. What is the chemical substance that carries a message from one cell to another?
   a) Axon fluid.
   b) Dendrite fluid.
   c) Neurotransmitter.
   d) Hormone.

4. Dendrites receive information from:
   a) The axon of other neurons.
   b) The dendrites of other neurons.
   c) The cell body of other neurons.
   d) The nucleus of other neurons.

5. _____ release neurotransmitters.
   a) Axons.
   b) Dendrites.
   c) Cell bodies.
   d) The nucleus.

6. Which of the following is NOT true about irritability?
   a) Plants do not experience irritability.
   b) Activates neurons in the brain.
   c) Requires axons in animals.
   d) Neurons act upon muscles.

7. The most important gland in the human body is:
   a) The pancreas.
   b) The pituitary.
   c) The ovaries.
   d) The thyroid.

Practice Drill: The Nervous System – Answers

1. **c)**
2. **d)**
3. **c)**
4. **a)**
5. **a)**
6. **a)**
7. **b)**

Chemistry

General chemistry examines the structure of matter as well as the reaction between matter and energy. It is the science that deals with the properties and transformations of materials. This section will cover the fundamental terms and processes of general chemistry, which include states of matter, chemical bonds, the periodic table, and principles and applications.

ELEMENTS, COMPOUNDS, AND MIXTURES

Matter

Matter is commonly defined as anything that takes up space and has mass. **Mass** is the quantity of matter something possesses, and usually has a unit of weight associated with it.

Matter can undergo two types of change: chemical and physical.

A **chemical change** occurs when an original substance is transformed into a new substance with different properties. An example would be the burning of wood, which produces ash and smoke.

Transformations that do not produce new substances, such as stretching a rubber band or melting ice, are called **physical changes**.

The fundamental properties which we use to measure matter are mass, weight, volume, density and specific gravity.

Extrinsic properties are directly related to the amount of material being measured, such as weight and volume.

Intrinsic properties are those which are independent of the quantity of matter present, such as density and specific gravity.

Atom

An atom is the ultimate particle of matter; it is the smallest particle of an element that still is a part of that element. All atoms of the same element have the same mass. Atomic chemical changes involve the transfer of whole atoms from one substance to another; but atoms are not created or destroyed in ordinary chemical changes.

An atom is made up of several parts. The center is called the **nucleus**, and is made up of two particles: a positively-charged particle, called a **proton**, and a particle that does not have a charge, called a **neutron**. The masses of a proton and neutron are about the same.

The nucleus of the atom is surrounded by negatively-charged particles called **electrons**, which move in orbits around the nucleus. The nucleus is only a small portion of the total amount of space an atom takes up, even though most of an atom's mass is contained in the nucleus.

Molecular Weight

A **mole** is the amount of substance that contains 6.02×10^{23} basic particles. This is referred to as **Avogadro's number** and is based on the number of atoms in C_{12} (Carbon 12). For example, a mole of copper is the amount of copper that contains exactly 6.02×10^{23} atoms, and one mole of water contains 6.02×10^{23} H_2O molecules. The weight of one mole of an element is called its **atomic weight**. The atomic weight of an element with isotopes, which are explained further below/on the next page, is the average of the isotopes' individual atomic weights.

The negatively-charged electrons are very light in mass. An atom is described as neutral if it has an equal number of protons and electrons, or if the number of electrons is the same as the atomic number of the atom. You may have already assumed – correctly! – from that information that the atomic number of an atom equals the number of protons in that atom. The **atomic weight** or **mass** of the atom is the total number of protons and neutrons in the atom's nucleus.

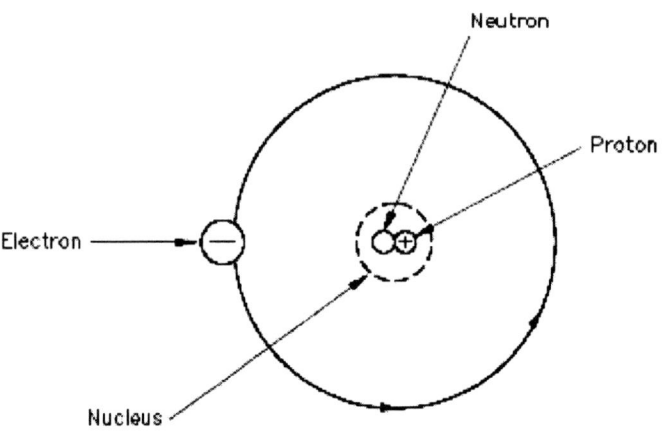

Elements
An element is a substance which cannot be broken down by chemical means; they are composed of atoms that have the same **atomic number** and are defined by the number of protons and neutrons they have. Some elements have more than one form, such as carbon; these alternate forms are called **isotopes.** There are approximately 109 known elements. Eighty-eight of these occur naturally on earth, while the others are **synthesized** (manufactured).

Hydrogen is the most abundant element in the Universe. It is found in 75% of all matter known to exist. **Helium** is the second most abundant element, found in approximately 25% of all known matter. The Earth is composed mostly of iron, oxygen, silicon, and magnesium, though these elements are not evenly distributed. 90% of the human body's mass consists of oxygen, carbon, hydrogen, nitrogen, calcium, and phosphorus. 75% of elements are metals, and eleven are gases in their natural state. We'll cover this more in-depth when we view the periodic table.

Molecules
A molecule is the smallest part of a substance that isn't chemically bonded to another atom. **Chemical formulas** are used to represent the atomic composition of a molecule. For example, one molecule of water contains 2 atoms of Hydrogen and 1 atom of Oxygen; its chemical formula is $2H + O = H_2O$.

Compounds and Mixtures
Substances that contain more than one type of element are called **compounds.** Compounds that are made up of molecules which are all identical are called **pure substances**. A **mixture** consists of two or more substances that are not chemically bonded. Mixtures are generally placed in one of two categories:

> **Homogeneous Mixture**: Components that make up the mixture are uniformly distributed; examples are water and air.

---

[7] Graphic from: http://www.circuitlab.org

Heterogeneous Mixture: Components of the mixture are not uniform; they sometimes have localized regions with different properties. For example: the different components of soup make it a heterogeneous mixture. Rocks, as well, are not uniform and have localized regions with different properties.

A uniform, or homogenous, mixture of different molecules is called a **solution**. If the solution is a liquid, the material being dissolved is the **solute** and the liquid it is being dissolved in is called the **solvent.** Both solids and gases can dissolve in liquids. A **saturated** has reached a point of maximum concentration; in it, no more solute will dissolve.

Practice Drill: Elements, Compounds, and Mixtures

1. Which statement best describes the density of an atom's nucleus?
    a) The nucleus occupies most of the atom's volume, but contains little of its mass.
    b) The nucleus occupies very little of the atom's volume, and contains little of its mass.
    c) The nucleus occupies most of the atom's volume, and contains most of its mass.
    d) The nucleus occupies very little of the atom's volume, but contains most of its mass.

2. Which of the following is not a physical change?
    a) Melting of aspirin.
    b) Lighting a match.
    c) Putting sugar in tea.
    d) Boiling of antifreeze.

3. A solid melts gradually between 85°C and 95°C to give a milky, oily liquid. When a laser beam shines through the liquid, the path of the beam is clearly visible. The milky liquid is likely to be:
    a) A heterogeneous mixture.
    b) An element.
    c) A compound.
    d) A solution.

4. The identity of an element is determined by:
    a) The number of its protons and neutrons.
    b) The number of its neutrons.
    c) The number of its electrons.
    d) Its atomic mass.

5. True or False? When a match burns, some matter is destroyed.
    a) True.
    b) False.

6. What is the reason for your answer to question **5**?
    a) This chemical reaction destroys matter.
    b) Matter is consumed by the flame.
    c) The mass of ash is less than the match it came from.
    d) The atoms are not destroyed, they are only rearranged.
    e) The match weighs less after burning.

7. An unsaturated solution:
    a) Hasn't dissolved as much solute as is theoretically possible.
    b) Has dissolved exactly as much solute as is theoretically possible.
    c) Is unstable because it has dissolved more solute than would be expected.
    d) None of the above.

8. A teaspoon of dry coffee crystals dissolves when mixed in a cup of hot water. This process produces a coffee solution. The original crystals are classified as a:
    a) Solute.
    b) Solvent.
    c) Reactant.
    d) Product.

Practice Drill: Elements, Compounds, and Mixtures – Answers

1. **d)**
2. **b)**
3. **c)**
4. **a)**
5. **b)**
6. **d)**
7. **a)**
8. **a)**

STATES OF MATTER

The physical states of matter are generally grouped into three main categories:

1. **Solids**: Rigid; they maintain their shape and have strong intermolecular forces.

2. **Liquids**: Cannot maintain their own shape, conform to their containers, and contain forces strong enough to keep molecules from dispersing into spaces.

3. **Gases**: Have indefinite shape; disperse rapidly through space due to random movement and are able to occupy any volume. They are held together by weak forces.

Two specific states of matter are **liquid crystals**, which can maintain their shape as well as be made to flow, and **plasmas**, gases in which electrons are stripped from their nuclei.

Gases

There are four physical properties of gases that are related to each other. If any one of these changes, a change will occur in at least one of the remaining three.

1. Volume of the gas.
2. Pressure of the gas.
3. Temperature of the gas.
4. The number of gas molecules.

The laws that relate these properties to each other are:

Boyle's Law: The volume of a given amount of gas at a constant temperature is inversely proportional to pressure. In other words; if the initial volume decreases by half, the pressure will double and vice versa. The representative equation is: $P_1V_1 = P_2V_2$.

Charles's Law: The volume of a given amount of gas at a constant pressure is directly proportional to absolute (Kelvin) temperature. If the temperature of the gas increases, the volume of the gas also increases and vice versa. The representative equation is: $V_1/T_1 = V_2/T_2$.

Avogadro's Law: Equal volumes of all gases under identical conditions of pressure and temperature contain the same number of molecules. The molar volume of all ideal gases at $0°$ C and a pressure of 1 atm. is 22.4 liters.

The **kinetic theory of gases** assumes that gas molecules are very small compared to the distance between the molecules. Gas molecules are in constant, random motion; they frequently collide with each other and with the walls of whatever container they are in.

Practice Drill: States of Matter

1. Under the same conditions of pressure and temperature, a liquid differs from a gas because the molecules of the liquid:
    a) Have no regular arrangement.
    b) Are in constant motion.
    c) Have stronger forces of attraction between them.
    d) Take the shape of the container they are in.

2. Methane (CH4) gas diffuses through air because the molecules are:
    a) Moving randomly.
    b) Dissolving quickly.
    c) Traveling slowly.
    d) Expanding steadily.

3. Which of the following would not change if the number of gas molecules changed?
    a) Volume of the gas.
    b) Type of gas.
    c) Pressure of the gas.
    d) Temperature of gas.

4. When the pressure is increased on a can filled with gas, its volume _____.
    a) Stays the same.
    b) Increases.
    c) Decreases.
    d) Turns to liquid.

5. Equal volumes of all gases at the same temperature and pressure contain the same number of molecules. This statement is known as:
    a) Kinetic theory of gases.
    b) Charles's Law.
    c) Boyle's Law.
    d) Avogadro's Law.

Practice Drill: States of Matter – Answers

1. c)
2. a)
3. b)
4. c)
5. d)

PERIODIC TABLE AND CHEMICAL BONDS

The Periodic table

The Periodic Table is a chart which arranges the chemical elements in a useful, logical manner. Elements are listed in order of increasing atomic number, lined up so that elements which exhibit similar properties are arranged in the same row or column as each other.

1a																	0
1 H 1.008	IIa											IIIb	IVa	Va	VIa	VIIa	2 He 4.00
3 Li 6.94	4 Be 9.01		12 Mg 24.31 <- Atomic number <- Chemical symbol <- Atomic weight									5 B 10.81	6 C 12.01	7 N 14.00	8 O 15.99	9 F 18.99	10 Ne 20.18
11 Na 22.99	12 Mg 24.31	IIIb	IVb	Vb	VIb	VIII			Ib	IIb		13 Al 26.98	14 Si 28.09	15 P 30.97	16 S 32.06	17 Cl 35.45	18 Ar 39.95
19 K 39.10	20 Ca 40.08	21 Sc 44.6	22 Ti 47.90	23 V 50.94	24 Cr 51.99	25 Mn 54.94	26 Fe 55.85	27 Co 58.93	28 Ni 58.71	29 Cu 63.54	30 Zn 65.37	31 Ga 69.72	32 Ge 72.59	33 As 74.92	34 Se 78.96	35 Br 79.91	36 Kr 83.80
37 Rb 85.47	38 Sr 87.62	39 Y 88.91	40 Zr 91.22	41 Nb 92.91	42 Mo 95.94	43 Tc 99	44 Ru 101.97	45 Rh 102.91	46 Pd 106.4	47 Ag 107.87	48 Cd 112.40	49 In 114.82	50 Sn 118.69	51 Sb 121.75	52 Te 127.60	53 I 126.90	54 Xe 131.30
55 Cs 132.91	56 Ba 137.34	57-71 see below	72 Hf 178.49	73 Ta 180.95	74 W 183.85	75 Re 186.2	76 Os 190.2	77 Ir 192.2	78 Pt 195.09	79 Au 196.97	80 Hg 200.59	81 Tl 204.37	82 Pb 207.19	83 Bi 208.98	84 Po 210	85 At 210	86 Rn 222
87 Fr 223	88 Ra 226	89-103 see below	104 Rf 261	105 Ha 260	106 Sg 263												

57 La 138.91	58 Ce 140.12	59 Pr 140.91	60 Nd 144.24	61 Pm 147	62 Sm 150.35	63 Eu 151.96	64 Gd 157.24	65 Tb 158.92	66 Dy 162.50	67 Ho 164.93	68 Er 167.26	69 Tm 168.93	70 Yb 173.04	71 Lu 174.97
89 Ac 227	90 Th 232.04	91 Pa 231	92 U 238.03	93 Np 237	94 Pu 242	95 Am 243	96 Cm 247	97 Bk 247	98 Cf 251	99 Es 254	100 Fm 253	101 Md 256	102 No 254	103 Lw 257

Note the following characteristics:

Each box contains the symbol of the element, its atomic number, and its atomic weight.

The elements appear in increasing order according to their atomic numbers, except for the two separate rows.

The vertical columns are called **groups**. Elements within a group share several common properties and often have the same outer electron arrangement. There are two categories: the main group and the transition elements.

The number of the main group corresponds to the number of valence electrons. Most of the transition elements contain 2 electrons in their valence shells.

The horizontal rows are called **periods** and correspond to the number of occupied electron shells of the atom.

The elements set below the main table are the **lanthanoids** (upper row) and **actinoids**. They also usually have two electrons in their outer shells.

---

[8] Graphic from: http://volcano.oregonstatevolcano.oregonstate.edu.

Most of the elements on the periodic table are metals. The alkali metals, alkaline earths, basic metals, transition metals, lanthanides, and actinides are all groups of metals.

In general, the elements increase in mass from left to right and from top to bottom.

The main difference between the modern periodic table and the one Mendeleev (the periodic table's creator) came up with is that Mendeleev's original table arranged the elements in order of increasing atomic weight, while the modern table orders the elements by increasing atomic number.

Electronic Structure of Atoms
The electrons of an atom have fixed energy levels. Those in the principle energy levels are said to be in **electron shells**. Shells which correspond to the highest energy levels, called **valance shells**, include the electrons usually involved in chemical bonding. Chemical formulas of simple compounds can often be predicted from valences. The valence electrons increase in number as you go across the periodic table.

The electrons in the outer orbit can combine with other atoms by giving up electrons or taking on electrons. Atoms that give up electrons (**cations**) change from being neutral to having a *positive* charge. Atoms that gain electrons (**ions**) change from being neutral to having a *negative* charge. The **octet rule** is a chemical rule which states that atoms of a low atomic number will share, gain, or lose electrons in order to fill outer electron shells with eight electrons. This is achieved through different types of bonding.

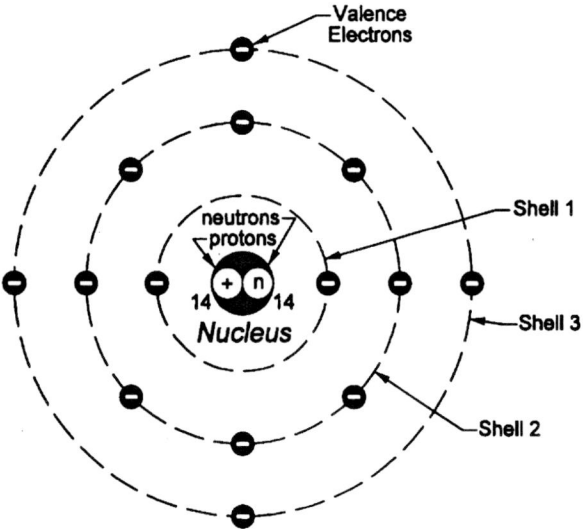

Chemical Bonds
Electromagnetism is involved in all chemical behavior, including the chemical bonds which hold atoms together to form molecules, as well as those holding molecules together to form all substances. **Electronegativity** measures the tendency of an atom to attract a bonding pair of electrons, and is affected by both the atomic number, and the distance between the valence electrons and the charged nucleus. The higher the assigned electronegativity number, the more an element or compound attracts electrons.

There are two main types of bonds formed between atoms: **Ionic** and **Covalent bonds.** Anions and cations, being negatively and positively charged respectively, exist because of the attraction of opposite charges, and usually form **ionic bonds**.

---

[9] Graphic from: http://www.circuitlab.org

A covalent bond forms when atoms share valence electrons. However, atoms do not always share electrons equally, resulting in a **polar covalent bond**. Electrons shared by two metallic atoms, form a **metallic bond**. Those electrons participating in metallic bonds may be shared between any of the metal atoms in the region.

If the electronegativity values of two atoms are similar, then:
- Metallic bonds form between two metal atoms.
- Covalent bonds form between two non-metal atoms.
- Non-polar covalent bonds form when the electronegativity values are very similar.
- Polar covalent bonds form when the electronegativity values are a little further apart.

If the electronegativity values of two atoms are different, then ionic bonds are formed.

Most metals have less than 4 valence electrons, which allows them to either gain a few electrons or lose a few; they generally tend to lose electrons, which causes them to become more positive. (This means that metals tend to form cations.)

A **hydrogen bond** is not considered a chemical bond. Instead, in a hydrogen bond, the attractive force between hydrogen is attached to an electronegative atom of one molecule and an electronegative atom of a different molecule. Usually the electronegative atom is oxygen, nitrogen, or fluorine, which have partial negative charges. The hydrogen has the partial positive charge. Hydrogen bonds are much weaker than both ionic and covalent bonds.

Practice Drill: Periodic Table and Chemical Bonds

1. When cations and anions join, they form what kind of chemical bond?
    a) Ionic.
    b) Hydrogen.
    c) Metallic.
    d) Covalent.

2. Generally, how do atomic masses vary throughout the periodic table of the elements?
    a) They decrease from left to right and increase from top to bottom.
    b) They increase from left to right and increase bottom to top.
    c) They increase from left to right and increase top to bottom.
    d) They increase from right to left and decrease bottom to top.

3. The force involved in all chemical behavior is:
    a) Electronegativity.
    b) Covalent bonds.
    c) Electromagnetism.
    d) Ionic bonds.

4. Which one of the following is not a form of chemical bonding?
    a) Covalent bonding.
    b) Hydrogen bonding.
    c) Ionic bonding.
    d) Metallic bonding.
5. Two atoms which do not share electrons equally will form what type of bond?
    a) Metallic bonds.
    b) Polar covalent.
    c) Ionic bonds.
    d) They cannot form bonds.

6. Chemical bonding:
    a) Uses electrons that are closest to the nucleus of the atoms bonding.
    b) Always uses electrons from only one of the atoms involved.
    c) Uses all the electrons in all atoms involved.
    d) Uses the valence electrons of all the atoms involved.

Practice Drill: Periodic Table and Chemical Bonds – Answers

1. a)
2. c)
3. c)
4. b)
5. b)
6. d)

ACIDS AND BASES

Acids

Naturally-occurring **acid solutions**, in which the solvent is always water, have several characteristic properties in common. They have a sour taste; speed up the corrosion, or rusting, of metals; conduct electricity; and introduce H^+ cations into aqueous solutions.

These characteristic properties can be changed by the addition of a base.

Bases (Alkalis)

Bases don't occur in as many common materials as do acids. A few examples of bases are: lime, lye, and soap. Basic solutions, as opposed to acidic solutions, have a bitter taste; conduct electricity, when their solvent is water; and introduce OH^- ions into an aqueous solution.

The characteristic properties can be changed by the addition of an acid.

The acidity or basicity of a solution is expressed by **pH values**. A neutral solution is defined by the following: it has equal concentrations of H^+ cations and OH^- ions, and a pH of 7. Neutrality is based on the pH of pure water. The more acidic a solution, the lower the pH is below 7. The more basic the solution, the higher the pH is above 7. The pH scale is based on logarithms of base 10. (If one solution has a pH of 8 and another has a pH of 10, then there is a 10^2 or 100 fold difference between the two.)

pH Scale

0	0.0 Hydrochloric acid (1M)
	2.0 Stomach acid
acids	3.0 Lemon juice
	5.0 Urine
	6.5 Saliva
7	**7.0 Pure water**
	7.4 Blood 8.0 Pancreatic juice
bases	11.0 Ammonia cleansers
	13.5 Oven cleaner
14	14.0 Sodium hydroxide (1 M) [10]

A **buffer** is used to make a solution which exhibits very little change in its pH when small amounts of an acid or base are added to it.

An acidic buffer solution is simply one which has a pH less than 7. Acidic buffer solutions are commonly made from a weak acid and one of its salts - often a sodium salt. A strong basic solution can be weakened by adding an acidic buffer.

---

[10] Graphic from: http://bioserv.fiu.edu

An alkaline buffer solution has a pH greater than 7. Alkaline buffer solutions are commonly made from a weak base and one of its salts. A strong acid can be made weaker by adding an alkaline buffer.

The human body contains many enzymes that only function at a specific pH. Once outside of this range, the enzymes are either unable to catalyze reactions or, in some cases, will break down. Our bodies produce a buffer solution that is a mixture of carbonic acid and bicarbonate, in order to keep the pH of blood at 7.4.

Practice Drill: Acids and Bases

1. One of the characteristic properties of an acid is that they introduce:
    a) Hydrogen ions.
    b) Hydroxyl ions.
    c) Hydride ions.
    d) Oxide ions.

2. A solution with a pH of 12 is:
    a) Very acidic.
    b) Neutral.
    c) Very basic.
    d) You can't have a solution with a pH of 12.

3. Buffers keep the pH of a solution from changing by:
    a) Converting strong acids to weak ones.
    b) Converting weak acids to strong ones.
    c) Converting weak bases to strong ones.
    d) More than one of the above answers is correct.

4. Proper blood pH level for humans is:
    a) 7.0.
    b) 7.2.
    c) 7.6.
    d) 7.4.

5. All of the following are properties of alkalis except:
    a) Bitter taste.
    b) Basic solutions are high conductors of electricity.
    c) Introduce OH⁻ ions into an aqueous solution.
    d) The characteristic properties can be changed by the addition of an acid.

Practice Drill: Acids and Bases – Answers

1. **a)**
2. **c)**
3. **a)**
4. **d)**
5. **b)**

Physics

Physics is the science of matter and energy, and of interactions between the two, grouped in traditional fields such as acoustics, optics, mechanics, thermodynamics, and electromagnetism.

MOTION

Speed is a scalar quantity and is defined as distance divided by time. (Ex: miles per hour.) **Velocity** is a vector quantity that describes speed and the direction of travel. **Magnitude of Acceleration** is defined as the change in velocity divided by the time interval. A **scalar quantity** is described only by its magnitude, whereas a **vector quantity** is described by magnitude and direction.

 Acceleration is change in velocity divided by time; an object accelerates not only when it speeds up, but also when slowing down or turning. The **acceleration due to gravity** of a falling object near the Earth is a constant $9.8 m/s^2$; therefore an object's magnitude increases as it falls and decreases as it rises.

Newton's Three Laws of Motion

1. An object at rest will remain at rest unless acted on by an unbalanced force. An object in motion continues in motion with the same speed and in the same direction unless acted upon by an unbalanced force. This law is often called "**the law of inertia**".

2. Acceleration is produced when a force acts on a mass. The greater the mass (of the object being accelerated) the greater the amount of force needed (to accelerate the object). Think of it like this: it takes a greater amount of force to push a boulder, than it does to push a feather.

3. Every action requires an equal and opposite reaction. This means that for every force, there is a reacting force both equal in size and opposite in direction. (I.e. whenever an object pushes another object, it gets pushed back in the opposite direction with equal force.)

An object's **density** is its mass divided by its volume. **Frictional forces** arise when one object tries move over or around another; the frictional forces act in the opposite direction to oppose such a motion. **Pressure** is the force per unit area which acts upon a surface.

There are **Three Important Conservation Laws** which are embodied within Newton's Laws. They offer a different and sometimes more powerful way to consider motion:

1. **Conservation of Momentum**: Embodied in Newton's first law (Law of Inertia), this reiterates that the momentum of a system is constant if no external forces act upon the system.

2. **Conservation of Energy**: Energy is neither created nor destroyed; it can be converted from one form to another (i.e. potential energy converted to kinetic energy), but the total amount of energy within the domain remains fixed.

3. **Conservation of Angular Momentum**: If the system is subjected to no external force, then the total angular momentum of a system has constant magnitude and direction. This is the common physics behind figure-skating and planetary orbits.

Energy and Forces

The energy stored within an object is called its **potential energy** – it has the potential to do work. But where does that energy come from? When gravity pulls down on an object (**gravitational energy**) the object receives potential energy. **Kinetic energy**, the energy of motion, is the energy possessed because of an object's motion.

The sum of an object's kinetic and potential energies is called the total **mechanical energy** (or, **internal energy**).

Frictional forces convert kinetic energy and gravitational potential energy into **thermal energy**. **Power** is the energy converted from one form to another, divided by the time needed to make the conversion. A **simple machine** is a device that alters the magnitude or direction of an applied force. Example: an inclined plane or lever.

Objects that move in a curved path have acceleration towards the center of that path. That acceleration is called a **centripetal acceleration. Centripetal force** is the inward force causing that object to move in the curved path. If the centripetal force is the action, the (opposite) reaction is an outwardly-directed **centrifugal force**.

THERMAL PHYSICS

Temperature and Heat

Heat and temperature are two different things. **Heat** is a measure of the work required to change the speeds in a collection of atoms or molecules. **Temperature** is a measure of the average kinetic energy of the atoms or molecules of a substance.

A **calorie** is the amount of heat required to raise the temperature of 1 gram of water by 1 degree Celsius. The **specific heat** of a substance is the ratio of the amount of heat added to a substance, divided by the mass and the temperature change of the substance.

The change of a substance from solid to liquid, or liquid to gas, etc., is called a **phase change**.

> **Heat of Fusion:** The amount of heat required to change a unit mass of a substance from solid to liquid at the *melting point*.

> **Heat of Vaporization:** The amount of heat needed to change a unit mass of a substance from liquid to vapor at the *boiling point*.

HEAT TRANSFER

Temperature Scales
There are three common temperature scales: **Celsius**, **Fahrenheit**, and **Kelvin**. Because it is based upon what we believe to be **absolute zero** (the lowest theoretical temperature possible before life ceases), the Kelvin scale is also known as the **absolute scale**.

Temperature Scale	Point at Which Water Freezes
Celsius	0° C
Fahrenheit	32° F
Kelvin	273K

The Two Mechanisms of Heat Transfer

> **Conduction**: Heat transfer via conduction can occur in a substance of any phase (solid, liquid, or gas), but is mostly seen in solids.

> **Convection**: Convection heat transfer occurs only in fluids (liquids and gases).

Both types of heat transfer are caused by molecular movement in the substance of interest.

WAVE MOTION (SOUND) AND MAGNETISM

Waves
Waves can be placed in one of two categories: **longitudinal** or **transverse**.

In a **transverse wave**, the motion of the medium is perpendicular to the motion of the wave; for example, waves on water. In a **longitudinal wave**, the motion of the medium is parallel to the motion of the wave. Sound waves are transverse waves.

A wave's **wavelength** is the distance between successive high points (**crests**) and low points (**troughs**). The **speed of a wave** is the rate at which it moves. **Frequency** – measured in **Hertz** (Hz) – is the number of repetitions, or cycles, occurring per second. The **amplitude** is the intensity (or strength) of the wave.

Sound
When vibrations disturb the air, they create sound waves. The **speed of a sound wave** is approximately 331m/s at 0° C. Human ears are capable of hearing frequencies between 20 to 16,000 Hz. The **decibel** (dB) scale is used to measure the loudness (amount of energy) of a sound wave. The scale starts at zero, which is the softest audio, and increases tenfold in intensity for every 10dB.

Magnetism is a force which either pulls magnetic materials together or pushes them apart. Iron and nickel are the most common magnetic materials. All magnetic materials are made up of tiny groups of atoms called domains. Each domain is like a mini-magnet with north and south poles. When material is magnetized, millions of domains line up.

Around every magnet there is a region in which its effects are felt, called its **magnetic field**. The magnetic field around a planet or a star is called the **magnetosphere**. Most of the planets in the Solar System, including Earth, have a magnetic field. Planets have magnetic fields because of the liquid iron in their cores. As the planets rotate, so does the iron swirl, generating electric currents which create a magnetic field. The strength of a magnet is measured in **teslas**. The Earth's magnetic field is 0.00005 teslas.

An electric current creates its own magnetic field. **Electromagnetism** (the force created together by magnetism and electricity) is one of the four fundamental forces in the Universe; the other three are gravity and the two basic forces of the atomic nucleus.

A magnet has two poles: a north pole and a south pole. Like (similar) poles (e.g. two north poles) repel each other; unlike poles attract each other. The Earth has a magnetic field that is created by electric currents within its iron core. The magnetic north pole is close to the geographic North Pole. If left to swivel freely, a magnet will turn so that its north pole points to the Earth's magnetic north pole.

Practice Drill: Physics

1. The temperature at which all molecular motion stops is:
   a) −460 °C.
   b) −273 K.
   c) 0 K.
   d) 0C.

2. What is the amount of heat required to raise the temperature of 1 gram of water by 1 degree Celsius?
   a) Specific heat
   b) Heat of fusion
   c) calorie
   d) Heat of vaporization

3. An object that has kinetic energy must be:
   a) Moving.
   b) Falling.
   c) At an elevated position.
   d) At rest.

4. The amount of heat required to melt an ice cube is called:
   a) Conduction.
   b) Specific Heat.
   c) A calorie.
   d) Heat of fusion.

5. A moving object has
   a) Velocity.
   b) Momentum.
   c) Energy.
   d) All of these.

6. Heat transferred between a pot of boiling water and the air above it is an example of:
   a) Conduction.
   b) Convection.
   c) Heat of vaporization.
   d) Phase change.

7. _____ increases, decreases, or changes the direction of a force.
   a) A simple machine.
   b) Energy.
   c) Momentum.
   d) Inertia.

8. _____ is a measure of the average kinetic energy of the atoms or molecules of a substance.
   a) Specific Heat
   b) Temperature
   c) Heat
   d) Force

9. Average speed is:
   a) A measure of how fast something is moving.
   b) The distance covered per unit of time.
   c) Always measured in terms of a unit of distance divided by a unit of time.
   d) All of the above.

10. Which of the following controls can change a car's velocity?
   a) The steering wheel.
   b) The brake pedal.
   c) Both A and B.
   d) None of the above.

11. The distance between two corresponding parts of a wave.
   a) Wavelength.
   b) Crest.
   c) Energy.
   d) Equidistance.

12. The high part of a transverse wave.
   a) Height.
   b) Period.
   c) Crest.
   d) Wavelength.

13. The magnetic field around a planet or a star is called a(an):
   a) Electromagnetic field.
   b) Magnetosphere.
   c) Magnetic field.
   d) Magnetic energy field.

14. The number of waves that pass a given point in one second.
  a) Trough.
  b) Energy.
  c) Crest.
  d) Frequency.

15. Unit of measurement for wave frequency.
  a) Crest.
  b) Decibel.
  c) Hertz (Hz).
  d) Period.

Practice Drill: Physics – Answers

1. **c)**
2. **c)**
3. **a)**
4. **d)**
5. **d)**
6. **b)**
7. **a)**
8. **b)**
9. **d)**
10. **c)**
11. **a)**
12. **c)**
13. **b)**
14. **d)**
15. **c)**

Geology

Geology is a branch of science which deals with the study of the Earth, the materials of which it is made, the structure of those materials, and the processes acting upon them. A very important part of geology is the study of how Earth's materials, structures, processes and organisms have changed over time. It includes such areas as volcanoes, rocks, minerals, gemstones, earthquakes, fossil fuels, and tectonics.

EARTH'S STRUCTURE

When the Earth first formed – about 4.54 billion years ago – it looked like a ball of bubbling-hot liquid rocks; rocks with different chemical elements, compounds, sizes, and weights. After a while, the heavier rocks started to "sink" towards the center of the Earth, while the lighter rocks moved towards the Earth's surface. This separation of rocks took millions of years. The Earth has a circumference of 24, 901 miles, and is made of several – sometimes overlapping – layers. These layers can be classified in two ways: by chemical composition, and by physical properties.

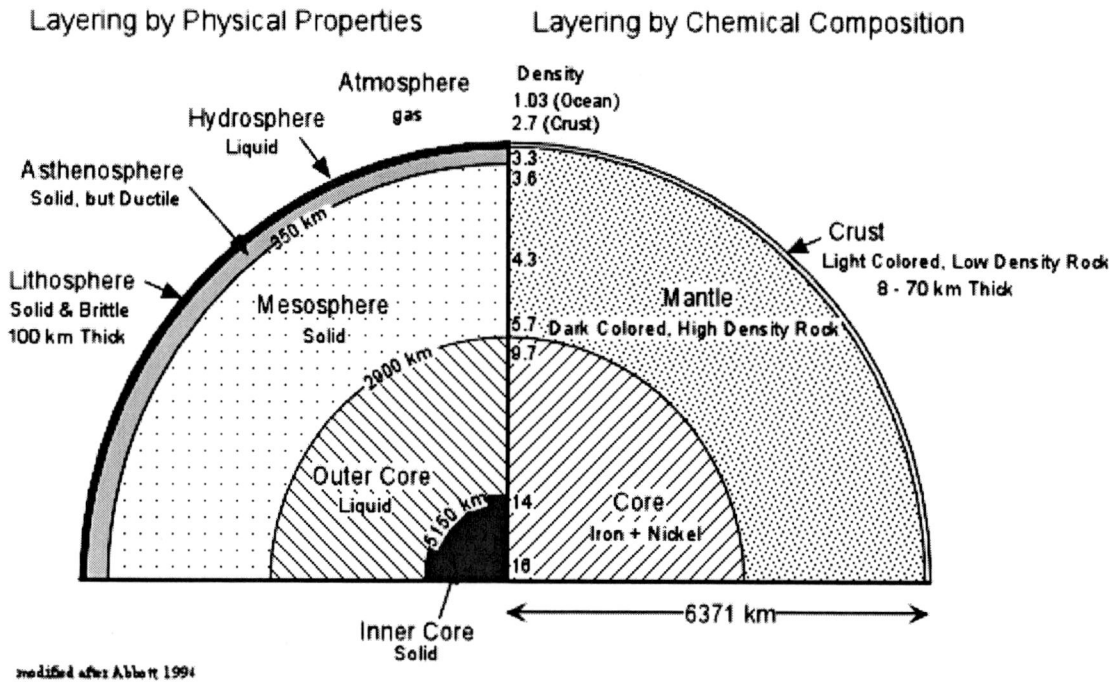

There are six levels to the Earth:

> **Inner Core:** Made of *solid* iron and nickel.
> **Outer Core:** *Molten* (hot liquid) iron and nickel, surrounding the inner core.
> **Mantle (mesosphere):** A large solid layer surrounding the **core**.
> **Asthenosphere:** The semi-fluid and flexible upper section of the mantle.
> **Lithosphere:** Includes the surface crust and the uppermost portion of the mantle.
> **Hydrosphere**: The liquid water component of the Earth.

81

Rocks

A **mineral** is a naturally-occurring inorganic solid that has a definite chemical composition and crystal structure. Mineral deposits are formed by many processes: separation by gravity, formation of placer deposits in streams (ex. gold) and lakes, chemical deposition of minerals in sea water, and more.

A **rock** is defined as a natural solid made up of minerals or other natural solids. For example, granite is a rock and quartz is a mineral.

Igneous rocks are formed directly from molten magma, or lava.

Sedimentary rocks are formed from sediments that are compressed or cemented together.

Metamorphic rocks are formed when other types of rock are heated and compressed over long periods of time.

Plate Tectonic Theory

Those independent sections of the Earth's lithosphere which move are called **tectonic plates**. Plate Tectonic Theory states that approximately 320 million years ago, the precursors to today's continents converged into a single land mass. Then, around 180 million years ago, that mass broke apart into seven tectonic plates: the African, North American, South American, Eurasian, Australian, Antarctic, and Pacific plates. Several minor plates also exist, including the Arabian, Nazca, and Philippines plates.

These plates all move around like cars in a demolition derby, at different speeds (from 2 cm to 10 cm per year--about the speed at which your fingernails grow!) and in different directions. A place where two plates meet is called a **plate boundary**. Boundaries have different names depending on how the two plates are moving in relationship to each other. If they are crashing, they are called **convergent** boundaries; pulling apart: **divergent** boundaries; sideswiping: **transform** boundaries.

Earthquakes generally occur where plates slip past each other; where one plate is sub-ducted (pushed under another; or at mid-ocean ridges, where plates are separating. **Volcanoes** occur when magma rapidly rises to the surface.

Mountain ranges are also formed through various processes – the Andes formed along a sub-duction zone, while the Himalayas were formed when two continental plates collided; the modern Rockies were formed by a compression followed by expansion.

Weathering is the deterioration of rock into small pieces, either through chemical or mechanical processes.

Chemical weathering involves the direct effect of atmospheric or biologically-produced *chemicals* on rocks.

Mechanical (or physical) weathering involves the breakdown of rocks through atmospheric *conditions* such as temperature changes, biological processes, moving water, wind, and glaciers.

Erosion is the movement of small bits of rock and soil. **Fossil fuel** deposits are partially decomposed organic debris. **Soil** is a mixture of pulverized rock and organic debris. Soil conditions are regulated by **humus:** a complex mixture of compounds resulting from the decomposition of plant tissue (stems and leaves).

THE HYDROLOGIC CYCLE (WATER CYCLE)

The movement of water on Earth is called the hydrologic cycle, the methods of which can be broken down into three different categories: **evaporation**, **precipitation**, and **run off**. The hydrologic cycle utilizes all three forms of water: vapor, liquid and solid.

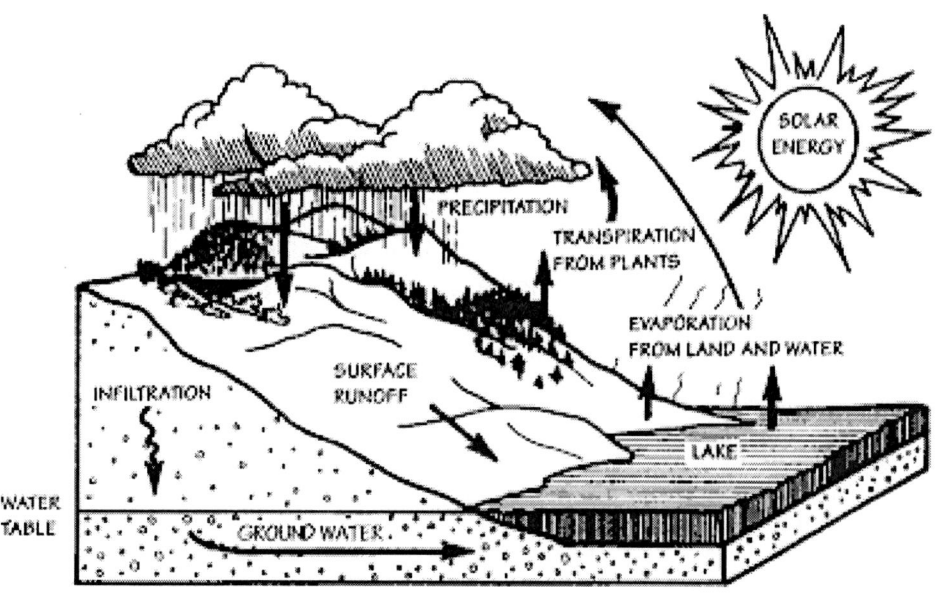

Evaporation is the transformation of liquid water to water vapor. Water can also vaporize through plant tissue, especially leaf surfaces. This process is known as **transpiration.**

Water which enters the atmosphere must first condense into a liquid (clouds and rain) or a solid (snow, hail, and sleet) before it can descend. **Precipitation** includes all forms by which atmospheric water falls to the Earth: snow, rain, hail, and sleet.

Runoff is the flow of water back to bodies of water, either by land (rivers and streams take this route) or through underground sources.

Ground water is found in spaces between soil particles underground (located in the zone of saturation). **Infiltration** is the process by which ground water accumulates and soaks into the ground. There it either replenishes shallow aquifers, or seeps into deep aquifers. **Aquifers** serve as underground beds of saturated soil or rock which yield significant quantities of water. **Shallow aquifers** flow into and replenish rivers and streams, while **deep aquifers** serve as large underground reservoirs of freshwater. Water may remain in deep aquifers for centuries, gradually moving towards and into the sea, where it then evaporates again into the atmosphere.

---

[11] Graphic from: greatswamp.org

TIDES

Most places on Earth have two high tides and two low tides which follow a cycle coinciding with the 24-hour 50-minute lunar day (or, the time it takes Earth to make one complete rotation relative to the moon). Along America's Atlantic Coast, two high and low tides occur daily, with relatively little difference between successive high and low waters. Such tides are called **semi-diurnal**. On the north shore of the Gulf of Mexico, the tide is **diurnal**, moving in and out again only once a day. The Pacific Northwest gets **mixed tides**, two highs and two lows day, characterized by significant gaps between successive tides.

An incoming tidal flow is called a **flood current** or **flood tide**; an outgoing flow is an **ebb current** or **ebb tide**. The time between the two tides, with little to no current, is called **slack water** or **slack tide**.

The moon's phases also greatly affect tides. Whenever the moon aligns with the earth and sun during its full-moon and new-moon phases, we have extremely high and extremely low tides, known as **spring tides**: a term that has nothing to do with the actual spring season.

Between these phases, when the moon is in its first and third quarters, the moon is at right angles to the sun. This position counterbalances the gravitational interaction of the moon and sun, resulting in a period when the range between high and low tides is minimal. These are known as **neap tides**. A **riptide** is a strong, subsurface tidal current that conflicts with another current or currents. They cause a violent underwater disturbance, usually in a direction contrary to that of the surface water.

Practice Drill: Geology

1. Which of the following is NOT a type of plate boundary?
    a) Transform.
    b) Translational.
    c) Divergent.
    d) Convergent.

2. In which scenario below would you be likely to hire a geologist to help better understand the situation?
    a) A spacecraft uses radar to map the surface of a planet in our Solar System.
    b) A volcano is erupting on a Pacific island.
    c) A small community is worried about contamination of their water wells from an industrial waste site.
    d) Geologists might be employed in all of these scenarios.

3. The most voluminous portion of the Earth is known to geologists as:
    a) The lithosphere.
    b) The mantle.
    c) The core.
    d) The crust.

4. The lithosphere is that portion of the Earth where rocks behave as:
    a) Rocks.
    b) Fluids.
    c) Plastic solids.
    d) Brittle solids.

5. Igneous, sedimentary, and metamorphic are:
    a) Three types of plate boundaries.
    b) Three divisions of Earth.
    c) Ways to describe soils.
    d) The three major classes of rocks.

6. Which of the following is **NOT** a subdivision of Earth's interior?
    a) The magnetosphere.
    b) The lithosphere.
    c) The core.
    d) The mantle.

7. What is transpiration?
    a) Transpiration is a process where water vapor enters the atmosphere when animals breathe.
    b) Transpiration is a process where water vapor forms clouds.
    c) Transpiration is a process where water vapor exits a plant through holes in the leaves.
    d) Transpiration is a process where water vapor enters the atmosphere as water and evaporates from the ground.

8. What are the three states of water on Earth?
    a) Groundwater, lakes, and clouds.
    b) Liquid water, frozen water, and water vapor.
    c) Gas, steam, and vapor.
    d) Groundwater, oceans, and ice.

9. What word means the change of state from liquid to a gas?
    a) Evaporation.
    b) Condensation.
    c) Eutrophication.
    d) Precipitation.

10. Spring tides occur:
    a) At new moon and first quarter moon.
    b) At first quarter and third quarter moons.
    c) At new moon and full moon.
    d) At third quarter and full moons.

Practice Drill: Geology – Answers

1. **b)**
2. **d)**
3. **b)**
4. **d)**
5. **d)**
6. **a)**
7. **c)**
8. **b)**
9. **a)**
10. **c)**

Meteorology

Meteorology is the study of the changes in temperature, air pressure, moisture, and wind direction in the troposphere.

ATMOSPHERE

Atmospheric Properties
The thin envelope of air surrounding our planet is a mixture of gases, each with its own physical properties. Two gases make up the bulk of the Earth's atmosphere: nitrogen, which comprises 78% of the atmosphere, and oxygen, which accounts for 21% of the volume of air.

The other 1% is composed of **trace** gases, the most prevalent of which is the inert gaseous element argon. The rest of the trace gases, although present in only minute amounts, are very important to life on earth. Two in particular, carbon dioxide and ozone, can have a large impact on atmospheric processes. Another gas, water vapor, also exists in small amounts and varies in concentration: almost non-existent over desert regions, and about 4% over oceans. Water vapor is important to weather production since it exists in gaseous, liquid, and solid phases; it also absorbs radiant energy from the earth.

Energy Balance
The energy balance of the Earth is achieved by an opposition of energy flow to and from the ground level and all the atmospheric layers. The general temperature gradient from the poles to the equator, as well as the change in seasons, is caused by the spherical nature of the Earth and its tilt.

Pressure Systems
Our global atmospheric circulation is dominated by four major pressure zones: high pressure at the poles; low pressure at 60 degrees latitude; high pressure at 30 degrees; and low pressure at the equator. A detailed explanation of why this is so would get into the weeds of complicated physics. However, it is possible to make a general argument that substantially explains things.

If the Earth didn't spin, but could somehow be heated at the equator (all the way around) while being cooled at the poles, then naturally air would rise at the equator and sink at the poles. Surface pressure would therefore be low at the equator and high at the poles; and surface winds would always and everywhere be from the north in the northern hemisphere and the south in the southern. But the Earth *does* spin. This introduces a force, the **Coriolis force**, on moving air. Now the surface winds are turning, and the north and south winds may be east winds – and these winds will have an equator-ward component in order to continue the transport of heat between equator and pole.

Air pressure is measured with **barometers** and reported in millibars (mb). One type of barometer is **mercurial**, which is very accurate but not portable. A mercurial barometer measures air pressure in inches of mercury, which are then converted to millibars. Another type of barometer is the **aneroid**, which measures air pressure in millibars and is portable.

Atmospheric Structure
The atmosphere is divided into four layers based on temperature: the **troposphere**, **stratosphere**, **mesosphere**, and **thermosphere**.

Troposphere

About 75% of the air in the atmosphere is compressed into the lowest layer, which is called the troposphere. In this layer, wherein clouds form and air masses continuously mix, the change of temperature in relation to height is relatively large. Within the troposphere, air consists of 78% nitrogen; 21% oxygen; and 1% argon, carbon dioxide, and minute amounts of other gases; tropospheric air also contains variable amounts of water vapor and a mixture of minute impurities, such as particles of dust and salt. The thickness of the troposphere varies with the season of the year.

Tropopause

The top of the troposphere is known as the tropopause. It is a transition zone between the troposphere and the stratosphere, and acts as a lid to "hold in" the lower atmosphere. This lid contains occasional breaks and overlaps, which provide paths for high-velocity winds called **jet streams**. The jet streams cause constant turbulence and a mixing of the lower atmosphere. This mixing of air masses causes our weather.

The Greenhouse Effect

Heat from the sun warms the Earth's surface, but most of it is radiated and sent back into space. Water vapor and carbon dioxide in the troposphere trap some of this heat, preventing it from escaping; this keeps the Earth warm. However, if there is too much carbon dioxide in the troposphere, then too much heat will be trapped.

Stratosphere

The layer immediately above the tropopause is the stratosphere. It has a stable temperature in the lower half of the layer and an almost complete lack of clouds. In the upper half of the stratosphere, at about 25 kilometers, the temperature begins to increase with height up to about 50 kilometers at the **stratopause**. In the stratopause, the temperature is about the same as that at the earth's surface; this warmth is caused by the presence of **ozone**, which absorbs part of the ultraviolet radiation from the sun. Without the ozone layer, life on Earth would be difficult, if not impossible.

The Ozone Layer is a thin layer of ozone which absorbs most of the harmful ultraviolet radiation from the sun. The ozone layer is being depleted ("holes" are appearing), growing thinner over Europe, Asia, North American and Antarctica.

Mesosphere

Extending 50 to 80 km above the Earth's surface, the mesosphere is a cold layer in which the temperature generally decreases as altitude increases. The atmosphere is very dense, and is thick enough to slow down meteors plunging into the atmosphere, until they burn up.

Thermosphere

The thermosphere extends from 80 km above the Earth's surface to outer space. The temperature is hot, with temperatures as high as thousands of degrees, because the few molecules present in the thermosphere receive extraordinarily large amounts of energy from the sun.

The Ionosphere

Scientists call the ionosphere an extension of the thermosphere; so technically, the ionosphere is not another atmospheric layer. The ionosphere represents less than 0.1% of the total mass of the Earth's atmosphere. But even though it is such a small part, it is extremely important! The upper atmosphere is ionized by **solar radiation**. This means that the Sun's energy is so strong at this level, that it breaks apart molecules. When the Sun is active, more and more ionization happens! Different regions of the ionosphere make long-distance radio communication possible by reflecting the radio waves back to Earth. It is also home to auroras. Temperatures in the ionosphere increase as altitude increases.

The Atmosphere:

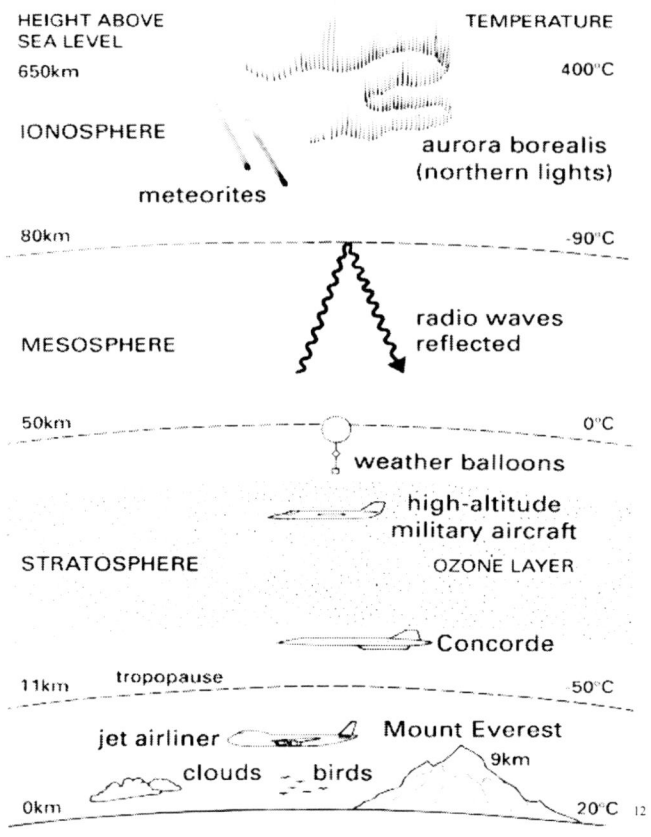

The General Circulation of the Atmosphere

The circulation on a spinning Earth is not really so much different from what we'd expect -- just a little more elaborate. The overall pattern includes two high-pressure systems and two low-pressure systems: high-pressure at the poles and at 30 degrees latitude, and low-pressure at the equator and at 60 degrees latitude.

The resulting wind systems are: **easterlies** between 60 degrees and the pole, known appropriately as **polar easterlies**; **westerly** winds from 30 to 60 degrees, commonly called the mid-latitude **westerlies**; and the **tropical easterlies**, known as **trade winds**. The **doldrums** is a region around the equator where heated air is rising. This air falls at the **horse latitudes**. Between the two, trade winds blow in a steady and predictable pattern. Many wind systems arise because the temperature of the oceans gradually changes in response to a change in solar radiation.

---

[12] Graphic from: http://media.photobucket.com

CLOUDS

Condensation is the process whereby water vapor is changed into small droplets of water; and may result from a decrease in temperature, a decrease of pressure, or an increase of water vapor in the air. In the atmosphere, condensation normally occurs when warm, moist air rises and cools by expansion. Frontal activity, terrain features, and unequal heating of land and sea surfaces cause the air to be lifted.

For condensation to occur, there must be something present in the atmosphere upon which the water vapor can condense. Virtually billions of minute particles – which result from ordinary dust, combustion products, and sea salt crystals – exist in the atmosphere. Condensation of water vapor upon these particles forms clouds and fog.

Clouds do not always produce precipitation; some clouds are only made of extremely small water droplets that simply float in the atmosphere. Still other forms of precipitation may fall from clouds and then evaporate, all without ever reaching the Earth's surface. This phenomenon is called **virga**.

Cloud Types

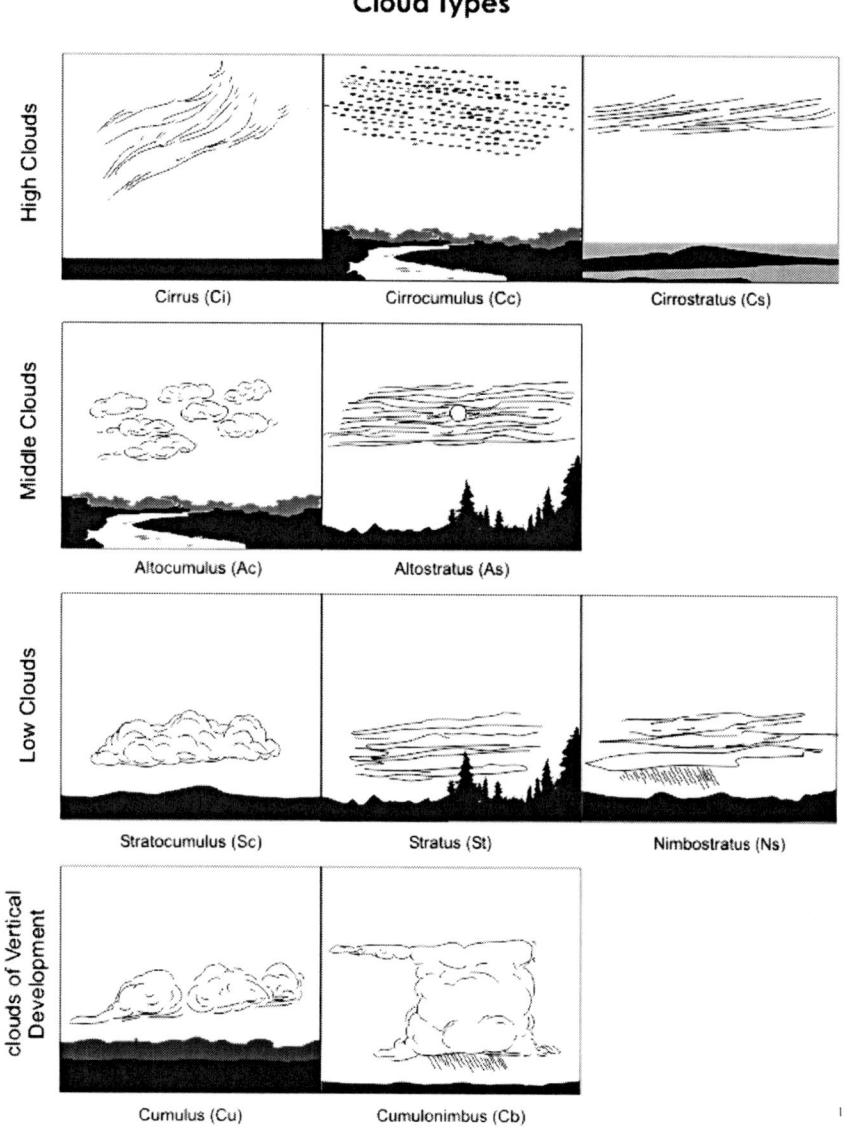

[13]

---
[13] Graphic from: cmos.ca
89

Cloud Categories

Clouds are classified by both their appearances and the physical processes which produce them. All clouds, by their shape, fall into two general categories: **cumuliform (cumulus)** and **stratiform (stratus)**

Cumulus means heaped or accumulated; and these heaped clouds are formed by rising air currents. Cumulus clouds may produce local showers or severe thunderstorms, as well as extremely strong vertical air currents.

Stratus, or sheet-like, clouds are formed when a layer of air is cooled below its saturation point without pronounced vertical motion. The vertical thickness of stratiform-type clouds may range from several meters, up to a few kilometers. Precipitation from stratiform clouds is generally continuous, with only gradual changes in intensity, and covers a relatively large area.

Cloud Classification

Clouds may be further classified as low, middle, high, and towering.

Low

When the bases of clouds are lower than 2,000 meters above the surface of the Earth, the clouds generally are designated as cumulus or stratus, unless they are producing precipitation. In that case, they are referred to as **cumulonimbus** or **nimbostratus**. (Nimbus means "rain cloud.")

A common cloud called **stratocumulus** has some characteristic of both cumulus and stratus clouds.

Middle

Between 2,000 and 6,000 meters, these clouds generally are identified with the prefix *alto*. **Altocumulus** and **altostratus** clouds are in this category.

High

Above 6,000 meters, high clouds are composed of ice crystals and generally have a delicate appearance. These clouds are designated as **cirrocumulus** and **cirrostratus. Cirrus** clouds exist at still greater altitudes, and are fibrous types of clouds composed of ice crystals. They appear as curly wisps.

Towering

Bases of towering clouds may be as low as the typical low clouds, but their tops may extend to, or even above, the tropopause.

Practice Drill: Meteorology

1. What are the two most abundant gases in the Earth's atmosphere?
   a) Nitrogen and oxygen.
   b) Oxygen and carbon monoxide.
   c) Water vapor and argon.
   d) Methane and hydrogen.

2. The layer of the Earth's atmosphere in which weather occurs is the:
   a) Stratosphere.
   b) Mesosphere.
   c) Thermosphere.
   d) Troposphere.

3. What causes the Earth's mesosphere (also known as the ozone layer) to be warmer than layers just above or below it?
   a) Chemical reactions involving ozone produce heat.
   b) Ozone absorbs solar energy.
   c) Heat is transported into the ozone layer by convection from the troposphere.
   d) Energetic particles hit the mesosphere to produce heat and aurorae.

4. The thick, dense region of the atmosphere is known as:
   a) Ionosphere.
   b) Mesosphere.
   c) Stratosphere.
   d) Hydrosphere.

5. The names of all three high-cloud genera contain which of the following words in some form?
   a) Alto.
   b) Cumulus.
   c) Cirrus.
   d) Stratus.

6. A cloud with some of the characteristics of both cumulus and stratus clouds is:
   a) Stratocumulus.
   b) Cirrus.
   c) Altostratus.
   d) Nimbostratus.

Practice Drill: Meteorology – Answers

1. a)
2. d)
3. b)
4. b)
5. c)
6. a)

ASTRONOMY

Astronomy is the scientific study of matter in outer space, especially the positions, dimensions, distribution, motion, composition, energy, and development of celestial bodies and occurrences.

OUR SOLAR SYSTEM

Our solar system is located in the **Milky Way Galaxy**, a collection of 200 billion stars and their solar systems. The Milky Way Galaxy is located in a group of 30+ galaxies we call the **Local Group**. The Local Group is a part of a local **super-cluster** of 100+ galaxies (called the Virgo Super-cluster). This super-cluster is one of millions of super-clusters in the universe.

Our solar system consists of the Sun, planets, **dwarf planets** (or **plutoids**), moons, an asteroid belt, comets, meteors, and other objects. The Sun is the center of our solar system; the planets, over 61 moons, the asteroids, comets, meteoroids, and other rocks and gas all orbit the Sun. The Earth is the third planet from the Sun in our solar system.

The Sun is about 26,000 light-years from the center of the Milky Way Galaxy, which is about 80,000 to 120,000 light-years across. Our solar system is located toward the edge of one of the Milky Way's spiral arms. It takes the Sun and our solar system roughly 200-250 million years to orbit once around the Milky Way. In this orbit, our solar system is traveling at a velocity of about 155 miles/sec (250 km/sec). A **light year** is a unit of length equal to about 6 trillion miles.

Planets

The nine planets that orbit the sun are, in order from closest to the Sun to farthest from the Sun: Mercury, Venus, Earth, Mars, Jupiter (the biggest planet in our solar system), Saturn (with large, orbiting rings), Uranus, Neptune, and Pluto (a dwarf planet or plutoid). A belt of asteroids, minor planets made of rock and metal orbits between Mars and Jupiter. These objects all orbit the sun in roughly circular orbits that lie in the same plane, referred to as the **ecliptic**. Pluto is an exception; this dwarf planet has an elliptical orbit tilted over 17° from the ecliptic.

The **inner planets**, planets that orbit close to the Sun, are quite different from the **outer planets**, those planets that orbit far from the Sun. The inner planets are Mercury, Venus, Earth, and Mars. They are relatively small, composed mostly of rock, and have few or no moons.

The **outer planets** include Jupiter, Saturn, Uranus, and Neptune. They are much larger, mostly gaseous, ringed, and have many moons. Pluto is a dwarf planet that has one large moon and two small moons.

Small Bodies

There are other smaller object that orbit the Sun, including **asteroids**, **comets**, **meteoroids**, and dwarf planets.

- Asteroids (also called minor planets) are rocky or metallic objects, most of which orbit the Sun in the asteroid belt between Mars and Jupiter.
- Comets are small, icy bodies that orbit the sun. They have very long dust tails.
- Meteoroids are small bodies that travel through space. They are stony and/or metallic and are smaller than asteroids. In fact, most are very tiny.

Practice Drill: Astronomy

1. What are the components of our solar system?
   a) Planets, the Sun, asteroids, meteors, and comets.
   b) Planets and asteroids.
   c) Meteors and comets.
   d) Planets, asteroids, the Sun.

2. What is the center of our solar system?
   a) The Milky Way.
   b) An asteroid belt.
   c) The Sun.
   d) The moon.

3. What planet is best known for its rings?
   a) Saturn.
   b) Uranus.
   c) Jupiter.
   d) Neptune.

4. The closest star to Earth is:
   a) The moon.
   b) The Milky Way.
   c) Venus.
   d) The Sun.

5. What is the name of a frozen chunk of ice and dust that orbits the sun?
   a) Comet.
   b) Meteorite.
   c) Asteroid.
   d) Meteor.

Practice Drill: Astronomy – Answers

1. **a)**
2. **c)**
3. **a)**
4. **d)**
5. **a)**

Chapter 2: Auto and Shop Information

AUTOMOTIVE

The modern car is an amazing combination of complex mechanical and electrical systems. A car's onboard computer is capable of finding the ambient temperature, pressure, relative humidity, and the position of each piston in the engine, as well as all of the other variables needed to start your engine. All of this, done in time it takes for you to turn the key in the ignition switch; and your engine can run smoothly after less than one rotation without assistance from the starter motor.

All of this requires a great deal of sensors and electrical signals to work flawlessly in cooperation with mechanical systems. In this chapter, we will review the major automotive systems, and the basic function of each.

Parts, Assemblies, and Systems

A **part** is the smallest piece of a car. It cannot be disassembled any further without destroying the part. The term **component** normally refers to a part in an electrical system, but is often used interchangeably to refer to mechanical parts.

An **assembly** is a group of parts that fit together to accomplish a single function, normally removed from a car together. You can buy complete assemblies at automotive parts stores; so when you are repairing a system, an assembly may be either disassembled and repaired, or simply replaced completely.

An automotive **system** is a collection of assemblies and parts which work together to accomplish a common goal.

In the human body, the circulatory system – a collection of body parts working together to deliver blood and oxygen to all parts of the body – is analogous to an automotive system. Breaking down the circulatory system further, the heart could be called an assembly which pumps blood throughout the system. Within the heart, a valve is a single part in the circulatory system.

Major Automotive Systems

The following systems are important to comprehend and remember:

1. **Frame and Body**: The frame gives the vehicle its rigidity and facilitates the mounting locations for all of the car's components. The body makes the car aerodynamic and aesthetically pleasing

2. **Engine**: Creates mechanical energy for moving the car and powering other systems.

3. **Cooling System**: Removes excess heat created during engine operation.

4. **Lubrication System**: Filters and circulates oil to high-friction zones of the engine to reduce part wear.

5. **Air Intake System**: Filters and delivers clean air to the engine.

6. **Fuel Delivery System**: Stores fuel and delivers the correct ratio of air and fuel to the engine.

7. **Ignition System**: Delivers high voltage to the engine's spark plugs at the correct time to facilitate efficient combustion.

8. **Emission Control System**: Guides engine exhaust gases to a safe deposit location, quiets engine noise, and reduces exhaust gas pollutants.

9. **Drive Train**: Delivers rotational power from engine to the driving wheels.

10. **Suspension System**: Allows vertical movement of the wheels in order to absorb shock; this gives passengers a smooth and safe ride.

11. **Steering**: Gives the driver control of the vehicle's trajectory.

12. **Brake System**: Allows the driver to slow and stop the vehicle.

13. **Safety System**: Prevents injury to the driver in the case of a collision.

Sensors and Gauges

All the systems described above must cooperate in order for a vehicle to operate smoothly. This means that the computer modules within the car must keep track of a wide variety of conditions in both the vehicle and the environment. In order to sample these conditions, the vehicle's onboard computers are linked to sensors.

A **sensor** is an automotive instrument that turns a physical quantity into an electrical signal. Sensors are sometimes referred to as transducers. A **transducer** is a device which converts energy into different forms. Sensors can be divided into two broad categories: active sensors and passive sensors.

An **active sensor** creates a small amount of voltage which depends on a particular condition. That voltage can then feed into a computer and be used to calculate that property.

A **passive sensor** is fed a specific voltage, known as the **reference voltage**, from the computer; the sensor's resistance changes depending on the condition being measured, such as temperature or pressure. The passive sensor's resistance creates a voltage drop seen by the computer that can be used to calculate the particular condition. The **variable resistor sensor** is also known as a **potentiometer**.

Common Automotive Sensors

Similar to the above systems, learn the following common automotive sensors and their characteristics:

1. **Temperature Sensor**: Measures temperature of a liquid or gas, through a change in resistance.
   - **Intake Air Temperature (IAT) Sensor**: AKA manifold air temperature (MAT) or intake manifold temperature sensor (IMTS). Measures intake manifold gas temperature.

   - **Engine Coolant Temperature (ECT) Sensor**: Also called the coolant temperature sensor (CTS). Measures the temperature of coolant in the engine.

2. **Pressure Sensor**: Measures pressure of a liquid or gas. This is accomplished through a change in the sensor's resistance that depends on the measured pressure.
   - **Ambient Air Pressure Sensor (APS)**: AKA the barometric pressure sensor (BARO). Measures the pressure of the environment outside the vehicle.

   - **Manifold Absolute Pressure (MAP) Sensor**: Makes the vacuum pressure in the air intake manifold relative to the ambient pressure.

3. **Position/Speed Sensor**: These types of sensors measure either the linear or angular position of a part, from which the speed can also be found. Magnetic sensors detect motion through induced voltage from a permanent magnet. A hall-effect sensor is a transducer that uses magnetism to generate voltage, generally to monitor speed. Optical sensors use light-emitting diodes (LEDs) to monitor speed.
   - **Engine Position Sensor (EPS)**: Measures the angle of the crankshaft so that the location of all pistons in the engine can be calculated.

   - **Throttle Position Sensor (TPS)**: Measures how far the throttle pedal is depressed, indicating how much power is desired from the driver.

4. **Piezoelectric Sensor**: Senses motion, vibration, or pressure by generating a voltage in response to stress.
   - **Knock Sensor (KS)**: Detects adverse engine noise from knocking, so that the air-fuel ratio or ignition timing can be adjusted appropriately.

   - **Impact Sensor**: Detects when the car is in a collision in order to: deploy air bags, and turn off both the fuel pump and the engine.

5. **Switching Sensor**: Either opens or closes a circuit depending on the condition being monitored.
   - **Brake Switch**: Detects when the brakes are being applied.

Common Automotive Gauges

A **gauge** is an instrument which gives a reading of a measurement's magnitude. They are often used in combination with sensors, since sensors are measure physical quantities. The gauge acts as a translator for the driver, giving the measurement found by the sensors an understandable, readable value.

As the capabilities of the modern vehicle expand, the need for a greater number of gauges increases. This is because the car's computer constantly monitors a great deal of variables which the operator may which to know.

For example, onboard computers have tracked ambient temperatures for many uses: shutting off the air conditioning pump below certain temperatures, calculating intake air mass, controlling engine performance parameters, etc. But say that operators wanted to know the outside temperature. Since vehicles were already tracking said temperature, it was easy for car manufactures to place gauges on the dashboard for drivers. More recently, many automotive manufacturers have been equipping cars with a fuel economy gauge that compares fuel consumption to the speed of the vehicle.

The following list details some of the gauges commonly found in an automobile. In addition to these, many more gauges can be attached to the car to monitor conditions not normally given to the driver, such as the pressure within the air conditioning system. Along with these gauges, a vehicle's dashboard will also have several warning lights to alert the driver to conditions such as: an engaged emergency brake, an unfastened seatbelt, a low-pressure tire having, or an engine needing service.

1. **Thermometer**: Gives a temperature in either degrees Fahrenheit (°F) or Celsius (°C).
   - **Ambient Temperature Gauge**: Shows temperature outside vehicle.

   - **Oil Temperature Gauge**: Shows temperature of oil in engine.

2. **Pressure Gauge**: Gives pressure or vacuum (negative) pressure, normally in pounds per square inch (psi), or kilopascals (kPa).
   - **Oil Pressure Gauge**: Shows the pressure of oil in an engine case.

   - **Boost Gauge**: Shows the pressure in a turbocharged or supercharged air intake system after the intercooler cools the air.

3. **Speed Gauge**: Shows the speed of a part's movement or rotation in units of length or angle per unit time, such as miles per hour (mph) or rotations per minute (rpm).
   - **Speedometer**: Shows the speed of the vehicle, normally in both miles per hour and kilometers per hour.

   - **Tachometer**: Shows the engine speed in rotations per minute.

4. **Fluid Level Gauge**: Shows the amount of fluid in a tank or reservoir
   - **Fuel Gauge**: Shows the amount of fuel left in the fuel tank in gallons (gal), liters (L), or percentage of the tank's capacity.

   - **Oil Level Gauge**: Shows the amount of oil in the engine's oil pan.

5. **Flow Meter**: Gives the rate of mass or volume flow of a fluid through a pipe or tube of interest, normally in gallons per minute (gpm) or liters per minute (L/min).
   - Fuel Consumption Gauge – Shows the rate at which fuel is flowing to the engine.

Frame and Body

The **frame** of a vehicle is the metal structure that creates the base around which the car is built. The frame has many purposes:

1. Strength: Supports the weight of the car and its cargo.

2. Rigidity: Resists twisting and warping when the car turns.

3. Support: Serves as the mounting location for most of the other parts of the car, such as: the engine, transmission, suspension components, and many other assemblies.

The outer shell of the vehicle is called the **body**, and is usually made of metal sheeting, fiberglass, plastic, or a composite skin. The body:
   - Protects the passengers and anything else in the interior of the vehicle. It also has aesthetic and aerodynamic purposes. The body is usually painted and makes the car look more attractive and sleeker.

- Reduces aerodynamic drag, increasing the fuel economy of the car. The body is usually painted, which makes the car look more aesthetically appealing and sleeker (aerodynamic).

- Includes a **firewall** that separates the interior of the car from the heat, noise, and debris in the engine compartment.

The term **chassis** is often used to refer to the main structural components of a vehicle. The chassis can be thought of as the skeleton of the car, and can refer to almost everything – frame, engine, transmission, suspension, tires, etc. – except the body. Many vehicles, such as most pickup trucks and sport-utility vehicles, have a body that can be unbolted and completely detached from the chassis.

This is known as a **body-over-frame construction** and can result in a strong vehicle with a fairly simple design.

However, a **unibody construction** (construction with an integrated frame and body, meaning the body cannot be simply unbolted from the frame) results in a lighter vehicle; for this reason, most smaller cars use a **unibody construction**. While this construction is often lighter and more fuel-efficient, the resulting vehicle is usually not as strong as one with a body-over-frame construction.

Some modern cars have a **monocoque construction**, which means the body and frame are truly integrated. This construction, also known as **stressed skin construction**, uses the body to bear the load of the vehicle. While this can result in a very light car, the design is more difficult and therefore currently restricted mostly to high-performance supercars.

Air Intake System
The engine of a car is often described as a glorified air pump, which would explain why the air intake system is such an important part of the vehicle.

The **air intake system** is responsible for supplying the engine with clean fresh air. If an impurity finds its way into the engine, it could cause damage. This is why air intake systems have **air filters** to block out airborne particles – like dust and pollen – while allowing clean air into the engine. While there are cleanable, reusable air filters, most are simply made of foam or paper and must be replaced occasionally. Running an engine with a dirty filter starves the engine of air and robs performance.

For maximum performance, it is also important that the engine is supplied with air at a high velocity that is laminar, or flowing smoothly; therefore, air intake systems are designed to speed up the air rushing to the engine while preventing the creation of turbulence (rough flow).

A **naturally aspirated** engine draws air from the atmosphere, at atmospheric pressure, without assistance. Adding pressure to the air going into an engine with a supercharger or turbocharger packs more air-fuel mixture into the cylinder, which can increase performance.

A **supercharger** is an air compressor – usually powered by the engine through a belt, pulley, or gear – whose purpose is to force more air into a car's engine. The engine is attached to a turbine within the supercharger that compresses and pushes air toward the engine. This means that the supercharger is paradoxically drawing power from the engine while it runs in order to increase the power of the engine.

In contrast, a **turbocharger** is an air compressor that is powered by the exhaust gases which flow from the engine – forcing more air into an engine. In a turbocharger, the exhaust gases rushing out of the engine turn the turbine, which compresses the air. While this means that the turbocharger does not place a direct load on the engine like the supercharger, it can create both backpressure and the complication of using extremely hot gases near the intake air.

An air intake with a supercharger or turbocharger is known as a **forced induction** system. Because cool air is less dense, it allows engines to run more efficiently. However, compressing the air through a supercharger or turbocharger increases the temperature, so forced induction systems normally have an **intercooler**: a heat-exchanger that cools the air after compression.

The engine is not always expected to operate at maximum power; the driver therefore must be able to control the amount of power created by the engine. This means that the air intake system must monitor and control the flow of air to the engine. A **mass air flow (MAF) sensor** monitors the speed of the air flowing through the intake system, from which the onboard computer can calculate the volume and mass of air flowing into the engine.

A **vane flow sensor** is, basically, a variable resistor with a spring-loaded, hinged flap which is pushed by the flow. The faster the fluid flows by the sensor, the farther the flap is pushed, which results in a resistance change seen by the computer.

Airflow restriction and turbulence can result from the drag caused by a vane flow sensor flap, and so most vehicles are equipped with a **hot wire sensor**. This type of sensor has a thin wire that is heated by the passing of currents through it. This increase in heat causes resistance in the wire.

However, the passing air flow cools the wire and decreases resistance; this is also seen by the computer, which uses the information to calculate the speed of the air. The hot wire sensor does not have moving parts which are subject to wear, like the vane flow sensor; but the hot wire sensor's wire is very thing and delicate. Usually, a car's computer will heat the wire when the car is first started, in order to burn off any deposits; but, if this cycle fails to initiate and/or remove all contaminates, then the wire can become blocked from the air flow. It is difficult to clean the wire without damaging it, so it is normally recommended to simply replace the sensor.

Air intake systems for engines with electric fuel delivery use a **throttle body** to control the amount of air flowing to the engine. The mass air flow sensor is usually located near the throttle body, sometimes attached directly to the intake manifold near the engine. The throttle body contains a butterfly valve known as the **throttle plate**, which is linked to the acceleration pedal. That way, the valve opens when the driver depresses the pedal. The opening and closing of the throttle plate controls the amount of air allowed to flow to the engine.

Automotive Fuels

Gasoline is derived from crude oil (petroleum) and is the most common type of fuel used in automobiles. Gasoline is given an **octane rating** that relates to the fuel's resistance to **autoignition** – which is the combustion of a fuel without the addition of a spark, usually due to a high pressure or temperature. Autoignition can result in one of two conditions: knock or preignition.

If an air-fuel mixture combusts before being reached by the spark plug's flame, it creates a noise called an **engine knock**, or **ping**. The loud banging of engine knock is actually a product of two pressure fronts colliding within the combustion chamber; it can destroy engine components within a matter of seconds cracking spark plugs, blowing gaskets, or creating holes in pistons.

Preignition is the detonation of air-fuel mixture within the combustion chamber without the addition of a flame from the spark plug. Preignition is very similar to engine knock, but occurs before the spark plug fires. There are three main causes for preignition: a hot carbon deposit in the cylinder, a sharp edge in the cylinder, or an overheated spark plug.

Gasoline's octane number serves as an indication of the fuel's resistance to combustion; the higher the octane number, the slower the fuel burns and the less likely it is to autoignite. You should always use a fuel with an octane number that matches the manufacturer's recommendation: usually between 87 and 93. Contrary to popular belief, using a fuel with an unnecessarily high octane number does not increase performance. However, many fuel distributors put additives into their "premium" fuels, which they claim help both clean and protect engine and fuel delivery components.

Diesel, which requires less refining than gasoline, is derived from crude oil, and is the second most-popular fuel for automobiles. Diesel is thicker than gasoline and has a higher **viscosity** (a measurement of a fluid's resistance to flow). This means that a diesel fuel delivery system uses greater pressure in order to force the fuel into movement.

Diesel also does not **vaporize,** or turn into a gas, as easily as gasoline, which further complicates its use in a car's engine. Remember that fuel cannot be injected into an engine as a liquid, because combustion requires that fuel be in a gaseous state. Diesel fuel is susceptible to water contamination, which can clog and corrode components of the fuel system, which is why diesel fuel delivery systems often have a water separator.

Since diesel has a higher energy density than gasoline, theoretically, a given amount of diesel could move a car further than the same amount of gasoline. Burning diesel also results in fewer exhaust emissions (which cause global warming). However, diesel engines do emit visible particulates like smoke and soot, which can harm the environment as well as humans. Diesel fuels are categorized by a diesel grade and cetane number.

Diesel fuel grades are determined by several fuel-based characteristics and ensure that the fuel meets the appropriate criteria recommended for that grade's particular use. There are many qualifications for determining diesel fuel grades: density, the number of impurities, viscosity, and the fuel's **cloud point**. One of the constituents of diesel fuel is paraffin, which is wax in solid form. The **cloud point** is the low temperature at which paraffin can separate from the rest of the diesel fuel and clog parts of the fuel delivery system.

Diesels No. 1 and No. 2 are the two most-commonly used grades in automotive applications. No. 2 diesel has a medium viscosity and is the most-frequently used fuel in diesel engines; it is often the only type of diesel offered at service stations. Since diesel tends to thicken at low temperatures, which can make a diesel engine harder to start and lead to poor fuel delivery while running during the winter, No. 1 diesel is sometimes used during the winter for its lower viscosity and thinness.

However, No. 1 diesel's thinness can become a problem in not providing enough lubrication, which leads to excess wear. Sometimes, No. 1 and No. 2 diesels are blended for winter use, but you should always consult the owner's manual for the manufacturer's recommendations.

A diesel fuel's **cetane rating** tells the fuel's flammability, which relates to the ease of starting an engine in colder weather. Most manufacturers recommend a cetane number between 40 and 50. A cetane number can be thought of as the opposite of an octane number. While a higher octane number means that the gasoline is less flammable and will burn more slowly, a higher cetane number indicates a more flammable diesel which will burn more quickly.

With the increased demand for cleaner, more renewable sources of energy for vehicles, several alternative fuels have become more available in recent years. **Methanol**, also known as wood alcohol because it can be made from wood chips, and **ethanol**, also known as grain alcohol because it is often made from crops like wheat and corn, are alcohols that have proven to be clean-burning automobile fuels. However, they are currently very expensive to produce, and engines require almost twice as much alcohol as gasoline, which halves the engine's fuel economy. Many service stations now mix alcohol in their gasoline, which has the added benefit of lowering the likelihood of knock.

Hydrogen, one of the most abundant elements on earth (and which can be created from water), has been studied a great deal and shows promise as an alternative fuel. When burned, hydrogen releases virtually no harmful byproducts. However, like alcohols, hydrogen is expensive to produce, and hydrogen fuel cell vehicles are not readily available for affordable to the general public. Also, hydrogen does not have nearly as high of an energy density as gasoline or diesel, which means that more hydrogen would need to be stored in the vehicle in order to travel the same distance as a gasoline-or-diesel-fueled vehicle.

Research has also gone into advancements in electric and fuel cell vehicles. Electric vehicles use rechargeable batteries to drive electric motors that move the car, while a fuel cell converts fuel's chemical energy into electricity in order to power electric motors.

Fuel Delivery System

The **fuel delivery system** stores the vehicle's fuel and, when the engine is running, delivers the correct amount of fuel to ensure the optimal air-fuel ratio (AFR) within the engine. **Air-fuel ratio** refers to either the mass or weight of the ratio of air to fuel which is supplied.

The term fuel-air ratio (FAR) is also sometimes used, especially when dealing with diesel engines. **Fuel-air ratio** is simply the inverse of air-fuel ratio; the mass of fuel divided by the mass of air supplied to the engine.

The air-fuel ratio supplied to an engine has an enormous impact on the engine's power and emissions. For this reason, automotive manufacturers do a great deal of testing in order to find the very best air-fuel ratio for their engine. If the fuel delivery system delivers an incorrect amount of fuel, the vehicle's performance, as well as the environment, can suffer.

Gasoline engines normally run at, or near, an air-fuel ratio that is **stoichiometric**. This means that there is exactly enough fuel to burn with the supplied air without leaving any extra fuel or air. The stoichiometric air-fuel ratio for gasoline is about 14.7:1 (stated as "fourteen point seven to one"), meaning that 1 gram of fuel is supplied for every 14.7 grams of air delivered.

Diesel engines, on the other hand, normally run at a **lean** air-fuel mixture, meaning that there is not enough fuel to completely react with the air in the engine. An engine running lean can experience many problems: difficulty starting, poor performance, lack of throttle response, high operating temperatures that can melt engine components, and knock.

An air-fuel mixture that has more fuel than is required to react with the air provided is said to be **rich**. A rich air-fuel mixture can cause: lowered fuel mileage and power, rough idling, increased pollutant emissions, black exhaust smoke, and fouled spark plugs. It is a common misconception that depressing the accelerator of a car simply adds more fuel to the engine. In fact, the air-fuel ratio is ideally kept constant; stepping harder on the throttle pedal adds both air and fuel, so that the engine is provided with a greater amount of the air-fuel mixture.

A vehicle's fuel is stored in a **fuel tank**, which is usually located near the rear of the vehicle (this balances the added weight of the engine in the front of the car). A **sending unit** extends into the fuel contained within the tank, monitoring the fuel-level while drawing fuel out of the tank to deliver to the vehicle's engine. **Fuel lines** are tubes made of strong, often double-walled steel which carry fuel throughout the vehicle.

The term **fuel hose** refers to flexible tubing, normally made of rubber, which carries fuel between those components which may vibrate or move relative to each other. Though the fuel system's sending unit usually has a filter, there is normally a finer, replaceable **fuel filter** in line with the main fuel line that prevents the engine from being exposed to fuel contaminants. A **fuel tank pressure sensor** monitors the fuel tank's pressure, which will increase if there is a clog in the fuel system and decrease if there is a leak.

Fuel flows through the lines of the fuel delivery system due pressure created by the **fuel pump**. Mechanical fuel pumps are normally powered by the engine's camshaft. Mechanical pumps are usually reciprocating pumps, meaning that they use a back-and-forth motion that causes pulsation in the fluid being pumped. Therefore, mechanical pumps not only produce an unsteady flow, but – since mechanical fuel pumps are often attached directly to the engine block – they can also unnecessarily heat the fuel.

Vapor lock is a condition in which fuel flow is decreased or stopped due to bubbles from the overheated fuel entering the fuel pump. Most modern cars have an electric fuel pump that creates a much smoother flow of fuel and greatly reduces the chances of vapor lock. Electric fuel pumps do not have to be mounted near the engine block, which means that they are not heated like a mechanical pump; also, they are able to pressurize all the fuel in lines close to the engine, decreasing the likelihood of it boiling.

> In fact, many vehicles are now made with the fuel pump integrated into the sending unit within the fuel tank. Electric fuel pumps also have a faster response. They pressurize the fuel system much more quickly than mechanical pumps, and can be shut off by two factors: low oil levels, detected by an oil-pressure sensor, or a collision detected by an impact sensor.

Before fuel enters the engine, it must be metered so that the air-fuel ratio is correct and the engine is receiving the correct amount of air-fuel mixture to create the amount of power desired by the driver. Again, this is done either mechanically or electrically. A **carburetor**, often shortened to carb, is a mechanism used to regulate the amount of fuel entering the airstream from the air intake system.

A carburetor utilizes a law of fluid dynamics known as **Bernoulli's principle**, which states that: a reduction of the cross-sectional area of a pipe through which a fluid is flowing will result in an increase of the fluid's speed and a decrease in the pressure. This is also known as the venturi effect.

As air flows through a carburetor, it encounters a section known as the **venturi**. There, the area of the tube decreases, which increases the speed of the air and reduces the pressure, pulling fuel stored in the carburetor's **bowl**. A **float** - which is hinged on the wall of the bowl and floats along the surface of the fuel – maintains the fuel level in the bowl. When the float is raised to a certain point, it blocks off the fuel inlet, preventing fuel from entering the bowl.

Carburetors will usually have at least two butterfly valves that restrict the flow through the carburetor.

> The **choke plate** cuts off the air supply as it is entering the carburetor and can be used to start a cold engine, when more fuel is needed. It is located before the venturi.

> The **throttle valve** is a butterfly valve connected the **throttle linkage**; it opens and closes in response to the driver's depression of the accelerator pedal. The throttle valve is located after the venturi and regulates the amount of air-fuel mixture allowed to enter the engine.

Carburetors can be adjusted to modify the air-fuel ratio. They usually have an adjustment screw for both high and low speed air-fuel ratios, and another to adjust the idle speed.

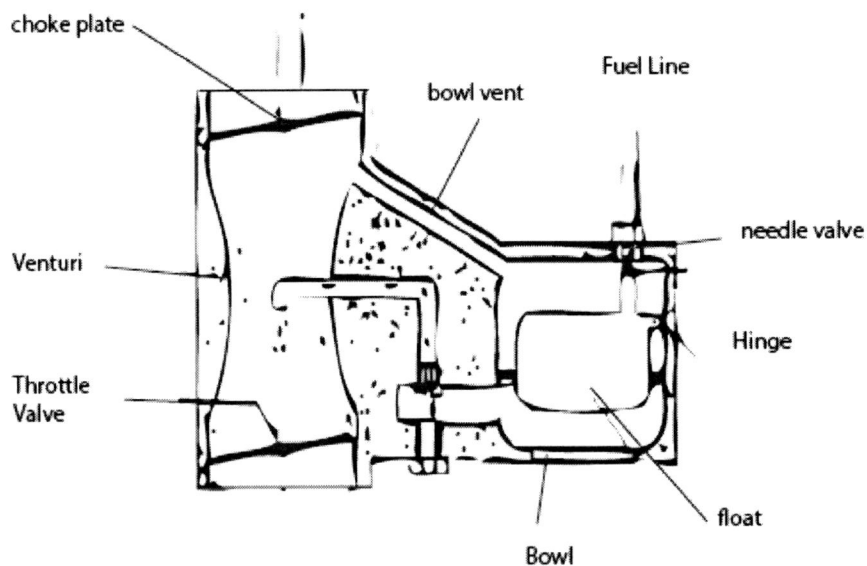

Instead of using a carburetor, cars built today are equipped with an electric fuel injection system. Diesel engines, for example, cannot use a carburetor. For diesel engines, fuel does not enter the airstream until it is already in the engine. Therefore, they must utilize an electric injection system; wherein instead of being drawn into the airstream, fuel is sprayed into the air by **injectors**.

Remember, fuel must be in vapor state before it can burn. For this reason, the injectors are usually located near the intake valve of the engine, where the heat of the engine and intake valves help evaporate the fuel. Often, the injectors are connected to a large fuel line known as the **fuel rail**, which ensures that all the injectors are pressurized by the fuel pump. Since the fuel is already pressurized by the fuel pump, the injectors merely open (to allow fuel to spray into the airstream) and close (to stop the flow of fuel).

The amount of time the injectors remain open is called the **pulse width**, which is designed to regulate the amount of fuel being injected. An increased pulse width will allow a longer time for the fuel to be sprayed, which means that more fuel mixes with the air.

Sometimes, especially in diesel engines, fuel is injected directly into the cylinder. This is known as **direct injection**.

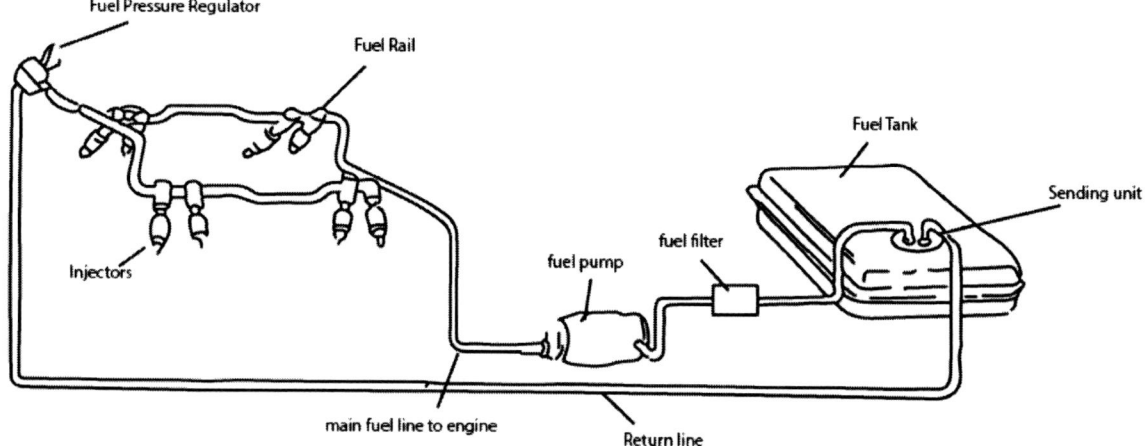

Internal Combustion Engines

An **internal combustion engine** converts the chemical energy of fuel into mechanical energy by burning the fuel and air within the engine. In contrast, external combustion engines require that a fuel – such as coal or wood – be burned on the outside of the engine to heat a working fluid.

> For example, a steam engine requires fire to heat water. That water turns into steam and powers the engine. Nowadays, since fuel is added to tanks with no external fire required, automotive engines are internal combustion engines.

There are several characteristics used to classify and differentiate engine types, them being: the engine's configuration, and the type of combustion process.

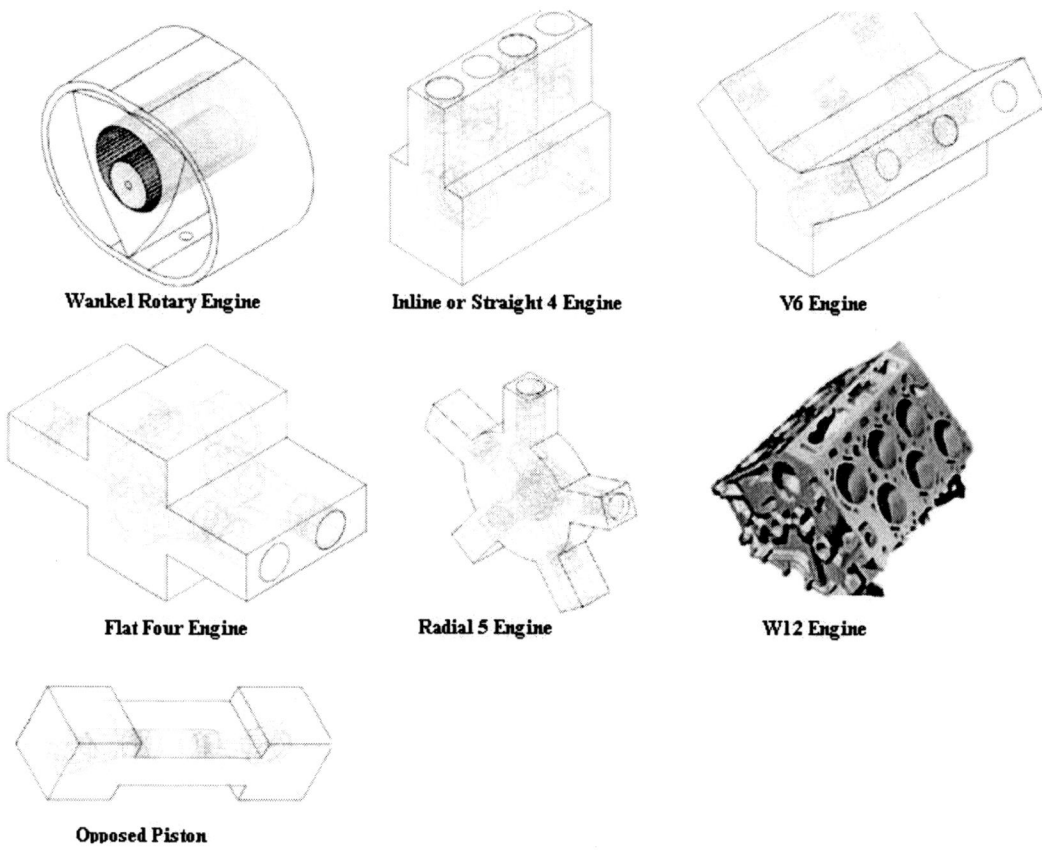

Wankel Rotary Engine **Inline or Straight 4 Engine** **V6 Engine**

Flat Four Engine **Radial 5 Engine** **W12 Engine**

Opposed Piston

Most automotive engines use a piston that moves up and down in a cylinder, and are categorized by the arrangement and number of cylinders. The **Wankel engine**, usually called a rotary engine, differs by using a triangular **rotor** that revolves around an eccentric shaft to transmit power.

Inline Engine: Parallel cylinders in a straight row within the engine block. (The block for an inline engine is fairly simple and inexpensive to manufacture. The cylinders can be either vertical or tilted, called a **slant engine**, to make room for other assemblies in the engine compartment.)

Flat or **Opposed Cylinder Engine**: Cylinders oriented horizontally on either side of the crankshaft. Improve a vehicle's handling by creating a lower center of gravity. However, they are also fairly wide.

> **Boxer Engines**: Flat engines whose pistons on opposite sides of the crankshaft move in and out at the same time, instead of alternating, reminiscent of the gloves of boxers exchanging punches.

V-Engines: Tilted cylinders on either side of the crankshaft, creating a V. The cylinders can be at any angle depending on the space needed in the compartment, but they usually form 60 or 90 degree angles.

W-Engines: Tilted and offset cylinders in more than just two rows. A W-engine can have a great number of cylinders without taking up a great deal of space.

Radial Engines: Cylinders extend radially outward from a central crankshaft, creating a circle around the crankshaft. This type of engine is nearly obsolete, but was once used in many aircrafts. Instead of the crankshaft rotating, sometimes the cylinders of a radial engine rotate around the stationary crankshaft. This requires more power to start the engine, but it does produce more rotational inertia to keep the engine running. These engines are sometimes call rotaries, which can be confusing as Wankel engines are sometimes called rotary engines.

Opposed Piston Engines: Two pistons in a cylinder move in and out towards each other. This type of engine is rare, but sometimes used in the marine industry.

Main Components of the Automotive Engine

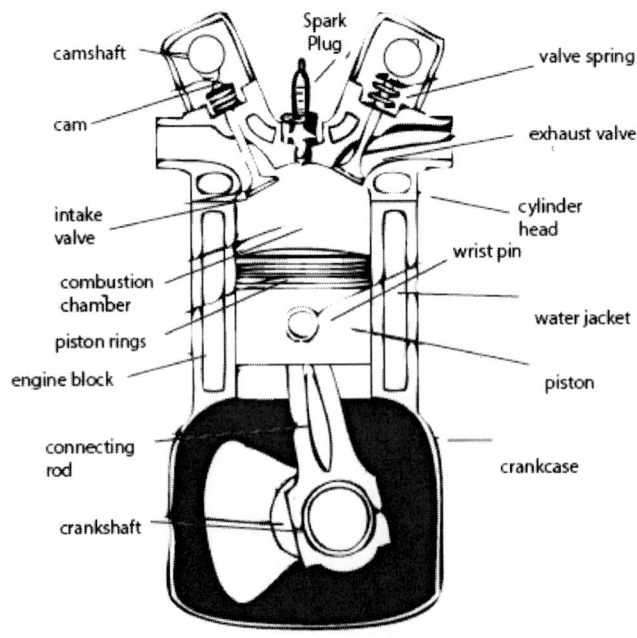

1. **Engine Block**: Metal casing forming the main body of the engine. Holds and houses all other parts of the engine.

2. **Cylinder**: Round hole bored into the engine block. Has a slightly bigger diameter than a piston, which fits into the cylinder to move up and down.

3. **Piston**: Metal cylinder that travels up and down in the cylinder, separating the crankcase from the combustion chamber. Compresses gases and captures the pressure of the combustion process. The top of the piston, the piston head, can be shaped to help mix the gases during combustion, direct burned gases out the exhaust port, and make room for the intake and exhaust valves.

4. **Deck**: The flat top of the cylinder block, around the cylinder bores, onto which the cylinder head attaches.

5. **Cylinder Head**: Attaches to the deck surface to form the top of the combustion chamber. Contains the intake and exhaust valve trains. The spark plug also threads into the cylinder head. A gasket is placed between the cylinder head and the deck surface to create a seal.

6. **Intake Valve**: Opens and closes the intake port to allow the flow of the air-fuel mixture into the combustion chamber during the intake process. An engine usually has one or two intake valves per cylinder.

7. **Exhaust Valve**: Opens and closes the exhaust port during the exhaust stroke, which allows burned gases to flow from the combustion chamber into the exhaust system. Since exhaust gases are at a high pressure, the exhaust valve is normally smaller than the intake valve. An engine usually has one or two exhaust valves per cylinder.

8. **Camshaft**: A shaft with lobes known as cams which open and close the intake and exhaust valves as the shaft rotates. If the camshaft is in the cylinder head, levers called rocker arms ride on the cams to push on the valves. If the camshaft is located in the engine block, lifters ride on the cams and transfer the linear motion to the rocker arms through push rods. Valve springs push on the other side of the rocker arms to keep the lifters in contact with the camshaft. An engine may have more than one camshaft, depending on its configuration.

9. **Crankshaft**: The shaft in the bottom of the engine block (the crankcase) which transmits power captured by the pistons during the combustion process. Converts the piston's linear motion into a rotational motion. Fits into the perfectly round main bearings of the engine block. Has counterweights to reduce vibrations.

10. **Camshaft Drive**: A belt, chain, or gear system that transmits the rotation of the crankshaft to the camshaft, turning the camshaft at one-half the speed of the crankshaft.

11. **Connecting Rod**: Connects the piston in the cylinder to the crankshaft in the crankcase. The connecting rod attaches to the piston through a cylindrical wrist pin and bolts to the crankshaft's smooth rod journal.

12. **Flywheel**: A large metal disk that attaches to the front of the crankshaft outside of the engine block. Smoothes engine operation through its large rotational momentum. Connects the engine to both the transmission, through the clutch, and the starter motor, through the flywheel's ring gear.

13. Harmonic Balancer: Sometimes called a vibration damper. A disk attached to the end of the crankshaft that absorbs vibrations in the crankshaft. Acts as a pulley for drive belts to other assemblies in the engine compartment.

While automobile engines do have many configurations, they all operate on only two basic processes: the four-stroke cycle and the two-stroke cycle. Both two-stroke and four-stroke engines have very similar components because the two cycles involve the same four steps:

1. **Intake**: Low pressure caused by downward movement of the piston draws air-fuel mixture into the combustion chamber.

2. **Compression**: The piston moves upward, compressing the air-fuel mixture and increasing the pressure (and therefore the combustibility of the air-fuel mixture).

3. **Combustion**: Also called the power stroke. The air-fuel mixture is ignited. The flame propagates throughout the combustion chamber, increasing pressure and forcing the piston back down in the cylinder.

4. **Exhaust**: The burned air-fuel mixture is evacuated out of the combustion chamber to the exhaust system, preparing the cylinder to repeat the cycle.

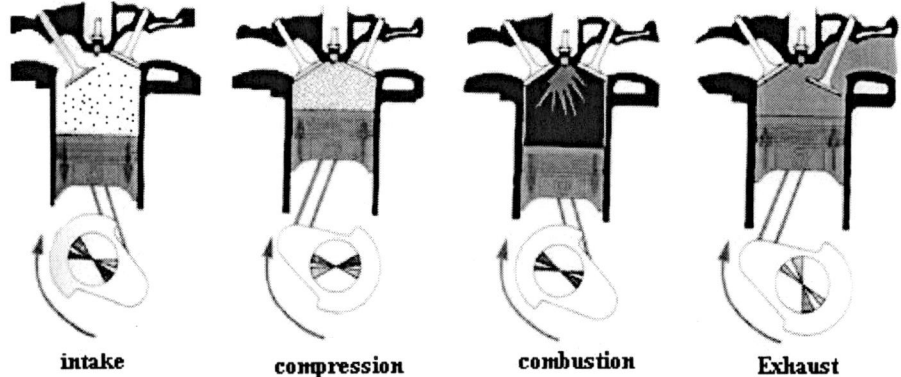

intake   compression   combustion   Exhaust

The difference between the two lies in their names. A *four-stroke* engine completes the four steps of the cycle and creates power through combustion, every *four strokes* of the piston (up-and-down twice) or two rotations of the cylinder. *Two-stroke* engines also complete the cycle, but they create power every time the piston reaches the top of the cylinder (every two strokes or one rotation of the crankshaft).

Two-stroke engines expel more pollution – since they require an oil mixture within their fuel – and are generally less efficient than four-stroke engines. Two-stroke engines also lack power at low speeds and need to be serviced more often. That is why most cars operate on the four-stroke cycle.

The gasoline four-stroke cycle is also called the **Otto cycle** after Nikolaus August Otto, the German engineer who made the first engine successfully run using this cycle.

In a gasoline four-stroke engine, the intake stroke occurs as the piston travels downward in the cylinder. The downward motion of the piston creates low pressure in the combustion chamber. The intake valve opens, which allows air-fuel mixture to be drawn into the cylinder from the air intake system. As the piston nears the bottom of the cylinder, the intake valve closes and the piston begins to travel upwards again, compressing the air-fuel mixture. This compression of the air-fuel mixture increases the pressure, temperature, and combustibility of the air-fuel mixture. When the piston gets close to the top of its travel again, the spark plug fires, igniting the air-fuel mixture.

While turbulence is not good in the air intake system, it does help spread the flame during combustion, so many piston heads are shaped to help mix the air-fuel mixture in the combustion chamber. As the flame propagates, the pressure in the combustion chamber is greatly increased, forcing the piston back down in the cylinder. The combustion stroke is the only step in the cycle that creates power instead of consuming it.

Once the piston reaches the bottom of its travel again, the exhaust valve opens. The piston's upward travel pushes the burned gases out of the cylinder and into the exhaust system. Ideally, all of the burned gases would be evacuated to make room for a fresh charge. However, there is usually a small amount of **residual gases** that remain in the engine after the exhaust stroke, especially around the rim of the piston head. Luckily, the piston head can be shaped to help direct exhaust gases out the exhaust port.

As the piston reaches the top of its travel, the exhaust valve closes and the intake valve re-opens, starting the cycle over again.

The **Wankel rotary engine**, named for another German engineer Felix Wankel, also operates on the gasoline four-stroke process. However, in Wankel rotary engines, the process occurs in three separate moving combustion chambers, between the three corners of the triangle.

The Wankel rotary engine has two advantages:

1. Eliminates the linear (up-and-down) motion of the piston, which required that the piston's momentum change between each stroke.

2. Creates three power strokes for every one revolution of the rotor.

A diesel four-stroke engine operates very similarly to a gasoline four-stroke engine. However, the intake stroke draws only air into the cylinder. Also, it does not use a spark plug. Instead, fuel is injected during the combustion stroke and combusts due to the high pressure in the combustion chamber. For this reason, gasoline engines are often called **spark ignition** (SI) engines, while diesel engines can be called **compression ignition** (CI) engines.

Diesel engines often have a **precombustion chamber**, or prechamber, above the cylinder. Combustion begins in the prechamber, and the flame propagates in the main combustion chamber in the cylinder. The prechamber can have a **glow plug**, which heats the diesel fuel. This helps start the engine in cold weather, particularly helpful since the fuel in diesel engines thickens in low temperatures.

The diesel cycle is generally less efficient than the Otto cycle. However, most diesel engines are more efficient than gasoline engines because they are capable of achieving much greater compression ratios.

The **compression ratio** of an engine is the maximum volume of the combustion chamber divided by the minimum volume.

> **Maximum Volume**: Occurs at the very bottom of the piston's stroke – known as **bottom dead center** (BDC) – when the piston is as far away from the cylinder head as possible.

Minimum Volume: Occurs when the piston is as close to the cylinder head as possible at the very top of its stroke, known as **top dead center** (TDC).

> For example, the volume between the piston and the cylinder head at BDC is 3 liters, and the volume between the piston and cylinder head is 1 liter at TDC. The compression ratio is therefore 3:1 (stated as "three to one").

> When the compression ratio in a gasoline engine is too high, the fuel will experience too high of a pressure during the compression stroke. This causes combustion before the spark plug is able to fire. Remember what this is called? Engine knock.

Since diesel engines use the high pressure generated in the compression stroke to ignite fuel, there is less concern over engine knock. Therefore, much greater compression ratios can be obtained. In fact, many naval engines are large enough that a person can stand comfortably in the combustion chamber. However, the increased pressure means that diesel engines must be made more durable, leading to greatly increased weights.

Two-stroke engines operate on the same principles as four-stroke engines, but do possess differences which enable them to complete their cycle in only two strokes (one rotation of the crankshaft).

A two-stroke engine requires oil to be mixed with its fuel in order to lubricate the engine parts in the crankcase. The fuel mixture enters the crankcase to lubricate the moving parts, and the rotating crankshaft helps force the fuel toward the intake port of the cylinder.

As the piston moves downward, it uncovers the intake port and allows the fuel mixture to flow into the combustion chamber. The intake port of a two-stroke engine usually has a **reed valve**, which is simply a flexible material that acts as a check valve. Sometimes, however, the intake port has a **rotary valve** that rotates in order to open and close the intake port at the appropriate time.

Just like in the four-stroke engine, the piston then travels back towards the top of its stroke to compress the air-fuel mixture before the spark plug ignites it. As the piston travels back downward, the exhaust port is uncovered to allow the burned gases to escape. As the piston travels farther down the cylinder, it uncovers the intake port so that a fresh charge begins to fill the combustion chamber while the exhaust gases are still leaving, known as **scavenging**.

Lubrication System

Fuel and oil do not travel through the crankcase of most engines, so a lubricant must be circulated throughout the engine to all the moving parts. **Motor oil**, which is usually refined from crude oil (petroleum), is the lubricant used in engines. **Synthetic oil** can be made from artificial materials like modified crude oil or vegetable oil. Synthetic oil offers many advantages: longer life, lower friction, and better fuel economy than **conventional oil**.

Oil weight refers to the oil's viscosity and is an important determinant of the oil's performance. Low-viscosity oil flows more easily, but if the oil is not viscous enough, the moving parts of the engine will rub on each other; that metal-to-metal contact can seize the engine. Ideally, the moving parts of the engine do not actually touch each other, but glide on a thin layer of oil in a small space between moving parts known as the **bearing clearance**.

For example, engines have removable soft metal inserts that fit into many of the areas where a round shaft rotates in a bore. **Main bearings** fit in the crankshaft main journal into which the crankshaft fits; **rod bearings** fit into the bottom of the connecting rods that attach to the crankshaft; and **rod bushings** are pressed into the connecting rods' small end through which the wrist pin is inserted.

However, these bushings do not prevent friction in these areas. Instead, the bearings have a small hole and recession known as an **oil groove**. These grooves allow oil to fill and flow through the bearing clearance. A too-thin oil will flow through the bearing clearance too quickly, allowing the moving parts to make contact.

Since oil viscosity is so important to the operation of the engine, the oil weight is always printed on the front of a container of oil as the oil's **viscosity index** or number. The Society of Automotive Engineers (SAE) established a system which assigns numbers in multiples of five based on the oil's viscosity. Oil with low viscosity is given a low number, while a higher number means that the oil has a higher resistance to flow.

> For example, which oil is more viscous? One with a SAE 50 weight, or one with a SAE 10? The answer: the SAE 50 oil.

Those two oils are examples of **single-grade oil**, meaning they only have one viscosity number. However many motor oils have a viscosity that varies with temperature, and therefore receive a rating with two numbers. These **multigrade oils** are thinner at low temperatures and thicken as the engine warms and approaches normal operating temperatures. Multiviscosity ratings have one number that is followed by the letter W, designating it as the oil's winter rating, and then a second number that gives the oil's weight at normal, warmer temperatures. For example, a 10W-30 will flow easily like a SAE 10 oil when the engine is cold, but thicken as the engine warms and exhibit the behavior of a SAE 30 at normal operating conditions.

Oil collects in the engine's **sump**, which is normally just the bottom of the crankcase, called the **oil pan**. Some engines have what is known as a **dry sump system** that uses an external oil reservoir to store the oil. Dry sump systems locate the oil reservoir close to the ground, lowering a vehicle's center of gravity and reducing the small resistance in the engine (caused by the crankshaft counterweights splashing through oil in the oil pan). For this reason, dry sump systems are usually used only in high-performance vehicles.

The **oil pump** is driven by either the camshaft or the crankshaft. It draws oil from the sump through the **pickup tube**, forcing it through the rest of the lubrication system. The oil passes through an **oil filter** to prevent particles from entering and damaging bearings in the engine.
The oil then flows through the engine's **oil galleries**, which are passages in the engine block, so that it can enter and lubricate the engine's moving parts. Though the main purpose of motor oil is to reduce friction and noise, it also helps transfer heat from the engine. An **oil cooler** is often used to transfer this collected heat to surrounding air, keeping the engine oil at a controlled temperature.

It is important that lubrication maintains a high enough pressure to properly lubricate all of the engine's components. Therefore, cars often have an **oil pressure sensor** which gives a reading through the **oil pressure gauge**. When the oil pressure is too low, the oil pressure sensor will either illuminate a warning light, or shut off the engine.

Since high oil pressure can reduce a vehicle's fuel economy, the lubrication system can also use an **oil pressure relief valve** to prevent the lubrication system from exceeding a maximum pressure.

Since engine oil is under pressure and it is important not to lose any oil, seals and gaskets are used to prevent leaks.

Seals: Used at the ends of the crankshaft.

Gaskets: Fitted between most engine parts. For example: between the oil pan and cylinder head, whose seam is exposed to the outside of the engine.

Piston rings are also fitted into slits known as **ring grooves** near the top of the piston, in order to seal the small space between the piston and the cylinder wall. This prevents both oil from entering the combustion chamber and air-fuel mixture from entering the crankcase.

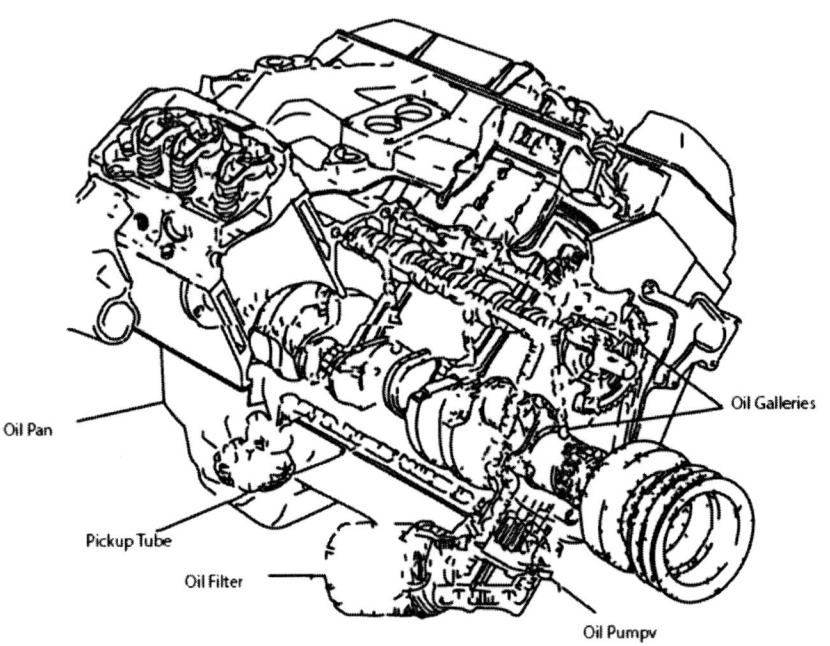

Cooling Systems
Though motor oil transfers some heat from the engine, it is not enough to maintain the engine's proper operating temperature. Therefore, a cooling system is required.

Many older engines are **air-cooled**, meaning that the only working fluid in the cooling system is air from the surroundings. The engine block of an air cooling system has fins around the cylinders in order to increase the surface area exposed to the air, which increases the rate of heat transfer.

Air cooling systems also use a fan to blow the air through the fins, utilizing a heat transfer method known as **forced convection**. Forced convection transfers heat much better than the simple conduction of still air, or natural convection to a slowly-moving airstream.

Most modern cars are **liquid-cooled**. As the name suggests, they use a liquid – instead of air – to cool the engine. Engines with liquid cooling systems are often called water-cooled, though water is not the main fluid used. Instead, liquid cooling systems use a mixture of water and antifreeze called **coolant** to extract heat from the engine. The coolant is usually a 50/50 mixture of water and antifreeze, meaning it is half (50%) water and half antifreeze.

Antifreeze increases the freezing temperature and boiling point of the liquid, reducing the risk of freezing, which can clog the system, or boiling, which can create bubbles in the system and damage the pump. The antifreeze also helps prevent rust and corrosion.

The **water pump** moves the coolant through the coolant system. The coolant flows through **water jackets**, which are hollow areas in the block that surround the cylinder. After flowing around the intake manifold, cylinder head, and engine block, the coolant travels through the **upper radiator hose** to a heat exchanger known as the **radiator**.

As the coolant flows downward through tiny tubes in the radiator, the **radiator fan** forces air around these tubes, transferring the heat from the coolant to the airstream. At the top of the radiator, the **radiator cap** seals the radiator filler neck to prevent leakage and keep the system pressurized. This further increases the boiling point of the liquid, while also relieving excess pressure that could damage the system. The radiator cap should never be removed unless the coolant has been given sufficient time to cool.

From the bottom of the radiator, the coolant flows through the **lower radiator hose** back to the water pump.

Since the coolant is heated by the engine, it can also be pumped to the vehicle's heater to warm the interior of the car. A **coolant reservoir** stores extra coolant and makes sure that the cooling system is always supplied with enough of the fluid. An engine is not hot when it is first started, so the cooling system does not need to transfer heat as efficiently.

This is why cooling systems are equipped with a **thermostat**, which cuts off the flow of coolant to the radiator when it is below a certain temperature. When the thermostat is closed, the coolant bypasses the radiator and simply flows back and forth from the water pump and engine. When the coolant approaches its operating temperature, the thermostat opens and allows the cooling system to operate normally.

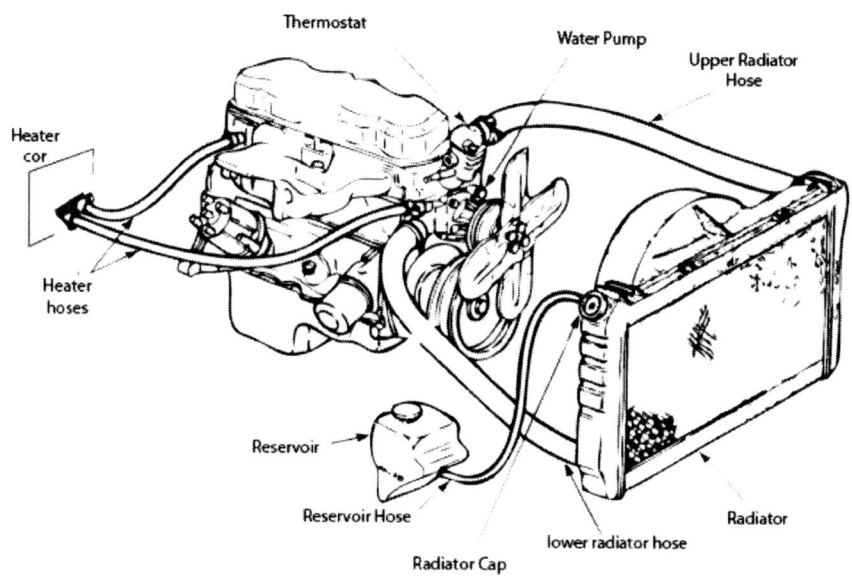

Electrical System

The electrical system includes all the sensors and conductors that transmit electrical power and signals throughout the vehicle. The electrical system encompasses several subsystems, including the accessory and safety systems. The electricity of the vehicle is provided by a **battery**, which converts chemical energy into electricity. The battery has a negative terminal, sometimes called the ground, and a positive terminal.

When the engine is running, it rotates the **alternator**, which is a device that converts rotational motion into electricity in order to recharge the battery. When the level of the liquid in the battery is low, water can be added. You should always be careful not to spill any of the battery acid. Also, make sure that the battery is reconnected properly: usually a red wire connects to the positive terminal, and a black wire connects to the negative terminal.

When jumpstarting a car with a dead battery, you should connect the red jumper cable to the positive terminals of both batteries, then attach the black jumper cable to the negative side of the good battery, and finally attach the other end of the black jumper cable to either the negative terminal of the dead battery or a good ground, such as the engine block, on the car with the dead battery.

Whenever working on any part of the electrical system, you should always disconnect the battery and make sure all stored charges are released. When installing or removing the battery, be very careful not to create an arc by letting any tools touch both terminals or connect the positive terminal to any surroundings. Once the battery is disconnected, it is a good idea to wrap electrical tape around the wires that connect to the positive terminal to make sure that they do not accidently make contact with the terminal and charge the system.

Ignition System

The performance of a car's engine depends on several electrical systems. The **Ignition System** is responsible for delivering the spark that ignites the air-fuel mixture during the combustion process. This has a great direct impact on the performance of the engine.

The ignition system must deliver a very high voltage to the spark plug at the correct time in each cylinder for the engine to operate properly. The engine does not operate at peak performance if the spark plug fires when the piston is exactly at TDC. Instead, the spark should occur just before the piston reaches the top of its travel, because pressure does not immediately occur when the air-fuel mixture is ignited.

The delay in pressure increase is known as **ignition delay**.

Ignition timing tells when the sparkplug fires in relation to the position of the piston within the cylinder; it is measured in degrees Before Top Dead Center (BTDC).

For instance, if an engine is set at 7° BTDC, this means that, when the spark plug fires, the crankshaft rotates seven more degrees before the piston reaches TDC. This gives the flames time to propagate through the combustion chamber, making the combustion process's peak pressure occur when the crankshaft is at the position to best create the maximum amount of power.

When the engine is moving faster, the flames do not have as much time to spread, so ignition must occur earlier in the cycle. Increasing the number of degrees BTDC at which the spark occurs is called **advancing the time**; making the spark occur closer to TDC is called **retarding the timing**.

The flame must travel through the entire combustion chamber before the pressure is too great. If the ignition timing is too late, air-fuel mixture trapped around the rim of the piston near the ring grooves, known as **end gases**, can ignite from the great pressure. When the two flame fronts in the combustion chamber collide, there is a huge pressure spike, resulting in the loud banging of engine knock and eventual engine damage. To avoid engine knock at low speeds while still obtaining higher performance at high speeds, many vehicles have a **variable timing ignition system**. This system advances the ignition timing at high speeds and retards the ignition timing at low speeds.

Older cars and lawnmowers have a simple **magneto system**, wherein a permanent magnet sends a pulse of electricity to the spark plug when the engine's crankshaft is at a particular position.

Modern vehicles require a more complex ignition system that sends more voltage to the spark plugs of multiple cylinders and different times. To keep the engine running smoothly and prevent vibrations, the spark plugs of an engine do not usually fire in an order as simple as front-to-back. Instead, they are staggered. The **firing order** dictates when the cylinders of an engine receive a spark.

For instance, a four-cylinder engine might have its cylinders number front-to-back and have the firing order 1-2-4-3 or 1-3-4-2. When working on the ignition system, you should make sure you know the differences between the cylinders, as well as their firing order.

High voltage electricity is delivered to the spark plug of each cylinder by the **distributor**, which is driven by the camshaft. The spark plugs are connected to the **distributor cap** by high tension cables known as **spark plug wires**.

A **rotor** inside the distributor rotates and, as its metal arm passes closely to the contact in the distributor cap for a cylinder, completes the electrical circuit, allowing high voltage electricity to flow to that cylinder's spark plug. A spark plug must be clean and have a properly-adjusted gap between its electrodes in order to fire efficiently. Similar to the hot wire MAF sensor, a spark plug must be heated to burn off deposits.

Based on the shape of their ceramic insulator, spark plugs are divided into two broad categories: hot plugs and cold plugs.

> **Cold Plugs** have an insulator that is shaped to maximize heat transfer away from the electrode, keeping it cooler and preventing preignition.

> However, a spark plug might not get hot enough to burn off deposits if it is only driven slowly. In this case, a **Hot Plug** can be used.

A spark plug will only fire when provided with a very high voltage, so the distributor cannot simply connect to the battery. Instead, the distributor is connected by the **coil wire** to the **ignition coil**, which uses two sets of **windings**, or wires wrapped in tight circles, to change the batteries low voltage to a much higher voltage. This is similar to a transformer.

> **Low Voltage**: Usually 12 V.

> **Higher Voltage**: 15,000 – 45,000 V, depending on the engine and spark plugs.

When no spark plugs are firing, a magnetic field builds in the **primary winding** of the ignition coil, which is made of thick wire wrapped several hundred times around or near the secondary winding. The distributor has either an electrical system or mechanical point system that acts as a switch for the coil.

When the switch is closed, the primary winding builds a magnetic field. When the switch opens and the distributor engages one of the cylinders' spark plug wires, the magnetic field is interrupted and a high voltage is discharged through the **secondary winding**. This secondary winding is made of thousands of windings of very thin wire.

The ignition system is often divided into two circuits:

The Primary Ignition Circuit: Includes all ignition components that receive low voltage

The Secondary Ignition Circuit: Includes all the high voltage ignition components.

Some modern cars now have an **electronic ignition module** to deliver high voltage and control ignition timing, instead of a mechanical system.

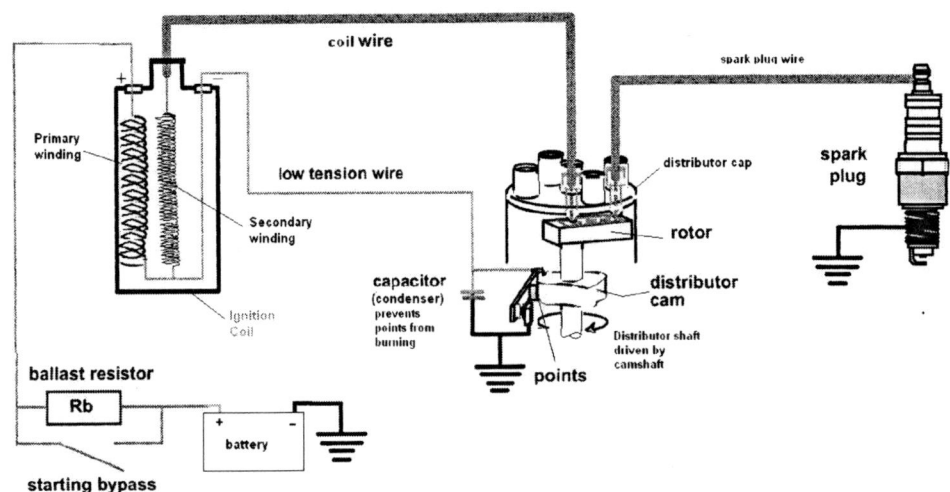

Emission Control System

The **emission control system** directs the toxic burned exhaust gases from the engine toward the rear of the vehicle, filters out most pollutants, and reduces exhaust noise. Emission control standards are mostly concerned with three main pollutants: hydrocarbons (HC), carbon monoxide (CO), and oxides of nitrogen (NOx).

Hydrocarbons are toxins that result from the burning of fuel and can cause illness and smog.

Carbon monoxide is a colorless, odorless toxin that is very harmful when inhaled. Carbon monoxide results from incomplete combustion and can cause headaches, nausea, blurred vision, and even death. CO emissions increase when there is less oxygen present in the air-fuel mixture, such as when the mixture is rich.

Oxides of nitrogen are formed by the reaction of nitrogen and oxygen in the air during combustion. NOx emissions are harmful to the eyes and lungs and form ozone. Most factors that cause NOx, like a lean air-fuel mixture and high temperature, improve fuel economy and

HC and CO emissions. This means that the engine cannot be tuned for zero emissions, but must be tuned to produce the least overall pollutants. The pollutants are then further reduced by the emission control system before being expelled to the atmosphere.

Many vehicles are equipped with an **exhaust gas recirculation (EGR) system** that allows exhaust gases to enter the intake manifold to reduce NOx emissions by replacing oxygen in the air-fuel mixture and lowering the combustion temperature. Oxygen (O_2) sensors track the amount of oxygen in the exhaust gases, which is used to adjust the air-fuel ratio, ignition timing, and EGR settings. Emissions released to the atmosphere are further reduced by the catalytic converter.

The **catalytic converter** contains a catalyst, which is a material that speeds up chemical reactions; the oxygen atoms in the NOx particles react with HC and CO particles to leave harmless nitrogen (N_2), carbon dioxide (CO_2), and water (H_2O) to be expelled out the tailpipe of the vehicle. When the catalytic converter is brand new, it is almost 100% efficient in eliminating all pollutants. However, over time, it grows less effective.

The exhaust system also has **resonator** and **muffler** inline with the exhaust pipe. These work together to reduce noise and give the vehicle its "exhaust note." These components do not only quiet the car to meet legal requirements, but also increase engine performance. An exhaust system can be tuned to help remove burned gases from the combustion chamber more efficiently, making the engine more fuel efficient and powerful.

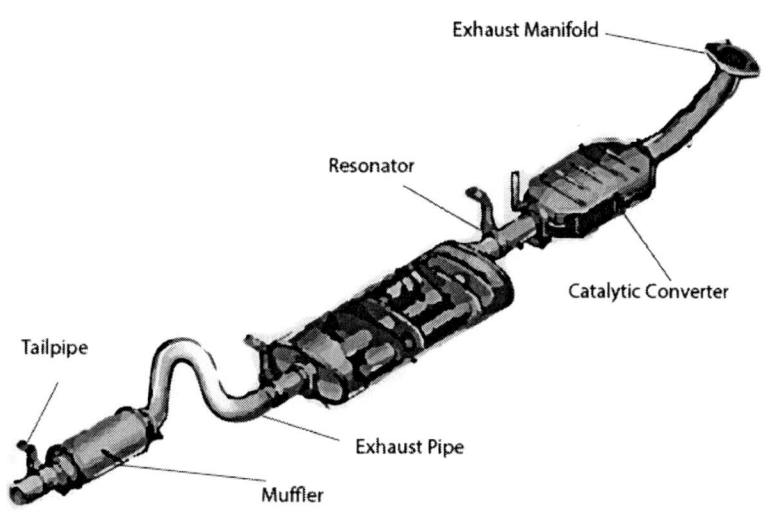

Drive Train
The **drive train**, also called the powertrain, of a vehicle includes all of the components necessary to create and transmit power to the road. This includes the engine, wheels, and everything that transmits the rotation of the engine to the wheels.

A **transmission** is a series of gear trains with various gear ratios which give the vehicle the ability to drive at a wide range of speeds while keeping the engine speed within its safe operating range. A low gear allows the vehicle to drive slowly while keeping the engine rpm's higher. It also facilitates quicker acceleration. Meanwhile, a high gear ratio allows the vehicle to travel faster while the engine's speed stays lower for better fuel mileage.

A **manual transmission** lets the driver choose which gear to engage for the driving conditions and desired power.

An **automatic transmission** uses electronic controls and a hydraulic system to shift gears without the assistance of the driver.

The transmission will have an electric **starter motor** mounted to it. This engages the flywheel and rotates the engine when starting. In order for the car's engine to be able to continue running while the car is stopped, it must be connected to a device that allows it to be disengaged from the transmission and then reengaged when the driver wants to continue.

A vehicle with a manual transmission has a **clutch** that is mounted to the flywheel of the engine. The clutch allows the driver to engage or disengage the engine from the transmission. When the driver presses the clutch pedal, the clutch disconnects the engine from the transmission so the engine no longer rotates the transmission's input shaft. The driver must disengage the clutch while shifting in between gears.

Instead of a clutch, automatic transmissions are connected to the engine by a **torque converter**: a hydraulic coupling that allows the engine and transmission input shaft to turn at different speeds.

Sometimes, such as in a front-engine rear-wheel-drive vehicle, the engine and the drive wheels are located on opposite sides of the car. In those cases, a cylindrical tube known as a **drive shaft** must be used to transmit the rotation of the transmission to the drive wheels. The drive shaft then connects to a **differential**: a gear assembly that transmits power to the wheels while allowing them to rotate at different speeds.

The differential must be able to travel up and down without bending the drive shaft. Therefore, the drive shaft must have a universal coupling, or **U-joint**, which transmits rotational power but does not require the shafts on either side to be parallel.

If the car is front-engine front-wheel-drive, or rear-engine rear-wheel-drive, then the engine is on the same side of the car as the drive wheels; therefore, a drive shaft is not needed. Instead, the transmission and differential are combined into one assembly known as a **transaxle**. **Axles**, shafts which connect the wheels to either side of the differential or transaxle, rotate the drive wheels.

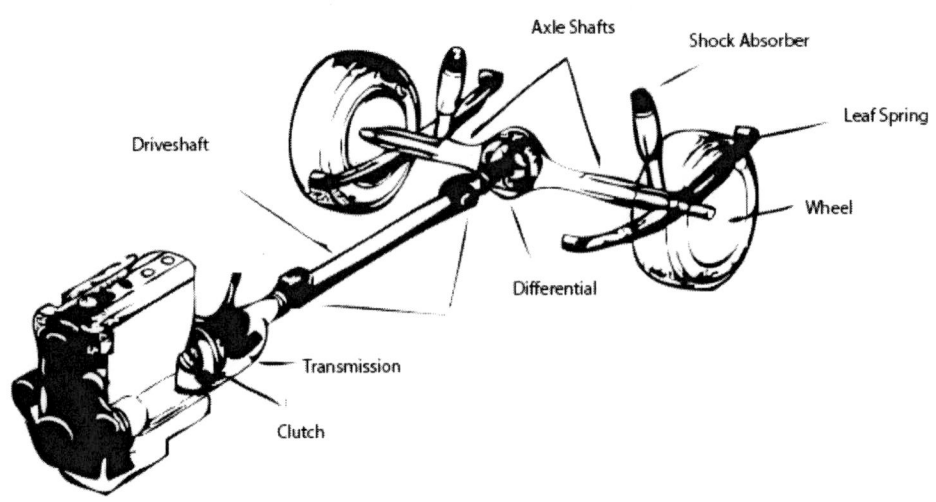

Steering, Suspension, and Braking Systems

The **steering system** allows the driver to control the vehicle's direction of travel by turning the front wheels. The **rack and pinion** set of gears can convert the rotation motion of the steering wheel into linear motion for turning the front wheels of the vehicle.

Most modern cars now have **power steering**, which is a system that uses hydraulics to assist the driver in steering the wheel. Without power steering, the steering wheel can be very difficult to turn.

Tie rods connect the steering mechanism to the wheels and are ultimately responsible for turning the wheels left and right. The tie rods have an adjustable length that can tune the vehicle's **toe**: a measurement of how parallel the front wheels are.

> **Toe-In**: The tires are closer at the front.

> **Toe-Out**: The tires are closer at the rear.

A wheel's **camber**, measured in degrees, is the angle of the wheel and tire relative to the horizontal plane.

> **Positive Camber**: The top of the tire leans outward, away from the center of the car.

> **Negative Camber**: The top of the tire tilts inward, toward the center of the car.

Caster is the angle relative to the ground of the line, around which the front tires pivot when the driver turns the steering wheel.

> **Positive Caster**: The top of this pivot line leans toward the rear of the vehicle. In a car with positive caster, the front wheels contact the ground behind the pivot line, which gives them a tendency to stay pointing toward the front of the car. This makes turning more difficult.

> **Negative Caster**: A car with negative caster turns more easily, but is less stable and can turn due to bumps in the road.

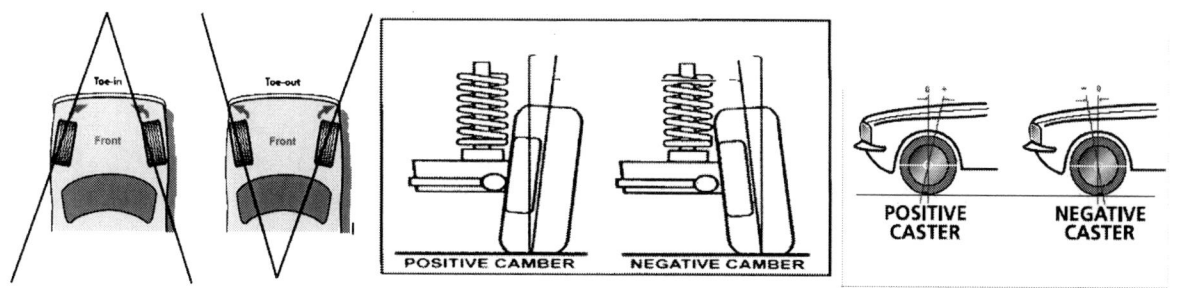

The **suspension system** provides the vehicle's handling characteristics, and allows the wheels and tires to travel up and down without affecting the driver. Joints and linkages, or **control arms**, connect the wheels to the rest of the car. This allows the wheels to travel up and down in relation to the body; it also controls the angle of the wheels as they travel up and down.

Springs in the suspension system support the weight of the vehicle while allowing movement of the wheels. **Shock absorbers**, or dampers, help absorb the impacts experienced by the wheels while driving and prevent the springs' tendency to oscillate or bounce.

Early automobiles had mechanical braking systems that connected the brake pedal or lever to the brakes via a metal rod or cable. Today, cars are made with hydraulic braking systems that give the driver a mechanical advantage. This improves the braking power and eliminates the hazard of suddenly failing (which would leave the driver without the ability to stop the car).

Most cars still have a separate mechanical brake linkage known as an emergency brake (e-brake), or **parking brake**, that can be engaged without relying on the hydraulics. Most vehicles also have a **brake booster**, which assists the driver in depressing the brake pedal. This means that less effort is required to push on the brake pedal; but when the engine is off, the brake pedal can become very difficult to press.

Modern cars also have an **anti-lock brake system (ABS)** that prevents the driver from completely stopping the rotation of the wheels while the car is in motion, which would cause loss of control. When the ABS senses the tires skidding, the brakes pulse slightly, allowing the tires to keep traction while still slowing their rotation.

The brake pedal is connected to the **master cylinder**, which converts the mechanical force applied to the brake pedal into hydraulic pressure in the **brake fluid** that is transmitted to the four wheels of the car. The hydraulic pressure is used to create a friction to slow the rotation of the wheels. In a **drum brake assembly**, the hydraulic pressure pushes friction plates, called **brake shoes**, outward. There, they make contact with the rotating **brake drum** to which the wheel is bolted.

A **disk brake assembly** uses the hydraulic pressure to clamp friction plates known as **brake pads** (held in place by a **caliper**) onto a rotating **brake disk**, onto which the wheel is bolted.

Though disk brakes are more efficient in cooling and less likely to fail, some vehicles only have disk brakes in the front. In those cases, they have drum brakes in the rear. This is because drum brakes are less expensive to manufacture; most of the work done in stopping a vehicle is done by the front wheels due to weight transfer, anyway.

Disk brakes also have the advantage of not needing frequent servicing, because the pads are self-adjusting, unlike the shoes of a drum brake. Whatever the brake-type, the hydraulic system can get air in its lines, which makes the brake pedal feel spongy.

To avoid this condition, brake lines should not be mounted near any hot engine parts, which can cause boiling of the brake fluid; also, the brake system should be bled, which is the process of removing air from the lines of the braking system.

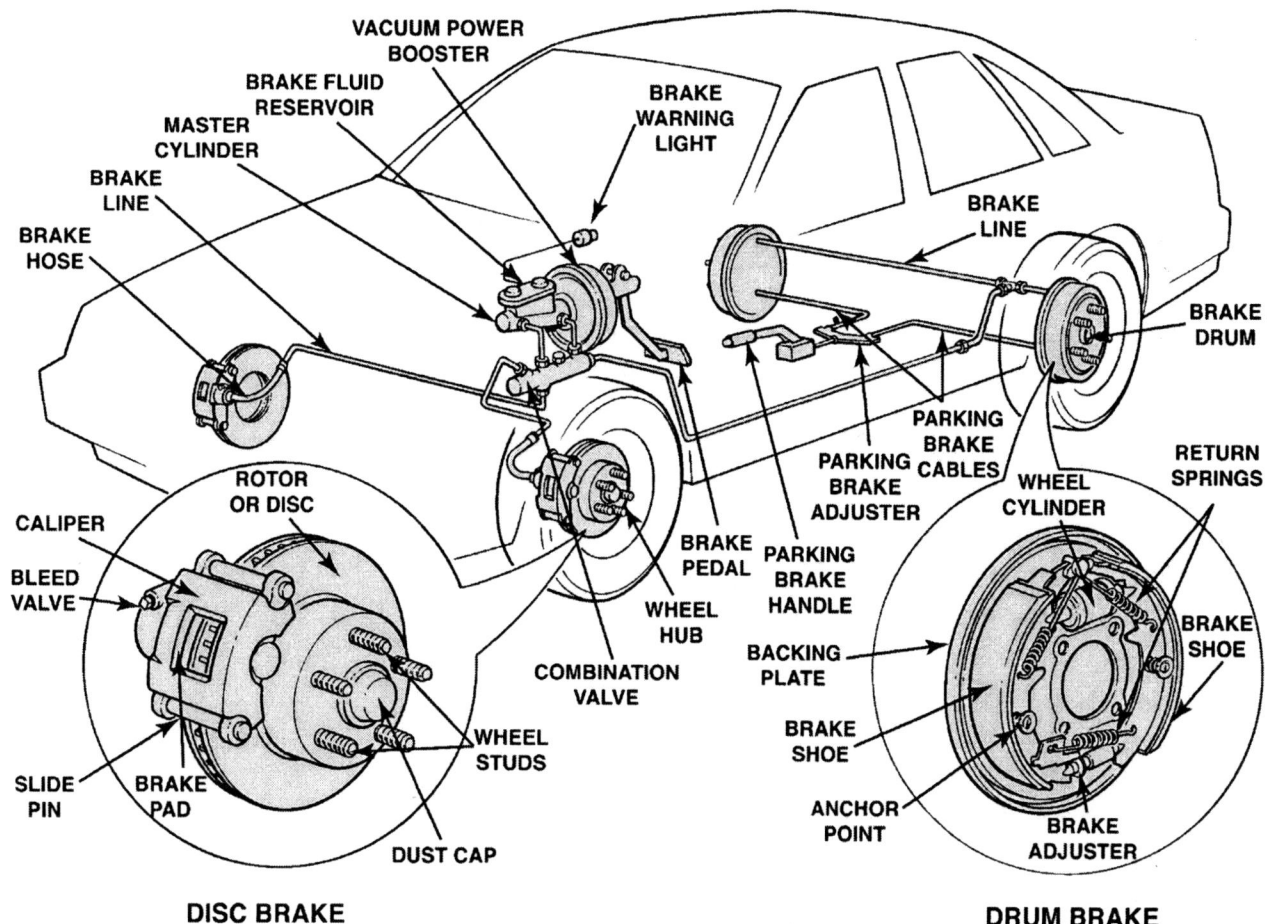

DISC BRAKE

DRUM BRAKE

Practice Drill: Automotive

1. What would you use to check the air pressure in a car's tires?
   a) Tachometer.
   b) Pressure sensor.
   c) Pressure gauge.
   d) Barometer.

2. What type of vehicle construction allows the body to be easily unbolted and removed from the frame?
   a) Monocoque.
   b) Body-over-frame.
   c) Unibody.
   d) Stressed skin.

3. When tire pressure is checked, the gauge gives:
   a) The absolute pressure of the air in the tire.
   b) The temperature of the air in the tire.
   c) The barometric pressure.
   d) The difference between the air pressure in the tire and atmospheric pressure.

121

4. What could be the cause of deposits building up on the spark plug?
   a) Using a cold spark plug.
   b) Using a hot spark plug.
   c) The spark plug does not extend far enough into the cylinder.
   d) Both a) and c).

5. A car's oil level drops and there is bluish smoke coming out of the tailpipe. What is the most likely cause?
   a) A leak in the lubrication system.
   b) Worn piston rings.
   c) A blown head gasket.
   d) A rich air-fuel mixture.

6. A car is billowing white smoke or water vapor out of its tailpipe. What is the most likely cause?
   a) A rich air-fuel mixture.
   b) A lean air-fuel mixture.
   c) A blown head gasket.
   d) Worn piston rings.

7. Which engine part is responsible for converting the linear motion of the combustion expansion into rotational power?
   a) The piston.
   b) The connecting rod.
   c) The camshaft.
   d) The crankshaft.

8. What happens when the driver depresses the gas pedal?
   a) The air-fuel ratio becomes rich.
   b) The throttle plate opens further.
   c) The clutch engages.
   d) The choke plate opens.

9. A car's battery is replaced, but quickly drains. What could be the cause?
   a) The new battery was not manufactured correctly.
   b) The car's alternator is not operating properly.
   c) The car's electrical system has a short.
   d) Any of the above.

10. Which of the following is NOT a part of the drive train?
   a) Driveshaft.
   b) Axle.
   c) Tie rod.
   d) Clutch.

11. A car's brake pedal is not difficult to push, but feels "mushy" and must be pressed very hard to slow the vehicle. What is the most likely cause?
    a) Air in the brake lines.
    b) Brake booster failure.
    c) ABS failure.
    d) Leak in the brake system.

12. What does motor oil accomplish in the engine?
    a) Reduces friction.
    b) Reduces engine noise.
    c) Cools engine parts.
    d) All of the above.

13. Which of the following absorbs vibrations in the crankshaft?
    a) Shock absorber.
    b) Harmonic balancer.
    c) Damper.
    d) Flywheel.

14. Why is a mechanical clutch not used with an automatic transmission?
    a) An automatic transmission does not change gears.
    b) An automatic transmission uses a torque converter instead.
    c) An automatic transmission uses a differential instead.
    d) An automatic transmission connects directly to the engine.

15. Which of the following is NOT a difference between gasoline and diesel four-stroke engines?
    a) The diesel engine does not use spark plugs.
    b) A diesel engine must use a prechamber while a gasoline engine cannot.
    c) A diesel engine can achieve a greater compression ratio.
    d) Both a) and c).

16. A transaxle is a combination of the following two assemblies:
    a) Transmission and differential.
    b) Differential and axle.
    c) Driveshaft and differential.
    d) Transmission and axle.

17. Gasoline and diesel are both refined from:
    a) Methane.
    b) Crude oil.
    c) Propane.
    d) Kerosene.

18. The ignition coil functions to:
    a) Produce a constant high voltage for use by the spark plugs.
    b) Reduce the amount of voltage supplied by the battery.
    c) Produce a pulse of high voltage from the lower voltage of the battery.
    d) Start the engine when the ignition key is turned on.

19. What part of the engine does the starter motor engage?
   a) Flywheel.
   b) Harmonic damper.
   c) Crankshaft.
   d) Clutch.

20. What step in the four-stroke process produces power?
   a) Exhaust stroke.
   b) Compression stroke.
   c) Combustion stroke.
   d) Intake stroke.

21. What could be the cause of high oil pressure?
   a) Low oil level.
   b) Oil with too low of a viscosity.
   c) Leak in the oil system.
   d) Clog in the oil system.

22. What forces the flow of fuel through the fuel delivery system to the engine?
   a) Fuel pump.
   b) Sending unit.
   c) Injectors.
   d) Fuel tank pressure.

23. What forces the flow of air through a naturally-aspirated intake system to the engine?
   a) Air pump.
   b) Turbocharger.
   c) Ambient pressure.
   d) Carburetor.

24. The inner portion of a tire is wearing out faster than the outside portion. What could be the cause?
   a) Toe.
   b) Caster.
   c) Camber.
   d) Pressure.

25. What is the most likely cause of a tire wearing out on the inner and outer portions faster than in the middle?
   a) Toe.
   b) Caster.
   c) Camber.
   d) Pressure.

26. What is the main reason that tractor-trailers transmissions have 10 or 15 forward gears, while normal passenger cars usually only have 4?
   a) Truck drivers go through much more training than the common driver.
   b) Semi-trailer trucks can drive much faster than passenger cars.
   c) Semi-trailer trucks are designed to pull very heavy loads.
   d) A 15-speed transmission would be too large to fit in a passenger car.

27. What kind of leak could cause excessive noise from the exhaust?
    a) Leak in the exhaust header.
    b) Leak in the resonator.
    c) Leak in the muffler.
    d) All of the above.

28. Which of the following is true about a gasoline's octane rating?
    a) A higher octane fuel offers better performance
    b) It is an indication of the fuel's viscosity
    c) It is an indication of the fuel's resistance to knock
    d) It is an indication of the fuel's density

29. Which of the following oils would be the thickest at high temperatures?
    a) 5 W-30.
    b) 10 W-40.
    c) SAE 10.
    d) SAE 30.

30. Which of the following oils would offer the least resistance to flow at low temperatures?
    a) 5 W-30.
    b) 10 W-40.
    c) SAE 10.
    d) SAE 30.

Practice Drill: Automotive – Answers

1. **c).** A pressure gauge is used to check pressure. A tachometer tells engine speed and a barometer tells atmospheric pressure. A pressure sensor measures pressure, but only gives an electrical signal, so a person would need a pressure gauge to read the pressure.

2. **b).** A unibody construction has a body attached to the frame. A monocoque, or stressed skin, construction has a body that acts as a part of the frame. A body-over-frame construction has a body separate from the frame.

3. **d).** Deposits can build up on the spark plug due to the spark plug not heating properly. Cold plugs have a ceramic insulator that is designed to efficiently transfer heat away from the electrode, keeping it cool. A spark plug might also not heat up if it is protruding into the combustion chamber.

4. **d).** A pressure gauge gives gage pressure, which is the difference between ambient pressure and the pressure being measured.

5. **b).** Bluish smoke results from burning oil. Though leaking oil could fall on a hot surface, the problem statement says the smoke is coming out of the tailpipe, so the oil was in the combustion chamber. If the piston rings are worn, they can allow oil into the combustion chamber, which burns and exits the tailpipe as smoke.

6. **c).** The most likely cause of white smoke or water vapor is coolant entering the combustion chamber, which is usually caused by a crack in the engine block or cylinder head or a blown head gasket.

7. **d).** The piston turns the expanding combustion gases into a linear motion; the connecting rod connects the piston to the crankshaft; and the crankshaft turns the linear piston motion into rotational motion. The camshaft is driven by the crankshaft.

8. **b).** The air-fuel ratio should remain constant for best engine performance. The clutch does not have any connection to the accelerator pedal, and the choke is normally only closed to block the airflow through the carburetor when starting the engine. The gas pedal is connected by the throttle linkage to the throttle plate. This provides more air flow to the engine when the gas pedal is depressed.

9. **d).** Any of these conditions would cause a battery to drain very quickly. Though it is rare, a battery with a manufacturing flaw may not be able to hold a charge for long. If the car's alternator is not working, the battery will not be recharged. If the car's electrical system has a short, electricity will constantly flow from the battery through the short.

10. **c).** Tie rods are a part of the steering system.

11. **a).** A booster failure can make the brake pedal very hard to press; the anti-lock brake system (ABS) keeps the driver from losing control of the vehicle when pushing on the brakes too hard; and a leak in the brake system can make the brakes feel as though they are fading while the brake pedal is held down. A leak can also make the hydraulic brake system fail completely.

12. **d).** Though the motor oil's main purpose is to reduce friction by preventing metal-to-metal contact, it also reduces noise and transfers heat from the engine.

13. **b).** The flywheel stores rotational inertia to continue the crankshaft's rotation. Shock absorbers and dampers are parts of the suspension system. Though the harmonic balancer is sometimes called a vibration damper, the term "damper" is normally used to refer to a device in the suspension system that deadens oscillations.

14. **b).** Though it is sometimes called a converter clutch, a torque converter is used to allow an automatic transmission's input shaft to turn at a different speed than the engine.

15. **b).** It is important to remember that the word "NOT" means we are looking for the answer that is false. Choices **a)** and **c)** are true. A diesel engine does not necessarily need a prechamber and a gasoline engine can use a precombustion chamber, so choice b is false.

16. **a).** A transaxle is a combination of a transmission and a differential in one housing.

17. **b).** Gasoline, diesel, and conventional motor oils are all derived from crude oil (petroleum).

18. **c).** The ignition coil uses the batteries low voltage to build a magnetic field in its primary winding so that it can supply a pulse of high voltage to the spark plugs when the magnetic field is interrupted and collapses.

19. **a).** The starter motor's pinion meshes with the flywheels ring gear to turn the engine over when starting the car.

20. **c).** The combustion stroke, also known as the power stroke, is the only step in the four-stroke process that generates instead of consuming power.

21. d). High oil pressure can be caused by deposits or clogs in the oil system or use of an oil that has too high of a viscosity. If the oil level is low, the oil's viscosity is too low, or there is a leak in the oil system, then the oil pressure will be lowered.

22. a). The fuel pump pressurizes the fuel in the fuel delivery system.

23. c). A naturally-aspirated intake system does not have a turbocharger or supercharger. The air flows into the cylinders due to the difference in pressure between the atmosphere and the combustion chamber, caused by the downward motion of the piston. One can either say that the low pressure in the combustion chamber sucks the air into the cylinder, or that the higher pressure of the atmosphere pushes the air into the cylinder.

24. c). If the vehicle has too much negative camber, most of the vehicle's weight will be on the inner side of the tire, leading to uneven wear.

25. d). If the tire's pressure is too low, then the middle of the tire may not wear as quickly as do the sides. If the tire's pressure is too high, then the tire will bulge and the middle will wear faster.

26. d). Because tractor-trailers pull enormous loads, their engines must stay in a narrow range to create enough torque to pull the weight of the load.

27. d). All of these leaks would cause an increase in noise levels. The muffler and resonator reduce exhaust noise and the exhaust header is located near the engine before any noise reduction devices.

28. c). The octane rating is an indication of the fuel's likelihood to cause knock; the higher the octane number, the more resistant the fuel is to knocking.

29. b). The oil weight tells the oils viscosity. A thick oil means high viscosity. Since the problem asks about the viscosity at high temperatures, the winter ratings can be ignored.

30. a). Low resistance to flow means a low viscosity. Since this question is asking about low temperatures, the winter rating of the multigrade oils should be used.

SHOP

Other sections have discussed many simple machines and assemblies, but there is one important part of these assemblies which we have not yet reviewed: fasteners. A **fastener** is any hardware responsible for joining or holding pieces of an assembly together. Though fasteners are often underappreciated, they play a vital role in every part of our lives. Our cars, homes, furniture, and home appliances are all held together by fasteners; and the failure or misapplication of one of these fasteners can mean disaster. That is why it is essential to know about the different types and proper use of fasteners and those tools used to apply them in order to repair machinery.

Bolts and Screws

Most assemblies are held together by threaded fasteners, the most common of which is the bolt. A **bolt** is a cylindrical fastener with an extern al threading, which allows the bolt to be tightened into any object with a similar internal threading. This type of fastener is also called a **machine screw**.

There is no universally-accepted distinction between a bolt and a machine screw, but the term "machine screw" is normally used to refer to a bolt that is small in diameter, usually below ½ inch. However, there are some machine screws that are ¾ inch, and some bolts which are below ¼ inch in diameter. Therefore the two terms can be, and sometimes are, used interchangeably.

Diameter and Length
A bolt, or machine, screw is defined by four characteristics:

1. Diameter.

2. Length.

3. Head type.

4. Thread.

The length and diameter of a bolt can be given in either inches or millimeters. Bolts measured in inches are called **standard** or American bolts, and those measured in millimeters are called **metric**. The thread diameter of a bolt is measured from the very edges of its threading. This is known as the bolt's **major diameter**. If you measure the diameter at the base of the threading, you are measuring the bolt's root, or **minor diameter**.

The length of a bolt is measured from the base of the bolt's head to the tip of the bolt. The **head** is the larger portion on the top of the bolt which allows the bolt to be tightened; it also prevents the bolt from travelling all the way through the hole into which it is being inserted. Some special bolts, such as studs and set screws, do not have heads while others, like some threaded plugs, have heads which are smaller than the fastener's diameter. Bolts have a variety of head sizes and shapes that require different tightening tools. These tools will be discussed in detail later.

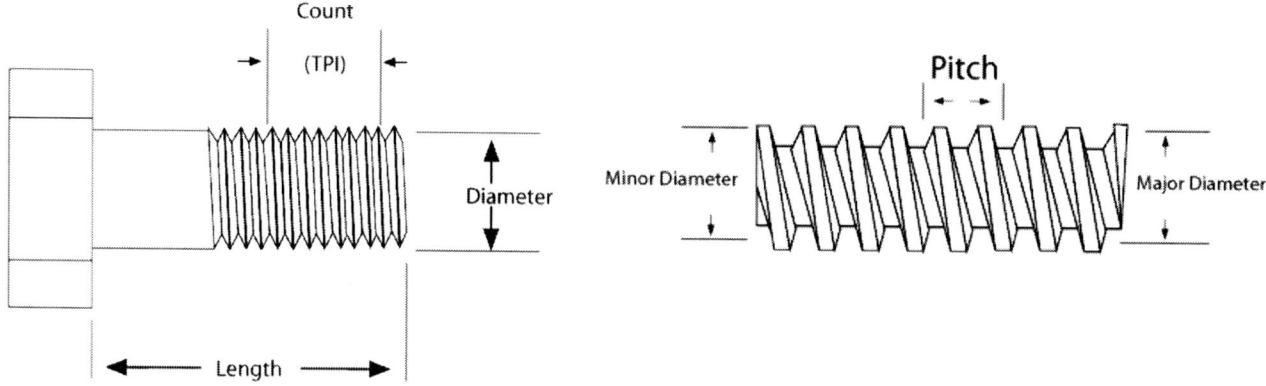

Thread Count and Pitch

A bolt's basic threading is described by its diameter, count (or pitch), and direction. Standard bolts use what is known as **thread count**, or threads per inch (TPI), to describe how tightly packed the thread teeth are. As its name suggests, TPI is the number of complete rotations of the helical edge around the bolt, threads, which are in one inch of the bolt. The higher a bolt's count, the more tightly packed, or fine, the threads. There are a variety of thread counts, but the most commonly used threads can be broken into two standardized categories: Unified National Fine Thread (UNF or UF) and Unified National Course Thread (UNC or UN).

Fine thread means that there are a greater number of threads per inch, so the helical wedge is much tighter and the threads appear smaller. Conversely, a bolt with **course thread** appears to have larger threads as there are fewer helix rotations per inch. Instead of thread count, metric bolts use what is called thread pitch to describe how tightly the helical wedge is wrapped around the bolt.

Thread pitch is the distance between each thread, measured in millimeters. This number indicates the distance which a bolt will penetrate or back out of a hole each time it is rotated. Contrary to TPI, a higher pitch results in the threading having larger "valleys," which means that the threads are less tightly packed.

Therefore, a fine threaded bolt has a high thread count but low pitch; and a course bolt has a low thread count and a high value for pitch. A bolt's thread count or pitch can be found by using a **thread gauge**: a series of thin metal plates with teeth that fit precisely into a bolt's threading.

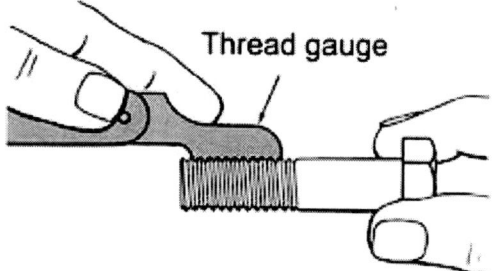

When compared to course threaded bolts of identical diameter and material, fine threaded bolts can generally support a greater load and are less likely to loosen due to vibrations. It's also best to use a fine thread pitch when the bolt is being used for the adjustment of a machine's performance parameters, because the bolt will not move as far for each rotation.

However, course threaded bolts are generally more durable than those of fine thread. For example, a course thread is less likely to be damaged when the bolt is dropped or struck on its side; a course thread is also less likely to be **stripped** or cross-threaded.

A bolt is said to have **s**tripped threads when the bolt's teeth fail and are unwrapped from inner cylinder. Care should always be taken to make sure that a bolt is being inserted straight into a hole and not skewed, otherwise a misalignment known as **cross-threading** can result. A bolt should rotate into a threaded hole without much initial effort. It should never be over-tightened, which could strip the bolt or hole.

Size Classification

There are several systems used to easily describe the characteristics of a bolt in one short abbreviation, but the most common basic notations give simply the diameter, pitch or count, and bolt length. For example, a 1 ¼ inch-long bolt with a ½ inch diameter and 20 tpi count would be described as ½ - 20 X 1 ½. It is worth noting that this 20 tpi count is a fine thread, so other codes may involve the abbreviation UNF. Also, standard bolts with diameters under ¼ inch are described by a number instead of their measured diameter. The diameter of a numbered bolt can be found with the equation:

$$D = N * 0.013 + 0.060$$

In this equation, "D" is the diameter of the bolt, and "N" is the number describing the size of the bolt. Using this equation, a #4 bolt would have a diameter of 0.112, which is about 7/64 inch. This means a bolt with a diameter of 7/64 inch, 40 tpi count, and ¾ inch length would be notated as #4 – 40 X 3/4. This particular bolt would have a course thread. Metric bolts are notated similarly, so a 40 mm long bolt with 6 mm diameter and 1.0 pith would be written as M 6 X 1.0 X 40. Bolts may also be fully or partially threaded, so it is important that the bolt's description is read carefully if a particular thread length is required.

Thread Direction

Most fasteners are tightened by rotating them to the right (clockwise) and loosened by rotating them to the left (counter-clockwise), following the famous phrase "righty tighty, lefty loosey." These bolts are said to have right-hand thread direction. However, some bolts are left-handed, meaning they are tightened when rotated counter-clockwise and loosened when rotated clockwise. You should always make sure a bolt matches the thread direction of the hole into which it is being tightened.

Specific Tools and Their Uses

For a bolt to be put through a material, a hole must exist for the bolt to be inserted. To create a hole in a material, a drilling or boring tool must be used. The drill press and handheld drill are the most common types of boring tools.

Drill

Many **drills** have a setting which reverses their direction; and many also have variable speed settings, often with the speed increasing as the trigger is squeezed harder. Electric drills use a type of clamp known as a **chuck** to hold the attachment which is to be rotated. The chuck is tightened onto the desired attachment using a **chuck key**, which is a specially-designed tool that has a post which fits into a hole on the side of the chuck. There, the teeth of the chuck key engage the teeth of the chuck.

When the chuck key is turned, the chuck either clamps down or releases the drill attachment. A chuck key is designed specifically for one particular tool, so most are not interchangeable. If the wrong chuck key is used, the teeth of the chuck and key may not properly mesh. When using the chuck key, you should first unplug the drill and always make sure that the teeth of the chuck and key fit together well and are fully-engaged to prevent damage to the chuck, the key, or yourself.

It is important to remember to remove the chuck key before using the drill; otherwise the chuck key will be thrown off the chuck and could cause serious harm to anyone in the area. To avoid this hazardous circumstance, many chuck keys are attached to the cord of the drill. This causes the user to unplug the drill before using the chuck key while preventing loss of the chuck key. If a drill is designed with a separate chuck key, a good practice is to either a) – buy a chuck key holder or b) – use electrical tape to attach the key to the drill's cord.

Keyless chucks are becoming more and more popular, because they enable the user to quickly change attachments without any extra tools. In those cases, instead of using a key, **keyless chucks** are simply twisted by hand to tighten or loosen the chuck's fingers. **Cordless drills** are becoming popular as well, because they can be easily transported and do not rely on an outlet or external power source.

When using a handheld drill, the boring tool can have a tendency to wander, or walk. To avoid this, a **center punch** or **center drill bit** should always be used first when drilling a hole with a handheld drill.

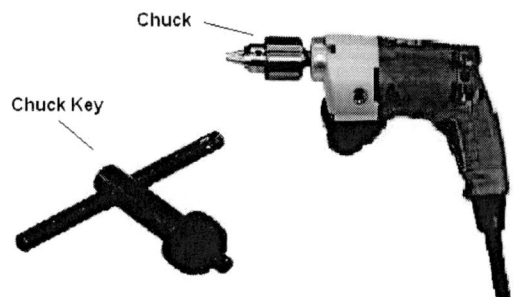

Chuck

Chuck Key

Drill Press
A **drill press**, also known as a bench drill, is very similar to a handheld drill in that they have the same basic parts, but a drill press rests on either the floor or a workbench. The workpiece is placed on the **table** and held in place by either clamps or magnets while the drill **head** is lowered through the material. This keeps the operator's hand clear of moving parts, allowing a drill press to have a more powerful motor than a handheld drill.

Bench drills also have a mechanical advantage in both the head-lowering rack and pinion, which allow holes to be drilled without much effort from the user. Another advantage of the drill press is that holes can be drilled straighter and more accurately.

Drill Bits
To create holes with a drill, a **drill bit** or boring tool must be inserted into the chuck. Drill bits have different **shank** sizes, so you should make sure that the shank of the attachment you want to use will fit properly into your drill's chuck.

Chucks have different opening diameters, but there are three chucks that are the most common: 1/4; 3/8; and 1/2 inch chucks. Drill bits can be made of many types of materials with different coatings and shapes, so it is important that the correct boring tool is being used for the workpiece's material and thickness. While most drill bits are right-handed, left-handed drill bits are also available, so the drill or press must be turning in the correct direction when drilling a hole.

The **lip**, or cutting edge of the **web**, should lead the rotation of the bit into the material. This allows the edge to cut into the material, while the **flute** removes chips from the hole being drilled. It is also important that the drill bit is lowered in a straight line and not subjected to any bending, which can break the drill bit, especially if the drill bit is of thin diameter. Drill bits eventually become dull with use, but can be sharpened using special bit-sharpening tools.

However, be aware that if a drill bit has a coating or surface treatment, sharpening will remove that treatment, therefore sharpened bits will not work as well as a bits.

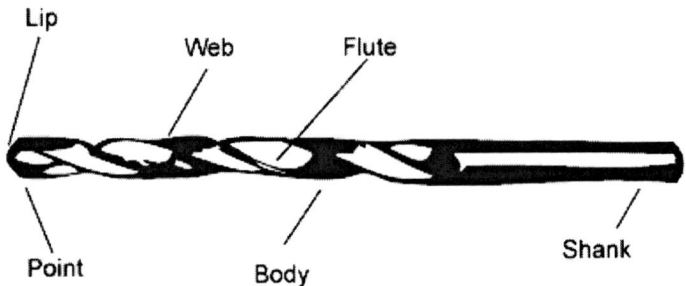

Taps and Dies
For a bolt to be threaded into a hole, the hole must first be tapped. Tapping refers to the process of creating internal, or female, threading. The easiest way to create internal threading is with a tool known as a **tap**. Most tap sets normally provide a table which details the size of hole needed to be drilled for each tap.

A **hand tap** is held with a special wrench. It must be aligned perfectly with the hole about to be tapped. A **jig**, or guide, is often used to make sure that the tap is going straight into the hole. The tap is then rotated into the hole, cutting the threads as it sinks. Taps are made of very hard and brittle materials that can easily break while being twisted. Therefore, you must remember three important things: do not bend the tap at all, use plenty of cutting lubricant, and occasionally reverse the rotation of the tap to relieve stress. (For instance, a tap might be rotated half a rotation counter-clockwise for every full clockwise rotation.)

A tap should never be forced, and if the hole feels too tight, you should stop and remove the tap. Always err on the side of caution. Taps can also be used to repair a damaged female thread, a process known as "**chasing**" the thread.

Taps are often sold with **dies**, which create external, or male, threading. Dies can also be used to chase the thread on a damaged bolt. The process of cutting external threading is basically the same as cutting internal threads. The die should be inserted and secured into the wrench or handle.

Make sure that the correct side of the die is facing towards the cylinder being cut. The cutting side of the die should have a slightly larger opening, and it often has the thread dimensions printed on it. Again, plenty of lubricant should be used, and the die should be cleaned frequently.

Nuts

Instead of tapping the materials being joined, which is sometimes not practical or possible, nuts are often used in combination with bolts. A **nut** is a type of fastener with internal threading.

The **hex nut** is the most commonly-used nut, because it has the same hexagonal shape as most bolts; but **square nuts** are frequently used as well.

Wing nuts have extensions resembling a bird's wings, which makes them easy to tighten or loosen by hand.

A **castellated, or castle, nut** is a special nut with notches cut on one side. A castle nut is used in combination with a threaded shaft or bolt that has one or more holes drilled through its side. The castle nut is tightened to its specified torque and then, if not done already, aligned so a **cotter pin** or wire can be inserted through a hole in the shaft to prevent the nut from loosening.

Lock nuts are also used to prevent loss of torque once the nut is tightened. Just as their name suggests, lock nuts are a type of nut that locks into place once threaded onto a bolt. Lock nuts usually have a nylon insert to achieve this locking effect.

Other nuts should always engage the bolt smoothly and should never be forced to tighten. A lock nut on the other hand should not tighten onto a bolt without any effort. If a lock nut does tighten onto a bolt too easily, it may be damaged and is no longer locking in place.

| Hex Nut | Square Nut | Wing Nut | Castle Nut | Lock Nut |

Wrenches

A tool is usually required to easily tighten or loosen bolts and nuts. For most bolts and nuts, a **wrench** is used for this purpose. Wrenches come in many different varieties. The most common wrench types are the open-end, box-end, and tubing or line wrenches.

An **open-end wrench** has the advantage of having an opening through which a nut or bolt head can be inserted. This means that an open-end wrench can tighten bolts and nuts in tight spaces with restricted access. However, an open-end wrench should never be used for very tight nuts or bolts because the wrench's jaws will flex and cause the wrench to slip and possibly damage the wrench or hardware.

A **box-end wrench** fully surrounds the bolt or nut being tightened, reducing the risk of the wrench slipping. Box-end wrenches have an opening with either six or twelve points and can be used for damaged, rusted, and very tight bolts and nuts.

A **combination wrench** has a box-end jaw on one side and an open-end on the other. Usually the jaws of a combination wrench are the same size.

A tubing, or **line wrench**, also sometimes called a flare nut wrench, is similar to a box-end wrench but has an opening on one side so that a tube can fit through the wrench; this makes a line wrench useful for tightening or loosening pipe fittings.

Whatever type of wrench you are using, you should always make sure the wrench is meant for the size of bolt or nut. The size of wrench needed is determined by the width of the bolt head or nut being tightened. The wrench should fit snuggly on the hardware.

Metric wrenches should always be used for metric hardware and standard wrenches should be used for bolts with standard dimensions. An adjustable **Crescent® wrench** can also be used if the correctly-sized wrench is not available. However, adjustable wrenches have a tendency to slip, and so should only be used as a last resort.

Combination Wrench   Crescent Wrench

Socket Wrenches

A socket wrench can also be used to quickly tighten and loosen hardware. A **socket** is a hollow cylinder with an opening on one end shaped to fit on a bolt, similar to a box-end wrench. The other end of the socket has a square opening that can fit on a **socket handle**. The width of this square opening determines the socket's **drive size**.

Sockets are available in several drive sizes, the most common of which are 1/4, 3/8, 1/2, and 3/4 inch. A small drive may need to be used for smaller hardware or in tight spaces, but should never be used for very tight bolts as this may damage the tool or hardware. The most popular socket handle is the **ratchet**, whose built-in ratcheting mechanism allows the user to loosen or tighten hardware with a simple back-and-forth motion.

A **breaker bar** can be used for very tight wrenches and usually comes with a very large drive size.

A **speed handle** has the ability to loosen or tighten hardware very quickly.

A **torque wrench** is used to tighten a bolt or nut to a specific torque. A torque wrench will either measure units of foot-pounds or inch-pound; and usually either has a dial indicating torque, or a mechanism which clicks once the desired torque is achieved.

An **extension,** or **universal joint** ("U-joint"), can also be used with a socket wrench so that the socket can reach hardware in tight places or extend around an obstruction.

Pneumatic, or air-powered, socket wrenches – like air impact wrenches and air ratchets – also exist, but should only be used with sockets specifically designed for use with pneumatic wrenches, which are normally a flat black color.

Socket Wrench & Head

Pliers

Pliers are another type of clamping or gripping tool. Pliers can be used to clamp, bend, and cut objects, but should not be used to tighten bolts and nuts. If pliers are used to tighten or loosen hardware, they may slip and cause damage to the hardware or injury to the user.

Needle nose pliers can be used to hold small parts in tight spaces and are often used when soldering. Needle nose pliers usually have a wire cutter built in near the handle. You should never apply too much force to needle nose pliers, as their long, skinny jaws can easily break. The jaws of **slip joint pliers** can be adjusted, allowing them to firmly grip objects of multiple sizes.

Tongue-and-groove pliers, more commonly known as **Channellock® pliers**, are a type of slip joint pliers that are also called water pump pliers (because they can be used on pipes and pipe fittings).

Locking pliers or **vise-grips** can be clamped onto a part and locked into place, freeing both of the user's hands.

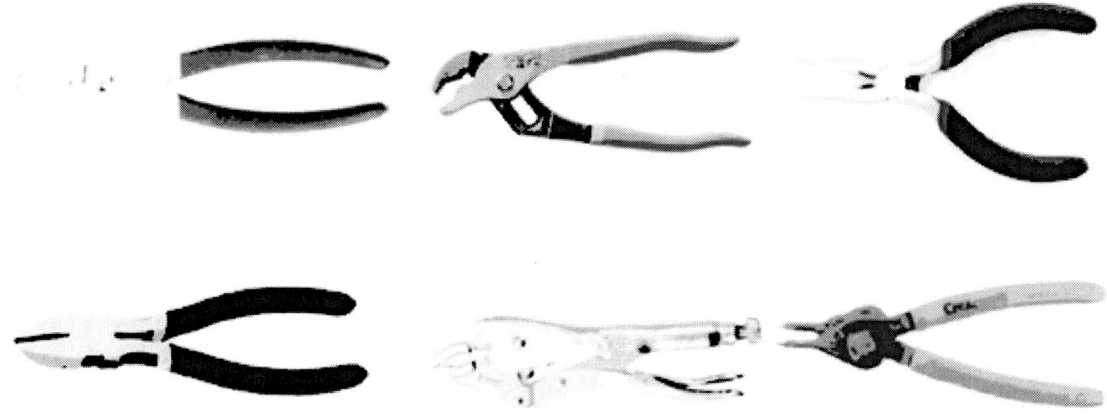

Names of Pliers from Left to Right:
Slip Joint, Bib Joint, Needle Nose, Diagonal Cutting, Vise Grips, Snap Wring

135

Screwdrivers

When securing or hanging an object on wood, a **wood screw** can be used, which may require a smaller hole to be drilled in the wood before inserting the screw. If a screw is being secured to drywall, a **drywall anchor** should be used.

A **screwdriver** tightens screws, but the type of screwdriver needed will depend on the head of each particular screw.

The most common types of screwdrivers are the **flat-head** and **Phillips-head**. Whatever the type of screwdriver, you should always make sure that the screwdriver being used fits the screw being tightened by completely filling the screw's slot. If an improperly-sized screwdriver is used, the tool or hardware may be damaged.

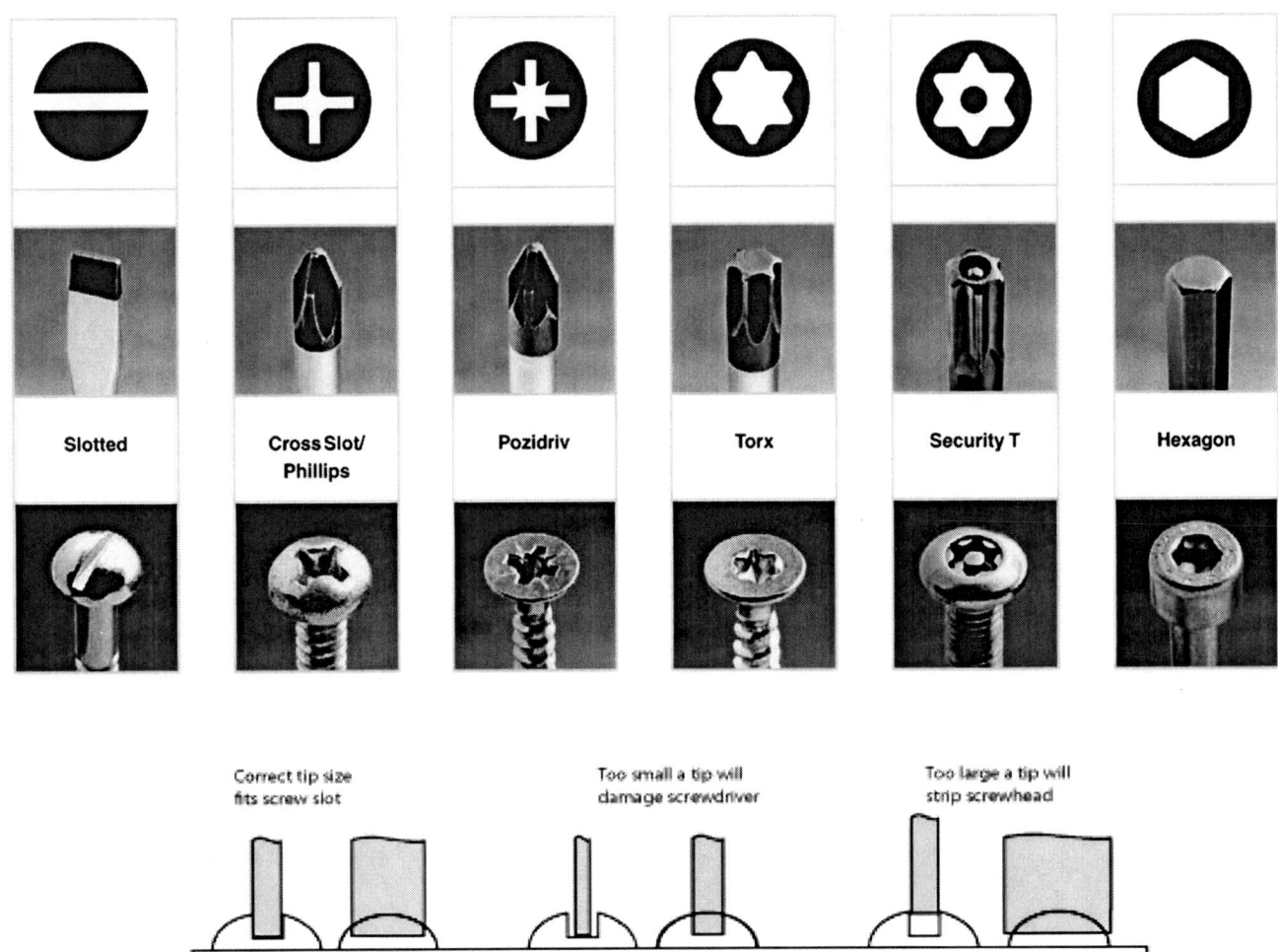

Nails

Nails can also be used to secure objects to wood. Nails, tacks, and brads come in many different shapes and sizes. The correct nail must be selected for the particular task for which the nail is being used. There are two ways in which nail size is normally designated.

The first is known as the nail's penny size. The **penny size** tells a nail's length and is given by a number followed by the letter *d*. The penny size originated in England and once represented the cost of one hundred nails of that particular size. Larger nails have a larger penny size because it would cost more to buy one hundred of the larger nails. For instance, a 2d is only one inch long while a 10d nail is three inches long.

Nail size can also be given as the nail's length and **gauge**, which is the nail's thickness, similar to a wire gauge. A higher gauge means a thinner nail. For instance, a 1/2" 20 ga (gauge) brad is very small, with a length of only half an inch and a diameter of about 0.035 inches; it is usually only used for holding wire or finishing work. A 3" 8 ga nail is three inches long with a 0.165 inch diameter and can be used for more demanding purposes, like framing.

Hammers

When a power source or compressed air is available, a **nail gun** can be used to quickly drive a great deal of nails. More often than not, however, a **hammer** is used to drive nails. Hammers are normally organized according to their weight. A ten ounce hammer might be used for jobs around the house, a twenty ounce hammer could be used for heavier jobs like framing, and a ten pound **sledge hammer** would be necessary for heavy-duty jobs such as demolition.

The most common type of hammer seen in the household or hardware store is the **claw hammer**, whose head has a flat surface on one side for driving nails and a claw on the other for pulling out nails or ripping apart material. When using the claw of a hammer, always be careful not to damage any surface around the nail being removed. A block of wood can be placed under the end of the hammer to give more leverage and prevent the hammer from contacting the surface in which the nail is driven.

The **finishing hammer**, also known as a tack hammer, is similar to the claw hammer, but is smaller and lighter with a head specifically designed for small brads and tacks.

Mechanics do not usually work with wood or drive nails, and so do not have a use for a claw or finishing hammer. Instead, mechanics most often use the **ball peen hammer** for jobs such as forming and shaping metal or striking a chisel or punch.

A mechanic might also use a **rubber mallet** when it is important that the object being struck is not damaged, or a **deadblow hammer** filled with sand or shot to reduce noise and risk of the mallet bouncing off the object.

Chisels and Punches

As briefly stated earlier, ball peen hammers are often used to strike chisels. A **chisel** is a tool designed to remove material from a workpiece when hammered. Chisels can be designed to remove material from wood, rock, or metal, so it is important to use the correct type of chisel for the material on which you are working. In addition, there are two types of chisels for metal; hot chisels and cold chisels.

A **cold chisel** can be used to cut metal without the application of heat and does not give a smooth finish. A cold chisel can also be used to separate two parts stuck together.

The metal should be heated when a **hot chisel** is being used. Chisels will become dull with wear and should be sharpened using a bench grinder. However, you should not grind a chisel too quickly, as excessive heat can temper the metal, making it more brittle.

A **punch** is also struck with a hammer and is used to mark or drive objects.

A **center punch** is used to make a small mark where a hole is to be drilled in order to prevent the drill bit from walking, shifting out of place before being drilled.

A nail or **set punch** is used to drive a nail flush with or below the surface of a piece of wood.

A **pin punch** is very similar to the set punch and is used to insert pins, such as a **spring pin** or **dowel**, into tight holes.

A **starting**, or drift, **punch** has a much longer taper – and is therefore stronger than – a pin punch. For this reason, a starting punch should be used to begin the removal of a pin and a pin punch should be used when a starting punch would be too large and would get stuck in the hole.

Planing Tools

Abrasives

Chisels are used to remove material for objects, but it is difficult to leave a smooth finish. For this, a smoothing tool must be used. The simplest tool used for smoothing is sandpaper. **Sandpaper** comes in many shapes and materials, some with adhesive backs to be mounted on electric sanders.

There are many variations of sandpaper, sanding discs, and electric sanders, but all have a **grit size**, which tells how coarse or how fine the abrasive surface is. Sandpaper with a low grit size (generally below 80 grit) is considered a coarse grade because it has a very rough abrasive surface with large particles.

Coarse sandpaper removes more material than fine sandpaper, but it will not leave as smooth a finish. The opposite is also true: because sandpaper with a higher grit size will have a relatively smoother abrasive surface, it will remove material less easily while leaving a very smooth finish.

You want to avoid leaving an uneven finish; for this reason, many use a **sanding block**, which is a simply a block with a flat side used to hold sandpaper. **Steel wool** can also be used to smooth surfaces, but its coarseness is determined by a graded scale instead of grit size: ranging from super fine at 0000 and very coarse at 4. Also, do not forget that it is important to protect your hands during the sanding process, so it is advisable to wear protective gloves.

Files

Instead of sandpaper, it can sometimes be easier to use a **file** to smooth a surface, especially when removing burrs and sharp edges. Like sandpaper, files can be coarse or fine, referred to as the file's cut. Files can also have many different shapes: flat, half-round, triangular, round, and square being the most popular. It is important to make sure that the type of file being used not only fits the desired shape, but also the material of the object being smoothed.

Files normally have a pointed end called a **tang**, which should always be fitted into a handle. Using a file without a handle is dangerous and can lead to serious injury. To use a file, you should hold firmly with one hand on the handle and the other on the file tip. Filing is a simple back-and-forth motion, with pressure exerted only on the forward stroke.

Files are designed to cut on the forward stroke; lifting on the backstroke reduces wear and extends the life of the file. You should also not file too quickly. More than one stroke every second will lessen the life of the file. Be sure not to press too hard, and never strike or pry with the files, as they are brittle and can easily break, sending sharp metal shards flying into the air.

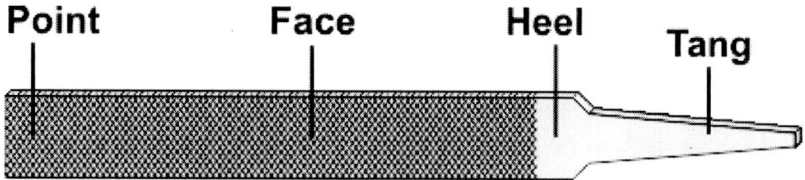

Rasp and Plane

A **rasp** is a woodworking tool that is very similar to a file, but is much coarser. Because a rasp is coarser, it is used to remove material very quickly, and it leaves a rough finish.

A **plane** is another tool used to remove wood in order to either smooth or trim a surface. While electric planes are available, the hand plane is more common. The **base** of the plane has an opening known as a **mouth**. When the plane is pushed across a wooden surface, the blade protruding from the mouth shaves off a layer of wood, which passes out of the mouth of the plane.

The **depth adjustment knob** can either extend the blade to make a deeper cut or retract the blade so that less material is removed. Two hands should always be used when planing to avoid slipping and cutting your hand on either the blade or wood shavings.

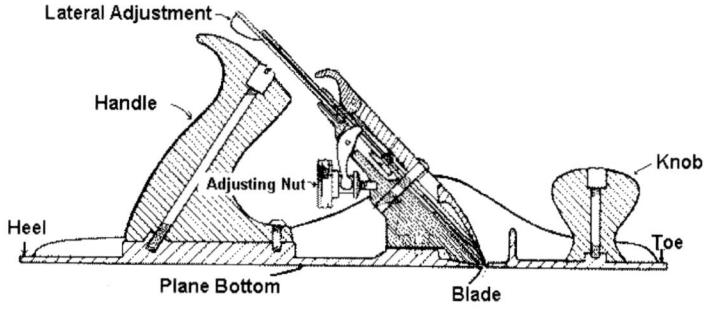

Saws

A **saw** can be used to remove a large part of a workpiece or to cut a material into two pieces. Saws can be powered by hand, electricity, or compressed air, and can be designed for cutting a variety of materials. Therefore, it is important to select the proper saw for the material and thickness of the object being cut. Popular types of **power saws** include circular, band, and reciprocating saws.

A **circular saw** has a rotating round blade and can either be handheld or mounted on a base or table, like the **miter saw** or **table saw**.

Band saws also have a continuously rotating blade, but the blade is a long strip of metal with teeth on one side. The band is held in tension between two pulleys, one of which is rotated by a motor, pulling the blade in a circle and the teeth through the material being cut.

The popular **chainsaw** is a special type of band saw used for making very rough cuts through thick wood. Like circular saws, band saws can either be handheld or mounted to a base.

A **reciprocating saw** has a straight blade that moves back and forth very quickly. Some reciprocating saws are very large and powerful while others, like the **jigsaw**, are smaller and can manage more complex, curved cuts. Reciprocating saws have changeable blades, so you should make sure that the blade is meant for the particular material and thickness being cut and is securely installed before attempting to use the saw.

Whether using a hand or power saw, a blade should be selected that is designed for the material being cut and has a **tooth count** high enough to ensure that at least two teeth are in contact with the material at all times. Finer saw blades have a higher tooth count, and will have a greater number of teeth in contact with the material at all times. This gives a cleaner cut, but a saw blade with a lower tooth count will cut more quickly.

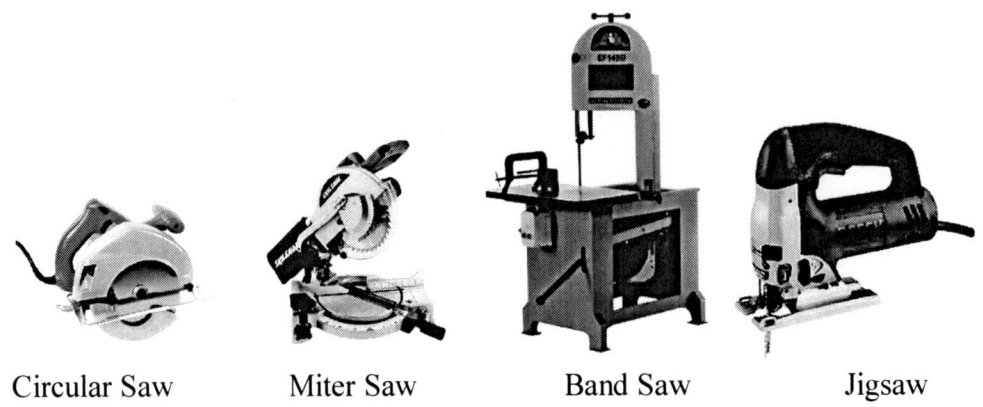

Circular Saw   Miter Saw   Band Saw   Jigsaw

While electric saws are very useful for quickly cutting through material, they are limited to areas where power outlets are available, making handsaws more common. In woodwork, two types of saw can be used for rough cuts, depending on the direction of the cut being made.

A **crosscut saw** is used to cut *across* the grain of wood, while a **ripsaw** is used to cut *with* the grain. A ripsaw has sharp teeth in a relatively straight line, while a crosscut saw has teeth that are offset from each other, creating a wide cut area or **kerf**.

A **backsaw** has a reinforced back that makes it more suitable for tasks requiring a precise cut.

For very intricate designs, a **coping saw** can be used to cut curved surfaces; a coping saw has a removable blade, enabling it to make internal cuts as well. A miter box can also be used to make precise angles.

A **miter box** is a saw guide for cutting 45 and 90 degree angles. A piece of wood is inserted into the miter box, and the saw is slid back and forth through the guides to make a cut at the desired angle.

A **hacksaw** is used when cutting metal, and has a removable blade attached to an adjustable frame. The frame of a hacksaw usually has two handles, one on either side of the blade. Both handles should always be used when cutting with a hacksaw.

When installing a blade, the teeth should point away from the handle so that cutting occurs on the forward stroke. As with filing, light pressure should be applied on the forward stroke and released when pulling the saw back. You should make no more than one stroke of the saw every second.

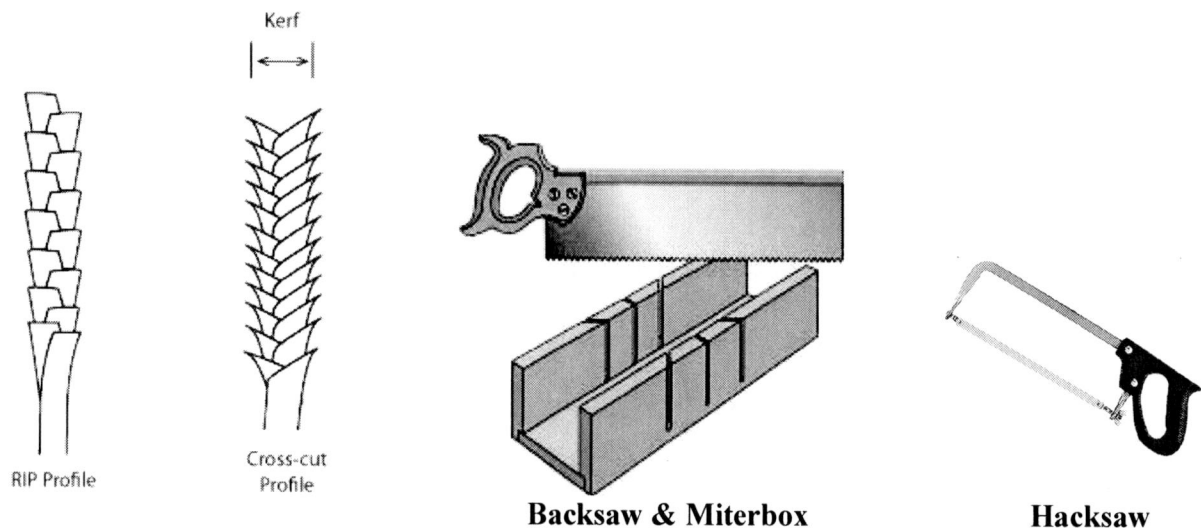

Backsaw & Miterbox   **Hacksaw**

Other Fastening Methods

Bolts and screws are the most common type of fasteners and have already been discussed. Snap rings and rivets are also fairly common fasteners.

Snap Rings and Rivets

Snap rings, also known as retaining rings or circlips, can be inserted with **snap ring pliers** into an internal or external groove to prevent endplay when two cylindrical parts are fitted together.

A **rivet** can be inserted into a hole and secured using either a hammer or **riveter**, depending on the type of rivet. This creates a semi-permanent joint, because the rivet has to be drilled out in order to separate the parts. However, it is sometimes either not feasible to have fasteners hold two parts together or it is necessary to have a more permanent joint. In these cases, soldering and welding can be used as a permanent way of joining parts.

Internal Snap Ring   External Snap Ring   Snap Ring Pliers

Soldering

Soldering is a process of joining two metal pieces, usually wires, by heating and melting a filler metal between the two pieces. A **soldering gun**, or iron, heats the metal to be joined – and a metal alloy, known as solder, with a low melting point is applied to the joint.

Any impurity in the area being soldered will result in a weak joint, so it is important to clean the joint before soldering. The metal to be joined should be cleaned with sandpaper or a metal brush. A chemical known as **flux** can also be applied to the metal to prevent oxidation after soldering. Brazing is a joining process similar to soldering, but much higher temperatures are required to melt the filler metal, so different equipment must be used.

Welding

Welding is a joining process for permanently bonding larger metal pieces. Unlike soldering, welding melts part of the workpiece as well as the filler metal.

In **oxyacetylene welding**, a torch supplied with oxygen and acetylene gases is used as the heat source; and a **filler rod** is fed into the melted joint as a filler metal.

Electric arc welding uses electricity as its heat source and is a much easier process.

Shielded metal arc welding (SMAW), more commonly known as **stick welding**, uses a rod called an **electrode**. Electrodes are coated in a material known as **flux**, which creates a gas when it melts that prevents contamination of the weld being created. Like a battery, a stick welder has a positive and negative terminal to create electrical current.

When stick welding, the **ground clamp** is attached to the workpiece and the **electrode** is inserted into the positively-charged electrode holder. When the electrode is placed near the workpiece, the electrical circuit is completed, and an electrical arc melts the workpiece and electrode. Whenever the electrode has been used to a point where there is no more flux, the rod is replaced.

This slows the welding process if a great deal of material is being welded, making **gas metal arc welding (GMAW)** another popular type of welding.

Metal inert gas (MIG) welding, sometimes called wire feed welding, is a very popular welding process due to its ease and versatility. MIG welding is similar to stick welding in that a ground clamp is attached to the workpiece and an electrode completes the circuit to create an arc and heat the base and filler metals. However, the electrode in this case is a wire that can be continuously fed into the molten metal, making the process much faster.

Flux cored arc welding uses a wire filled with flux, but normally a shield gas is used to prevent contamination. Like the electrode, the shield gas must be chosen to match the material that is being welded; the most popular shield gases are carbon dioxide and argon. The arc created during welding is very bright and a great amount of heat is generated, so special welding face-shields, leather gloves, and thick protective clothing should be worn. Even if your skin is not touched by splashing molten metal, the ultraviolet light given off by the arc can quickly burn your skin, with a resulting burn similar to sunburn.

Measuring Instruments

Rules

When working in the shop, it is often necessary to measure distances such as the length of a fastener, the width of a board, or the diameter of a hole. Simple rulers are normally used to quickly make measurements when a great deal of accuracy is not needed.

A **steel rule** is normally used in the shop because metal is less flexible and more durable than other materials like plastic or wood. Though they are available in many sizes, steel rules are normally 6, 12, or 18 inches long. Steel rules are also available in various thicknesses. Thicker rules are less flexible, but thinner rules make reading measurements easier because the markings are closer to the workpiece.

A **folding rule** can be used to measure greater distances and has the advantage of being able to fold into a smaller size for storage. However, folding rules cannot be relied upon for accuracy because the segments may not line up perfectly, resulting in an imperfectly straight measure.

A **tape measurer** or tape rule is a flexible rule that can be wound up for easy storage. Common tape measurers are metal and curved across their width so they are less likely to bend while measuring. Longer plastic or cloth tape rules are available for measuring greater distances.

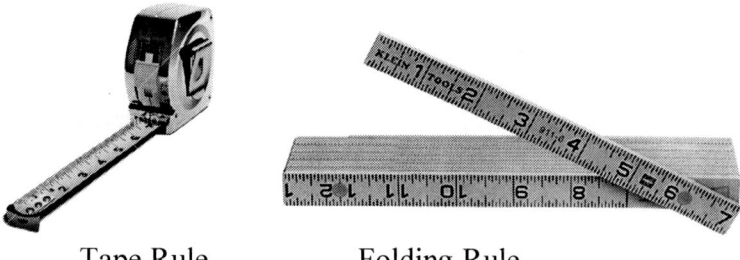

Tape Rule   Folding Rule

All rules will have marks or lines known as **graduations**. Many rules will have multiple sets of graduations, so it is important to know the units of each graduation and how to read the measurement. Rules will have long lines marking the major units and shorter lines in between marking smaller increments.

For instance, a metric rule will usually have lines showing centimeters and then nine shorter lines in between each centimeter designating millimeters (or 0.1 cm).

A standard rule could also have longer lines marking inches and nine small lines designating tenths of an inch. However, it is more common for a standard rule to have a slightly shorter line marking half inches, even shorter lines in between designating quarters of an inch, still shorter lines showing eighths of an inch, shorter lines marking sixteenths of an inch, and so on, sometimes up to 1/64 of an inch.

Calipers

Calipers can be used to achieve greater accuracy when taking a measurement. A caliper is a tool used to measure the distance between two points. The caliper's tips are adjusted to touch the two points being measured then the caliper is removed and compared to a rule.

Firm joint or **friction joint calipers** use friction to make the legs hard to open or close. When using friction joint calipers, the legs must be firmly tapped open or closed to adjust the points to the desired points. In contrast, **spring calipers** have a spring attached to the legs and an adjustment nut must be turned to separate or bring together the legs.

Inside calipers have legs that bend slightly outward near the tip while **outside calipers** have bowed legs, enabling them to reach around obstructions while measuring outer widths.

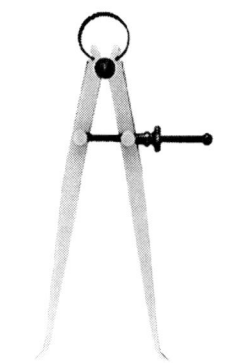

Inside Spring Caliper   Outside Friction Joint Caliper

Vernier, **dial**, and **digital** calipers are the most commonly used types of calipers because they can give a direct reading of a variety of length types without the use of a separate rule. These calipers include a built-in scale, outside jaws for measuring outer widths, inside jaws for measuring inner lengths, and a slender depth probe. The jaws are simply adjusted to fit the desired length and the measurement is read directly off of the caliper.

> **Vernier calipers** have a sliding mark that points out the value of the length being measured on the built-in scale. Vernier calipers will often have a standard and metric scale, so it is important to know what units are desired.

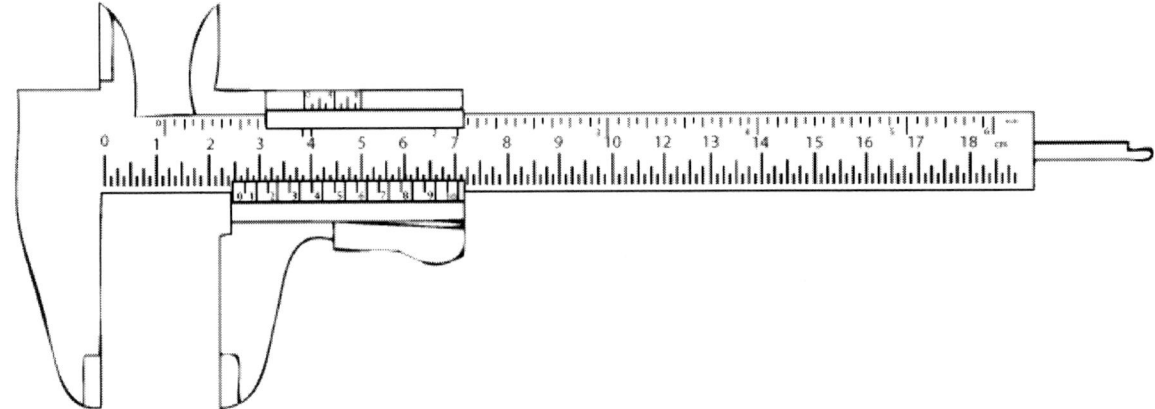

> **Dial calipers** have a rotating dial, similar to the hand of a clock, which points at the value of the measurement.
>
> **Digital Calipers** are simple to use because they have a digital readout that gives the length in either standard or metric units.

A **micrometer** can be used to measure thicknesses when even greater precision is desired. A micrometer, or mike, is a special type of caliper that incorporates a calibrated screw for precise measurements. The thimble of a micrometer is turned until the anvil and spindle touch the points being measured and the value is read from the graduations on the sleeve and thimble.

On standard calipers, the sleeve has increments of tenths of an inch (0.1") with smaller graduations marking twenty five hundredths of an inch (0.025") and the thimble has graduations indicating thousandths of an inch (0.001"). When a measurement is made, the values shown on the sleeve and thimble are added together to find the total measurement.

Metric calipers have millimeters and graduations showing half a millimeter (0.5mm) on the sleeve and graduations of hundredths of a millimeter (0.01mm) on the thimble.

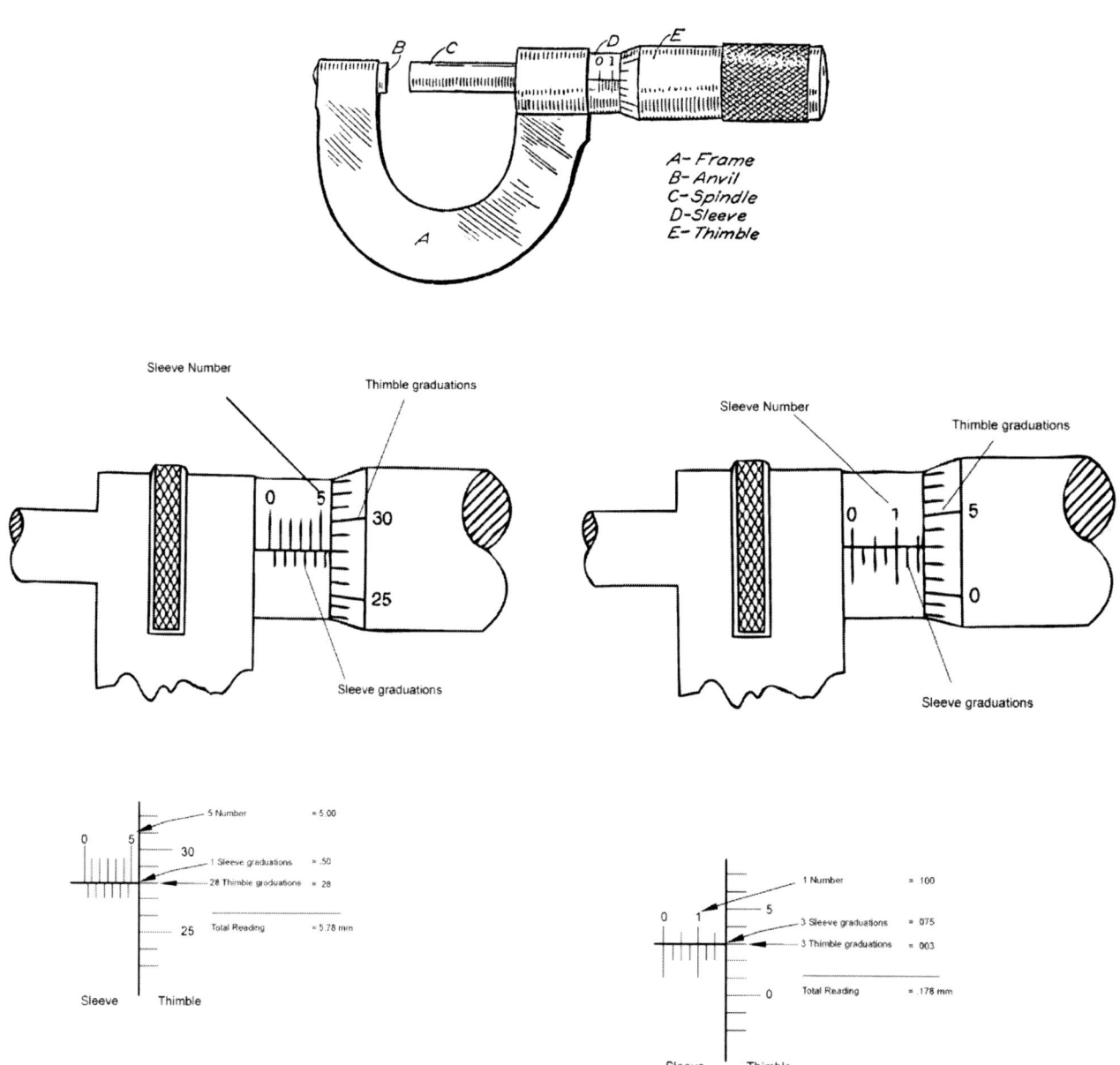

Angle

A **carpenter's square** is an L-shaped steel beam with length graduations, usually inches, on the sides. A carpenter's square can be used to both lay out a right angle and to measure distances. Other types of squares include the **try square**, which is usually smaller than a carpenter's square and made of a wooden stock and metal blade for testing how close an angle is to ninety degrees, and the **combination square**, which has a sliding head with edges for measuring 45 and 90 degree angles.

A **level** is a straightedge that has a tube of liquid with a bubble that indicates whether a surface is exactly horizontal or vertical. A **protractor** can also be used to measure the angle between two lines, but digital protractors and **angle finders** have become popular because they can easily find a horizontal or vertical line and measure any angle.

A **plumb bob** is another tool used to find a vertical, or plumb, line. A plumb bob is simply a pointed weight attached to a string. It can be held over a point and used to align objects vertically.

Temperature

Temperature can be measured with a digital or analog **thermometer** in either degrees Celsius or Fahrenheit. Originally, 0° C was defined as the freezing point of water and 100° C was the boiling point of water. The following equation can be used to convert a temperature from degrees Celsius to degrees Fahrenheit:

$$[° F] = [° C] * 9/5 + 32$$

This means that the freezing point of water is about 32° F and the boiling point is about   212° F.

Pressure

Pressure can be measured using a **pressure gauge**, usually in units of pounds per square inch (psi) or bars (bar). A pressure gauge does not give absolute pressure, but the difference between atmospheric pressure and the pressure being measured, known as **gage pressure**. When the pressure being measured is below atmospheric pressure, a **vacuum gauge** is used.

Practice Drill: Shop

1. What is the diameter of a 3/4 – 16 X 1 bolt?
   a) 1".
   b) 16 mm.
   c) 3/4".
   d) 1/2".

2. What is the pitch of a M 12 X 1.5 X 40 bolt?
   a) 12 mm.
   b) 1.5 tpi.
   c) 12 tpi.
   d) 1.5 mm.

3. Which of the following is true about a UNF bolts?
   a) They have a higher pitch.
   b) They are left-handed.
   c) They have a higher thread count.
   d) They are metric.

4. A rusted bolt has a head that has been slightly rounded. Which wrench would be best for loosening it?
   a) Open-end wrench.
   b) Line wrench.
   c) Box-end wrench.
   d) Crescent wrench.

5. What is the best tool to drive a finishing nail flush with the surface of a wooden table?
   a) Set punch.
   b) Wooden mallet.
   c) Pin punch.
   d) Center punch.

6. What tool would be best for repairing the damaged threads of a bolt?
   a) Tap.
   b) File.
   c) Die.
   d) Sandpaper.

7. What type of file should be used to remove burs from a soft metal?
   a) Coarse file.
   b) Rounded file.
   c) Rasp.
   d) Fine file.

8. Which nut is meant to be tightened by hand, without the assistance of tools?
   a) Square nut.
   b) Castle nut.
   c) Wing nut.
   d) Lock nut.

9. Which of the following handsaws is best suited for cutting curved shapes into wood?
   a) Coping saw.
   b) Back saw.
   c) Hacksaw.
   d) Crosscut saw.

10. Which of the following power saws is best suited for cutting curved shapes into wood?
   a) Miter saw.
   b) Band saw.
   c) Jigsaw.
   d) Chainsaw.

11. When should vise caps be used?
   a) When clamping soft metal.
   b) When clamping a precisely machine part.
   c) When clamping a delicate part.
   d) All of the above.

12. The following allows a socket to reach around an obstruction to tighten a bolt:
   a) Extension.
   b) Universal joint.
   c) Breaker bar.
   d) T-handle.

13. What should always be done while tapping a hole?
   a) Turn the tap to the right and only back out once the entire hole has been tapped.
   b) Use plenty of oil or lubricant.
   c) Start tapping at an angle and straighten as the tap sinks in the hole.
   d) Use a tap that is larger than the hole.

14. A bolt is to be tightened to 50 lb-ft. What is the best tool for this job?
   a) Torque wrench.
   b) Breaker bar.
   c) Impact wrench.
   d) Speed handle.

15. What pliers would be best for pulling a thin wire out of a small hole?
   a) Channellock ® pliers.
   b) Slip joint pliers.
   c) Needle nose pliers.
   d) Vise grips.

16. Which of these jobs would call for the largest gauge nail?
   a) Hanging a picture.
   b) Framing.
   c) Installing a shelf.
   d) Installing a decorative panel.

17. When can you use a deadblow hammer?
   a) When using a chisel.
   b) When hammering a sharp edge.
   c) When you don't want the hammer to rebound.
   d) When hammering a nail.

18. What should be used to fasten a shelf on drywall?
   a) Center.
   b) Anchor.
   c) Nail.
   d) Rivet.

19. Which should be used before drilling?
   a) Center punch.
   b) Set punch.
   c) Cold chisel.
   d) Starting punch.

20. What handsaw should be used to make a rough cut across the grain of wood?
   a) Backsaw.
   b) Hacksaw.
   c) Crosscut saw.
   d) Ripsaw.

21. Which socket can be used by a 1/2" drive impact wrench?
    a) 3/4" chrome plated socket.
    b) 1/4" flat black socket.
    c) 1/2" blue titanium socket.
    d) 3/4" flat black socket.

22. What instrument is best suited for finding a line perfectly vertical from a point?
    a) Level.
    b) Plumb bob.
    c) Protractor.
    d) Square.

23. What instrument is best suited for aligning a surface perfectly horizontal?
    a) Level.
    b) Plumb bob.
    c) Protractor.
    d) Square.

24. What screwdriver is used to tighten a screw with a single slot in its head?
    a) Flat-head.
    b) Philips.
    c) Reed and prince.
    d) Torx.

25. Which sandpaper will remove material the fastest?
    a) 140 grit.
    b) 20 grit.
    c) 80 grit.
    d) 200 grit.

26. Which sandpaper will leave the smoothest finish?
    a) 140 grit.
    b) 20 grit.
    c) 80 grit.
    d) 200 grit.

27. Which of these saws leaves the widest kerf?
    a) Backsaw.
    b) Coping saw.
    c) Crosscut saw.
    d) Rip saw.

28. What should be done to create the strongest soldered joint?
    a) Clean the sections to be joined with sandpaper or a wire brush.
    b) Clean the sections to be joined with soap and water.
    c) Treat the sections to be joined with flux.
    d) Both a) and c).

29. When should you use a Crescent® wrench?
    a) When tightening a square nut.
    b) When tightening a wing nut.
    c) When tightening a bolt or nut that is slightly rounded.
    d) Only when no other wrench fits the bolt or nut.

30. Why is gas blown on metal when it is being welded?
    a) To clean the area.
    b) To prevent oxygen contamination.
    c) To contain hot sparks cause by the arc.
    d) To cool the metal being welded.

Practice Drill: Shop – Answers

1. **c)**. This bolt has a diameter of three quarter inches.

2. **d)**. Remember that metric bolts are assigned a pitch, which is the distance between teeth in millimeters (mm). Standard bolts have a thread count in number of teeth per inch (tpi).

3. **c)**. UNF stands for United National Fine Thread, which has a greater number of threads per inch, which is its thread count.

4. **c)**. The box-end wrench completely surrounds the head of the bolt and reduces the risk of rounding the head even more.

5. **a)**. A set punch, also called a nail punch, is used to drive a nail flush with a surface.

6. **c)**. A die is the best tool for repairing external threads. A tap is used to repair internal threading.

7. **d)**. A fine file does not remove material as quickly and leaves a smooth finish. If a coarse file is used on soft material, it may be too abrasive and leave deep scratches.

8. **c)**. A wing nut has two "wings." This makes it easy to tighten or loosen by hand.

9. **a)**. A coping saw has a high back and removable blade, and so is well-suited for making curved or interior cuts.

10. **c)**. A jigsaw is a handheld reciprocating saw that can manage complex curved and interior cuts.

11. **d)**. Vise caps are metal covers for the jaws of a vise. They protect the part being clamped and give a more secure grip on delicate parts.

12. **b)**. A universal joint, or U-joint, allows a socket to reach at an angle around an obstruction.

13. **b)**. You should always use plenty of lubrication while tapping a hole. You should always make sure the hole is the right size for the tap, ensure that the tap is entering the hole straight (using a guide or jig if possible), and frequently release the stress in the tap by reversing direction.

14. a). A torque wrench should be used when a particular torque is desired. An impact wrench or breaker bar is likely to over tighten the bolt, which can cause damage to either the bolt or hole. A speed wrench will tighten the bolt quickly but does not have much mechanical advantage (and still has no torque indication).

15. c). Needle nose pliers have a long thin nose specifically meant for gripping small objects in tight spaces, especially when working on electrical equipment.

16. b). A nail's gauge tells how thick it is. Nails used in framing must be thick to support the loads of the building.

17. c). A deadblow hammer is soft and filled with shot or sand to prevent the hammer from rebounding. A deadblow hammer should never be used on a chisel or sharp edge.

18. b). A drywall anchor should be used when attaching something to a drywall.

19. a). A center punch is used to make a small mark to keep the drill bit from walking.

20. c). A crosscut is used to cut across the grain of wood.

21. d). An impact wrench is a pneumatic socket wrench and should only be used with sockets specifically designed for pneumatic wrenches. A ½" drive is normally only used for sockets between 1/2" and 1", so a 1/4" socket would fit a smaller drive size.

22. b). A plumb bob is specifically designed for finding a line vertical from a point.

23. a). A level has a bubble in a tube with a slight bulge in the middle that is used to align a surface horizontally or vertically.

24. a). A flat-head screwdriver has a single flat blade that fits into a screw head with a single slot.

25. b). A sandpaper's grit tells the size of the abrasive particles; the higher the number the smaller the particle and the less abrasive the sandpaper. Choice b is the most coarse sandpaper, which will remove material the fastest.

26. d). The 200 grit is the finest choice of sandpaper, which will not remove material as quickly, but will leave the smoothest finish.

27. c). A crosscut saw has teeth that are staggered and create a wide kerf while the other saws have teeth that are relatively straight, leaving a smaller cut.

28. d). Metals to be soldered together should be cleaned with sandpaper or a wire brush to prevent contamination and treated with flux to prevent oxidation.

29. d). Adjustable wrenches should only be used when no other wrench is available to fit the bolt or nut because there is an increased risk of the wrench slipping.

30. b). Gas is blown onto the area being welded to lower the concentration of oxygen in the area, which oxidizes the weld, which weakens it and leads to rust.

Chapter 3: Electrical Information

In the modern world, electronics are all around us and we each rely on electricity for our basic needs. Despite its presence in all aspects of our lives, electricity is not often fully understood. However, as electronics become more and more prevalent in everyday life, it is becoming increasingly important for one to have a basic knowledge of electricity.

Atoms and the Electrical Current
Many find the concept of electricity difficult to comprehend because electricity cannot be seen. This is because electricity originates at the subatomic level. All objects are made of **atoms**, including this book, the chair you are sitting in, and even you.

Atoms are made of protons, neutrons, and electrons. Protons and neutrons make up the **nucleus** of an atom, and electrons orbit around the nucleus in layers known as **shells**.

Protons: Positively charged particles.

Electrons: Negatively charged particles.

Neutrons: Particles without charge.

Let's have an example.

The picture below shows the basic structure of an aluminum atom. Aluminum's atomic number is 13, as seen on a periodic table of elements. This **atomic number** tells the total number of electrons in a single atom. To balance the negative charge of the electrons, an atom has the same number of protons as electrons, so the aluminum atom in the figure has 13 protons in its nucleus.

Aluminum's Atomic Structure

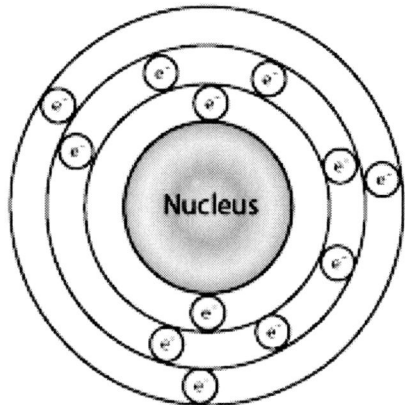

Also note that the aluminum atom only has three electrons in its outer shell. This outer shell, known as the **valence shell**, is what determines the conductivity of an object. **Conductivity** refers to the willingness of atoms to exchange electrons. Aluminum is highly conductive because its outer shell is capable of holding eight electrons, like the noble gas argon, but a single atom only has three electrons in its valence shell. This means it has a tendency to steal or share electrons through ionic and covalent bonds when it is combined with other atoms.

Materials can be divided into three broad categories: **conductors**, **insulators**, and **semi-conductors**.

Conductors

When the atoms of a material easily exchange electrons, the material is said to be a **conductor**.

Valence electrons in conductors have low ionization energy, which means that it does not take as much energy to separate valence electrons from the atom. This is because the valence shell is not filled, which allows the valence electrons to easily move to a neighboring atom.

As we will find later, it is this movement of electrons that gives rise to electricity. Metals are good conductors in their solid state and often have **free electrons** that do not belong to a single atom but move freely throughout the material's volume. Silver, copper, and gold are the most conductive metals. While silver is more conductive than copper, it is also more expensive, which is why it is common to see copper used in household items.

Insulators

Atoms in **insulators** do not easily exchange electrons. The ionization energy of these elements is much greater than conductors because the valence shells are filled (or the electrons present in the outer shell are bonding with neighboring atoms).

Rubbers, plastics, and ceramics are categorized as insulators, which is why these are also often seen in home appliances, such as plastic insulation around metal wires, ceramic circuit boards, and PVC conduit.

Semi-conductors

Semi-conductors behave as neither conductors nor insulators. However, they can have very interesting uses that will be discussed in detail later.

As was stated earlier, the flow of electrons gives rise to electricity. However, we have not yet mentioned what makes these electrons move from one atom to another. The answer is an **electrical potential** difference, or change in **voltage**, across the material, usually provided by a battery or power source.

A battery has two terminals: one positive and one negative. The negative terminal has a negative charge because it has an excess of electrons relative to the positive terminal (remember that electrons are negatively charged).

When a wire is used to connect the two terminals, there is a voltage difference across the wire that creates an electric field within the wire. This begins to push electrons toward the positive terminal in an attempt to neutralize the voltage difference.

This is similar to a situation in which two tanks, one full and one empty, are connected by a pipe near the base. If the pipe is opened, the water will flow from the full tank into the empty tank until the levels are equal.

This is why electrical potential, or the ability to accomplish electrical work, is also called **electrical pressure**; it is the driving force of electricity through a conductor, just as pressure is the driving force of water through a pipe.

Electrical potential is also known as **electromotive force** (emf) because it can be thought of as the force that causes electrons to move through a conductor. In equations, electrical potential is represented with the letter *E*. Electrical potential is measured as voltage in units called **volts** (V). To measure voltage, a **voltmeter** is connected to the two points of the circuit across which the voltage drop is being found.

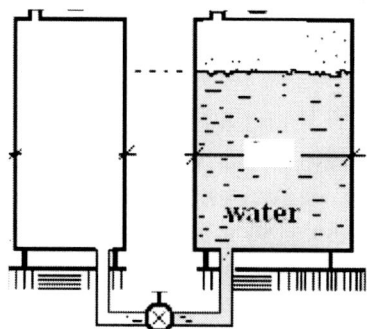

Think again about the wire connected to a battery's terminals; a certain number of electrons will flow past a given point each second, and each of these electrons carries a certain **charge** (Approximately - $1.602 * 10^{-19}$ Coulombs).

The flow rate of electrical charge is called **current**, which can be measured by attaching an **ammeter** into a circuit at the point through which it is desired to measure current. Current is measured in amperes (A), or **amps**, and one amp is equal to one coulomb per second. In formulae, current is represented by the letter *I*, which can be remembered by thinking of current as the *intensity* of electrical flow.

Current is the flow rate of electrical charge, but electrons are negatively charged. This means that current is not given by the direction of the flow of electrons, but opposes the flow of electrons. While electrons flow from lower to higher electric potential, electricity flows from high to low electric potential. This convention can be confusing, but the thing to remember is that electrons flow in order to equalize electric potential and, because electrons are negative, current flows in the opposite direction.

In our battery example, excess electrons flow from the negative terminal towards the positive, and because the electrons have a negative charge, the charge is actually said to be flowing from the positive terminal toward the negative terminal. Thus electrical current can always be thought of as opposing the flow of electrons.

So far in our discussion of electricity, we have only considered the battery as a power source. In this example, we are provided with a relatively constant voltage, so the current flowing through our wire will be constant as well. This flow of current in a single direction is known as **direct current** (DC) and can be seen in cars and other battery-powered appliances as well as thermocouples and solar cells.

The electricity provided by the outlets in our houses, however, is known as **alternating current** (AC) and does not flow in a single direction. Instead, the voltage oscillates, changing directions to back and forth very quickly, usually creating a smooth sine-wave when graphed against time (See figure on the next page).

The advantage to supplying this AC power to residents and businesses is that it can be transmitted through great distances at high voltages; transformers can be used to either increase or decrease the voltage. AC does not always create a nice sine-wave when graphed, though. In some applications, it will create a square or triangular wave or any other shape imaginable.

In laboratories, an instrument called an oscilloscope is used to create various AC wave patterns, such as the ones shown in the graphs below, with a given frequency and wavelength. **Frequency** is measured in units of hertz (Hz), which is the number of complete cycles per second. **Wavelength** is the distance between two consecutive peaks or troughs in a wave. The waves shown below all have the same wavelength and frequency.

In America, electricity is provided at 120 V and 60 Hz. This means that in America the current from our outlets changes directions a total of 120 times, creating 60 full waves, every second. Often home appliances will have an AC/DC adapter, known as a recifier. Other countries do not necessarily provide electricity at the same voltage and frequency, so it is important not to attempt to use American appliances outside of the country without knowing the type of power being supplied and using the appropriate adapter.

Figure 1.4: Wave created by alternating current

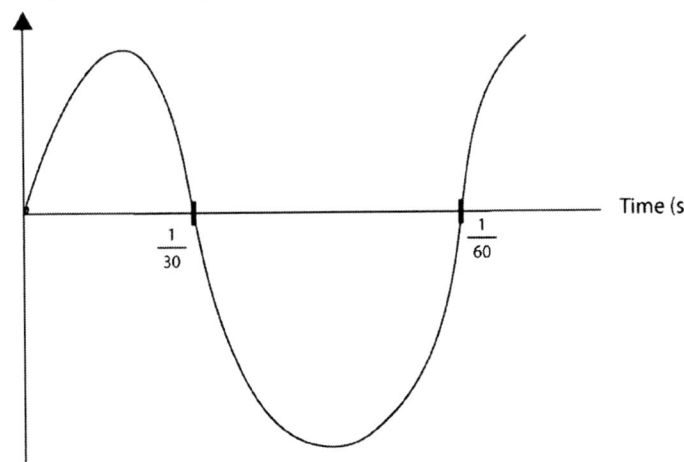

Figure 1.5: Common AC Wave Patterns

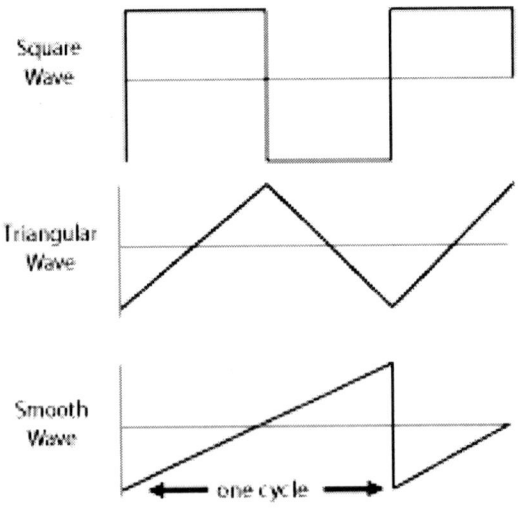

Circuits and Diagrams

A **circuit** is a chain of electrical components that includes a power source, conductors, and loads. A **closed-loop**, meaning a continuous path connecting the positive and negative ends of a power supply, is necessary for the flow of electricity to be possible. We have considered a circuit with a battery and a wire conductor. This circuit accomplishes nothing besides draining our battery and creating heat in the wire. Usually an electrical circuit is designed to convert electrical energy into some other useable form of energy such as movement or light.

A **circuit diagram** is a schematic that visually represents an actual electrical circuit. The common symbols used in a circuit diagram are shown on the following page. Characteristics of a component can be noted near its symbol on a circuit diagram. For instance, an AC power supply's voltage and frequency might be written above their symbols, and resistors often have their resistance noted.

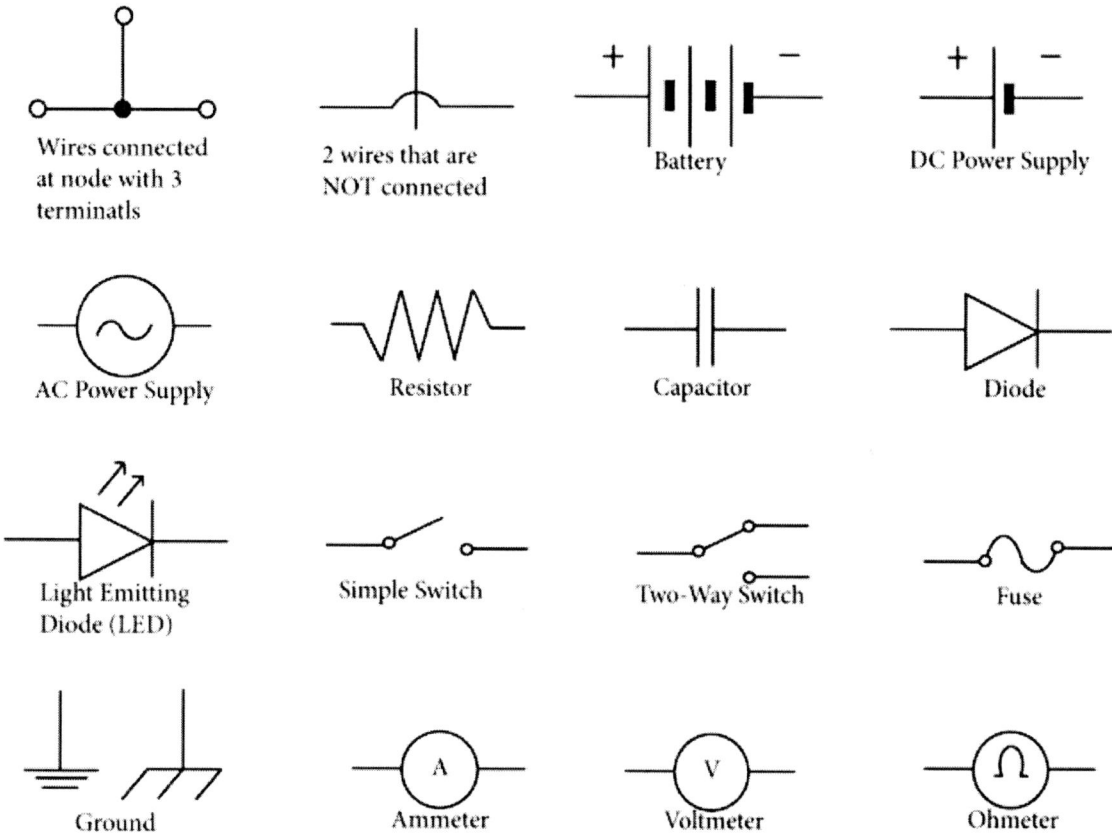

Wires connected at node with 3 terminatls	2 wires that are NOT connected	Battery	DC Power Supply
AC Power Supply	Resistor	Capacitor	Diode
Light Emitting Diode (LED)	Simple Switch	Two-Way Switch	Fuse
Ground	Ammeter	Voltmeter	Ohmeter

Resistors

Resistivity is the opposite of conductivity; **conductivity** refers to an object's willingness to allow the flow of electrons, while **resistivity** is the object's resistance to the flow of electrons. In fact, if a material's conductivity is known, its resistivity is found by taking the reciprocal.

Just as every material has some measurement of conductivity, every material also has some amount of resistance. Even a wire in a circuit has a little bit of resistance; but, unless a wire is extremely long or thin, the resistance in the wires of a circuit is usually so small when compared to the loads in the circuit that it is ignored. Therefore, wires are normally treated as perfect conductors with no resistance.

Resistance of an electrical component can be measured in units of **ohms** (Ω) with an **ohmmeter**. In equations, resistance will be represented by the letter *R*. A **resistor** is a simple electronic component that offers a given amount of resistance and is often used to achieve a desired voltage and current.

Not all resistors offer a constant resistance; some are adjustable or vary in response to environmental conditions, as in the cases of variable or adjustable resistors, rheostats, and potentiometers. For simplicity, any load in a circuit that offers a constant resistance can be replaced by a resistor without affecting the characteristics of the circuit.

For instance, if we add a light into our battery and wire example, the situation will look like the two equivalent circuits below. Although resistance in some components, like light bulbs, will actually increase with higher temperature, we ignore these effects when we don't know anything about the characteristics of this increase.

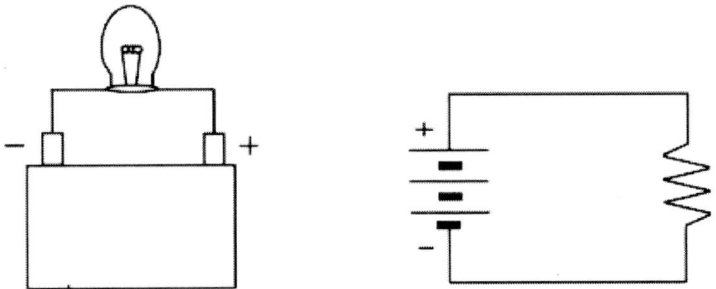

Equivalent Circuits (Ignoring effects of temperature)

We said earlier that the flow of electrons is similar to the flow of water. If we increase the pressure forcing water through a pipe, the water will flow faster. Now let's look more closely at the circuit shown above. Similar to water flowing through a pipe, if we increase the voltage in our power source, the increased potential will cause a faster flow of charge, meaning our current is increased.

However, if we increase the resistance in our light bulb, the greater load will slow down the current. This relationship is expressed as Ohm's Law:

$$E = I * R$$

Remember that *E* is electrical potential in volts (V), *I* is intensity of current in amps (A), and *R* is resistance in ohms (Ω). Given any two of these values, we can always find the third. For example, if we use a 12 V battery and measure the current to be 2.5 A, then the resistance of the light bulb is 4.8 Ω.

Remember that every material, even air, has some amount of conductivity, and even if the material's resistivity is very high it can conduct electricity. This makes high voltage circuits very dangerous because it is possible for a current to flow through air.

Electrical Power
Power, represented by the letter *P*, is defined as the rate at which work is done and. Since work is measured in joules (*J*), power is in units of joules per second, which is called a **watt** (*W*). In electronics, power is the rate at which energy is consumed by the circuit, and is given by the equation:

$$P = I * E$$

So with our light bulb and 12 V battery providing 2.5 A of current, we are consuming 30 W (or doing 30 J of work) each second. Notice that, using Ohm's Law and the power equation, given any two values of current, voltage, or resistance, we can always calculate power consumption. The following equation is a combination of Ohm's Law and the power equation:

$$P = I^2 * R = E^2/R$$

This does not need to be memorized; it is merely a combination of the two equations and an illustration that, given two values of voltage, current, resistance, or power, the other two values can always be calculated.

Resistors in Series and Parallel

Most electrical circuits are not as simple as a single load connected to a source. They can become very complicated, with multiple components connected **in series** or **parallel**. For more complicated circuits, it can be easier to combine the resistances of multiple components and branches to create a simpler equivalent circuit.

Resistors in Series (a) and Parallel (b)

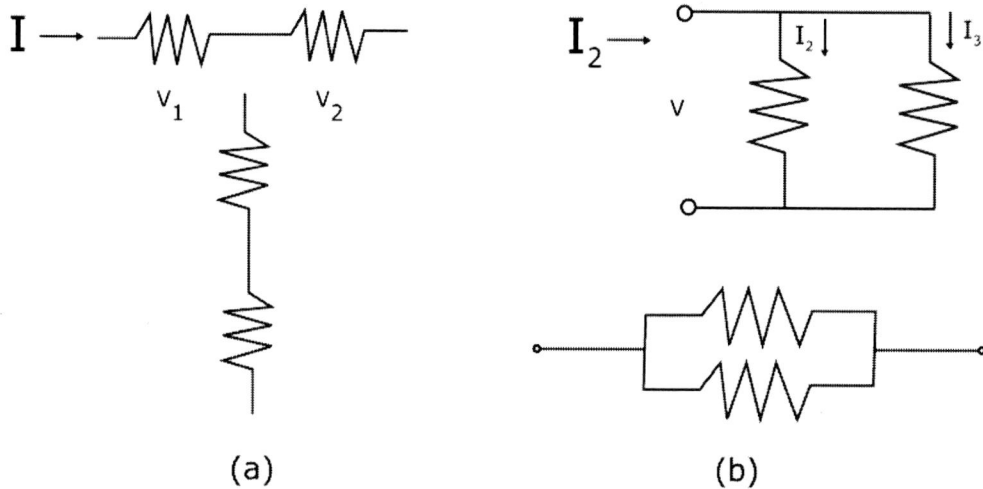

(a) (b)

Electrical components that are linked together one after another on a single branch of an electrical circuit, resembling links in a chain, are said to be **in series**. When components are linked in series, the current through all those components will be the same, similar to several water pipes fitted together. If water is not collecting in any of these pipes, the amount of water flowing through all of the pipes will be the same. However, the pressure drop across each pipe may not necessarily be the same.

Similarly, the voltage drops across each of the electrical components linked in series may not be equal depending on each components resistance. The total, or equivalent, resistance of components in series can be found by adding all of the resistances in that branch:

$$R_{series} = R_1 + R_2 + \text{...}$$

This equivalent resistance can be used with Ohm's Law to find the current flowing through that branch. In order to find the voltage drop across a single component, Ohm's Law is used again, this time using the current of the branch and only that component's resistance.

Example: A 5 Ω and a 10 Ω resistor are connected in series to a 30 V power source. What is the voltage drop across the 5 Ω resistor?

Answer: First, we find the equivalent resistance of the circuit by adding the resistances in series. This gives us an equivalent resistance of 15 Ω.

Now, using Ohm's Law, we find the current in this circuit is 2 A.

The same current is flowing through both of the resistors, so we use Ohm's Law again to find that the voltage of a 5 Ω resistor with 2 A of current is 10 V.

Additional Comments: If we calculate the voltage drop of the 10 Ω resistor, we find it is 20 V. Summing up the two voltage drops, 10 V + 20 V = 30 V, which is the potential of the power source. Also notice that the voltage drop is twice as much across the resistor with twice the resistance. This makes since as a higher resistance should lead to a higher voltage, just like higher friction in a pipe would lead to a larger pressure drop.

When components are linked **in parallel**, the current through the components may not be the same; and an equivalent resistance cannot be found by merely adding the individual resistances. We now have a case similar to two water pipes diverging. The pressure pushing water into the two pipes will be the same, but the same amount of water may not be flowing through each pipe.

However, if we add together the rate of flow through each pipe, it should add up to the amount of water flowing into the point where the pipes split. If we look at the parallel resistors in the diagram above, the current I_1 is equal to $I_2 + I_3$. The currents through the resistors in parallel are different, but the voltage across the resistors will be the same.

Finding an equivalent resistance in this case is not as straight forward as resistors in series.

For resistors in parallel, we can find an equivalent resistance with this equation:

$$1/R_{parallel} = 1/R_1 + 1/R_2 + ...$$
$$\text{OR}$$
$$R_{parallel} = 1/(1/R_1 + 1/R_2 + ...)$$

Keeping in mind that the voltage drop across the parallel branches will be the same and the currents will add up to the total current of the circuit, which is the current drawn from the power source, we can now analyze a parallel circuit similarly to a series circuit.

Example: A 5 Ω and a 10 Ω resistor are connected in parallel to a 30 V power source. What is the current flowing through the 5 Ω resistor?

Answer: This time the voltage across both resistors will be equal to the electrical potential of our power source, 30 V.

We use Ohm's Law to find the current through the 5 Ω resistor, which is 6 A.

Additional Comments: Though this problem may seem more intimidating than the series circuit example, it actually takes fewer steps. We did not need to find an equivalent resistance to answer the question, but let's look at the situation.

If we calculate the current through the 10 Ω resistor, we find that it is 3 A. The current is twice as high through the resistor with half the resistance. Just like water flowing through two pipes, electrical current seeks the path of least resistance.

Furthermore, we can calculate the equivalent resistance of this circuit to be about 3.33 Ω. Applying Ohm's Law to the power source, we find that the current being drawn from the source is 9 A. Just like water splitting into two pipes, the sum of the current through the two branches is equal to the current flowing into the branches, $I_{5\Omega} + I_{10\Omega} = I_{source}$.

Grounds and One-Wire Circuits

If you have spent time working on cars, you may have noticed that some electrical circuits do not seem to return to the battery's negative terminal. For instance, some lights appear to have a single wire attached to the light bulb. An arrangement like this is known as a **one-wire circuit**, which seems like an oxymoron.

We have already said that a closed circuit is required for the flow of electricity, so a one-wire setup may seem impossible. However, a wire does not have to be used to complete the circuit; only a conductor does. In the case of **frame-ground circuits**, the chassis of the car is used as a conductor. This saves the manufacturer time and the cost of excessive electrical wires.

A **ground** refers to a common connection in a circuit that is used as either a reference voltage or return to the power source. In most homes, an **earth-ground** is used as a reference, or zero, voltage and is protection against a short circuit or insulation failure.

A **short circuit**, or short, refers to a situation in which two conductors that are meant to be separated contact each other, allowing current to flow between them. This creates a shortcut for the flow of electrons and, because electrical current will choose the path of least resistance, some components will no longer receive any voltage. This drop in resistance increases current and can melt wires and electrical components. When a short circuit occurs, a circuit may seemingly be turned off, but power is still being drawn from the source, leading to drained batteries and safety risks.

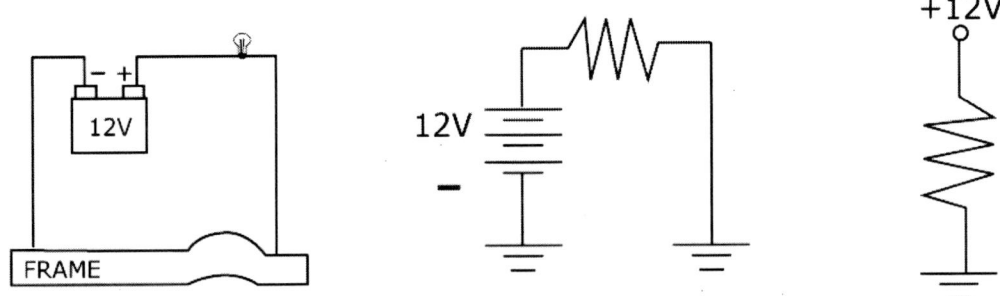

Capacitors

So far, we have looked at circuits that only have current flowing when the power source is attached to a closed-loop circuit. However, a circuit can have potential without being connected to a battery or outlet.

A **capacitor**, or condenser, is a component that stores electrical energy. The simplest type of capacitor is a parallel-plate capacitor: two thin metal sheets separated by a material known as a **dielectric**, which helps increase the capacitor's ability to store energy.

In practice, a second dielectric layer is added, and the layers are rolled together to increase the conductive plates' areas without increasing the size of the capacitor. Increasing the plates' areas further increases the capacitor's ability to store energy. The ability to store electrical energy is known as **capacitance**, which is represented in equations by the letter C and can be measured with a **capacitance meter** in units of **farads** (F).

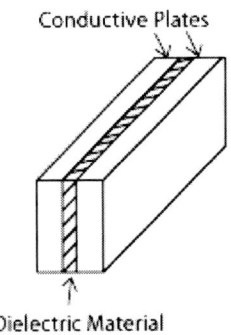

Conductive Plates

Dielectric Material

When a capacitor is attached to a power source, electrons begin to build on one of the plates. Electrons on the other plate are repelled by the negative charge; it loses electrons to equalize the total charge of the capacitor. This means that the current flows through the capacitor while the plates build charges.

However, as the first plate becomes filled with electrons and the second with protons, it becomes more and more difficult for current to flow through the capacitor. Since the plates of the capacitor have charges, the capacitor now has its own electrical potential and will discharge when a wire is attached to its plates.

In this sense, a charged capacitor can act as a power source while its plates discharge. These charging and discharging characteristics can be seen in the graphs below.

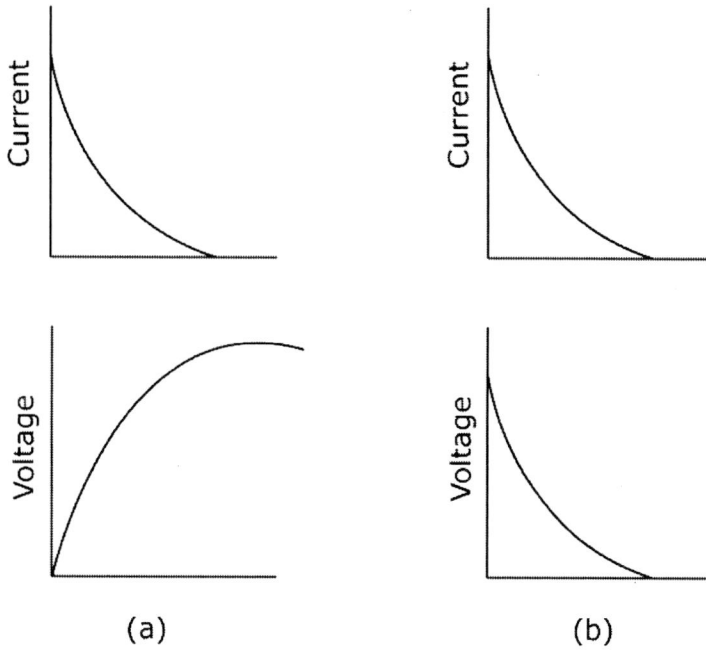

(a)   (b)

One way of remembering these time-response characteristics is that, when attached to a power source, a capacitor initially acts as a wire in the circuit, but begins to act as a break in the circuit as charge builds. Once a capacitor is charged, it acts like a battery with a very short life.

In our water analogy, a capacitor would be similar to a storage tank with a membrane, such as a balloon or bladder, separating the inlet from the outlet. In this situation, water can freely flow into the tank and push water out of the outlet until the membrane is fully stretched, at which time the storage tank will be filled and no more water will be allowed to flow through the inlet. Once the tank is filled and pressure is taken off the inlet, the membrane will want to force water back out the inlet.

Similarly, a capacitor allows the flow of current when it is first attached to a circuit, but begins to deny the current over time. This opposition to the flow of current is known as **impedance** and can be thought of as a time-dependent resistance. Once the capacitor is filled, it can be connected to a circuit and the plates will discharge.

When introduced to alternating current, capacitors exhibit very useful behaviors. If the current has a very high frequency, the capacitor is not allowed to fully charge, so its impedance remains low and the current is not greatly interrupted.

When the alternating current has a very low frequency, the current's direction does not change as often; this means the circuit's characteristics approach that of a DC circuit, so the capacitor has a greater impedance and current flow is restricted.

The energy storage and impedance characteristics of capacitors are used in applications such as noise cancellation in radios and power supplies in alternators, ignition systems, and camera flashes.

Magnetism and Inductors

Electricity and magnetism have a fascinating relationship. The flow of electricity gives rise to magnetic fields, and magnetism can be used to create electricity, which is how motors, relays, and generators work.

All wires in an electrical circuit have a magnetic field around them. If a wire is wrapped into a coil, it will create a magnetic field through the center of the coil. A magnetic material such as iron (a ferrous material) can be placed in the center of the coil to help strengthen the magnetic field. This setup is the basic construction of an **electromagnet,** as well as another type of energy storage component known as an **inductor**.

Inductance is a conductor's ability to use a magnetic field to create a voltage in itself, known as **self-inductance**, and other close-by conductors, known as **mutual-inductance**. In equations, self-inductance is represented by the letter L and is given in **henries** (H).

Simple Electromagnet with Magnetic Field

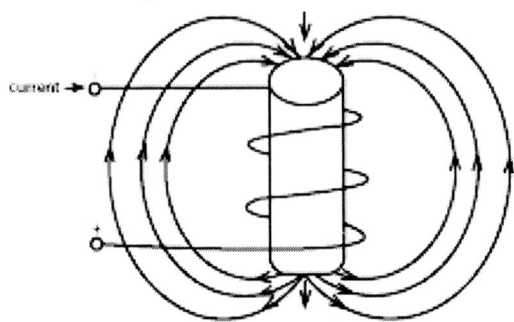

Though capacitors and inductors are both energy storage devices, they are based on separate principles and behave very differently. While capacitors store energy through the use of an electric field, inductors store energy through the use of a magnetic field. This leads to a drastic difference in the behavior of the two devices' impedances.

When an inductor is first introduced to a power source, it will resist the flow of current while a magnetic field builds in its core. Once the magnetic field has been created, if the current through the inductor is suddenly reduced, the inductor will create, or induce, its own current. The behavior of an inductor can be seen in the graphs below.

The time-response of an inductor can be thought of as the opposite of that of a capacitor in that an inductor initially acts as a break in the circuit when introduced to a power source. As the magnetic field builds in the inductor, the inductor begins to act as a wire in the circuit.

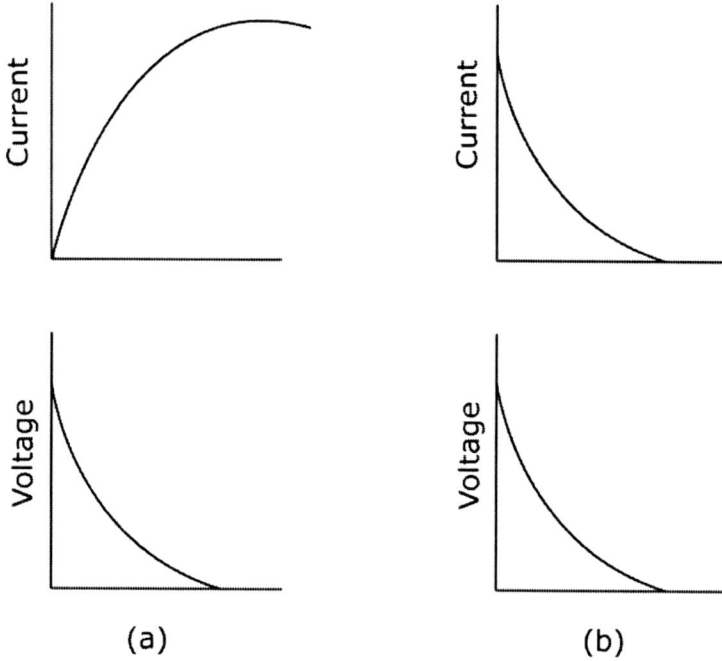

(a)　　　　　　　　(b)

Going back to our water analogy, an inductor is similar to a water wheel or turbine. When water first begins to flow through a watermill, the water wheel will be difficult to turn, because it has a large mass. This will slow down the water until the water wheel begins to turn. Once the water wheel is turning, it has a great amount of inertia. If the flow of water is slowed, the water wheel will want to continue spinning at its faster speed, pushing the water forward. In the same way, an inductor always opposes change in current, impeding the flow when current is increased and creating its own current when the current is decreased.

Inductors have behavior nearly the opposite of that of capacitors when introduced to alternating current. When an inductor is given a high frequency signal, the current changes too quickly for the inductor to build a magnetic field, resulting in a high impedance. Given a low frequency, the inductor's impedance decreases because the signal is becoming more like DC; the inductor builds a magnetic field and resists a change in current by inducing its own current.

Because of their differing behaviors, inductors and capacitors are often used together in signal processing.

Transformers
Another common application of magnetic fields in the creation and control of electricity is in **transformers**. As in an inductor, a wire is wrapped around a magnetic core, but unlike the core of an inductor, the magnetic core of a transformer protrudes out of the conductive coil and continues in a loop through a second coil.

In a transformer, the object of the magnetic core is to strengthen the magnetic field all the way through the second coil. A simple transformer is shown below.

Transformer

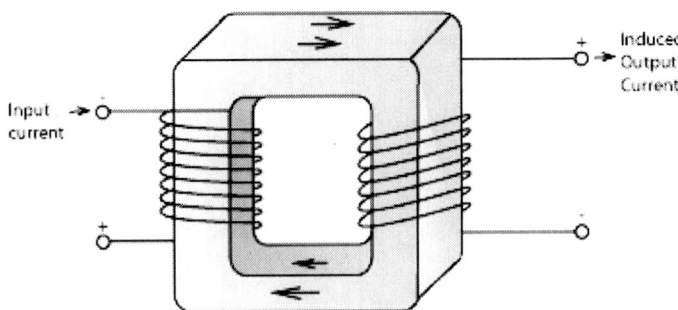

While the inductor takes advantage of a property known as self-inductance, the transformer creates something known as mutual-inductance. We said before that a wire with current has a magnetic field, which can be strengthened and controlled by wrapping the wire into a coil.

A magnetic field can also create current by passing a magnetic field through a coil. This creates a current in the second wire. The output voltage of a transformer can be either higher or lower than its input voltage, depending on the number of turns in the primary (input) and secondary (output) coils. The input and output voltages are related through the equation:

$$V_{in}/V_{out} = N_{in}/N_{out}$$

Here, V_{in} and V_{out} are the input and output voltages and N_{in} and N_{out} are the number of turns in the input and output coils, respectively. From this equation, we can see that if the secondary coil has a greater number of turns than the primary coil, then the output voltage will be greater than the input. This is known as a step-up transformer.

Conversely, a step-down transformer has a greater number of turns in the input coil so that the output voltage is lower than the input. Step-down transformers can be seen on many electrical poles outside of homes and businesses, where they enable electricity to be transmitted at high voltages in power lines and then reduced to a safer voltage for residential use.

Semi-Conductors
As we said earlier, **semi-conductors** have electrical properties in between conductors and insulators. Semi-conductors do not have full valence shells, but the bonds between atoms are somewhat strong, making it difficult for electrons to flow through the material.

However, when impurities are added through a process called **doping**, a semiconductor's conductivity can be greatly improved. For instance, silicon is a semiconductor with four electrons in its valence shell.

In its pure form, silicon atoms will share their valence electrons through covalent bonds, so it is difficult to induce a current. However, doping can increase the conductivity of silicon.

If an impurity with five valence electrons such as phosphorous or arsenic is added to a semiconductor like silicon or germanium, an **n-type semiconductor** is created. The **dopant** atoms take the place of atoms in the original structure.

However, the dopant has one more valence electron than the host substance, so a free electron is created and conductivity is increased. This type of semiconductor is known as n-type because it has extra negatively-charge particles.

If the impurity introduced has three valence electrons, as is the case when adding boron or indium, a **p-type semiconductor** is created. The dopant atom again replaces one of the original substance's atoms, but this time there is a missing electron and a "hole" is created. This semiconductor is known as p-type because it has more protons than electrons and when a voltage is introduced to the material, the holes move across the material to facilitate the flow of electrons.

Diodes

These n- and p-type semiconductors are interesting enough on their own, but have amazing characteristics when they are joined together in what are known as **junctions**. When a p- and n-type semi-conductor is joined with a terminal on each, the resulting electrical component is known as a **diode**. The n-type material has excessive electrons and is known as a **cathode**. The p-type material has "holes" from missing electrons and is known as an **anode**.

When the cathode of the diode is attached to the negative side of a power source, the flow of electrons pushes the excess electrons toward the p-type semiconductor on the anode side. In this case, the diode is said to be in **forward-bias**, and current flows through the diode with very little resistance.

However, when the anode is connected to the negative side of the power source and the cathode to the positive, the excess electrons in the n-type material repel the electrons attempting to flow from the negative side of the power source. The diode is now in **reverse-bias**, and current is not allowed through the diode. The diode allows current to flow in one direction and resists it in the other, like a one-way valve in a water pipe.

In circuit diagrams, the symbol for a diode appears to point toward the cathode, or n-type, terminal, so that the diode points in the direction in which current is allowed to flow. Diodes are frequently used when converting AC to DC, known as **rectification**.

Characteristics of a Diode

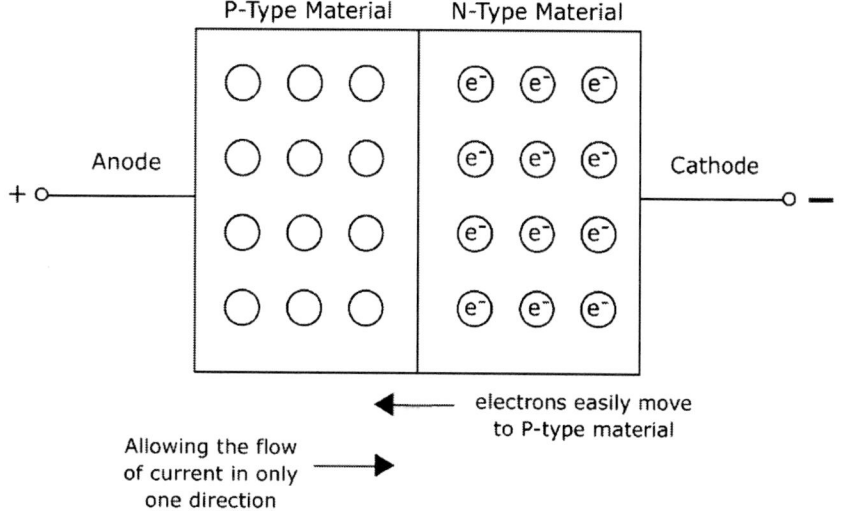

167

Transistors

Transistors are another device made of n- and p-type semiconductors and are commonly used as switches, amplifiers, or current regulators. They have come to replace mechanical relays because they are more efficient and are a solid-state device, meaning they do not have moving parts that will wear and limit their speed. Transistors have at least three terminals: a **collector**, **base**, and **emitter**.

On the diagram symbol for a transistor, the arrow will always be on the side of the emitter. The arrow will also always point toward the n-type semi-conductor. In an **NPN transistor**, a p-type material is sandwiched between two n-type layers and a small voltage on the p-type base allows current to flow from the collector to the emitter. A **PNP transistor**, on the other hand, is an n-type material between layers of p-type material and behaves in the opposite manner of an NPN transistor.

With a PNP transistor, a negative voltage at the base allows current to flow from the emitter to the collector.

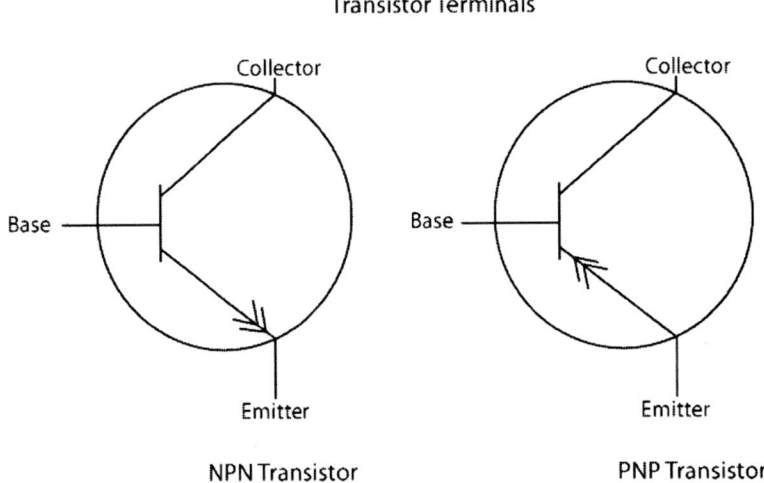

Transistor Terminals

NPN Transistor   PNP Transistor

Modern Circuits

Today, many appliances like televisions, computers, and mobile phones contain **integrated circuits** (IC), or microchips, which are tiny circuits of microscopic components, like resistors, capacitors, and transistors, created by depositing layers overlapping semi-conductors.

Most of these circuits do not use wires, but flat conductor strips laminated into an insulator board connecting circuit components. This type of small panel is known as a **printed circuit** and can support and connect thousands of small electrical components, creating vastly complicated circuits.

Household appliances also often use multiple wires in a single insulated cable. One example of this is the **coaxial cable**, which has two conductive materials, one wrapped around the other so that the two conductors share the same axis. Coaxial cables are often used in audio and video applications, and their cords can have several different wires bundled together. In this case, each wire will have its own insulation with a particular color.

It is important to pay close attention to the colors of each wire in order to ensure that the wires are being attached to the correct components. Some plugs also have one larger prong so that the plug will only fit easily into an outlet in one direction. These are known as **polarized plugs** and should never be forced to fit into an outlet the wrong way.

Electrical circuits can safely be inspected and maintained as long as basic safety precautions are observed, such as disconnecting power and releasing all stored energy before servicing and frequently inspecting for worn insulation.

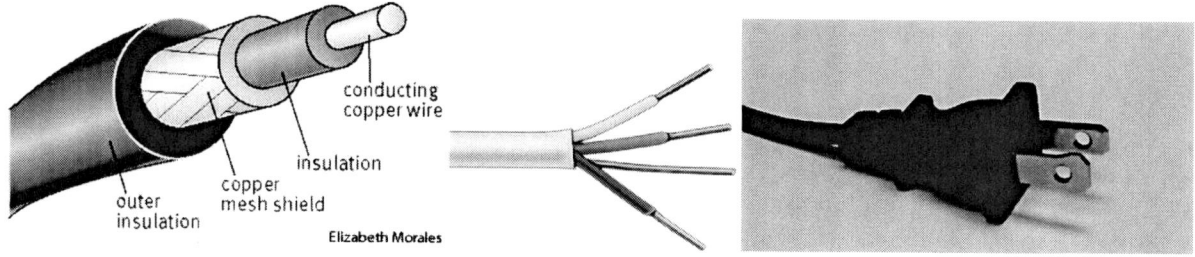

conducting copper wire
insulation
copper mesh shield
outer insulation
Elizabeth Morales

Practice Drill: Electrical Information

1. A single electron has a charge of $-1.602 * 10^{-19}$ C. Every minute, $60 * 10^{20}$ electrons pass a given point in a wire. What is the current in this wire?
    a) 1.602 kA.
    b) 16.02 A.
    c) 267 mA.
    d) 961.2 A.

2. A 1-kΩ resistor is attached to a 1.5-V battery. What will be the current through the resistor?
    a) 15 A.
    b) 1.5 mA.
    c) 1.5 kA.
    d) 150 A.

3. Two identical light bulbs are attached to a power source in series. What will happen if one of the bulbs burns out?
    a) The other bulb will shine brighter.
    b) The other bulb will dim.
    c) The other bulb will go out.
    d) There will be no effect on the other bulb.

4. Two identical light bulbs are attached to a power source in parallel. What will happen if one of the bulbs burns out?
    a) The other bulb will shine brighter.
    b) The other bulb will dim.
    c) The other bulb will go out.
    d) There will be no effect on the other bulb.

5. In problem #4, what will happen to the battery?
    a) More power will be drawn from the battery.
    b) Less power will be drawn from the battery.
    c) The battery will explode.
    d) Nothing.

6. Two identical light bulbs are attached to a battery. Will they shine brighter when attached in series or parallel?
    a) The bulbs will shine brighter in series.
    b) The bulbs will shine brighter in parallel.
    c) Brightness will not change.
    d) The brightness of the bulbs cannot be predicted.

12V

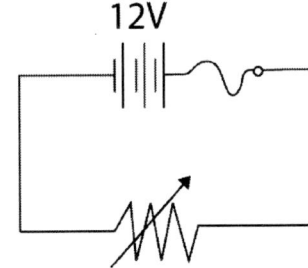

7. The fuse in the picture above is rated for 3 A. To what values can the variable resistor be adjusted without blowing the fuse?
    a) 4 Ω only.
    b) Anything below 4 Ω.
    c) Anything above 4 Ω.
    d) The fuse is not rated for this high of voltage.

8. What is the core of an electromagnet normally made of?
    a) Magnesium.
    b) Iron.
    c) Aluminum.
    d) Gold

9. What device is used to convert AC to DC?
    a) Transformer.
    b) Rectifier.
    c) Transistor.
    d) Diode.

10. What are the units of the component represented by the symbol above?
    a) Farads.
    b) Henries.
    c) Amps.
    d) Ohms.

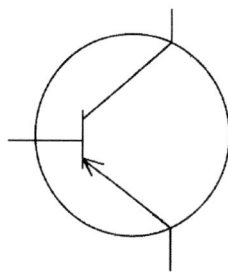

11. What does the symbol shown above represent?
   a) Transformer.
   b) NPN transistor.
   c) Diode.
   d) PNP transistor.

12. Which American wire gauge (AWG) size can be used for the highest current application?
   a) 1.
   b) 10.
   c) 20.
   d) 36.

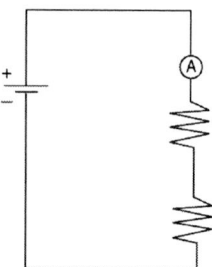

13. The resistors in the circuit above both have a resistance of 2 Ω. If the ammeter reads 10 A, what is the current through the lower resistor?
   a) 20 A.
   b) 5 A.
   c) 10 A.
   d) 40 A.

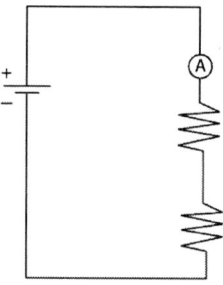

14. In the figure above, what is the voltage of the source if the resistors are both 2 Ω resistors and the ammeter reads 10 A?
   a) 5 V.
   b) 10 V.
   c) 20 V.
   d) 40 V.

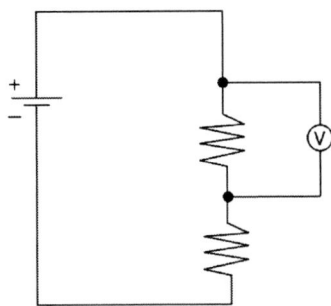

15. In the figure above, the resistors both have a resistance of 5 Ω. If the voltmeter reads 6 V, what is the voltage supplied by the source?

    a) 30 V.
    b) 12 V.
    c) .6 V.
    d) 60 V.

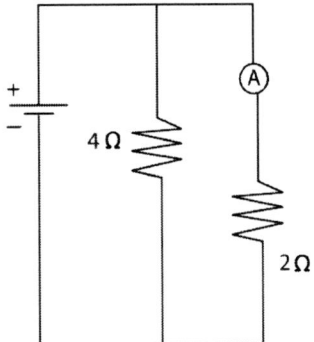

16. If the ammeter in the circuit above reads 4 A, what is the voltage supplied by the source?

    a) 2 V.
    b) 4 V.
    c) 8 V.
    d) 16 V.

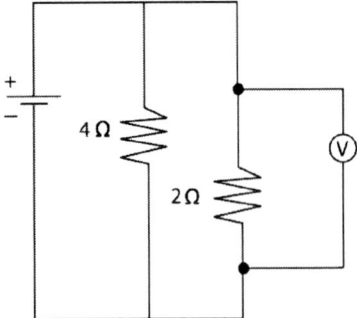

17. If the voltmeter in the figure above reads 8 V, what is the current through the 4 Ω resistor?

    a) 2 A.
    b) 16 A.
    c) 32 A.
    d) 64 A.

18. Are a car's headlights connected in series or parallel?
   a) Series.
   b) Parallel.
   c) Both.
   d) Neither.

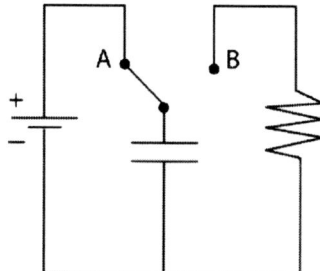

19. The switch in the circuit above has been in position A for a long time. How will the current through the resistor behave if the switch is suddenly put to position B?
   a) Remain constant.
   b) Start at zero and increase to a certain value.
   c) Start at a certain value and then decrease to zero.
   d) There will be no current.

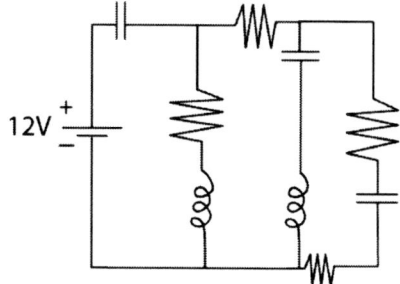

20. Which of the following diagrams shows an equivalent circuit to the one shown above?

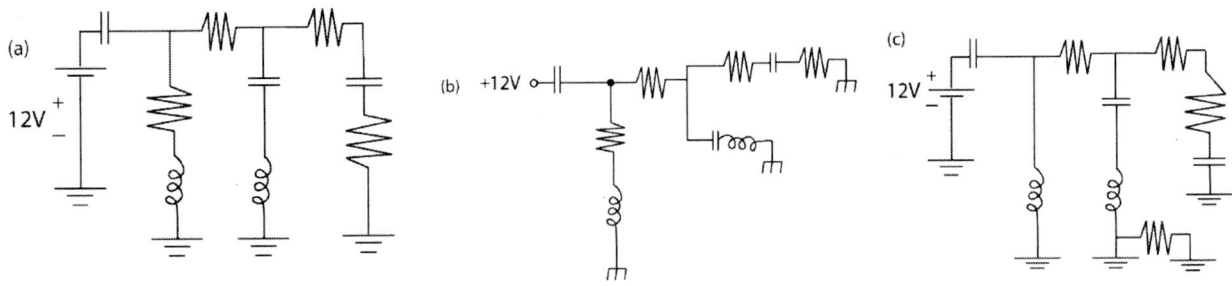

(a)

12V

(b) +12V

(c)

12V

d) Both a) and b).

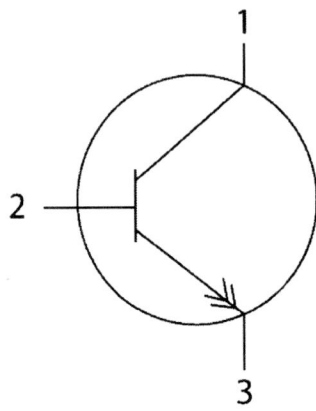

1

2

3

21. Which of the terminals in the figure above is the emitter?
   a) 1.
   b) 2.
   c) 3.
   d) None of the above.

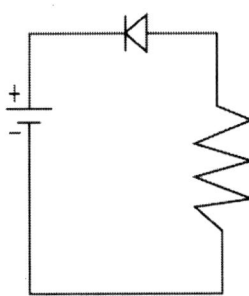

22. If the source in the figure above supplies 12 V and the resistance of the resistor is 2 Ω, what is the current through the resistor?
   a) 6 A.
   b) 24 A.
   c) 3 A.
   d) 0 A.

23. What does DC stand for in electronics?
   a) Direct circuit.
   b) Direct current.
   c) Divided circuit.
   d) Dry coil.

24. Which electrical component can replace a mechanical switch?
  a) Diode.
  b) Oscilloscope.
  c) Relay.
  d) Transformer.

25. What is the purpose of the third prong on a plug?
  a) To make sure the plug is inserted into the outlet the correct way.
  b) To supply a direct current to the appliance.
  c) To supply a ground source to the appliances housing.
  d) To supply a signal to the building's energy meter to track power consumption.

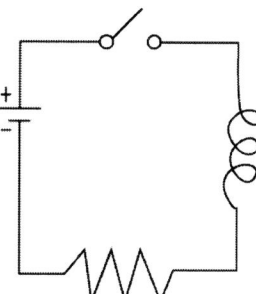

26. The switch in the circuit above is suddenly closed after being open for a long time. How will the current through the conductor behave?
  a) Stay constant.
  b) Start at zero and increase to a certain value.
  c) Start at a certain value and decrease to zero.
  d) Start at zero and increase forever.

27. Which of these metals has the least resistance?
  a) Aluminum.
  b) Tin.
  c) Silver.
  d) Iron.

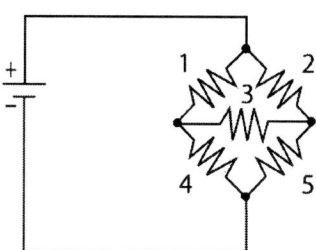

28. If the power source in the circuit above supplies 12 V and each of the fiver resistors offers 2 Ω of resistance, what will be the current through resistor number 3?
  a) 3 A.
  b) 36 A.
  c) 0 A.
  d) 24 A.

29. What characteristic is measured in henries?
- a) Capacitance.
- b) Resistance.
- c) Translucence.
- d) Inductance.

30. What is the cathode of a diode made of?
- a) Silicon.
- b) N-type material.
- c) Iron.
- d) P-type material.

Practice Drill: Electrical Information – Answers

1. **b) 16.02 A**. Current is defined as the flow rate of charge, measured in amps, or coulombs per second. This means we are trying to find the amount of charge passing a given point every second. The problem tell us how much charge each electron is carrying ($-1.602 * 10^{-19}$ C) and how many electrons pass a point every minute ($60 * 10^{20}$ electrons per minute). To find the number of electrons passing every second, we divide $60 * 10^{20}$ electrons per minute by 60, giving simply 10^{20} electrons per second.

   To find the total charge passing per second, we just multiply the number of electrons passing with the charge of each electron:

   $(-1.602 * 10^{-19}$ C per electron$) * (10^{20}$ electrons per second$) = 16.02$ C/s $= 16.02$ A.

2. **c) 1.5 kA**. According to Ohm's Law, $I = V/R$. In this case, the voltage is 1.5 V and the resistance is 1 kΩ, which is the same as 1,000 Ω. Dividing voltage by resistance, we get 0.0015 A, which is the same as 1.5 kA

3. **c) The other bulb will go out**. When the filament on one of the bulbs breaks, there will no longer be a closed-loop circuit and electricity will no longer be able to flow through the other bulb.

4. **d) There will be no effect on the other bulb**. When a bulb is attached to a power source, it draws or receives the same voltage, whether it is parallel with another component or not. Ohm's Law is $E = I * R$. Since the resistance and voltage input are the same in both cases, the current will also be the same. According to the power equation, $P = I * E$, this means that the single battery will draw the same amount of power in both cases as well.

5. **b) Less power will be drawn from the battery**. This is tricky since Problem 4 said that the bulb would still draw the same amount of power. However, this problem is looking at the power drawn from the battery, meaning the power dissipation of the entire circuit, which will be twice as high when the two bulbs are still drawing current in parallel. When one bulb burns out, the power dissipation is cut in half.

   Another approach would be to look at the total resistance of each circuit. When the bulbs are attached in parallel, the total resistance will be half the resistance of a single bulb, or $R/2$. If we choose a resistance for the bulbs of 2 Ω, this would mean the total resistance of the parallel circuit is 1 Ω. When one bulb burns out, the resistance of the circuit becomes simply the resistance of the bulb, R, for which we chose the value 2 Ω. Since the case of the bulbs in parallel has a lower total resistance, it will take less power to illuminate both bulbs. One combination of Ohm's Law and the power equation is $P = E^2/R$, so power is inversely proportional to resistance. The potential of the battery does not change when one of the bulbs burns out, but the resistance doubles, meaning that the power drawn from the battery is cut in half.

6. **b) The bulbs will shine brighter in parallel.** The light bulbs will shine brighter when they are attached to the battery in parallel.

There are a couple ways to approach this problem, but the main point of the question is that, regardless of the type, the brightness of a bulb will depend on the power being dissipated by the bulb. Remember that the power equation is $P = E * I$.

Looking at a single bulb in the series circuit, both bulbs will receive the same current but only half of the battery's voltage. One of the combinations of Ohm's Law with the power equation is $P = E^2/R$. So the power dissipated by a single bulb in series will be the square of half the battery's voltage divided by the bulb's resistance, or $(V/2)^2/R = V^2/4R$. Instead of doing this algebra, we can also choose values for the voltage and resistance, such as 6 V and 2 Ω, which would give us 9/2 W = 4.5 W power dissipation.

A single bulb in parallel will receive the full voltage from the battery. Using the same form of the power equation, $P = E^2/R$, the power dissipated by a single bulb will simply be V^2/R or, plugging in our 6 V and 2 Ω, 18 W. This is four times larger than the other case!

The other approach we can take to this problem is creating an equivalent circuit. If the bulbs are attached in series, the total resistance will be twice the resistance of a single bulb, 2R, or 4 Ω if we plug in our chosen value of 2 Ω for each bulb. If the bulbs are attached in parallel, the equivalent resistance will only be half that of a single bulb, R/2 or 1 Ω, so electricity can more easily flow when given a voltage. With the equation $P = E^2/R$, both equivalent circuits would have the same potential, but the resistance is lower for the parallel case, giving a higher power consumption because power is inversely related to resistance.

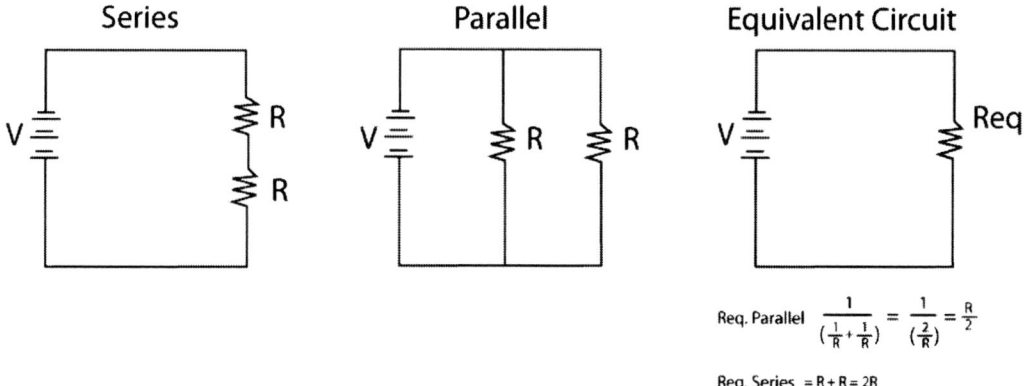

This answer makes sense when we consider the hydraulic analogy. The series case is similar to two pipes attached in a row, which will resist flow for twice as long, so it is like a pipe that is half the diameter. However, the parallel case is similar to two pipes beside each other, which gives the same length but offers two paths through which the water can flow, so more water can more easily flow quickly through two pipes attached in parallel.

7. **c) Anything above 4 Ω**. The first step is to find the value of resistance that will give a current of 3 A. Using Ohm's Law, $R = E/I$, and seeing in the diagram that it is a 12 V battery, the resistance at which the fuse will blow is 4 Ω. But this is not the end of the problem. The fuse can support any current lower than 3 A. Knowing that current is inversely proportional, we want a current lower than 3 A and, therefore, a resistance higher than 4 Ω. To test this, we can also choose values for the variable resistance that are higher and lower than 4 Ω and see what current we get. For instance, if we choose a resistance of 3 Ω, the current will be 12 V/3 Ω = 4 A. At this value, the current will be too high and the fuse will fail.

   However, if we choose a resistance higher than 4 Ω, such as 6 Ω, we will find a current lower than 3 A. 12 V/6 Ω = 2 A. Therefore we want resistance that is above 4 Ω.

8. **b) Iron**. The core of an electromagnet is made of a ferrous metal to strengthen the magnetic field created by the coil.

9. **b) Rectifier**. A rectifier is a device used to convert alternating current to direct current, which is known as rectification.

10. **a) Farads**. The symbol shown represents a capacitor. The unit of capacitance is a farad. Henries are the units for inductance, amps are the units for current, and ohms are the units for resistance.

11. **d) PNP transistor**. The arrow in the symbol for a transistor always points towards the n-type material, so this is a symbol for a PNP transistor, an n-type semiconductor sandwiched between two p-type semiconductors.

12. **a) 1**. A wire's gauge describes the wire's diameter; the higher the number, the smaller the wire's diameter. Choice A has the largest diameter. Don't forget that if too small of a wire is used for an application with a high current draw, it may melt.

13. **c) 10 A**. The resistors in this circuit are connected in series, so they will have the same current flowing through them, just like to pipes connected in series would have the same amount of water flowing through them.

14. **d) 40 V**. The total resistance of this circuit is the sum of the two resistors, 2 + 2 = 4 Ω, and the ammeter gives the current of the circuit. According to Ohm's law, voltage is current times resistance, $V = I * R = 10 * 4 = 40$ V.

15. **b) 12 V**. Since the resistors are connected in series, they will have the same current flowing through them. Because the resistors have the same resistance and the same current, they will also have the same voltage, which is measured by the voltmeter. The voltage supplied by the source is equal to the sum of the voltage across the resistors: 6 + 6 = 12 V.

16. **c) 8 V**. Since the resistors are connected in parallel, they will have the same voltage drop, just like two pipes connected in parallel would have the same pressure difference. This voltage drop will be the same as the potential supplied by the source. According to Ohm's law, the voltage across the 2 Ω resistor is $V = I * R = 4 * 2 = 8$ V, which is equal to the voltage supplied by the source.

17. a) 2 A. Since the resistors are connected in parallel, they will have the same voltage, which is given by the voltmeter. According to Ohm's law, the current through the resistor is $I = V/R = 8/4 = 2$ A.

18. b) Parallel. A car's headlights are connected to the battery in parallel so that one of them can still illuminate if one of them goes out. If they were connected to the battery in series and one headlight went out, the circuit would no longer be a closed-loop and the other headlight would go out as well.

19. c) Start at a certain value and then decrease to zero. When the switch is left is position A, the resistor is not part of a complete loop, so it will receive no voltage and the current is equivalent to the following figure.

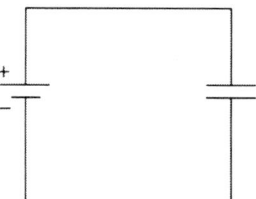

In this setup, the capacitor will build a charge while storing energy provided by the source. When the switch is moved to position B, the source will no longer be part of a complete loop and the resulting circuit is shown below.

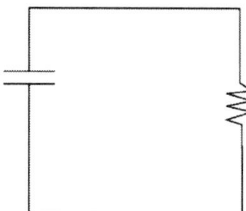

In this circuit, the now fully-charged capacitor will act as a source, providing the resistor with a voltage, and the current through the resistor will start at a value dependent on the resistance of the resistor. As time goes on, the capacitor will lose charge and no longer act as a source of potential for the resistor. The current through the resistor will be zero when the capacitor is fully discharged.

20. d) – Both a) and b). In these circuits, the negative side of the source is replaced by a common ground. For two circuits to be equivalent, each branch of one should correspond to exactly one branch of the other, so you can follow the conductor with your finger and encounter the same components in the same order. This condition holds for both choices **a)** and **b)**.

21. c) 3. The arrow in the symbol for a transmitter is always on the side of the emitter. Also, since the arrow is pointing toward the outside of the symbol, this is an NPN transistor because the arrow always points towards the n-type semiconductor.

22. d) 0 A. The diode in the circuit diagram is pointing towards the positive terminal, which means it is in reverse-bias and will not allow current to flow. For the diode to be in forward-bias, it should point toward the negative terminal, in the direction of the flow of electricity. In forward bias, the cathode is connected to the negative side of the source and the anode is connected to the positive.

23. b) Direct current. DC stands for direct current. AC stands for alternating current.

24. c) Relay. A relay acts as an electrical switch.

25. c) To supply a ground source to the appliances housing. For the user's safety, some appliances housings are grounded to provide a route for electricity to follow in case of a short circuit.

26. b) Start at zero and increase to a certain value. When the switch is first closed, the inductor will block any flow of current, initially acting like a break in the wire, until it is able to build a magnetic field. Once the inductor has built a magnetic field, it will act as a simple conductor, showing no resistance. This means that after a long time the current in the circuit will be determined by only the voltage supply and resistor.

27. c) Silver. Resistance is the opposite of conductivity, so this question is asking for the most conductive metal. Silver has the highest conductivity of any element in the periodic table.

28. c) 0 A. Because of the symmetry of this setup, the voltage will be equal on either side of resistor number 3. If there is no potential difference across a resistor, there will be no current. Resistor number 3 can be taken out of this setup without affecting the current through or voltage drop across the other resistors. Also note that because of the symmetry, all the resistors except number 3 will have the same voltage and current.

29. d) Inductance. Inductance is measured in henries, capacitance is measured in farads, and resistance is measured in ohms. Translucence is the transparency of a material, not an electrical property.

30. b) N-type material. The cathode of a diode is made of n-type material and has excess electrons. When the cathode is connected to the negative side of a source, it allows the flow of electrons, so the diode is in forward-bias.

Chapter 4: Mechanical Comprehension

Physics is a fascinating subject, but it can be very confusing. Before diving into the topics covered in the mechanical section of the ASVAB, we should first define two types of values used in physics; **scalars** and **vectors**.

In most basic math, simple numerical values are calculated (for instance 1 + 1 = 2). These simple numbers are known as **scalar** values, meaning they have a magnitude, but no direction, associated with them. Mass is an example of a scalar value commonly used in physics.

However, we live in a three-dimensional universe, so normally a simple number cannot sufficiently describe a physical characteristic. Instead, we need a magnitude as well as a direction, which is known as a **vector**. A vector not only tells how large a value is, but also whether it acts upward, to the left, to the right, etc.

For example, **speed** is a scalar value that tells you how fast an object is going. But if you are driving, knowing only the speed of your car, it will be impossible to navigate. Instead, you need to know your speed as well as the direction in which you are traveling, which is a vector value known as **velocity**. Velocity tells the direction and speed that an object is traveling.

Force and Newton's Laws of Motion

A **force** is a push or pull that can result in an object's motion or change of shape, and has a magnitude and direction, making it a vector. Force is measured in **Newtons** (N) in the metric system of units, but can also be measured in the standard unit of **pounds force** (lbf).

Though its effects can be noticed, a force cannot be seen; it can be thought of as an interaction between two bodies. The basic rules of forces are described by **Newton's Laws of Motion**, which are the foundation of the field of **mechanics.**

1. **First Law of Motion**: Until acted on by an external force, an object's velocity will remain constant, meaning speed and direction will not change. You may recognize: "An object at rest will remain at rest and an object in motion will remain in motion until a force is applied." An object's natural resistance to a change in its motion is known as **inertia**, so Newton's first law is also known as the **Law of Inertia**.

   Intuitively, the law of inertia makes sense. If a soccer ball is resting in a field, it is not going to move until someone kicks it. Once the ball is kicked, though, it does not continue to travel forever, which seems like it is a violation of Newton's first law.

   However, there are forces such as drag from the air and friction from the field that eventually cause the ball to come to stop again. In the same way, if a moving car is put into neutral, it will slow down and eventually stop due to parasitic losses in the car's wheels and drivetrain, aero drag, and friction.

2. **Second Law of Motion**: Describes a force's effect on the motion of a body. It states that the acceleration of the object will be proportional to the sum of the forces being applied. Algebraically, Newton's second law is written as: $F = m * a$.

Here, F is force, m is mass in kilograms (kg) or pounds mass (lbm), and a is acceleration in meters per second squared (m/s^2) or feet per second squared (ft/s^2). Notice that force and acceleration are both vectors, so the acceleration of an object will be in the direction of the force being applied to it.

Acceleration is defined as the rate of change of an object's velocity. Acceleration does not have to result in a change in speed; it can also cause a change in direction, as is the case in centripetal, or rotational, acceleration. Remember that velocity and acceleration are two separate and distinct values. Just because the acceleration is positive does not mean that the object's velocity is positive and vice versa.

A negative velocity would mean the object is going backward (or opposite of the direction designated as "positive") and a positive acceleration means the object's velocity is increasing in the positive direction (or decreasing in the negative direction). Though the term "deceleration" is often used to describe a decrease in speed, this is not technically correct. Instead, a change in velocity is always called acceleration and can either be positive or negative, depending on direction.

3. **Third Law of Motion**: Involves the coupling of forces and reactions. The law is often stated as, "For every action there is an equal and opposite reaction." The actions and reactions we are considering are forces. For example, if you lean against a wall, you are applying a force on the wall. According to Newton's third law, the wall is applying the same force back on you. These two forces will be the same magnitude, but in opposite directions; you push toward the wall and the wall pushes back on you. Because there is no motion involved when you lean again a wall, this is considered a **static** example.

    A **dynamic** example of Newton's third law is two cars crashing. If one car collides into a second, stationary car, both cars feel the same amount of force. The force applied to the stationary car is in the direction of the collision and causes the car to begin moving in the same direction as the first car. The moving car would have a force applied to it in the opposite direction by the stationary car, resulting in, among other things, a decrease in speed. Since the force on the two cars will be in opposite directions, the acceleration of the cars will also be in opposite directions; the stationary car speeds up and the moving car slows down.

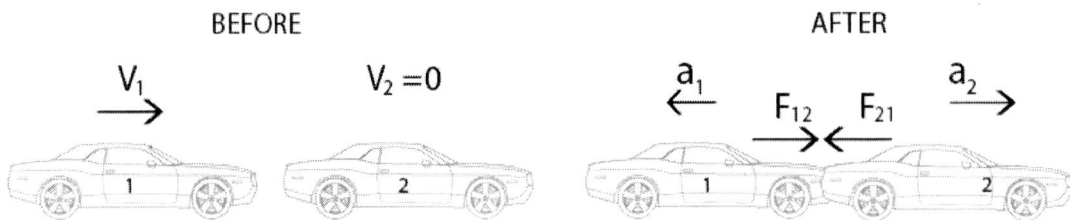

Collision of a car moving at velocity V_1 into the second stationary car with the force car 1 applies on car 2 F_1, the equal force car 2 applies on car 1 F_{21}, and the resulting accelerations a_1 and a_2.

Centrifugal Force
The terms centripetal and centrifugal force are often incorrectly used interchangeably. A **centripetal force** is a force that makes an object travel along a curved path. This means a centripetal force creates a **centripetal acceleration** toward the center of the curved path.

For example, when a car is driven in a circle, the front tires exert a centripetal force on the car, accelerating it toward the center of the circle. Passengers in the car feel as though they are being pulled toward the outside of the circle, and this pull is **centrifugal acceleration**, which results from **centrifugal force**.

A centrifugal force is the reaction force of a centripetal force that pulls an object toward the outside of the curved path being traveled. This all means that a centrifugal force and a centripetal force are of equal magnitude and opposite directions, just as would be expected of a force and reaction according to Newton's third law. As Newton's second law states, centripetal force equals the mass of the object multiplied by centripetal acceleration:

$$F_c = m * a_c = m * v^2/R$$

Here, a_c is the centripetal acceleration and is equal to the square of the object's linear velocity (v) divided by the radius of the curved path, R.

When a ball on a string is swung in a circle, the string exerts a centripetal force on the ball, preventing it from leaving the circular path, and the resulting centrifugal force pulls the ball outward, causing tension in the string and keeping it taut.

The Law of Gravity and Weight
Sir Isaac Newton also formulated the **law of universal gravitation**. Although it is not considered one of Newton's three laws of motion, this is a very important law of physics and has profound implications in our world. Many people are familiar with the story of Isaac Newton observing a falling apple and coming up with the idea of gravity.

Though the authenticity of this story, and even whether Newton was the original formulator of the law, is unclear, Newton's law of universal gravitation is nonetheless named after him, and it describes the mutual attraction between celestial bodies, such as planets and stars. It states that the **gravitational force** two bodies exert on each other is proportional to their masses and inversely proportional to the square of the distance between them:

$$F_g = G * m_1 * m_2 \, r^2$$

Here, G is the **universal gravitation constant** ($6.674 * 10^{-11}$ Nm^2/kg^2), m_1 and m_2 are the masses of the two bodies, and r is the distance between them. You may notice that there is no vector on the right side of this equation. The product of scalar values cannot equal a vector because no direction is specified, so this equation is not technically correct.

This is because the right side of this equation normally has a unit vector with a length of 1 in the direction of the measurement of the distance between the two planets. This has been left out, but remember that gravity is an attractive force; it will always tend to pull two bodies toward each other with equal force.

$$F_{e,s} \qquad F_{s,e} \qquad F_c$$

Sun

$$F_{e,s} = F_{s,e} = F_c$$

The gravitational force exerted by the sun on the Earth $F_{s,e}$ is equal to the gravitational force applied to the sun by the earth $F_{e,s}$ and is balanced (equal to) the centrifugal force resulting from the Earth's movement.

Newton's law of universal gravitation is a fairly complex concept and would seem difficult to apply to an object on the earth since there are so many objects applying a gravitational force on each other. Just look around; every object you see is applying a gravitational force on you, and you are pulling all those things toward you with the same force!

Thankfully, the law of gravity can be greatly simplified when dealing with objects on the earth's surface. The earth has a mass so much greater than any of the other objects around you that the force of gravity pulling objects toward the earth's center is much stronger than the attraction between any objects on the earth's surface. This means that we can ignore all gravitational forces besides the earth's gravity, which proves accurate when making calculations except in very rare cases, such as when a person is standing next to the Himalayan Mountains. (Next to the Himalayan Mountains, a plumb line will not point directly toward the center of the earth, but skew slightly toward the mountains, but even in this case the error in measurements is small.)

Another simplification arises from the huge radius of the earth. No matter how good of an arm you have, if you throw a ball into the air, it will not go very far at all when compared to the earth's radius. This means that even if you take an elevator to the top of a very tall building, you really haven't changed your distance from the center of the earth, so you'll still feel approximately the same gravitational force.

Therefore, we can reduce the universal gravitation equation to a simple equation for the earth's force of gravity on an object:

$$F_g = m * g$$

Here, m is the mass of the object in kilograms (kg) or pounds mass (lbm) and g is the **acceleration due to gravity**, which is 9.81 m/s^2 or 32.2 ft/s^2 towards the center of the earth. This constant acceleration of gravity near the surface of the earth means that any object, no matter what its mass, will fall to the ground at the same rate, as long as there is not significant aero drag. If a bowling ball and an orange are dropped from a building at the same time, they will accelerate toward the earth at the same rate and hit the ground at the same time.

The constant acceleration of gravity also gives rise to the concept of **weight**. The weight of an object is merely a measure of the force of gravity on the object ($m * g$), and is measured in Newtons (N) or pounds force (lbf).

The object's mass is a constant scalar value that cannot be changed. However, if the object is taken to another planet, its weight, which is a vector, may be different depending on that planet's acceleration of gravity. The fact that weight is a force means that an object, such as this book, resting on your table exerts a force on the table; the table exerts a force of the same magnitude, the object's weight, back on the object.

This force exerted back on the object opposing the object's weight is known as a **normal force** because it is normal, or perpendicular, to the surface of the table. If you hold this book flat in your hands, you must apply an upward force to keep the book stationary; therefore you are supplying the normal force equal to the book's weight.

Table Supporting the Weight of a Book

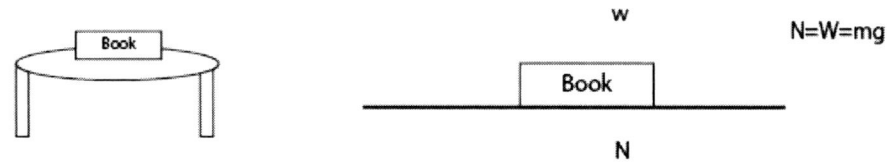

Gravity exerts a force equal to the book's weight onto the table and the table exerts an normal force back on the book so the book does not fall to the ground.

Another concept arising from the idea of weight force is an object's **center of gravity** or **center of mass**. The center of mass is essentially the average location of the object and is often used in physics to simplify problems, treating the object as a single particle with all of its mass at its center of gravity.

An object's stability is also determined by the location of its center of gravity. For example, if you stand flat-footed with straight legs and try to reach for an object fairly far in front of you, you may feel off-balanced. When you lean forward and reach out your arms, you are shifting your center of gravity forward in front of your feet, creating a torque that will cause you to fall forward once it is too great for your feet to overcome.

However, if you either bend your knees or stick one of your legs out behind you as you reach forward, the extra weight behind your grounded foot counteracts the weight in front of your foot so that your center of gravity does not shift, keeping you balanced.

This is very similar to a crane that has a large weight just behind the operator's cab to counteract added weight on the crane's arm when lifting. This weight's position is often adjustable, so it can be moved farther away from the crane's base when picking up objects that are either heavy or near the end of the crane's arm; without this large counterweight, a crane could not lift heavy objects without tipping over.

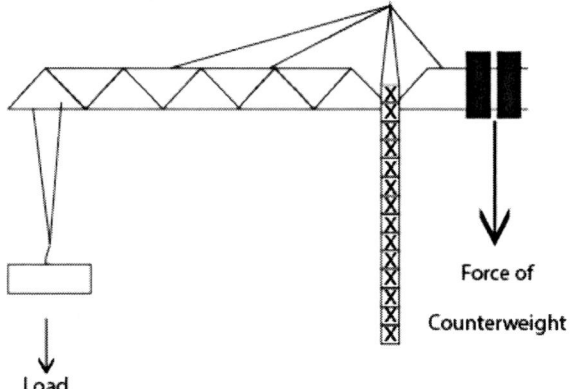

Torque

Torque (twisting force which attempts to rotate an object), or **moment** due to a force, equals the distance of the force from the **fulcrum**, or pivot point, multiplied by the tangential force: $T = F * r$.

F is the force and r is the **torque arm**, or distance from the fulcrum.

In the crane example, the middle of the crane acts as a fulcrum and the counterweight and load apply forces downward, creating two moments in opposite directions; the load is twisting the crane counterclockwise and the counterweight twists clockwise. Torque is measured in Newton-meters (Nm) or foot-pounds-force (lbf-ft).

It is important to remember that the force and distance are both vectors, which means that the component of force and the torque arm considered must be perpendicular. Applying force to the handle of a wrench is another example.

If the 10lbf force is applied to a 10-inch wrench, then the torque on the bolt is 100 in-lbf. If the force is not applied at a 90 degree angle, the resulting torque will not be as high. For instance, if the force is applied at a 30 degree angle to the wrench handle, then the component of the force perpendicular to the wrench is only 5 lbf, and the resulting torque is just 50 in-lbf.

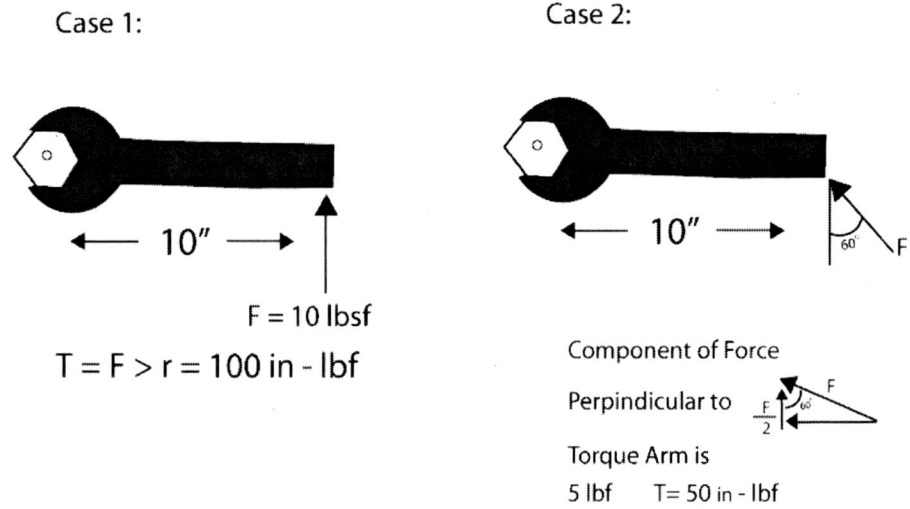

Case 1:

F = 10 lbsf

T = F > r = 100 in - lbf

Case 2:

Component of Force

Perpindicular to

Torque Arm is

5 lbf   T= 50 in - lbf

Friction

The normal force created by gravity also gives rise to a resistance to sliding known as **friction**. If you try to slide a refrigerator across a floor, you may find it very hard to move the object. Newton's third law suggests that there must be a force opposing your attempts to push the refrigerator; if not, it would easily slide across the floor and continue to slide until acted on by another force, such as a wall. This force opposing your efforts to move the refrigerator is friction. There are two types of friction: static and kinetic.

As you might have guessed, **static friction** is the force of friction between two objects that are not moving relative to each other. Static friction arises from the attempt to slide two surfaces past each other. In our refrigerator example, there is no force of friction until you attempt to push the refrigerator.

If you are not applying a force on the refrigerator, the only forces felt by the refrigerator are the force of gravity and the normal force of the floor holding it up, both of which are equal to the refrigerator's weight. When you start to push on the refrigerator and it does not move, static friction is holding the refrigerator in place.

The force of static friction is equal to the force that you are applying to the refrigerator; however, once pushed hard enough, the refrigerator will begin to move. The force necessary to start sliding an object is called **stiction** and is given by the equation: $F_{f,s} = \mu_s * N$.

$F_{f,s}$ is the maximum force of static friction (stiction), N is the normal force applied on the object by the surface across which it is sliding, and μ_s is the **coefficient of static friction**. Past this stiction point, the object will begin to move, and the force of **kinetic friction** will oppose the sliding motion: $F_{f,k} = \mu_k * N$. This is the same as the equation for static friction, except that the coefficient μ_k is the **coefficient of kinetic friction**.

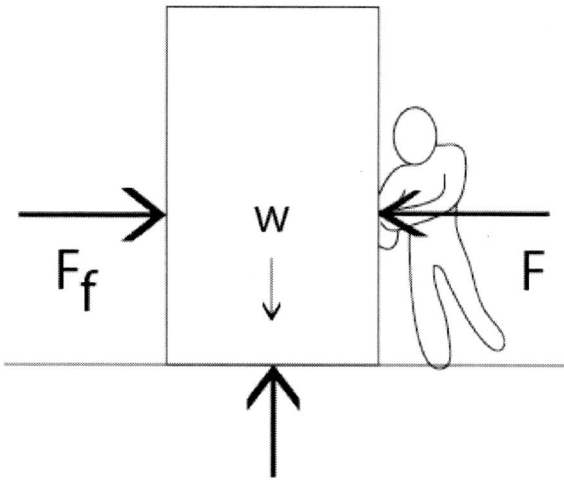

The force of friction, whether static or kinetic, will always oppose the direction of the force causing the sliding. Also, both coefficients of friction are always less than one, and the coefficient of static friction is usually greater than the coefficient of kinetic friction.

This means that it takes a greater force to get an object to start sliding across a surface than it does to keep the object sliding once it has already started. The figure following shows a graph of the force of friction versus the sliding force applied to an object.

Considering this graph in relation to our refrigerator example, if you start pushing on the refrigerator, the force of static friction will prevent sliding until you have applied enough force to overcome the stiction point. After this, the force of kinetic friction will give a constant opposition to the sliding, no matter how hard or fast you push.

Force of Friction (F_f) with Increasing Applied Force (F)

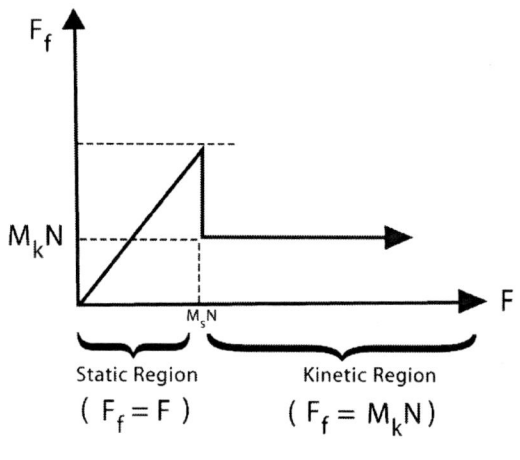

Energy
An object raised to a height above the ground will have an amount of stored energy known as **gravitational potential energy**. The higher an object is moved, the more potential it has. Gravitational potential energy is defined as: $PE = m * g * h$.

Here, m is the mass of the object, g is the acceleration of gravity (9.81 m/s^2), and h is the height of the object from the surface of the earth.

Sometimes, gravitational potential energy is represented by the letter U instead of PE.

Gravitational potential energy, like all types of energy, is given in units of joules (J) or foot-pounds-force (ft-lbf). You may notice that gravitational potential energy is simply the force of gravity on an object multiplied by the objects height.

Since the force of gravity, or weight, is given in units of Newtons, one joule is the same as one Newton multiplied by one meter (1J = 1Nm). When an object is dropped, its gravitational potential energy is converted into **kinetic energy**, which is defined as: $KE = \frac{1}{2} m * v^2$.

Here, m is again the mass of the object and v is the object's velocity.

Kinetic energy also has units of joules and is sometimes represented by the letter E instead of KE. Energy is always conserved, meaning it cannot be created or destroyed. This is known as the law of **conservation of energy**. The law of conservation of gravitational energy can be written as:
$PE + KE = m * g * h + \frac{1}{2} m * v^2$ = constant.

However, all types of energy are always conserved, whether mechanical, electrical, chemical, nuclear, solar, etc. Even the power plants that supply our homes with electricity do not create energy; they simply convert kinetic, chemical, nuclear, or solar energy into electrical energy.

If an object is brought to a certain height, it has a particular amount of gravitational potential energy. When the object is dropped, its potential energy is converted to kinetic energy, so the amount of gravitational potential energy that the object had at its highest point will be exactly how much kinetic energy it has as it hits the ground (ignoring aero drag).

The law of conservation of energy applies to all objects in a gravitational field, so the velocity of a falling object will depend only on the height through which it has fallen and not the path. This means that the same laws used to find the speed of a falling baseball can also be used to find the speed of a rollercoaster.

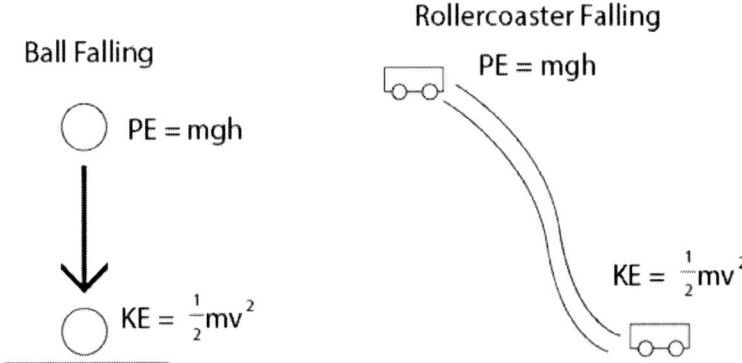

Work

In physics, the term **work** refers to a force applied over some distance: $W = F * d$.

F is the force being applied, and d is the distance of movement in the direction of the force.

It is important to remember that the distance measured is the **displacement** in the direction of the force, which is not the same as total distance traveled; displacement is the distance between the starting and ending points.

If you are holding a book and either keep it stationary or move it to the side, no work has been accomplished because you are pushing upward on the book and there has been no upward movement.

If you move the book upward, work has been done against gravity, and if you allow the book to move downward while holding it, you have done negative work because the movement was opposite the direction of the force you are applying.

In the case of downward movement, one can also say that gravity has done the work; the gravitational force is pulling the book downward in the same direction as the book's movement, so gravity has done positive work on the book.

Work is given in units of joules (J) or foot-pounds-force (ft-lbf). This is the same unit as energy because work can also be thought of as a change in the state of energy of an object, known as the **work-energy theorem**.

In our example of the book, if it weighs 1N and you lift it 1m upward, you have done 1 J of work, or added 1 J of gravitational potential energy. You can verify this by comparing the equations for work and potential energy. Since the force you are exerting to hold up the book is equal to the weight of the book, the work equation is the same as the equation for gravitational potential energy ($m * g * h$).

Power

Power is the rate at which work is done: $P = W/t$.

W is the amount of work done in joules (J) and t is the time over which the work was accomplished in seconds (s). One joule per second (J/s) is equal to a watt (W), the common metric unit of power.

Power can also be given in units of foot-pounds-force per second (ft-lbf/s) or horsepower (hp). One horsepower is equal to 550 ft-lb/s or 746 W. Work is force times distance, so if a force is being applied to an object to move it at a constant velocity, we can also say that power is force times velocity:
$P = F * d/t = F * v$.

F is force, and v is velocity either in meters per second (m/s) or feet per second (ft/s).

Simple Machines

These physics definitions of work and power can be counterintuitive. If you hold dumbbells in front of you with your arms outstretched, you will eventually grow tired. However, if the weights are not moving, according to the laws of physics, no work has been done and, no matter how long you hold the weights, no power will ever be used. Your physical exhaustion results not from the work done, but the force you have to apply to hold the weights in place.

This is the basis for the simple machines that we use to make our lives easier every day. **Simple machines** are devices that change the direction or magnitude of a force. The **mechanical advantage** of simple machine is defined as the output force divided by the force that is applied: $MA = F_{out}/F_{in}$.

F_{out} is the machine's output force or load and F_{in} is the force input or effort to the simple machine. The mechanical advantage is, in a sense, the percentage of the input force that is applied as the output of the simple machine. A simple machine does not do work or create power, instead work and power are said to be conserved, meaning that a simple machine can multiply force only by sacrificing displacement and speed.

Levers

The first type of simple machine we will look at is the lever. A **lever** is simply a beam with a pivot or hinge known as a **fulcrum**, which can either multiply the input force by sacrificing output travel distance or multiply distance and speed with a decreased output force. The mechanical advantage of lever is given by: $MA_{lever} = d_{in}/d_{out}$.

Here, d_{in} is the distance from the fulcrum to the point where the input force is applied, or input arm, and d_{out} is the output arm, or distance from the fulcrum to the point of the output force. Levers are divided into three types or classes: **first class**, **second class**, and **third class**.

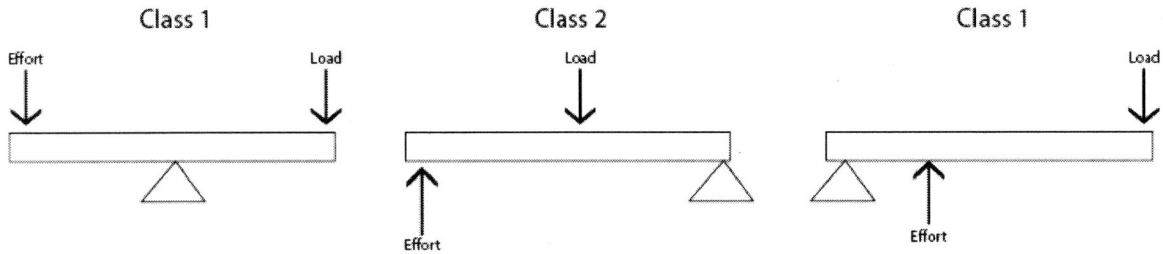

When an input force is applied to a lever, it creates a moment, or torque, about the fulcrum, which is then balanced by the output force. This means the input force multiplied by the input arm is equal to the output force multiplied by the output arm.

1. **First Class Lever**: The fulcrum is between the input and output forces, which are in opposite directions. A popular example of a first class lever is a seesaw. On a seesaw, when one person is in the air, their weight is applying a downward force on one end of the lever and the other person must apply an upward force to bring them back to the earth. A seesaw has input and output arms of equal length, so the mechanical advantage is one, meaning the input and output force and the distances traveled by the two riders are equal.

   A first class lever like this is said to have no mechanical advantage, or a mechanical advantage of one, because it merely changes the direction of the input force. If it is desired to multiply the input force, the input arm should be lengthened. This will give the lever a mechanical advantage greater than one.

Conversely, by lengthening the input arm, the output force will not move as far. If the output arm is longer, it will move faster and farther than the input arm, but a greater input force is required. A lever like this would have a mechanical advantage less than one.

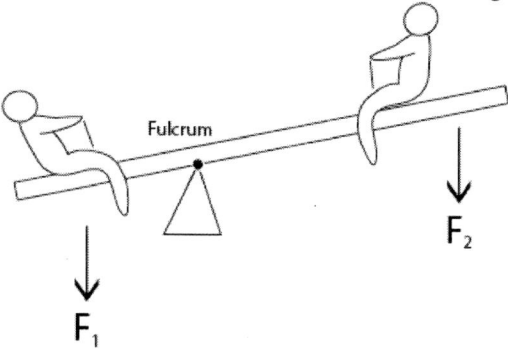

2. **Second Class Lever**: The input and output forces are on the same side of the fulcrum, with the output force closer to the fulcrum, meaning that a second class lever will always have a mechanical advantage greater than one. The most popular example of a second class lever is a wheelbarrow. The front wheel of a wheelbarrow acts as its fulcrum and the user lifts far behind the location of the load in order to lift very heavy objects.

3. **Third Class Lever**: The input and output forces are on the same side of the fulcrum on a **third class lever** as well. In contrast to a second class lever, the input force of a third class lever is applied closer to the fulcrum than the load.

This means third class levers have a mechanical advantage less than one and are used to increase the output distance or speed. For example, take a swinging baseball bat: The batter places both hands near the end of the handle and swings; the top hand moves faster than the other, so the slower hand acts as a fulcrum. The end which makes contact with the ball is moving very quickly when the ball is hit.

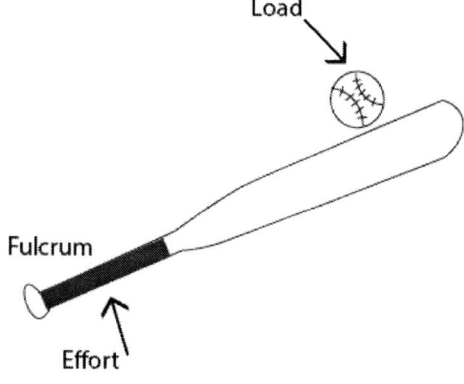

Inclined Planes

The **inclined plane** is another simple machine. Basic inclined planes are often used to do work against gravity, as is the case with a ramp. When an inclined plane is used to move an object upward, the user does not have to use as much force as if they lifted the object vertically upward.

However, the user must apply the force over a greater distance, so the work required is the same for both cases if we ignore friction. The mechanical advantage of an inclined plane is: $MA_{\text{inclined plane}} = L/H$.

L is the length of the inclined plane and H is the height, as shown in the figure below. This equation can be confusing when compared to our original mechanical advantage equation ($MA = F_{out}/F_{in}$), but in the case of an inclined plane, we can think of the output force as the force required if the load were lifted vertically upward, and the input force as the actual effort required when using the inclined plane.

It would seem that the most efficient inclined plane would have an extremely long length because this increases the mechanical advantage. However, increasing the length not only increases the travel distance up the ramp but also the strength requirement of the plane. This is similar to breaking a stick by bending it. If you have a very long twig, it can be easily broken in half.

Once the stick has been broken in half, the shorter resulting halves will be harder to break. If the process is repeated a few times, you may no longer be able to break the stick by hand. When an inclined plane is used to lift a load, the item being lifted applies a downward force to the ramp, bending and possibly breaking it if the ramp is too long or weak.

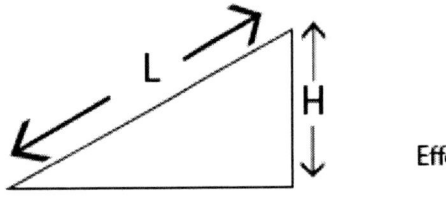

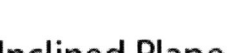

Inclined Plane

Screws

A **screw** is a specific application of the inclined plane; it is simply an inclined plane wrapped around a cylinder. If you look closely at a single-threaded screw, a triangle can be formed out of the threading by connecting consecutive teeth. The mechanical advantage of the screw will depend on the length of the tool used to turn the screw.

A screw can also be used for lifting heavy objects with the setup shown below, known as a **screw jack**. The mechanical advantage for this assembly is: $MA_{\text{screw jack}} = 2\pi r/P$.

Here, r is the torque arm, or distance from the center of the bolt (the fulcrum) and P is the distance between two consecutive teeth on the screw threading, known as the thread's pitch.

This mechanical advantage is found by considering the total distance that the input force must travel ($2\pi r$) and the total height that the screw will rise (P) in one turn of the input torque arm. Sometimes the mechanical advantage of only the screw is given, without specifying a tool or setup used to turn the screw.

In these cases, the radius of the shaft around which the inclined plane is wrapped is used as the torque arm r in the mechanical advantage equation.

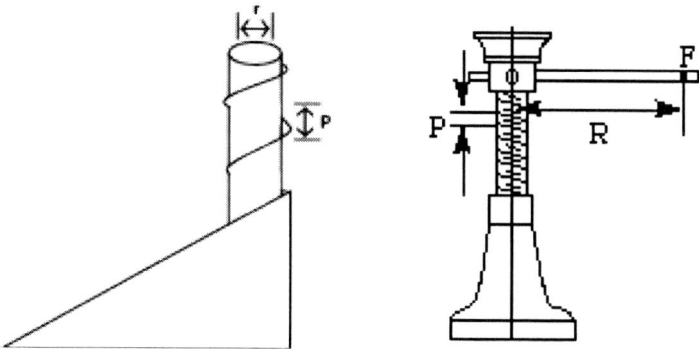

Wedges

The **wedge** is another variation of the inclined plane. A wedge can be thought of as two inclined planes placed back-to-back. Wedges are normally used for cutting and splitting as well as securing an object in place. An axe or knife is an example of a wedge used for cutting or splitting. A wedge is also used to secure the head of a hammer to its handle and to hold open doors as a doorstop. The mechanical advantage equation of a wedge differs only slightly from that for an inclined plane: $MA_{wedge} = L/t$.

The thickness, t, is measured across the end of the wedge. Again, it would seem that a wedge should be as long and sharp as possible, but a thinner, sharper wedge not only is transversely weaker (to side-loading), but also has a tendency of binding when used to chop. For instance, if a log-splitting axe is too sharp, it can become lodged in the wood with the log flexing back onto the blade, increased friction and making the axe difficult to remove.

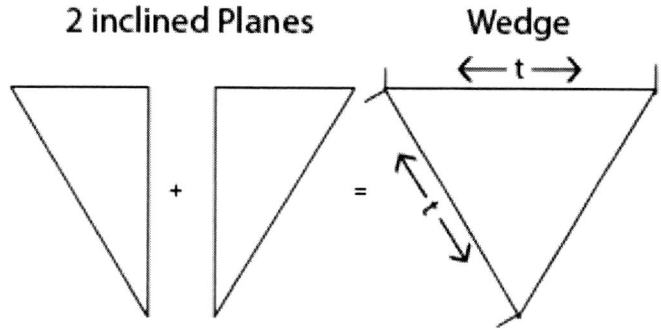

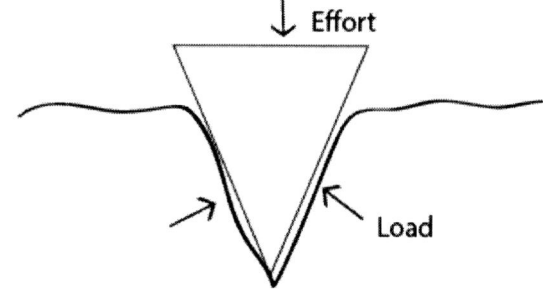

An Axe (Wedge) Splitting Wood

Pulleys and the Block and Tackle

The next type of simple machine we'll look at is the **pulley**. Pulleys are not used alone; they are used to support a cable, rope, belt, or chain, so we should discuss these items, which we will refer to simply as "cords" from now on, before trying to understand pulleys. Cords can be thought of simply as force transmitters.

However, unlike solid bodies and fluids, cords can only transmit pulling force, known as **tension**. If you try to bend or push on a cord it flexes, providing no resistance; if you secure a cord to an object and pull on it, though, it will transmit this pull as tension to the object to which it is attached.

When loaded, the tension throughout a cord is uniform, meaning that every piece of a cord along its length sees the exact same load. This is where the phrase, "A chain is only as strong as its weakest link" comes from. Each link in the chain will see the same load and be under the same amount of stress, so the entire chain can only hold the amount that the weakest link can hold before breaking.

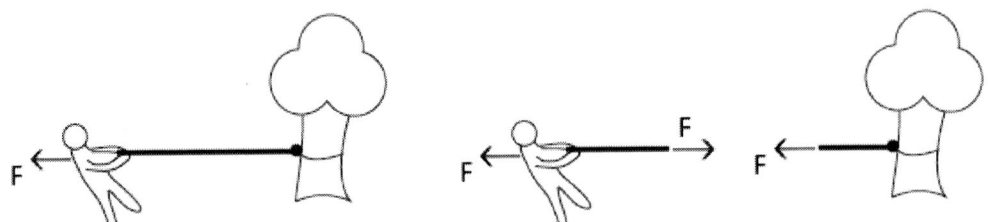

When you pull on a rope, the force is uniformly distributed through the length of
the rope as tension.

A **pulley** is a wheel and axle that supports a cord and, in doing so, changes the direction of cord's orientation and therefore the direction of the tension in the cord. Although pulleys have some frictional losses, they are small enough that we can ignore them and say that the tension in the cord is uniform. This means that the pulling force's direction is changed while its magnitude stays the same. This means that a single pulley offers no mechanical advantage ($F_{in} = F_{out}$ so $MA_{pulley} = 1$).

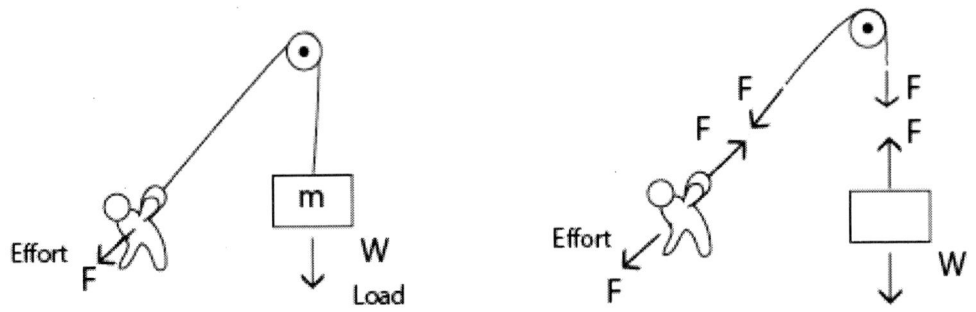

When a pulley is used to suspend an object, the tension in the rope is uniform
and equal to the weight of the object.

However, a series of pulleys, known as a block and tackle, can be used to give a mechanical advantage and make it possible to more easily lift heavy objects. When the input force is applied to a single cord, the mechanical advantage of a block and tackle can be found by counting the number of cord segments whose tension is being applied to lift the object: $MA_{b\&t} = N$.

Here, N is the number of cord segments extending from the moving output block, as shown in the pictures below. Again, this mechanical advantage comes at the cost of moving distance, so if the mechanical advantage is 4, then the output block will only move one quarter of the distance traveled by the input force.

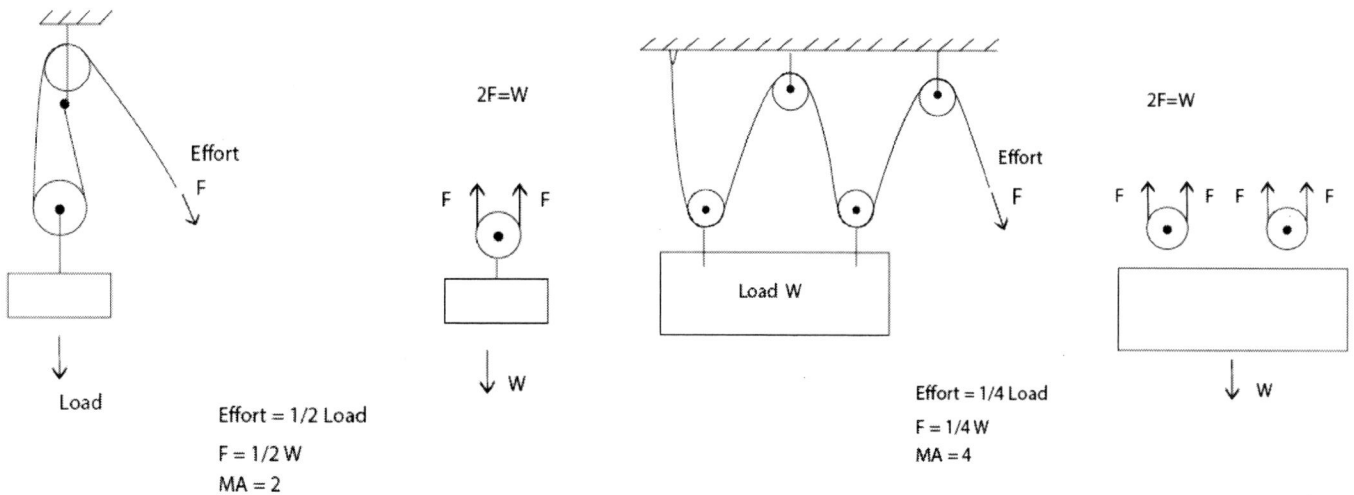

The Wheel and Axle

We said that a pulley is a wheel and axle, but the wheel and axle is, in its own right, a simple machine. **Wheel and axle** refers to two cylinders that are attached to each other coaxially that are allowed to rotate about their center, as shown below. The wheel and axle can be thought of as a variation of the lever, with the fulcrum at the center and the forces applied tangentially to the surface of the wheel and the axle, sometimes using belts or rope wrapped around the wheel and/or axle. In this way, the wheel and axle creates a continuous lever. The mechanical advantage of a wheel and axle assembly is given by:

$MA_{w\&a} = R_{wheel}/R_{axle}$

Here, R_{wheel} and R_{axle} are the radii of the wheel and axle, respectively.

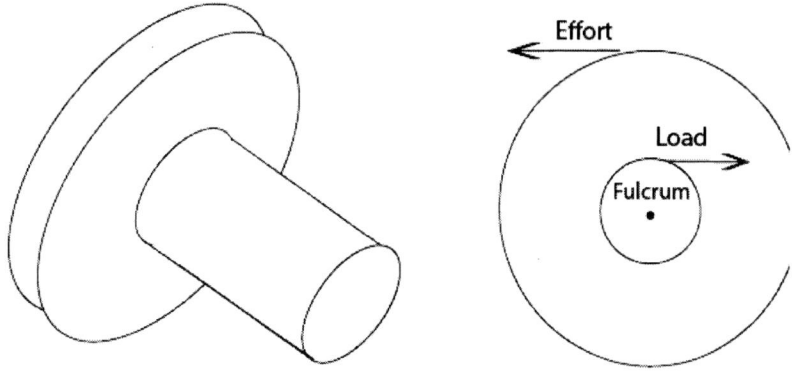

However, an axle does not have to have only one wheel and each wheel does not have to be the same size. The wheels on a car are the same size, but sometimes wheel and axles are required to turn various machine parts at different speeds. For this, assemblies like the one shown below are necessary. The mechanical advantage between two different wheels can be found as: $MA_{wheels} = R_{in}/R_{out}$.

Here, R_{in} and R_{out} are the radii of the input wheel and output wheel, respectively. The mechanical advantage of the wheel and axle and two-wheel assembly are both found by comparing the input and output moments about the axis; the input and output torques must be equal. Remember again that this mechanical advantage will be gained by sacrificing the distance traveled.

For instance, if the input wheel has a radius four times as large as the output, the mechanical advantage will be four. This means the output force will be four times as large as the input, but the circumference of the output wheel is a quarter of that of the input wheel, so a belt attached to the output wheel will turn only a quarter as far as one attached to the input wheel.

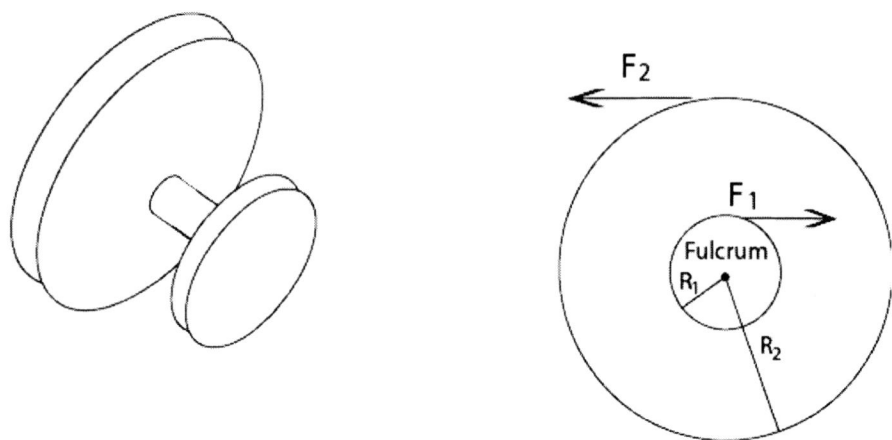

Gears
The rotation and torque of a wheel can be transmitted a great distance by connecting two wheels with a belt or chain, as shown below The mechanical advantage of this setup is given by: $MA_{gears} = R_{out} / R_{in.}$

R_{out} and R_{in} are again the output and input radii, respectively. Notice that this mechanical advantage is the inverse of the mechanical advantage between two wheels on the same axle (MA_{wheels}) and is denoted as MA_{gears}. This is because this pulley assembly is the same basic concept as two gears; it is two disks rotating with the same tangential velocity at their contact point.

However, two gears will rotate in opposite directions. **Gears** are simply interlocking wheels with their **effective radii** given by the point at which the two wheels have the same velocity.

Effective radii at two gears are given by the point at which their linear velocities are equal. Pulleys connected by a bolt or chain are two discs that turn with the same velocity at their radii, just like gears, and the assembly's mechanical advantage is calculated the same way as a pair of gears. However, a pair of gears will rotate in opposite directions.

To find the mechanical advantage of a long **gear train**, or series of gears interlocked together, we only need to worry about the input and output gear radii, not the radii of the gears in between, as long as they are interlocked and not on the same shaft.

Again, if the output gear has a radius four times that of the input gear, the mechanical advantage will be four but the output gear will only rotate once for every four rotations of the input gear.

For two interlocking gears, the force applied at the effective radius, or meshing point, is the same for both gears. Since the gears are different radii, this creates different moments on the two gears. If the input gear is driving a larger output gear, the output force is greater than the input and the assembly is called a torque-multiplier or speed-reduction assembly. If the output gear is smaller than the input, the assembly is a speed-multiplying or torque-reducing assembly.

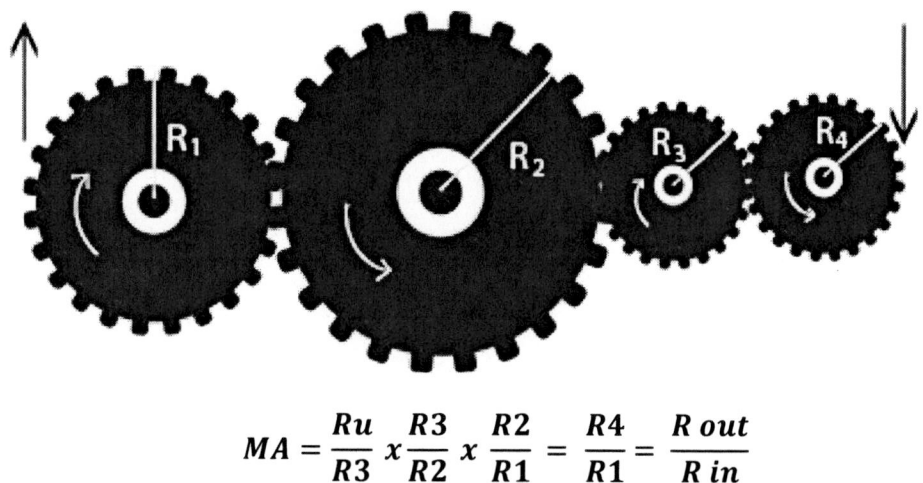

$$MA = \frac{Ru}{R3} \; x \frac{R3}{R2} \; x \; \frac{R2}{R1} = \frac{R4}{R1} = \frac{R\,out}{R\,in}$$

Fluids and Hydraulics

If a force needs to be transmitted a great distance, it may not be convenient to use any of the mechanical simple machines discussed above. Instead, fluids can be used to transmit the force through hydraulic and pneumatic systems. The term fluid is not synonymous with liquid. A **fluid** is any material that conforms to the shape of its container and is not compressible, so we consider any liquid or gas to be an incompressible fluid.

In fluids, we define **pressure** as a force per unit area, given in pounds per square inch (psi); Pascals (Pa), which is the equivalent of one Newton (N) per square meter (m^2); or **inches of mercury** (in Hg), which is defined as the pressure exerted by a one-inch high column of liquid mercury.

The principle of transmission of pressure, also known as **Pascal's law**, states that pressure applied to one part of the fluid will be distributed evenly to the entire rest of the fluid. In large containers of liquid, the pressure relies on the pressure applied at the surface as well as the depth within the container, so the pressure increases deeper in the container due to the weight of the water.

However, in containers of gas or shallow containers of liquids, the effects of gravity can be ignored and the pressure is constant throughout the container. This principle is utilized in **hydraulics** through the setup shown in the picture below.

In this simplified hydraulic system, one piston is applying a pressure that is equal to the input force spread over the area of the piston's face. This pressure is distributed throughout the fluid, so the face of the second piston will see the same force per unit area. This relationship is stated mathematically as:

$$P_{in} = P_{out}$$
$$F_{in} / A_{in} = F_{out} / A_{out}$$

P_{in} is the pressure on the face of the input piston, which is the input force divided by the area of the input piston's face and is equal to the output pressure P_{out}. Since the output piston in this case is larger, the output force will be greater. For this dual-piston setup, we can define a mechanical advantage by dividing the output force by the input (the definition of mechanical advantage): $MA_{pistons} = A_{out} / A_{in}$.

Remember, this mechanical advantage is gained through decreasing the output motion, so if the output piston has an area four times that of the input, the mechanical advantage will be four, so the output force will be four times the input; however, the output piston will only move a quarter of the distance of the input piston's travel, assuming incompressibility of the fluid.

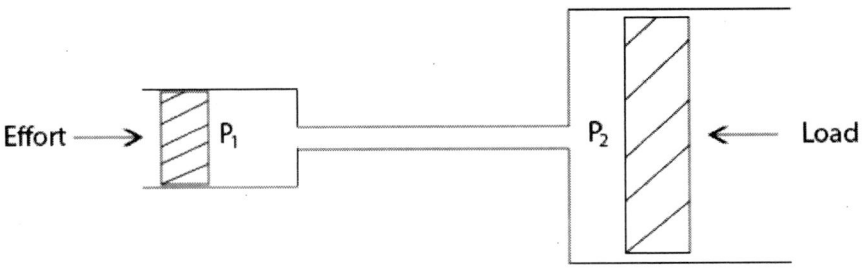

Basic Piston setup of Hydraulic System
The input force is distributed over the face of the input piston and transferred to the fluid
as pressure, which is applies an output force to the second piston.

This difference in piston motion can also be explained by considering volume displacement of the fluid. When the input piston moves, it displaces a volume of fluid equal to the area of the piston multiplied by the distance of the piston's motion.

This volume displaced causes the output piston to move to make room for the volume entering the cylinder, but since the output piston has a larger area, it will not need to move as far to displace the same amount of fluid.

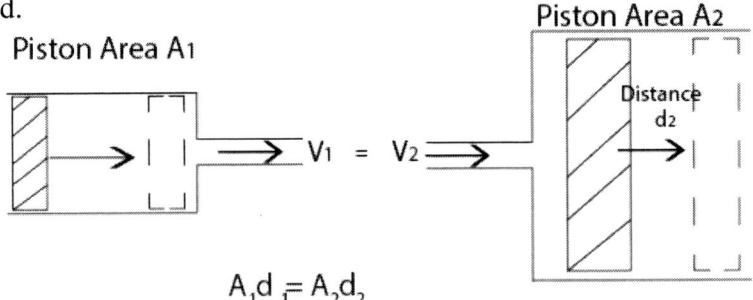

The movement of the pistons in the hydraulic system can also be explained by fluid
displacement. The volume of fluid displaced by the movement of the first piston
($V_1 = A_1 d_1$) flows into the second cylinder ($V_1 = V_2$) and causes the piston to move to
make room for the incoming fluid.

This volume displacement concept can also be applied to a fluid flowing through a pipe. When a fluid is flowing through a pipe, mass must be conserved, meaning that no amount of fluid is gathering anywhere in the pipe; the amount of fluid flowing into the pipe is equal to the amount flowing out.

Since the flow is constant through all points in the pipe, the flow velocity must increase whenever the cross-sectional area of the pipe decreases. Mathematically, the law of **conservation of mass** is stated as:

$$Q_1 = Q_2$$
$$v_1 * A_1 = v_2 * A_2$$

Here, Q_1 and Q_2 are the volumetric flow rates of the fluid, v_1 and v_2 are the velocities of fluid particles, and A_1 and A_2 are the cross-sectional areas of the pipe at points 1 and 2, respectively.

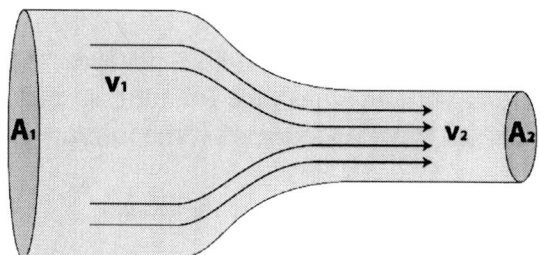

Energy must also be conserved in the flow of a fluid, just like any other body subjected to gravity. Unlike solid bodies, however, fluids also have a defined pressure energy. This means that between any two points, the sum of a fluid's pressure, kinetic, and potential energies must remain constant. Mathematically, this is stated in a force per unit area basis:

$$p + \tfrac{1}{2} \rho v^2 + \rho g h = \text{constant}$$
$$p_1/\rho + v_1^2/2 + g h_1 = p_2/\rho + v_2^2/2 + g h_2$$

Here, p is pressure, ρ is the density of the fluid (which we assume remains constant), v is the velocity of the fluid, g is the acceleration of gravity (9.81 m/s^2 or 32.2 ft/s^2), and h is the height of the fluid.

This relationship is known as **Bernoulli's principle** and can be applied to any points along a streamline. A **streamline** is an imaginary line through a smoothly flowing fluid that is always tangential to the fluid's velocity, and can be thought of as a line that would follow the path of a particle flowing through the fluid.

Practice Drill: Mechanical Comprehension

1. A person moves forward ten steps and then backwards ten steps. What is the total distance traveled?
   a) -10 steps.
   b) 0 steps.
   c) 10 steps.
   d) 20 steps.

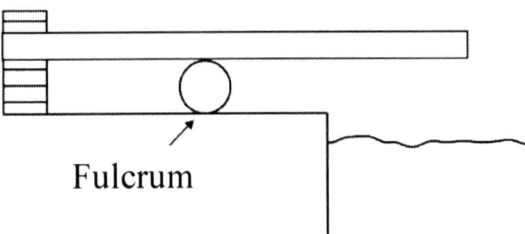

Fulcrum

2. A springboard is a diving board made out of a flexible platform that acts like a spring and is held stationary by a hinge on one end with an adjustable fulcrum, so that a person can dive off the other end, as shown in the picture above. What will happen if the fulcrum is moved away from the diver?
   a) The board will be stiffer.
   b) The board will flex more under the weight of the diver.
   c) Fulcrum position makes no difference.
   d) The platform will be less likely to break.

3. A car travels 60 miles south in one hour, and then 90 miles north in two hours. What is the total displacement during this time?
   a) -30 miles.
   b) 0 miles.
   c) 30 miles.
   d) 150 miles.

4. For the car described in problem #3, what is the average speed during the first hour of travel?
   a) -60 mph.
   b) 1 mph.
   c) 50 mph.
   d) 60 mph.

5. For the car described in problem #3, what is the average speed during the 3 hours of travel?
   a) -10 mph.
   b) 0 mph.
   c) 10 mph.
   d) 50 mph.

6. For the car in problem #3, what is the average velocity during the 3 hours of travel, if we define north as the positive direction?
   a) -10 mph.
   b) -1 mph.
   c) 1 mph.
   d) 10 mph.

7. A 10 kg person stands on a scale. Approximately what will the scale read?
   a) 10 N.
   b) 32 N.
   c) 98 N.
   d) 196 N.

8. A 10 kg person travels to the Moon, which has a smaller acceleration due to gravity than the Earth. What will happen to the person's mass?
   a) The person's mass will decrease.
   b) The person's mass will stay the same.
   c) The person's mass will increase.
   d) It is impossible to tell from this information.

9. A 10 kg person travels to the Moon, which has a smaller acceleration due to gravity than the Earth. What will happen to the person's weight?
   a) The person's weight will decrease.
   b) The person's weight will stay the same.
   c) The person's weight will increase.
   d) It is impossible to tell from this information.

10. A person travels to a distant planet and finds that their weight has increased from their weight on Earth. Assuming the person's mass has not changed, what can we say about the planet's radius?
   a) The planet's radius is smaller than that of Earth.
   b) The planet's radius is equal to that of the Earth.
   c) The planet's radius is larger than that of the Earth.
   d) It is impossible to tell from this information.

11. What force is required to accelerate a 10 kg object from rest to 10 m/s in 5 seconds? (Assume no resistive forces.)
   a) 15 N.
   b) 20 N.
   c) 100 N.
   d) 500 N.

12. A 50 kg object begins at rest on a surface with a static coefficient of friction at 0.6 and a kinetic coefficient of friction at 0.5. If you push horizontally on the object with a force of 27 N, how quickly will it move across the surface? (Assume that the object does not tip over.)
   a) 0 m/s.
   b) 5 m/s.
   c) 20 m/s.
   d) 30 m/s.

W in ... W out

13. Which of these best describes the gear train above?
- a) Torque-multiplier.
- b) Speed-multiplier.
- c) Frequency-multiplier.
- d) None of the above.

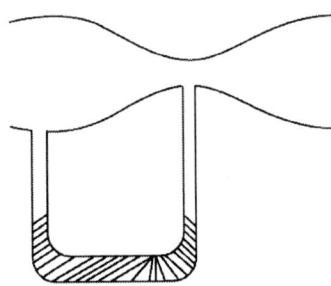

14. The figure above shows an air duct that narrows at a point. A U-tube is attached as shown and the bottom is filled with water. What will happen to the water when air starts flowing through the duct?
- a) The left side will go up and the right side will go down.
- b) Both sides will go down.
- c) The left side will go down and the right side will go up.
- d) Both sides will go up.

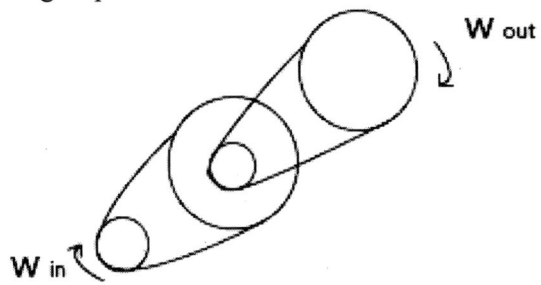

W out

W in

15. Which of these describes the pulley train shown above?
- a) Rotation-inverter.
- b) Speed-multiplier.
- c) Torque-multiplier.
- d) None of the above.

16. To have the best leverage in the scissors above, you should:
    a) Hold the scissors at D and cut at A.
    b) Hold the scissors at D and cut at B.
    c) Hold the scissors at C and cut at A.
    d) Hold the scissors at C and cut at B.

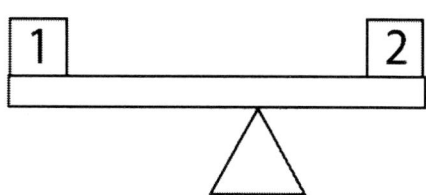

17. Which of the objects in the picture above weighs more?
    a) Object 1.
    b) Object 2.
    c) They weigh the same amount.
    d) It is impossible to tell.

18. Which of these statements is true about a car's transmission?
    a) Higher gears have a higher mechanical advantage.
    b) Lower gears have a higher mechanical advantage.
    c) All the gears have the same mechanical advantage.
    d) The mechanical advantage depends on the weight of the car.

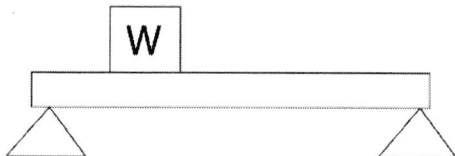

19. In the picture above, does the support on the left or right carry more of the object's weight?
    a) Left supports more weight.
    b) Right supports more weight.
    c) They carry the same amount of weight.
    d) It is impossible to tell.

20. Three cubes of equal volume are put in a hot oven. The cubes are made of three materials: wood, iron, and silver. Which cube will heat the fastest?
    a) The wooden cube.
    b) The iron cube.
    c) The silver cube.
    d) The cubes all heat up at the same rate.

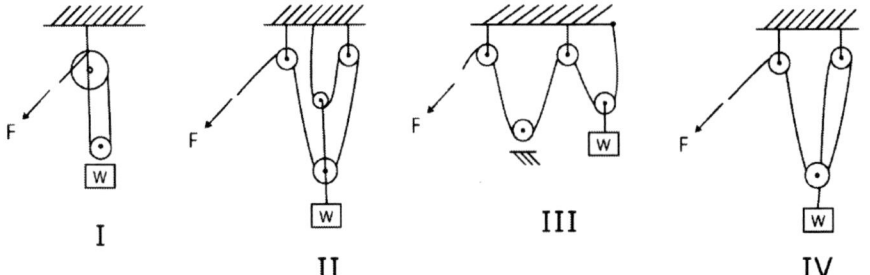

21. Which of block and tackle pictured above requires the least effort to lift a weight of W?
 a) I.
 b) II.
 c) III.
 d) IV.

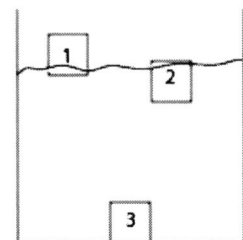

22. What can be said about the three objects shown above in a tank of water?
 a) Object 3 weighs the most.
 b) Object 1 has the lowest density.
 c) Objects 1 and 2 have the same density.
 d) None of the above.

23. Two gears create a mechanical advantage of 4:1 and the larger gear has 24 teeth. How many teeth does the pinion have?
 a) 6 teeth.
 b) 12 teeth.
 c) 24 teeth.
 d) 96 teeth.

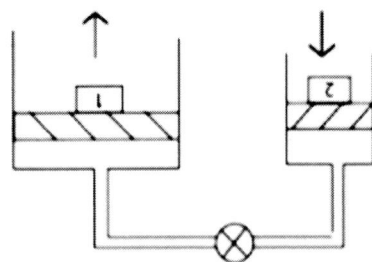

24. In the hydraulic system shown above, the valve is originally closed and the two objects are level. When the valve is opened, the object on the right begins to move downward and the object on the left moves upward. What can be said about the two objects?
 a) Object 1 weighs more.
 b) Object 2 weighs more.
 c) The objects weigh the same amount.
 d) It is impossible to tell from this information.

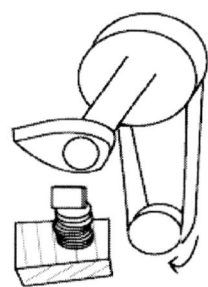

25. The figure above is a simplified model of the camshaft in a car's engine. The pulley attached to the crankshaft is of half the diameter of the pulley attached to the camshaft. About how far must the crankshaft turn before the camshaft pushes the valve all the way open?
   a) 90 degrees.
   b) 180 degrees.
   c) 270 degrees.
   d) 540 degrees.

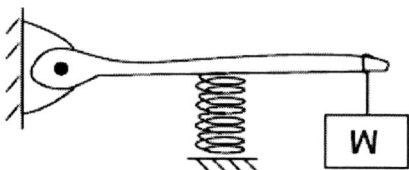

26. The picture above shows a hinged arm attached to a weight and being held horizontal by a spring. If the weight is moved to the left (closer to the hinge), what will happen?
   a) The spring will compress more.
   b) The spring will extend.
   c) Nothing.
   d) It is impossible to tell.

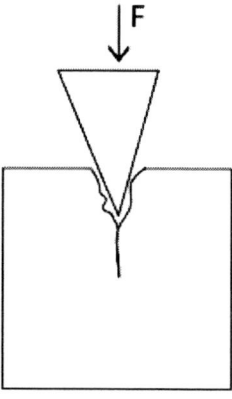

27. The picture above shows an axe splitting a piece of wood. What type of simple machine is this?
   a) Lever.
   b) Blade.
   c) Inclined plane.
   d) None of these.

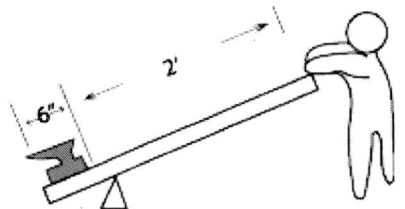

28. The picture above shows a person lifting a heavy object with a lever. What is the mechanical advantage?

    a) 0.25.

    b) 0.3.

    c) 3.

    d) 4.

29. Which of these best describes the gear train shown above?

    a) Torque-multiplier.

    b) Speed-multiplier.

    c) Frequency-multiplier.

    d) None of the above.

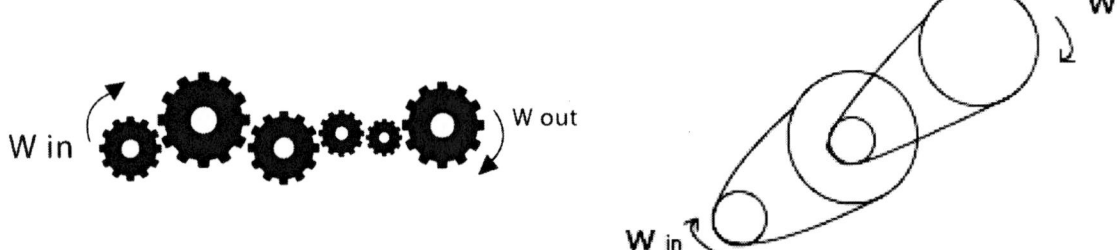

30. If the input gear on the left has the same diameter as the input pulley on the right and the output gear on the left has the same diameter as the output pulley on the right, which assembly gives the higher mechanical advantage?

    a) The gear train on the left.

    b) The pulley train on the right.

    c) The assemblies have the same mechanical advantage.

    d) It is impossible to tell.

Practice Drill: Mechanical Comprehension – Answers

1. **d) 20 steps**. Total distance traveled does not take direction into account, so we can add the two distances: $10 + 10 = 20$ steps.

2. **b) The board will flex more under the weight of the diver**. The distance between the fulcrum and the diver is being lengthened, so the torque arm is being increased; the weight of the diver will apply a greater moment to the platform, resulting in the platform flexing a greater amount.

    You can also consider the two extremes of the fulcrum either being adjusted directly underneath the diver or as far away from the diver as possible. If the fulcrum is underneath the diver the board will not flex at all, and if the fulcrum is the farthest point away from the diver the board will flex the maximum amount.

    This means that the board flexes more as the fulcrum is adjusted away from the diver. Since the board is flexing more, it would be more likely to break because there is a greater moment.

3. **c) 30 miles**. Displacement is the distance between the starting and ending points, so we cannot simply add the two distances together. If we take north as the positive direction, the car moves 60 miles in the positive direction and then 90 miles in the negative direction.

    Adding these values, $60 + (-90) = 60 - 90 = -30$ miles. However, displacement is always positive. Displacement is not a vector, but a scalar. It is just the distance between the start and end points, NOT the vector distance between the two points.

4. **d) 60 mph**. Speed is distance traveled divided by time and does not take direction into account. In this case, the car travels 60 miles in one hour, 60 miles / 1 hour = 60 miles per hour.

5. **d) 50 mph**. Speed is a scalar value, so it does not take direction into account. Average speed is distance traveled divided by time (x/t), so we first find the distance traveled, $60 + 90 = 150$ miles, then the total time, $1 + 2 = 3$ hours, and finally divide the distance by time, $150/3 = 50$ miles per hour.

    While it is also possible to find the average speed during the two legs of the trip and calculate a weighted average, this is much more complicated and reduces to the same equation.

6. **a) -10 mph**. Notice in this question we have to define a positive direction because the question asks for a vector value, which has a magnitude and direction. Similar to problem #4, we must first find the total displacement of the car, which is 30 miles. However, we have to remember that this is 30 miles south, the NEGATIVE direction.

    Like average speed, average velocity is distance divided by time, 30 miles/3 hours = 10 mph, but since the distance traveled is in the negative direction, the average velocity must be negative: $-30/3 = -10$ mph.

    Again, we could also find the average velocity during each leg of the trip and find a weighted average, but this is even more complicated when working with vector values and still reduces to the same equation of total distance divided by total time.

7. **c) 98 N.** A scale measures weight, and since it is the earth's gravitational pull on the object which is being weighed, the force of gravity is the mass of the object times the constant acceleration due to gravity (9.8 m/s^2). mg = 10 * 9.8 = 98 N

8. **b) The person's mass will stay the same.** Mass is a scalar vector depends on the density and volume of an object, both of which will stay constant. A person's mass will stay the same no matter what planet they are on.

9. **a) The person's weight will decrease.** Weight is a measurement of force, so it is a vector value which has a magnitude that depends on mass and acceleration. We already found in problem #8 that the person's mass will not change, so their weight will be proportional to the acceleration of gravity.

Since the acceleration due to gravity on the moon is less than that of the earth, the acceleration of gravity will decrease when the person travels to the moon, meaning their weight will also decrease.

10. **d) It is impossible to tell from this information.** Since the person's weight has increased, the acceleration of gravity on this distant planet is higher than that on Earth. It is tempting to say this must be a smaller planet. However, we cannot say anything about the planet's radius because gravitational force depends on both the mass and distance from the center of an object.

Acceleration due to gravity on a planet depends on the planet's mass and radius; it varies directly with mass and proportionally to the inverse square of the radius (m/r^2). If this planet has the same mass as the Earth, its radius must be smaller so that the planet is denser than the earth. If the radius of the planet is the same as the Earth's, it must have a larger mass and density. However, we are not given any of this information, so the only thing we can say is that the value of m/r^2 for the planet is larger than the Earth's.

11. **b) 20 N.** This problem involves Newton's second law ($F = ma$). To find the force required, we must first calculate the desired acceleration, which is the rate of change of velocity,
$a = \Delta v/\Delta t = 10/5 = 2$ m/s^2. Newton's second law states that $F = ma = 10 * 2 = 20$ N.

12. **a) 0 m/s.** The key to this question is that the object "begins at rest". In order for an object at rest to begin moving, the maximum static friction force must first be overcome,
$F_{f,s} = \mu_s * N = 0.6 * 50 = 30$ N.

Since the force being applied is less than the "stiction" force, the object will not move. The force of friction in this case is equal to the 27 N being applied. Had the force been greater than 30 N, the object would move, a kinetic friction force of $F_{f,k} = \mu_k * N = 0.5 * 50 = 25$ N would resist the motion, and the speed at steady state would be much more difficult to find.

13. **b) Speed-multiplier.** Remember that in a gear train it is only necessary to look at the input and output gears. Since the input gear is larger than the output, the output gear will turn faster, making this a speed-multiplying gear train.

14. **c) The left side will go down and the right side will go up.** Air flowing through the duct will have to speed up at the narrow portion. According to Bernoulli's principle, the pressure in the air will decrease when the speed increases, so the pressure on the right side of the U-tube will be less than the pressure on the left side. This will push the water downward in the left side of the pipe and, since the

volume of the water will stay constant (the water is incompressible), the water in the right side will rise.

15. **b) Speed-multiplier**. Pulley trains are not as simple as gear trains; you can't just look at the input and output pulleys. Instead, you have to look at each step of the pulleys. Fortunately, both steps of this system increase the speed, so this assembly is a speed-multiplier.

16. **b) Hold the scissors at D and cut at B**. For the best leverage, the input arm should be long and the output arm should be short. This means the load should be close to the fulcrum at B and the effort should be far from the fulcrum at D.

17. **b) Object 2**. Object 1 is farther away from the fulcrum, giving it a greater torque arm and therefore higher mechanical advantage that object 2. Since the lever is horizontal, the moments cause by the two objects must be equal, $F_1R_1 = F_2R_2$. $R_1 > R_2$, so therefore $F_2 > F_1$.

18. **b) Lower gears have a higher mechanical advantage**. When driving a car, the transmission is shifted into higher gears when the car is moving faster, so the higher gears are able to produce a higher speed at the expense of torque, meaning they have less of a mechanical advantage. If a person puts a manual transmission in a high gear and tries to move a car from rest, the engine speed will drop and the engine will most likely not have enough power to start because there is not enough of a mechanical advantage. This can also break the car's clutch.

19. **a) Left supports more weight**. The support on the left will carry more of the object's weight. Several approaches can be taken to analyze this problem.

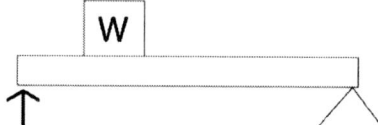

If the support on the left is treated as a fulcrum and the support on the right as a force, similar to a class 2 lever, the force will not have to be large because it has a high mechanical advantage.

However, if the support on the right is treated as a fulcrum and the support on the left treated as an effort force, the force will not have much of a mechanical advantage.

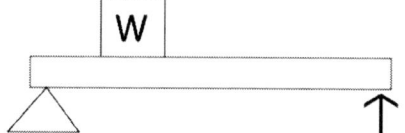

The question is analogous to finding which object weighs more on a balance, as shown below. The weight on the left represents the reaction force of the support on the left in the original question and the weight on the right represents the reaction force of the support on the right.

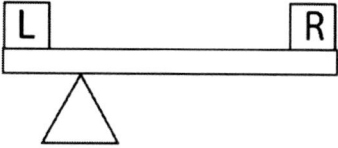

You can also think of the two extremes; if the weight is all the way to the left over the left support, the right support can be removed because it carries no load. Similarly, if the object is all the way on the right side, the right support carries the entire load. Since the object is closer to the left, the left support should carry more of the weight.

20. **c) The silver cube**. The speed at which the cubes will heat up depends on their thermal conductivity. Wood does not have a very high thermal conductivity. In metals, thermal conductivity generally follows the same trend as electrical conductivity; metals with high electrical conductivity have high thermal conductivity. This means the silver cube has the highest coefficient of thermal conductivity and will therefore heat the fastest.

21. **d) IV**. Looking closely at the figure: the two pulleys above the weight in II are attached, and the weight in setup II has four rope segments extending from it, so the mechanical advantage is four and $F = W/4$. Setups I and III have two rope segments extending from the weight, giving a mechanical advantage of 2, and setup IV has three rope segments extending from it, so setup IV's mechanical advantage is 3.

22. **b) Object 1 has the lowest density**. How high an object floats in water depends on that object's density. The objects are acted on by the force of gravity, which depends on the objects mass and a buoyancy force that depends on the volume of the liquid displaced. If the question stated that the three objects had the same volume, then object 3 would be the heaviest because it has the highest density and density is mass per unit volume. However, the problem does not state this and the height at which an object floats only gives its density.

23. **a) 6 teeth**. The pinion refers to the smaller of the two gears, so whether the mechanical advantage is 1:4 or 4:1, the pinion will have one quarter the number of teeth as the gear.

24. **d) It is impossible to tell from this information**. Though it is tempting to say object 2 weighs more, this hydraulic system gives the force applied to the piston on the right a mechanical advantage, so object 2 could actually weigh the same or less than object 1 and still push object 1 upward. Remember, the weight of object 1 is spread over a greater area, causing less pressure, while the weight of object 2 is concentrated on a smaller area and causes greater pressure.

25. **d) 540 degrees**. It is important to note first that the lower pulley attached to the crankshaft is rotating clockwise. This means that the camshaft is also rotating clockwise. The camshaft must turn 270 degrees (3/4 turn) before the cam is aligned with the valve stem so it is pushed as far down as it will go. The crankshaft turns at twice the speed of the camshaft, so it must rotate twice as far, 540 degrees (1.5 turns).

26. **b) The spring will extend**. This is a class three lever, where the weight is the load and the spring is the effort. If the weight is moved to the left, the load's torque arm is shortened and the weight has less leverage. This means the spring does not have to apply as much force and therefore expands.

27. **c) Inclined plane**. The axe in the picture is a wedge. Remember that a wedge is a type of inclined plane.

28. **d) 4**. The mechanical advantage of the lever is the length of the input arm divided by the length of the output arm (d_{in}/d_{out}), but the two lengths must be in the same units first. The input arm is two feet or 24 inches and the output arm is 6 inches, which is half a foot. Either way, 24/6 = 2/.5 = 4

29. d) None of the above. Normally, it is only necessary to consider the input and output gears. However, in this gear train three consecutive gears are touching, which means that this gear train will not be able to turn since two consecutive gears will turn in the opposite direction.

30. b) The pulley train on the right. The pulley system has a greater mechanical advantage. For the gear train, the mechanical advantage can be found from the diameters of the input and output gears. The pulley system has two steps, both of which are torque-multipliers. The pulley system's input and output pulleys may have the same diameter of the gear train's input and output gears, but the wheel and axle in the pulley system give it a greater mechanical advantage.

Chapter 5: Assembling Objects

The Assembling Objects section is a bit different from the rest - you cannot "study" for it like you do for math, reading, or science. It calls for a set of skills that some people just "get." In fact, many recruiters will advise that you not even complete this section; but since it won't hurt to do so, we'll include a brief review.

There is a 16 minute time limit to answer 16 questions of which there are two types. The first will require you to match up points on objects as indicated. The second is similar to a puzzle: connect various shapes together to form one cohesive unit. The easiest way to solve both of these types of questions is through process of elimination. Look at those answer choices which cannot possibly be correct. Perhaps they do not have the same points as those indicated in the question, or maybe they have different shapes than those listed in the question. Eliminate those, and you'll only have one or two selections that can be correct. From there, you can reason your way to the right answer!

The best way to understand these concepts is through practice - but don't spend too much time on this section. The others are a much higher priority.

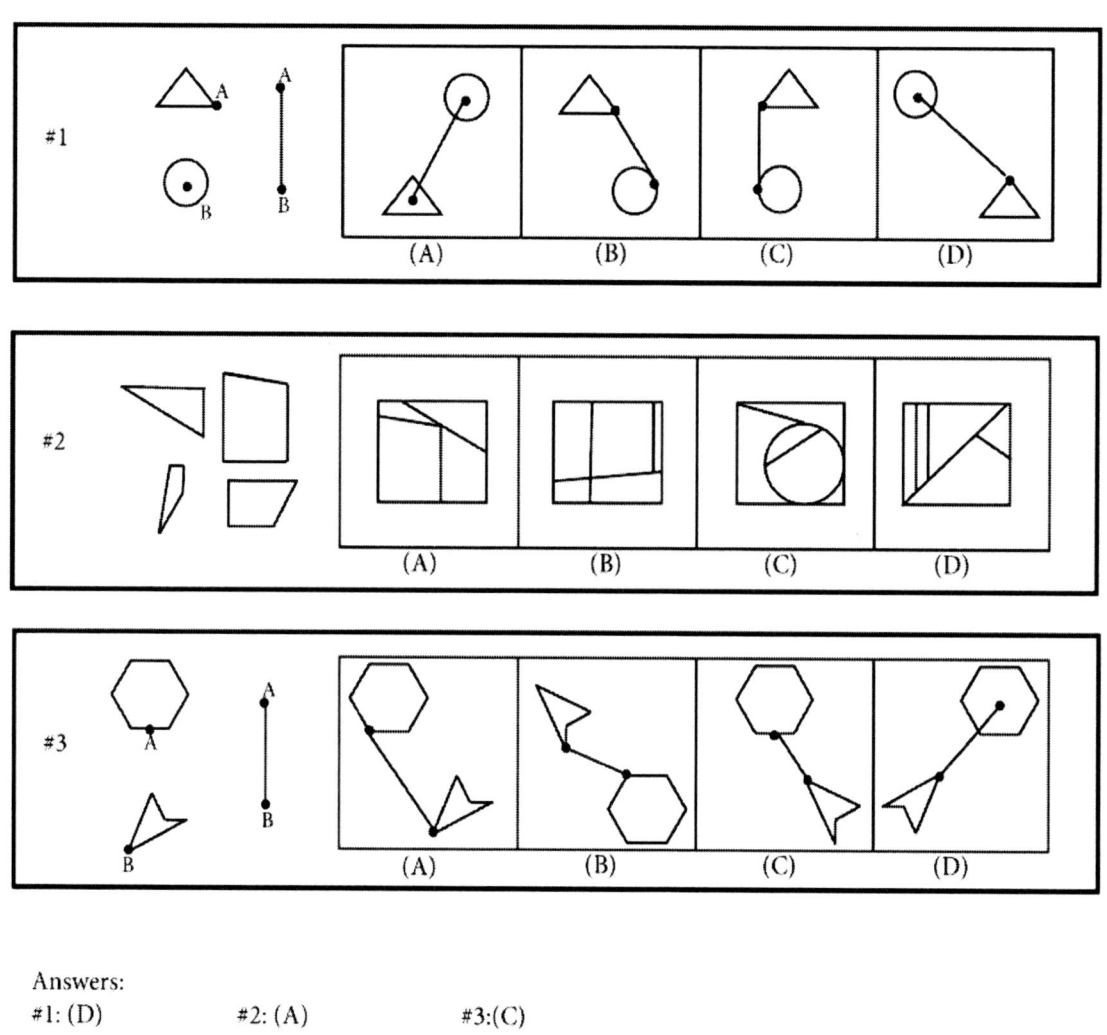

Answers:

#1: (D) #2: (A) #3:(C)

Chapter 6: Word Knowledge

The Word Knowledge subtest is one of the four core AFQT tests used to determine your eligibility to enlist. The military considers clear and concise communication so important that it is taught and graded at all levels of leadership training. If you are planning a military career, you will be tested on your verbal skills as you move through the ranks.

Your score is also used to determine if you qualify for many specialized jobs, such as military security and intelligence, air traffic control, medical, and administrative positions. The good news is that most individuals have been exposed to all of the vocabulary words used on the subtest by the time they have reached the tenth grade. This doesn't mean that you are going to recognize every single word. It *does* mean, however, that you won't be expected to know advanced Latin or graduate science terminology.

This section of the test gives you 35 questions to answer in 11 minutes. This may seem like a disproportionate amount of time – it comes out to about 18 seconds per question – but don't worry! We're going to arm you with all of the knowledge you'll need in order to work quickly and efficiently through this section.

You will encounter two types of questions on the ASVAB Word Knowledge subtest:

1. To define the word without context:

   Garner most nearly means:
   a) Create.
   b) Propose.
   c) Demonstrate.
   d) Gather.

2. To define the word within the context:

   The chemicals in the water were benign.
   a) Natural.
   b) Undisturbed.
   c) Harmless.
   d) Dangerous.

(The correct answers are: **d) Gather** and **c) Harmless**)

VOCABULARY BASIC TRAINING

The first step in getting ready for this section of the ASVAB consists of reviewing the basic techniques used to determine the meanings of words you are not familiar with. The good news is that you have been using various degrees of these techniques since you first began to speak. Sharpening these skills will help you with the paragraph comprehension subtest.

Following each section you will find a practice drill. Use your scores on these to determine if you need to study a particular subject matter further. At the end of each section, you will find a Practice Drill to test your Knowledge.

The questions found on the practice drills are not given in the two formats found on the Word Knowledge subtest; rather they are designed to <u>reinforce</u> the skills needed to score well on the Word Knowledge subtest.

Context Clues

The most fundamental vocabulary skill is using the context of a word to determine its meaning. The military considers this ability of considerable importance, and it is one of the two styles of questions on this subtest. Your ability to observe sentences closely is extremely useful when it comes to understanding new vocabulary words.

Types of Context
There are two different types of context that can help you understand the meaning of unfamiliar words: **sentence context** and **situational context**. Regardless of which context is present, these types of questions are not really testing your knowledge of vocabulary; they are testing your ability to comprehend the meaning of a word through its usage.

Situational context is the basis of the Paragraph Comprehension subtest and will be discussed in chapter two.

Sentence context occurs in the sentence containing the vocabulary word. To figure out words using sentence context clues, you should first determine the most important words in the sentence.

For Example: I had a hard time reading her <u>illegible</u> handwriting.
a) Neat.
b) Unsafe.
c) Sloppy.
d) Educated.

Already, you know that this sentence is discussing something that is hard to read. Look at the word that **illegible** is describing: **handwriting**. Based on context clues, you can tell that illegible means that her handwriting is hard to read.

Next, look at the choices. Choice **a) Neat** is obviously wrong, because neat handwriting would not be difficult to read. Choice **b) Unsafe** and **d) Educated** don't make sense. Therefore, choice **c) Sloppy** is the best answer choice.

216

Types of Clues
There are four types of clues that can help you understand the context, which in turn helps you define the word. They are **restatement, positive/negative, contrast,** and **specific detail.**

Restatement clues occur when the definition of the word is clearly stated in the sentence.

> For Example: The dog was <u>dauntless</u> in the face of danger, braving the fire to save the girl.
> a) Difficult.
> b) Fearless.
> c) Imaginative.
> d) Pleasant.

Demonstrating **bravery** in the face of danger would be **fearless,** choice **b)**. In this case, the context clues tell you exactly what the word means.

Positive/negative clues can tell you whether a word has a positive or negative meaning.

> For Example: The magazine gave a great review of the fashion show, stating the clothing was **sublime**.
> a) Horrible.
> b) Exotic.
> c) Bland
> d) Gorgeous.

The sentence tells us that the author liked the clothing enough to write a **great** review, so you know that the best answer choice is going to be a positive word. Therefore, you can immediately rule out choices **a)** and **c)** because they are negative words. **Exotic** is a neutral word; alone, it doesn't inspire a **great** review. The most positive word is gorgeous, which makes choice **d) Gorgeous** the best answer.

The following sentence uses both restatement and positive/negative clues:

"Janet suddenly found herself <u>destitute</u>, so poor she could barely afford to eat."

The second part of the sentence clearly indicates that destitute is a negative word; it also restates the meaning: very poor.

Contrast clues include the opposite meaning of a word. Words like **but, on the other hand,** and **however** are tip-offs that a sentence contains a contrast clue.

> For Example: Beth did not spend any time preparing for the test, but Tyron kept a <u>rigorous</u> study schedule.
> a) Strict.
> b) Loose.
> c) Boring.
> d) Strange.

In this case, the word **but** tells us that Tyron studied in a different way than Beth. If Beth did not study very hard, then Tyron did study hard for the test. The best answer here, therefore, is choice **a) Strict**.

Specific detail clues give a precise detail that can help you understand the meaning of the word.

For Example: The box was heavier than he expected and it began to become <u>cumbersome</u>.
- a) Impossible.
- b) Burdensome.
- c) Obligated.
- d) Easier.

Start by looking at the specific details of the sentence. Choice **d)** can be eliminated right away because it is doubtful it would become **easier** to carry something that is **heavier**. There are also no clues in the sentence to indicate he was **obligated** to carry the box, so choice **c)** can also be disregarded. The sentence specifics, however, do tell you that the package was cumbersome because it was heavy to carry; something heavy to carry is a burden, which is **burdensome**, choice **b)**.

It is important to remember that more than one of these clues can be present in the same sentence. The more there are, the easier it will be to determine the meaning of the word, so look for them.

Denotation and Connotation

As you know, many English words have more than one meaning. For example, the word **quack** has two distinct definitions: the sound a duck makes; and a person who publicly pretends to have a skill, knowledge, education, or qualification which they do not possess.

The **denotations** of a word are the dictionary definitions.

The **connotations** of a word are the implied meaning(s) or emotion which the word makes you think.

For Example:

"Sure," Pam said excitedly, "I'd just love to join your club; it sounds so exciting!"

Now, read this sentence:

"Sure," Pam said sarcastically, "I'd just love to join your club; it sounds so exciting!"

Even though the two sentences only differ by one word, they have completely different meanings. The difference, of course, lies in the words "excitedly" and "sarcastically."

Look back to the underlined word – **reinforce** - in the second paragraph of page 13. Can you think of several words that could be used and the sentence have the same meaning?

218

Practice Drill: Vocabulary Basic Training

Use context clues to determine the meaning of each underlined word.

1. His story didn't seem very <u>realistic</u>; even though it was a documentary.
   a) Believable.
   b) Humorous.
   c) Poetic.
   d) Exciting.

2. Listening to music too loudly, especially through headphones, can <u>impair</u> your hearing.
   a) Damage.
   b) Heighten.
   c) Use.
   d) Ensure.

3. Kelly's game happened to <u>coincide</u> with the Sue's recital.
   a) Happen before.
   b) Occur at the same time.
   c) Occur afterward.
   d) Not happen.

4. The weather has been very extreme lately; thankfully, today it's much more <u>temperate</u>.
   a) Troubling.
   b) Beautiful.
   c) Cold.
   d) Moderate.

5. He knew he couldn't win the race after falling off his bike, so he had to <u>concede</u>.
   a) Continue.
   b) Give up.
   c) Challenge.
   d) Be thankful.

6. The editor, preferring a more <u>terse</u> writing style, cut 30% of the words from the article.
   a) Elegant.
   b) Factual.
   c) Descriptive.
   d) Concise.

7. Victor Frankenstein spent the last years of his life chasing his <u>elusive</u> monster, which was always one step ahead.
   a) Unable to be compared.
   b) Unable to be captured.
   c) Unable to be forgotten.
   d) Unable to be avoided.

8. Certain <u>passages</u> were taken from the book for the purpose of illustration.
   a) Excerpts.
   b) Contents.
   c) Paragraphs.
   d) Tables.

9. The investigator searched among the <u>ruins</u> for the cause of the fire.
   a) Terminal.
   b) Foundation.
   c) Rubble.
   d) Establishment.

10. To make her novels more engaging, Cynthia was known to <u>embellish</u> her writing with fictitious details.
   a) Add to.
   b) Detract.
   c) Isolate.
   d) Disavow.

11. Robert's well-timed joke served to <u>diffuse</u> the tension in the room and the party continued happily.
   a) Refuse.
   b) Intensify.
   c) Create.
   d) Soften.

12. I had a difficult time understanding the book because the author kept <u>digressing</u> to unrelated topics.
   a) Deviating, straying.
   b) Regressing, reverting.
   c) Changing the tone.
   d) Expressing concisely.

13. The senator <u>evaded</u> almost every question.
   a) Avoided.
   b) Answered indirectly.
   c) Refused to answer directly.
   d) Deceived.

14. Sammie hasn't come out of her room all afternoon, but I would <u>surmise</u> that it is because she is upset about not being able to go to the mall.
   a) Confirm.
   b) Surprise.
   c) Believe.
   d) Guess.

15. The details can be worked out later; what's important is that the company follows the <u>crux</u> of the argument, which is that everyone be paid equally.
- a) Overall tone.
- b) Specific fact.
- c) Main point.
- d) Logic, reasoning.

Use context clues to choose the best word to complete the sentence.

16. Mr. Collins _____ tomatoes so vehemently that he felt ill just smelling them.
- a) Resented.
- b) Disliked.
- c) Detested.
- d) Hated.

17. We were rolling on the ground with laughter during the _____ new movie.
- a) Comical.
- b) Humorous.
- c) Amusing.
- d) Hilarious.

18. Tina's parents made us feel right at home during our visit to their house with their generous _____.
- a) Unselfishness.
- b) Politeness.
- c) Hospitality.
- d) Charity.

19. Although his mother was not happy that he broke the window, she was pleased that he was _____ about it.
- a) Honest.
- b) Trustworthy.
- c) Authentic.
- d) Decent.

20. The soldiers _____ to their feet immediately when then officer walked into the room.
- a) Stood.
- b) Leapt.
- c) Rose.
- d) Skipped.

Practice Drill: Vocabulary Basic Training – Answers

1. **a) Believable**. Realistic means accurate, truthful, and believable.

2. **a) Damage**. This is the only logical choice.

3. **b) Occur at the same time**. According to information in the sentence, the game was scheduled at the same time as the recital.

4. **d) Moderate**. The context says that the weather has been "extreme." It does not say if the weather has been extremely hot or cold; therefore, choices **b) Beautiful** and **c) Cold** can be ruled out. The sentence also indicates a change from negative to positive making moderate the best choice.

5. **b) Give up**. The speaker of the sentence knows they cannot win, so choice **b)** is the best choice.

6. **d) Concise**. Terse means concise, using no unnecessary words. The main clue is that the editor cut words from the article, reducing its wordiness.

7. **b) Unable to be captured**. Elusive means evasive, difficult to capture.

8. **a) Excerpt**. An excerpt is a passage or quote from a book, article, or other publication

9. **c) Rubble** is synonymous with ruin.

10. **a) Add to**. To embellish is to add details to a story to make it more appealing.

11. **d) Soften**. The clues *tension* and *continue happily* tell you that **d)** is the best choice

12. **a) To deviate, stray**. To digress means to deviate; to stray from the main subject in writing or speaking.

13. **a) To avoid**. To evade means to avoid by cleverness. The senator avoids answering the question by changing the subject.

14. **d) Guess**. The speaker is guessing why Samantha is upset based on circumstances; she has not actually given a reason.

15. **c) Main point**. Crux means the central or main point, especially of a problem. The main context clue is that the speaker isn't concerned with the details but is focused on getting agreement on the main point.

16. **c) Detested**. The knowledge that Mr. Collins feels ill just smelling tomatoes suggests that his hatred for tomatoes is intense; therefore, the best choice will be the most negative. To **dislike** tomatoes – choice **b)** – is the most neutral word, so this choice can be ruled out. **Resented** is a word that generally applies to people or their actions, ruling out choice **a)**. Given the choice between **c)** and **d)**, the most negative is **c) Detested**.

17. d) Hilarious. The movie must be extremely funny for the audience to have this sort of reaction, and, while all of the answer choices are synonyms for funny, the only one that means extremely funny is choice **d) Hilarious.**

18. c) Hospitality. Although all four choices describe different types of kindness, **unselfishness** – choice **a)** – can be ruled out because it has the same basic meaning as the adjective, generous. Choice **d) Charity** is a kindness usually associated with those less fortunate; since nothing in the context indicates this type of relationship, this choice can also be eliminated. Left with choices **b) Politeness** and **c) Hospitality**, hospitality best describes the kindness of welcoming someone into your home.

19. a) Honest. Again we have a case in which all of the word choices are synonyms for the word honest. In this case, the most neutral word is the best choice. Choice **b) Trustworthy, c) Authentic,** and **d) Decent** do not make as much sense as the most basic synonym, **honest.**

20. b) Leapt. The word immediately is the main clue. **a) Stood** and **c) Rose** are neutral words that do not convey a sense of urgency. Choice **b) Leapt** is the only word that implies the immediacy demanded by the sentence context.

ROOTS, PREFIXES, and SUFFIXES

Word Knowledge questions will also require you to determine the meaning of a word without sentence context. Although you are not expected to know every word in the English language, you are expected to have the ability to use deductive reasoning to find the choice that is the best match for the word in question, which is why we are going to explain how to break a word into its parts of meaning

prefix – root – suffix

One trick in dividing a word into its parts is to first divide the word into its **syllables**. To show how syllables can help you find roots and affixes, we'll use the word **descendant,** which means one who comes from an ancestor. Start by dividing the word into its individual syllables; this word has three: **de-scend-ant**. The next step is to look at the beginning and end of the word, and then determine if these syllables are prefixes, suffixes, or possible roots. You can then use the meanings of each part to guide you in defining the word. When you divide words into their specific parts, they do not always add up to an exact definition, but you will see a relationship between their parts.

Note: This trick won't always work in every situation, because not all prefixes, roots, and suffixes have only one syllable. For example, take the word **monosyllabic** (which ironically means "one syllable"). There are five syllables in that word, but only three parts. The prefix is "mono," meaning "one." The root "syllab" refers to "syllable," while the suffix "ic" means "pertaining to." Therefore, we have one very long word which means "pertaining to one syllable."

The more familiar you become with these fundamental word parts, the easier it will be to define unfamiliar words. Although the words found on the Word Knowledge subtest are considered vocabulary words learned by the tenth grade level of high school, some are still less likely to be found in an individual's everyday vocabulary. The root and affixes list in this chapter uses more common words as examples to help you learn them more easily. Don't forget that you use word roots and affixes every day, without even realizing it. Don't feel intimidated by the long list of roots and affixes (prefixes and suffixes) at the end of this chapter, because you already know and use them every time you communicate with some else, verbally and in writing. If you take the time to read through the list just once a day for two weeks, you will be able to retain most of them and understand a high number of initially unfamiliar words.

Roots

Roots are the building blocks of all words. Every word is either a root itself or has a root. Just as a plant cannot grow without roots, neither can vocabulary, because a word must have a root to give it meaning.

> For Example: The test instructions were **unclear.**

The root is what is left when you strip away all the prefixes and suffixes from a word. In this case, take away the prefix "un-", and you have the root **clear**.

Roots are not always recognizable words, because they generally come from Latin or Greek words, such as **nat**, a Latin root meaning **born**. The word native, which means a person born of a referenced placed, comes from this root, so does the word prenatal, meaning before birth. Yet, if you used the prefix **nat** instead of born, just on its own, no one would know what you were talking about.

Words can also have more than one root. For example, the word **omnipotent** means all powerful. Omnipotent is a combination of the roots **omni-**, meaning all or every, and **-potent**, meaning power or strength. In this case, **omni** cannot be used on its own as a single word, but **potent** can.

Again, it is important to keep in mind that roots do not always match the exact definitions of words and they can have several different spellings, but breaking a word into its parts is still one of the best ways to determine its meaning.

Prefixes and Suffixes

Prefixes are syllables added to the beginning of a word and suffixes are syllables added to the end of the word. Both carry assigned meanings. The common name for prefixes and suffixes is **affixes**. Affixes do not have to be attached directly to a root and a word can often have more than one prefix and/or suffix. Prefixes and suffixes can be attached to a word to completely change the word's meaning or to enhance the word's original meaning. Although they don't mean much to us on their own, when attached to other words affixes can make a world of difference.

We can use the word **prefix** as an example:

Fix means to place something securely.
Pre means before.
Prefix means to place something before or in front.

An example of a suffix:

Femin is a root. It means female, woman.
-ism means act, practice or process.
Feminism is the defining and establishing of equal political, economic, and social rights for women.

Unlike prefixes, **suffixes** can be used to change a word's part of speech.

For example, take a look at these sentences:

Randy raced to the finish line.
Shana's costume was very racy.

In the first sentence, raced is a verb. In the second sentence, racy is an adjective. By changing the suffix from **-ed** to **-y**, the word race changes from a verb into an adjective, which has an entirely different meaning.

Although you cannot determine the meaning of a word by a prefix or suffix alone, you *can* use your knowledge of what root words mean to eliminate answer choices; indicating if the word is positive or negative can give you a partial meaning of the word.

Practice Drill: Roots, Prefixes, and Suffixes

Try to find the root in each of the underlined words.

1. The bridge was out, so the river was <u>impassable</u>.
    - a) Im-
    - b) -pass-
    - c) -a-
    - d) –able

2. I am usually on time, but my husband is <u>chronically</u> late.
    - a) Chron-
    - b) -chronical-
    - c) -ally-
    - d) -ic

3. The only way to succeed is by <u>striving</u> to do your best.
    - a) Str-
    - a) Striv-
    - b) Strive-
    - c) -ing

4. We drifted along lazily on the <u>tranquil</u> river.
    - a) Tra-
    - b) -qui-
    - c) Tranq-
    - d) -uil

5. A <u>pediatrician</u> is a doctor who takes care of children.
    - a) Ped-
    - b) -ia-
    - c) -tri-
    - d) -cian

Choose the word that shares the same root as the given word.

6. Audible
    - a) Auditorium.
    - b) Because.
    - c) Dribble.
    - d) Bagel.

7. Nominate
    - a) Eaten.
    - b) Minute.
    - c) Hated.
    - d) Synonym.

8. Disappoint
    a) Disappear.
    b) Appointment.
    c) Interest.
    d) Potato.

9. Dilute
    a) Flute.
    b) Dictate.
    c) Pollute.
    d) Hesitate.

10. Sympathy
    a) System.
    b) Empathy.
    c) Pattern.
    d) Rhythm.

11. Science
    a) Conscious.
    b) Once.
    c) Alien.
    d) Parasite.

12. Incline
    a) Recline.
    b) Independent.
    c) Cluster.
    d) Twine.

For each question below, use the Latin word root to determine underlined word's meaning.

13. An underline{amiable} person is:
    a) Talkative, loud.
    b) Truthful, honest.
    c) Highly educated.
    d) Friendly, good-natured.

14. A lucid argument:
    a) Is very clear and intelligible.
    b) Is loosely held together, tenuous.
    c) Frequently digresses.
    d) Errs repeatedly in its logic.

15. A complacent person:
    a) Frequently makes mistakes, but does not accept responsibility.
    b) Likes to pick fights.
    c) Is contented to a fault, self-satisfied.
    d) Is known to tell lies, embellish the truth.

16. To <u>exacerbate</u> a problem means:
   a) To solve it.
   b) To analyze it.
   c) To lessen it.
   d) To worsen it.

17. To measure the <u>veracity</u> of something is to measure its:
   a) Value or worth.
   b) Truthfulness.
   c) Weight.
   d) Life force.

18. Something that is <u>eloquent</u> is:
   a) Dull, trite, hackneyed.
   b) Expressed in a powerful and effective manner.
   c) Very old, antiquated.
   d) Equally divided or apportioned.

19. To <u>indict</u> someone is to:
   a) Pick a fight with that person.
   b) Stop or block that person from doing something.
   c) Charge that person with a crime.
   d) Love that person dearly.

20. A <u>quiescent</u> place is:
   a) Very isolated.
   b) Tumultuous, chaotic.
   c) Sacred.
   d) Still, at rest.

21. An individual with <u>equanimity</u>:
   a) Has a violent temper.
   b) Is very stubborn.
   c) Enjoys the company of others.
   d) Is even-tempered and composed.

What are the affixes in each word?

22. Disease
   a) Dis-
   b) -ise-
   c) -eas-
   d) -ase

23. Uncomfortable
   a) Un-
   b) Un-, -com-
   c) -fort-
   d) Un-, -able

24. Disrespected
   a) Re-, -spect, -ed
   b) Dis-, -ed
   c) Dis-, re-, -ed
   d) Respect-, -ed

25. Impressive
   a) Im-, -ive
   b) -ive
   c) Press-, -ive
   d) Impre-, -ive

26. Predated
   a) Pre-
   b) Pre-, -d
   c) Pre-, -ed
   d) –d

Using your knowledge of prefixes and root words, try to determine the following words' meanings.

27. To take <u>precaution</u> is to:
   a) Prepare before doing something.
   b) Remember something that happened earlier.
   c) Become aware of something for the first time.
   d) Try to do something again.

28. To <u>reorder</u> a list is to:
   a) Use the same order again.
   b) Put the list in a new order.
   c) Get rid of the list.
   d) Find the list.

29. An <u>antidote</u> to a disease is:
   a) Something that is part of the disease.
   b) Something that works against the disease.
   c) Something that makes the disease worse.
   d) Something that has nothing to do with the disease.

30. Someone who is <u>multiethnic</u>:
   a) Likes only certain kinds of people.
   b) Lives in the land of his or her birth.
   c) Is from a different country.
   d) Has many different ethnicities.

31. Someone who is <u>misinformed</u> has been:
   a) Taught something new.
   b) Told the truth.
   c) Forgotten.
   d) Given incorrect information.

Choose the best answer to each question. (Remember you are looking for the closest meaning.)

32. Exorbitant means:
- a) Belonging to a group.
- b) To orbit.
- c) Beneath conscious awareness.
- d) Far beyond what is normal or reasonable.

33. Denunciation means:
- a) To denounce or openly condemn.
- b) Critical, of or like a condemnation.
- c) One who denounces or openly condemns another.
- d) The act of denouncing or openly condemning.

34. Metamorphosis means:
- a) To transform.
- b) One who has changed.
- c) A transformation.
- d) Tending to change frequently.

35. To reconcile means:
- a) To reestablish a close relationship between.
- b) To move away from.
- c) To undermine.
- d) To surpass or outdo.

36. Didactic means:
- a) A teacher or instructor.
- b) Intended to instruct, moralizing.
- c) To preach or moralize.
- d) The process of instructing.

37. Unilateral means:
- a) To multiply.
- b) Understated.
- c) Literal.
- d) One-sided.

38. Subordinate means:
- a) Under someone else's authority or control.
- b) Organized according to rank; hierarchical.
- c) Something ordinary or average, without distinction.
- d) Repeated frequently to aid memorization.

39. Incisive means:
- a) Insight.
- b) Worthy of consideration.
- c) Penetrating.
- d) To act forcefully.

40. <u>Intermittent</u> means:
    a) Badly handled.
    b) Occurring at intervals
    c) Greatly varied.
    d) A number between one and ten.

41. <u>Miscreant</u> means:
    a) Someone who is unconventional.
    b) Someone who lacks creativity.
    c) A very naive person.
    d) An evil person or villain.

Practice Drill: Roots, Prefixes, and Suffixes

1. **b) –pass-**

2. **a) Chron-**

3. **c) Strive-**

4. **b) –qui-.** *Quies* is a Latin root meaning rest or quiet.

5. **a) Ped-.** *Ped* is a Latin root meaning child or education. You might recognize that the suffix **-cian** refers to what someone does, such as physician or beautician. The suffix **-iatr** relates to doctors, as you can see in the words psychiatry and podiatry. Both suffixes support the root of the word.

6. **a) Auditorium.** From the Latin root **aud,** meaning hearing or listening.

7. **d) Synonym.** The words nominate and synonym share the root, **nom,** meaning name. Remember, roots are not necessarily going to be in the same position in other words.

8. **b) Appointment.** Greek root **poie,** meaning to make.

9. **c) Pollute.** Both dilute and pollute come from the root **lut,** meaning to wash.

10. **b) Empathy.** The words sympathy and empathy come from the Greek root **path,** meaning feeling, suffering, or disease.

11. **a) Conscious.** Science and conscious share the Latin root **sci,** which means to know.

12. **a) Recline.** Incline and recline both share the Greek root *clin,* meaning to lean toward or bend.

13. **d).** The root **am** means love. Amiable means friendly, agreeable, good natured, likeable, or pleasing.

14. **a).** The root **luc/lum/lus** means light. Lucid means very clear, easy to understand, intelligible.

15. **c).** The root **plac** means to please. Complacent means contented to a fault; self-satisfied.

16. **d).** The root **ac** means sharp, bitter. Exacerbate is to increase the severity, violence, or bitterness of.

17. b). The root **ver** means truth. Veracity means truth or truthfulness.

18. b). The root **loc/log/loqu** means word or speech. Eloquent means expressed in a powerful, fluent, and persuasive manner.

19. c). The root **dic/dict/dit** means to say, tell, or use words. To indict means to formally accuse of or charge with a crime.

20. d). The root **qui** means quiet. Quiescent means inactive, quiet, or at rest.

21. d). The root **equ** means equal or even. Equanimity means calmness of temperament, even-temperedness, or patience and composure, especially under stress.

22. a) Dis-. The prefix **dis-** means away from, deprive of, reversal, or not. If someone has a **disease** they are not well.

23. d) Un-, -able. The prefix **un-** means not. The suffix **-able** means ability or worthy of. **Uncomfortable** means not able to be in a state of comfort.

24. c) Dis-, re-, -ed. The prefix **dis-** means away from, reversal, or not. The prefix **re-** means back or again. The suffix **-ed** indicates that the word is in the past tense. **Disrespected** means showed a lack of respect towards.

25. a) Im-, -ive. The prefix **im-** means in, into, or within. The suffix **-ive** means having the nature of. **Impressive** means having the ability inspire an internal feeling of awe.

26. c) Pre-, -ed. The prefix **pre-** means before. The suffix **-ed** indicates that the word is in the past tense. **Predated** means came before the date.

27. a) Prepare before doing something. Pre- means before; **caution** means to be careful or take heed.

28. b) Put the list in a new order. *Re-* means again. In this case, order means organize. Reorder then means to organize the list again or to put the list into a different order.

29. b) Something that works against the disease. The prefix **anti-** means against. An **antidote** is something that works against a disease or a poison.

30. d) Has many different ethnicities. The prefix **multi-** means many. Someone who is **multiethnic** has relatives from many different ethnic groups.

31. d) Given incorrect information. Mis- means opposite, and to be **informed** is to have the correct information.

32. d) Far beyond what is normal or reasonable. The prefix **ex-** means out, out of, away from.

33. a) The act of denouncing or openly condemning. The prefix **de-** means against, the root **nounc** means to state or declare, and the noun suffix **-tion** means the act or state of.

34. c) A transformation. The prefix **meta-** means change, while the root **morph** means shape or form, and the **noun** suffix **-sis** means the process of. **Metamorphosis** means a marked change of form or a transformation.

35. a) Means to reestablish a relationship. The prefix **re-** means back or again and, the root **con** means with. Together they mean back together again or reestablishing a relationship.

36. b) Intended to instruct or moralize. The adjective suffix **-ic** means pertaining or relating to, having the quality of. Only choices **b)** and **d)** define a quality, and choice **d)** would require an additional suffix.

37. d) One-sided. The prefix **uni-** means one.

38. a) Under someone else's authority or control. The prefix **sub-** means under, beneath or below.

39. c) Penetrating. The adjective suffix **-ive** means having the nature of.

40. b) Occurring at intervals. The prefix **inter-** means between or among.

41. d) An evil person or villain. The prefix **mis-** means bad, evil, or wrong. The suffix **–ant** means an agent or something that performs the action.

SYNONYMS and ANTONYMS

Synonyms are groups of words that mean the same, or almost the same, thing as each other. The word synonym comes from the Greek roots **syn-,** meaning same, and **-nym,** meaning name. **Hard, difficult, challenging,** and **arduous** are synonyms of one another.

Antonyms are sets of words that have opposite, or nearly opposite, meanings of one another. The word antonym comes from the Greek roots **ant-,** meaning opposing, and **–nym** (name). **Hard** and **easy** are antonyms.

Synonyms do not always have exactly the same meanings, and antonyms are not always exact opposites. For example, scalding is an adjective that means burning. Boiling water can be described as scalding or as hot. **Hot** and **scalding** are considered synonyms, even though the two words do not mean exactly the same thing; something that is scalding is considered to be extremely hot.

In the same manner, antonyms are not always exact opposites. **Cold** and **freezing** are both antonyms of scalding. Although freezing is closer to being an exact opposite of scalding, cold is still considered an antonym. Antonyms can often be recognized by their prefixes and suffixes.

Here are rules that apply to prefixes and suffixes of antonyms:

- **Many antonyms can be created simply by adding prefixes.** Certain prefixes, such as *a-, de-, non-,* and *un-,* can be added to words to turn them into antonyms. **Atypical** is an antonym of **typical,** and **nonjudgmental** is an antonym of **judgmental.**

- **Some prefixes and suffixes are antonyms of one another.** The prefixes **ex-** (out of) and **in-/il-/im-/ir-** (into) are antonyms, and are demonstrated in the antonym pair **exhale/inhale.** Other prefix pairs that indicate antonyms include **pre-/post-, sub-/super-,** and **over-/under-.** The suffixes **-less,** meaning without, and **-ful,** meaning full of, often indicate that words are antonyms as well. For example: **meaningless** and **meaningful** are antonyms.

Practice Drill: Synonyms and Antonyms

In each sentence or group of sentences, choose whether the underlined words are synonyms, antonyms, or neither.

1. I think Mrs. Robinson is <u>honest</u>, but Jordan thinks she's <u>treacherous</u>.

2. Marley is making a <u>stew</u> for the class potluck, while Tara is cooking a <u>roast</u>.

3. The doctors agreed that the disease was not <u>terminal</u>. This came as welcome news to the man's family, who feared it might be <u>life-threatening</u>.

4. My grandfather <u>built</u> his house on the side of a mountain. He <u>erected</u> the house with his own two hands in the 1960s.

5. I always assumed Lisa was <u>sociable</u>; at the dance, however, she seemed rather <u>bashful</u>.

6. Many animals prey on rabbits, so rabbits tend to move <u>cautiously</u>. Lions do not have any natural predators, so they walk very <u>boldly</u>.

7. Our basement was full of old <u>junk</u>, so we gathered up all the <u>trash</u> and put it in bags.

8. Most people in the class were <u>excited</u> to go on a field trip, but Janet was <u>unenthusiastic</u>.

9. Terrah likes <u>English</u> class the most, while Durrell prefers <u>Spanish</u>.

10. The villagers ran for <u>safety</u> during the <u>dangerous</u> storm.

Choose the best answer choice for the following questions.

11. <u>Awe</u> is most dissimilar to:
    a) Contempt.
    b) Reverence.
    c) Valor.
    d) Distortion.

12. <u>Intricate</u> is most similar to:
    a) Delicate.
    b) Costly.
    c) Prim.
    d) Complex.

13. <u>Skeptic</u> is most dissimilar to:
    a) Innovator.
    b) Friend.
    c) Politician.
    d) Believer.

14. <u>Hypothetical</u> is most dissimilar to:
    a) Uncritical.
    b) Actual.
    c) Specific.
    d) Imaginary.

15. <u>Enhance</u> is most dissimilar to:
    a) Diminish.
    b) Improve.
    c) Digress.
    d) Deprive.

16. <u>Manipulate</u> is most similar to:
    a) Simplify.
    b) Deplete.
    c) Nurture.
    d) Handle.

17. <u>Subjective</u> is most dissimilar to:
   a) Invective.
   b) Objectionable.
   c) Unbiased.
   d) Obedient.

18. <u>Succinct</u> is most dissimilar to:
   a) Distinct.
   b) Laconic.
   c) Feeble.
   d) Verbose.

19. <u>Enthusiastic</u> is most similar to:
   a) Adamant.
   b) Available.
   c) Cheerful.
   d) Eager.

20. <u>Adequate</u> is most similar to:
   a) Sufficient.
   b) Mediocre.
   c) Proficient.
   d) Average.

21. <u>Uniform</u> is most dissimilar to:
   a) Dissembling.
   b) Diverse.
   c) Bizarre.
   d) Slovenly.

22. <u>Ecstatic</u> is most similar to:
   a) Inconsistent.
   b) Positive.
   c) Wild.
   d) Thrilled.

Practice Drill: Synonyms and Antonyms

1. **Antonyms**.

2. **Neither**.

3. **Synonyms**.

4. **Synonyms**.

5. **Antonyms**.

6. **Antonyms**.

7. **Synonyms**.

8. **Antonyms**.

9. **Neither**.

10. **Neither**.

11. **a) Contempt**. To be in **awe** of something is to admire it; to have **contempt** for something is to consider it worthless.

12. **d) Complex**. Intricate means having many elaborately arranged elements; **complex** means complicated or involved.

13. **d) Believer**. A **skeptic** is someone who doubts; a **believer** is one who thinks something is true.

14. **b) Actual**. To be **hypothetical** is to be contingent on being tested; to be **actual** is to exist in fact.

15. **a) Diminish**. To **enhance** is to increase; to **diminish** is to decrease.

16. **d) Handle**. To **manipulate** is to manage or to **handle** in a governing manner.

17. **c) Unbiased**. To be **subjective** is to be influenced by one's own emotions or beliefs without regard to evidence presented; to be **unbiased** is to be objective or impartial.

18. **d) Verbose**. To be **succinct** is to be brief and to the point; to be **verbose** is to use excessive words, to be wordy.

19. **d) Eager**. Enthusiastic bother mean showing great earnestness.

20. **a) Sufficient**. If something is **adequate**, it is considered to be **sufficient**.

21. **b) Diverse**. To be **uniform** is to be consistent or the same as others; to be **diverse** is to have variety.

22. **d) Thrilled**. A person who is **ecstatic** is delighted or **thrilled**.

REVIEW

So far, you have learned that context clues are words within the sentence that help convey the meaning of the word you are looking for. There are two different kinds of context: sentence context and situational context.

> **Sentence context** occurs immediately in the sentence surrounding the vocabulary word. The first thing you should do when looking for sentence context clues is determine the most significant words in the sentence and derive their meanings. Next, look at the answer choices and choose the one that makes the most sense in the sentence, considering those words.

> **Situational context** is context that comes from understanding the situation in which a word or phrase occurs.

There are four types of clues:

> **Restatement** clues are clues in which the word is openly defined.

> **Positive/negative** clues tell you whether the word has a positive or negative meaning.

> **Contrast** clues include the opposite meaning of a word.

> **Specific Detail** clues give details about the word, though not its exact meaning.

These four types of clues are often used in combination.

Remember that roots are the basic unit of meaning in words. When you read a word that is unfamiliar to you, divide the word into syllables and look for the root by removing any prefixes and suffixes.

You have also learned that prefixes and suffixes are known collectively as **affixes**. Although affixes are not words by themselves, they are added to roots or words to change the meaning of roots or change a word's part of speech. **Prefixes** that change or enhance the meanings of words, and are found at the beginning of words. **Suffixes** change or enhance the meanings of words and/or change parts of speech and are found at the end of words.

You have also learned that **synonyms** are words that have the same or almost the same meaning, while **antonyms** are words that have opposite or nearly opposite meanings. Synonyms and antonyms of a word will always share the same part of speech. That is, a synonym or antonym of a verb has to be a verb; a synonym or antonym of an adjective has to be an adjective; and so forth. We also learned that not all words have synonyms or antonyms, and that synonyms do not always have exactly the same meaning, just as antonyms do not have to be exact opposites.

Tips

Look carefully at the context of the sentence itself to avoid bringing your own contextual meaning.

Don't forget to pay attention to the connotation of all the important words in the sentence in addition to the question word.

Look for introductory words and phrases, such as these: unfortunately, however, surprisingly, however, and on the other hand. These words have a strong influence on the question word's meaning.

Remember to look for specific details that provide clues to meaning.

Use words that you are very familiar with as examples when you study word roots. The more familiar the word is to you, the easier it will be for you to remember the meaning of the root word. Use words that create a vivid picture in your imagination.

Be sure to look at all parts of the word as well as the context, if there is any, to determine meaning.

Remember the power of elimination on an exam. Use your knowledge of word roots to eliminate incorrect answers. The more you narrow down your choices, the better your chances of choosing the correct answer.

Roots do not always match the exact definitions of words. Another important thing to keep in mind is that sometimes one root will have several different spellings.

Affixes do not have to be attached directly to a root. A word can often have more than one affix, even more than one prefix or suffix. For instance, the word **unremarkably** has two prefixes (un- and re-) and two suffixes (-able and -ly).

Root or Affix	Meaning	Examples
a, ac, ad, af, ag, al, an, ap, as, at	to, toward, near, in addition to, by	aside, accompany, adjust, aggression, allocate, annihilate, affix, associate, attend, adverb
a-, an-	not, without	apolitical, atheist, anarchy, anonymous, apathy,
ab, abs	away from, off	absolve, abrupt, absent
-able, -ible	Adjective: worth, ability	solvable, incredible
acer, acid, acri	bitter, sour, sharp	acerbic, acidity, acrid, acrimony
act, ag	do, act, drive	active, react, agent, active, agitate
acu	sharp	acute, acupuncture, accurate
-acy, -cy	Noun: state or quality	privacy, infancy, adequacy, intimacy, supremacy
-ade	act, product, sweet drink	blockade, lemonade
aer, aero	air, atmosphere, aviation	aerial, aerosol, aerodrome
ag, agi, ig, act	do, move, go	agent, agenda, agitate, navigate, ambiguous, action
-age	Noun: activity, or result of action	courage, suffrage, shrinkage, tonnage
agri, agro	pertaining to fields or soil	agriculture, agroindustry
-al	Noun: action, result of action	referral, disavowal, disposal, festival
-al, -ial, -ical	Adjective: quality, relation	structural, territorial, categorical
alb, albo	white, without pigment	albino, albeit
ali, allo, alter	other	alias, alibi, alien, alloy, alter, alter ego, altruism
alt	high, deep	altimeter, altitude
am, ami, amor	love, like, liking	amorous, amiable, amicable, enamored
ambi	both	ambidextrous

ambul	to walk	ambulatory, amble, ambulance, somnambulist
-an	Noun: person	artisan, guardian, historian, magician
ana, ano	up, back, again, anew	anode, anagram
-ance, -ence	Noun: action, state, quality or process	resistance, independence, extravagance, fraudulence
-ancy, -ency	Noun: state, quality or capacity	vacancy, agency, truancy, latency
andr, andro	male, characteristics of men	androcentric, android
ang	angular	angle
anim	mind, life, spirit, anger	animal, animate, animosity
ann, annu, enni	yearly	annual, annual, annuity, anniversary, perennial
-ant, -ent	Noun: an agent, something that performs the action	disinfectant, dependent, fragrant
-ant, -ent, -ient	Adjective: kind of agent, indication	important, dependent, convenient
ante	before	anterior, anteroom, antebellum, antedate, antecedent antediluvian
anthrop	man	anthropology, misanthrope, philanthropy
anti, ant	against, opposite	antisocial, antiseptic, antithesis, antibody, antinomies, antifreeze, antipathy
anti, antico	old	antique, antiquated, antiquity
apo, ap, aph	away from, detached, formed	apology, apocalypse
aqu	water	aqueous
-ar, -ary	Adjective: resembling, related to	spectacular, unitary
arch	chief, first, rule	archangel, architect, archaic, monarchy, matriarchy, patriarchy
-ard, -art	Noun: characterized	braggart, drunkard, wizard

aster, astr	star	aster, asterisk, asteroid, astronomy, astronaut
-ate	Noun: state, office, function	candidate, electorate, delegate
-ate	Verb: cause to be	graduate, ameliorate, amputate, colligate
-ate	Adjective: kind of state	inviolate
-ation	Noun: action, resulting state	specialization, aggravation, alternation
auc, aug, aut	to originate, to increase	augment , author, augment, auction
aud, audi, aur, aus	to hear, listen	audience, audio, audible, auditorium, audiovisual, audition, auricular
aug, auc	increase	augur, augment, auction
aut, auto	self	automobile, automatic, automotive, autograph, autonomous, autoimmune
bar	weight, pressure	barometer
be	on, around, over, about, excessively, make, cause, name, affect	berate, bedeck, bespeak, belittle, beleaguer
belli	war	rebellion, belligerent, casus belli, bellicose
bene	good, well, gentle	benefactor, beneficial, benevolent, benediction, beneficiary, benefit
bi, bine	two	biped, bifurcate, biweekly, bivalve, biannual
bibl, bibli, biblio	book	bibliophile, bibliography, Bible
bio, bi	life	biography, biology biome, biosphere
brev	short	abbreviate, brevity, brief
cad, cap, cas, ceiv, cept, capt, cid, cip	to take, to seize, to hold	receive, deceive, capable, capacious, captive, accident, capture, occasion, concept, intercept, forceps, except, reciprocate
cad, cas	to fall	cadaver, cadence, cascade
-cade	procession	motorcade
calor	heat	calorie, caloric, calorimeter

capit, capt	head	decapitate, capital, captain, caption
carn	flesh	carnivorous, incarnate, reincarnation, carnal
cat, cata, cath	down, with	catalogue, category, catheter
caus, caut	burn, heat	caustic, cauldron, cauterize
cause, cuse, cus	cause, motive	because, excuse, accusation
ceas, ced, cede, ceed, cess	to go, to yield, move, go, surrender	succeed, proceed, precede, recede, secession, exceed, succession
cent	hundred	centennial, century, centipede
centr, centri	center	eccentricity, centrifugal, concentric, eccentric
chrom	color	chrome, chromosome, polychrome, chromatic
chron	time	chronology, chronic, chronicle, synchronize
cide, cis, cise	to kill, to cut, cut down	homicide, incision, circumcision, scissors
circum	around	circumnavigate, circumflex, circumstance, circumference, circumvent, circulatory
cit	call, start	incite, citation, cite
civ	citizen	civic, civil, civilian, civilization
clam, claim	cry out	exclamation, clamor, proclamation, reclamation, acclaim
clin	lean, bend	decline, inclination
clud, clus claus	to close, shut	include, exclude, clause, claustrophobia, enclose, exclusive, reclusive, conclude
co, cog, col coll, con, com, cor	with, together	cohesiveness, collaborate, convene, commitment, compress, contemporary, converge, compact, convenient, conjoin, combine, correct
cogn, gnos	to know	recognize, cognizant, diagnose, incognito, prognosis

com, con	fully	complete, compel, conscious, condense, confess, confirm
contr, contra, counter	against, opposite	contradict, counteract, contravene, contrary, counterspy, contrapuntal
cord, cor, cardi	heart	cordial, concord, discord, courage, encourage
corp	body	corporation, corporal punishment, corpse, corpulent
cort	correct	escort, cortege
cosm	universe, world	cosmos, microcosm, cosmopolitan, cosmonaut
cour, cur, curr, curs	run, course	occur, excursion, discourse, courier, course
crat, cracy	rule	autocrat, aristocrat, theocracy, technocracy
cre, cresc, cret, crease	grow	create, crescent, accretion, increase
crea	create	creature, recreation, creation
cred	believe	creed, credo, credence, credit, credulous, incredulous, incredible
cresc, cret, crease, cru	rise, grow	crescendo, concrete, increase, decrease, accrue
crit	separate, choose	critical, criterion, hypocrite
cur, curs	run	current, concurrent, concur, incur, recur, occur, courier, precursor, cursive
cura	care	curator, curative, manicure
cycl, cyclo	wheel, circle, circular	Cyclops, unicycle, bicycle, cyclone, cyclic
de-	from, down, away, to do the opposite, reverse, against	detach, deploy, derange, decrease, deodorize, devoid, deflate, degenerate
dec, deca	ten, ten times	decimal, decade, decimate, decathlon
dec, dign	suitable	decent decorate dignity
dei, div	God	divinity, divine, deity, divination, deify

dem, demo	people, populace, population	democracy, demography, demagogue, epidemic
dent, dont	tooth	dental, denture, orthodontist, periodontal
derm	skin, covering	hypodermic, dermatology, epidermis, taxidermy
di-, dy-	two, twice, double	divide, diverge
dia	through, across, between	diameter, diagonal, dialogue dialect, dialectic, diagnosis, diachronic
dic, dict, dit	say, speak	dictation, dictionary, dictate, dictator, Dictaphone, edict, predict, verdict, contradict, benediction
dis, dif	not, opposite of, reverse, separate, deprive of, away	dismiss, differ, disallow, disperse, dissuade, divide, disconnect, disproportion, disrespect, distemper, disarray
dit	give	credit, audit
doc, doct	teach, prove	docile, doctor, doctrine, document, dogma, indoctrinate
domin	master, that which is under control	dominate, dominion, predominant, domain
don	give	donate, condone
dorm	sleep	dormant, dormitory
dox	thought, opinion, praise	orthodox, heterodox, paradox, doxology
-drome	run, step	syndrome, aerodrome
duc, duct	to lead, pull	produce, abduct, product, transducer, viaduct, aqueduct, induct, deduct, reduce, induce
dura	hard, lasting	durable, duration, endure
dynam	power	dynamo, dynamic, dynamite, hydrodynamics
dys-	bad, abnormal, difficult, impaired, unfavorable	dysfunctional, dyslexia

e-	not, missing, out, fully, away, computer network related	emit, embed, eternal, ether, erase, email
ec-	out of, outside	echo, eclipse, eclectic, ecstasy
eco-	household, environment, relating to ecology or economy	ecology, economize, ecospheres
ecto-	outside, external	ectomorph, ectoderm, ectoplasm
-ed	Verb: past tense	dressed, faded, patted, closed, introduced
-ed	Adjective: having the quality or characteristics of	winged, moneyed, dogged, tiered
-en	Verb: to cause to become	lengthen, moisten, sharpen
-en	Adjective: material	golden, woolen, silken
en-, em-	put into, make, provide with, surround with	enamor, embolden, enslave, empower, entangle
-ence, -ency	Noun: action or process, quality or state	reference, emergency, dependence, eminence, latency
end-	inside, within	endorse, endergonic, endoskeleton, endoscope,
epi-	upon, close to, over, after, altered	epicenter, epilogue, epigone
equi-	equal	equidistant, equilateral, equilibrium, equinox, equation, equator
-er, -ier	Adjective: comparative	better, brighter, sooner, hotter, happier
-er, -or	Noun: person or thing that does something	flyer, reporter, player, member, fryer, collector, concentrator
-er, -or	Verb: action	ponder, dishonor, clamor
erg	work, effect	energy, erg, allergy, ergometer
-ery	collective qualities, art, practice, trade, collection, state, condition	snobbery, bakery, greenery, gallery, slavery

-es, -ies	Noun: plural of most nouns ending in -ch, -s, -sh, -o and -z and some in -f and -y	passes, glasses, ladies, heroes
-es, -ies	Verb: third person singular present indicative of verbs that end in -ch, -s, -sh, - and some in -y	blesses, hushes, fizzes, defies
-ess	female	actress, goddess, poetess
-est, -iest	Adjective or Adverb: superlative	latest, strongest, luckiest
ev-, et-	time, age	medieval, eternal
ex-	out of, away from, lacking, former	exit, exhale, exclusive, exceed, explosion, ex-mayor
exter-, extra-, extro-	outside of, beyond	external, extrinsic, extraordinary, extrapolate, extraneous, extrovert
fa, fess	speak	fable, fabulous, fame, famous, confess, profess
fac, fact, fec, fect, fic, fas, fea	do, make	difficult, fashion, feasible, feature, factory, effect, manufacture, amplification, confection
fall, fals	deceive	fallacy, falsify, fallacious
femto	quadrillionth	femtosecond
fer	bear, carry	ferry, coniferous, fertile, defer, infer, refer, transfer
fic, feign, fain, fit, feat	shape, make, fashion	fiction, faint, feign
fid	belief, faith	confide, diffident, fidelity
fid, fide, feder	faith, trust	confidante, fidelity, confident, infidelity, infidel, federal, confederacy,
fig	shape, form	effigy, figure, figment
fila, fili	thread	filigree, filament, filter, filet, filibuster
fin	end, ended, finished	final, finite, finish, confine, fine, refine, define, finale

fix	repair, attach	fix, fixation, fixture, affix, prefix, suffix
flex, flect	bend	flex, reflex, flexible, flexor, inflexibility, reflect, deflect, circumflex
flict	strike	affliction, conflict, inflict
flu, fluc, fluv, flux	flow	influence, fluid, flue, flush, fluently, fluctuate, reflux, influx
-fold	Adverb: in a manner of, marked by	fourfold
for, fore	before	forecast, fortune, foresee
forc, fort	strength, strong	effort, fort, forte, fortifiable, fortify, forte, fortitude
form	shape, resemble	form, format, conform, formulate, perform, formal, formula
fract, frag, frai	break	fracture, infraction, fragile, fraction, refract, frail
fuge	flee	subterfuge, refuge, centrifuge
-ful	Noun: an amount or quantity that fills	mouthful
-ful	Adjective: having, giving, marked by	fanciful
fuse	pour	confuse, transfuse
-fy	make, form into	falsify, dandify
gam	marriage	bigamy, monogamy, polygamy
gastr, gastro	stomach	gastric, gastronomic, gastritis, gastropod
gen	kind	generous
gen	birth, race, produce	genesis, genetics, eugenics, genealogy, generate, genetic, antigen, pathogen
geo	earth	geometry, geography, geocentric, geology
germ	vital part	germination, germ, germane

gest	carry, bear	congest, gestation
giga	billion	gigabyte, gigaflop
gin	careful	gingerly
gloss, glot	tongue	glossary, polyglot, epiglottis
glu, glo	lump, bond, glue	glue, agglutinate, conglomerate
gor	to gather, to bring together	category, categorize
grad, gress, gree	to gather, to bring together, step, go	grade, degree, progress, gradual, graduate, egress
graph, gram, graf	write, written, draw	graph, graphic, autograph, photography, graphite, telegram, polygraph, grammar, biography, lithograph, graphic
grat	pleasing	congratulate, gratuity, grateful, ingrate
grav	heavy, weighty	grave, gravity, aggravate, gravitate
greg	herd	gregarious, congregation, segregate
hale, heal	make whole, sound	inhale, exhale, heal, healthy, healthiness
helio	sun	heliograph, heliotrope, heliocentric
hema, hemo	blood	hemorrhage, hemoglobin, hemophilia, hemostat
her, here, hes	stick	adhere, cohere, cohesion, inherent, hereditary, hesitate
hetero	other, different	heterodox, heterogeneous, heterosexual, heterodyne
hex, ses, sex	six	hexagon, hexameter, sestet, sextuplets
homo	same	homogenize, homosexual, homonym, homophone
hum, human	earth, ground, man	humus, exhume, humane

hydr, hydra, hydro	water	dehydrate, hydrant, hydraulic, hydraulics, hydrogen, hydrophobia
hyper	over, above	hyperactive, hypertensive, hyperbolic, hypersensitive, hyperventilate, hyperkinetic
hypn	sleep	hypnosis, hypnotherapy
-ia	Noun: names, diseases	phobia
-ian, an	Noun: related to, one that is	pedestrian, human
-iatry	Noun: art of healing	psychiatry
-ic	Adjective: quality, relation	generic
-ic, ics	Noun: related to the arts and sciences	arithmetic, economics
-ice	Noun: act	malice
-ify	Verb: cause	specify
ignis	fire	ignite, igneous, ignition
-ile	Adjective: having the qualities of	projectile
in, im	into, on, near, towards	instead, import
in, im, il, ir	not	illegible, irresolute, inaction, inviolate, innocuous, intractable, innocent, impregnable, impossible, imposter
infra	beneath	infrared, infrastructure
-ing	Noun: material made for, activity, result of an activity	flooring, swimming, building
-ing	Verb: present participle	depicting
-ing	Adjective: activity	cohering
inter	between, among	international, intercept, interject, intermission, internal, intermittent,
intra	within, during, between layers, underneath	intramural, intranet

intro	into, within, inward	interoffice, introvert, introspection, introduce
-ion	Noun: condition or action	abduction
-ish	Adjective: having the character of	newish
-ism	Noun: doctrine, belief, action or conduct	formalism
-ist	Noun: person or member	podiatrist
-ite	Noun: state or quality	graphite
-ity, ty	Noun: state or quality	lucidity, novelty
-ive	Noun: condition	native
-ive, -ative, -itive	Adjective: having the quality of	festive, cooperative, sensitive
-ize	Verb: cause	fantasize
jac, ject	throw	reject, eject, project, trajectory, interject, dejected, inject, ejaculate, adjacent
join, junct	join	adjoining, enjoin, juncture, conjunction, injunction, conjunction
judice	judge	prejudice
jug, junct, just	to join	junction, adjust, conjugal
juven	young	juvenile, rejuvenate
labor	work	laborious, belabor
lau, lav, lot, lut	wash	launder, lavatory, lotion, ablution, dilute
lect, leg, lig	choose, gather, select, read	collect, legible, eligible
leg	law	legal, legislate, legislature, legitimize
-less	Adjective: without, missing	motiveless
levi	light	alleviate, levitate, levity

lex, leag, leg	law	legal, college, league
liber, liver	free	liberty, liberal, liberalize, deliverance
lide	strike	collide, nuclide
liter	letters	literary, literature, literal, alliteration, obliterate
loc, loco	place, area	location, locally, locality, allocate, locomotion
log, logo, ology	word, study, say, speech, reason, study	catalog, prologue, dialogue, zoology, logo
loqu, locut	talk, speak	eloquent, loquacious, colloquial, circumlocution
luc, lum, lun, lus, lust	light	translucent, luminary, luster, lunar, illuminate, illustrate
lude	play	prelude
-ly	Adverb: in the manner of	fluently
macr-, macer	lean	emaciated, meager
magn	great	magnify, magnificent, magnanimous, magnate, magnitude, magnum
main	strength, foremost	mainstream, mainsail, domain, remain
mal	bad, badly	malformation, maladjusted, dismal, malady, malcontent, malfunction, malfeasance, maleficent
man, manu	hand, make, do	manual, manage, manufacture, manacle, manicure, manifest, maneuver, emancipate, management
mand	command	mandatory, remand, mandate
mania	madness	mania, maniac, kleptomania, pyromania
mar, mari, mer	sea, pool	marine, marsh, maritime, mermaid
matri	mother	matrimony, maternal, matriarchate, matron
medi	half, middle, between, halfway	mediate, medieval, Mediterranean, mediocre

mega	great, million	megaphone, megaton, megabyte, megalopolis
mem	recall, remember	memo, commemoration, memento, memoir, memorable
ment	mind	mental, mention
-ment	Noun: condition or result	document
meso	middle	mesomorph, mesosphere
meta	beyond, change	metaphor, metamorphosis, metabolism,
meter	measure	meter, voltammeter, barometer, thermometer
metr	admeasure, apportion	metrics, asymmetric, parametric, telemetry
micro	small, millionth	microscope, microfilm, microwave, micrometer,
migra	wander	migrate, emigrant, immigrate
mill, kilo	thousand	millennium, kilobyte, kiloton
milli	thousandth	millisecond, milligram, millivolt
min	little, small	minute, minor, minuscule
mis	wrong, bad, badly	misconduct, misinterpret, misnomer, mistake
mit, miss	send	emit, remit, submit, admit, commit, permit, transmit, omit, intermittent, mission, missile
mob, mov, mot	move	motion, remove, mobile, motor
mon	warn, remind	monument, admonition, monitor, premonition
mono	one	monopoly, monotype, monologue, mononucleosis,
mor, mort	mortal, death	mortal, immortal, mortality, mortician, mortuary
morph	shape, form	amorphous, dimorphic, metamorphosis, morphology, polymorphic, morpheme, amorphous

multi	many, much	multifold, multilingual, multiply, multitude, multipurpose, multinational
nano	billionth	nanosecond
nasc, nat, gnant, nai	to be born	nascent, native, pregnant, naive
nat, nasc	to be from, to spring forth	innate, natal, native, renaissance
neo	new	neolithic, neologism, neophyte, neonate
-ness	Noun: state, condition, quality	kindness
neur	nerve	neuritis, neuropathic, neurologist, neural, neurotic
nom	law, order	autonomy, astronomy, gastronomy, economy
nom, nym	name	nominate, synonym
nomen, nomin	name	nomenclature, nominate, ignominious
non	nine	nonagon
non	not	nonferrous, nonsense, nonabrasive, nondescript
nov	new	novel, renovate, novice, nova, innovate
nox, noc	night	nocturnal, equinox
numer	number	numeral, numeration, enumerate, innumerable
numisma	coin	numismatics
nunci, nunc, nounc	speak, declare, warn	pronounce, announcement
ob, oc, of, op	toward, against, in the way	oppose, occur, offer, obtain
oct	eight	octopus, octagon, octogenarian, octave
oligo	few, little	Oligocene, oligosaccharide, oligotrophic, oligarchy
omni	all, every	omnipotent, omniscient, omnipresent, omnivorous

onym	name	anonymous, pseudonym, antonym, synonym
oper	work	operate, cooperate, opus
-or	Noun: condition or activity	valor, honor, humor, minor
ortho	straight, correct	orthodox, orthodontist, orthopedic, unorthodox
-ory	Noun: place for, serves for	territory, rectory
-ous, -eous, -ose, -ious	Adjective: having the quality of, relating to	adventurous, courageous, verbose, fractious
over	excessive, above	overwork, overall, overwork
pac	peace	pacifist, pacify, pacific ocean
pair, pare	arrange, assemblage, two	repair, impair, compare, prepare
paleo	old	Paleozoic, Paleolithic,
pan	all	Pan-American, pan-African, panacea, pandemonium
para	beside	paradox, paraprofessional, paramedic, paraphrase, parachute
pat, pass, path	feel, suffer	patient, passion, sympathy, pathology
pater, patr	father	paternity, patriarch, patriot, patron, patronize
path, pathy	feeling, suffering	pathos, sympathy, antipathy, apathy, telepathy
ped, pod	foot	pedal, impede, pedestrian, centipede, tripod,
pedo	child	orthopedic, pedagogue, pediatrics
pel, puls	drive, push, urge	compel, dispel, expel, repel, propel, pulse, impulse, pulsate, compulsory, expulsion, repulsive
pend, pens, pond	hang, weigh	pendant, pendulum, suspend, appendage, pensive, append
per	through, intensive	persecute, permit, perspire, perforate, persuade

peri	around	periscope, perimeter, perigee, periodontal
phage	eat	macrophage, bacteriophage
phan, phas, phen, fan, phant, fant	show, make visible	phantom, fantasy
phe	speak	blaspheme, cipher, phenomenon, philosopher
phil	love	philosopher, philanthropy, philharmonic, bibliophile
phlegma	inflammation	phlegm, phlegmatic
phobia, phobos	fear	phobia, claustrophobia, homophobia
phon	sound	telephone, phonics, phonograph, phonetic, homophone, microphone, symphony, euphonious
phot, photo	light	photograph, photoelectric, photogenic, photosynthesis, photon
pict	paint, show, draw	picture, depict
plac, plais	please	placid, placebo, placate, complacent
pli, ply	fold	reply, implicate, ply
plore	cry out, wail	implore, exploration, deploring
plu, plur, plus	more	plural, pluralist, plus
pneuma, pneumon	breath	pneumatic, pneumonia,
pod	foot, feet	podiatry, tripod
poli	city	metropolis, police, politics, Indianapolis, megalopolis, acropolis
poly	many	polytheist, polygon, polygamy, polymorphous
pon, pos, pound	place, put	postpone, component, opponent, proponent, expose, impose, deposit, posture, position, expound, impound

pop	people	population, populous, popular
port	carry	porter, portable, transport, report, export, import, support, transportation
portion	part, share	portion, proportion
post	after, behind	postpone, postdate
pot	power	potential, potentate, impotent
pre, pur	before	precede
prehendere	seize, grasp	apprehend, comprehend, comprehensive, prehensile
prin, prim, prime	first	primacy, primitive, primary, primal, primeval, prince, principal
pro	for, forward	propel
proto	first	prototype, protocol, protagonist, protozoan,
psych	mind, soul	psyche, psychiatry, psychology, psychosis
punct	point, dot	punctual, punctuation, puncture, acupuncture,
pute	think	dispute, computer
quat, quad	four	quadrangle, quadruplets
quint, penta	five	quintet, quintuplets, pentagon, pentane, pentameter
quip	ship	equip, equipment
quir, quis, quest, quer	seek, ask	query, inquire, exquisite, quest
re	back, again	report, realign, retract, revise, regain
reg, recti	straighten	regiment, regular, rectify, correct, direct, rectangle
retro	backwards	retrorocket, retrospect, retrogression, retroactive
ri, ridi, risi	laughter	deride, ridicule, ridiculous, derision, risible

rog, roga	ask	prerogative, interrogation, derogatory
rupt	break	rupture, interrupt, abrupt, disrupt
sacr, sanc, secr	sacred	sacred, sacrosanct, sanction, consecrate, desecrate
salv, salu	safe, healthy	salvation, salvage, salutation
sanct	holy	sanctify, sanctuary, sanction, sanctimonious, sacrosanct
sat, satis	enough	saturate, satisfy
sci, scio, scientia	know	science, conscious, omniscient
scope	see, watch	telescope, microscope, kaleidoscope, periscope, stethoscope
scrib, script	write	scribe, scribble, inscribe, describe, subscribe, prescribe, manuscript
se	apart, move away from	secede
sect, sec	cut	intersect, transect, dissect, secant, section
sed, sess, sid	sit	sediment, session, obsession, possess, preside, president, reside, subside
semi	half, partial	semifinal, semiconscious, semiannual, semimonthly, semicircle
sen, scen	old, grow old	senior, senator, senile, senescence, evanescent
sent, sens	feel, think	sentiment, consent, resent, dissent, sentimental, sense, sensation, sensitive, sensory, dissension
sept	seven	septet, septennial
sequ, secu, sue	follow	sequence, consequence, sequel, subsequent, prosecute, consecutive, second, ensue, pursue
serv	save, serve, keep	servant, service, subservient, servitude, preserve, conserve, reservation, deserve, conservation, observe

259

-ship	Noun: status, condition	relationship, friendship
sign, signi	sign, mark, seal	signal, signature, design, insignia, significant
simil, simul	like, resembling	
sist, sta, stit	stand, withstand, make up	assist, insist, persist, circumstance, stamina, status, state, static, stable, stationary, substitute
soci	to join, companions	sociable, society
sol, solus	alone	solo, soliloquy, solitaire, solitude, solitary, isolate
solv, solu, solut	loosen, explain	solvent, solve, absolve, resolve, soluble, solution, resolution, resolute, dissolute, absolution
somn	sleep	insomnia, somnambulist
soph	wise	philosophy, sophisticated
spec, spect, spi, spic	look, see	specimen, specific, spectator, spectacle, aspect, speculate, inspect, respect, prospect, retrospective, introspective, expect, conspicuous
sper	render favorable	prosper
sphere	ball, sphere	sphere, stratosphere, hemisphere, spheroid
spir	breath	spirit, conspire, inspire, aspire, expire, perspire, respiration
stand, stant, stab, stat, stan, sti, sta, stead	stand	stature, establish, stance
-ster	person	mobster, monster
strain, strict, string, stige	bind, pull, draw tight	stringent, strict, restrict, constrict, restrain, boa constrictor
stru, struct, stroy, stry	build	construe, structure, construct, instruct, obstruct, destruction, destroy, industry, ministry

sub, suc, suf, sup, sur, sus	under, below, from, secretly, instead of	sustain, survive, support, suffice, succeed, submerge, submarine, substandard, subvert
sume, sump	take, use, waste	consume, assume, sump, presumption
super, supra	over, above	superior, suprarenal, superscript, supernatural, superimpose
syn, sym	together, at the same time	sympathy, synthesis, synchronous, syndicate
tact, tang, tag, tig, ting	touch	tactile, contact, intact, intangible, tangible, contagious, contiguous, contingent
tain, ten, tent, tin	hold, keep, have	retain, continue, content, tenacious
tect, teg	cover	detect, protect, tegument
tele	distance, far, from afar	telephone, telegraph, telegram, telescope, television, telephoto, telecast, telepathy, telepathy
tem, tempo	time	tempo, temporary, extemporaneously, contemporary, pro tem, temporal
ten, tin, tain	hold	tenacious, tenant, tenure, untenable, detention, retentive, content, pertinent, continent, obstinate, contain, abstain, pertain, detain
tend, tent, tens	stretch, strain	tendency, extend, intend, contend, pretend, superintend, tender, extent, tension, pretense
tera	trillion	terabyte, teraflop
term	end, boundary, limit	exterminate, terminal
terr, terra	earth	terrain, terrarium, territory, terrestrial
test	to bear witness	testament, detest, testimony, attest, testify
the, theo	God, a god	monotheism, polytheism, atheism, theology
therm	heat	thermometer, theorem, thermal, thermos bottle, thermostat, hypothermia
thesis, thet	place, put	antithesis, hypothesis, synthesis, epithet
tire	draw, pull	attire, retire, entire

tom	cut	atom (not cutable), appendectomy, tonsillectomy, dichotomy, anatomy
tor, tors, tort	twist	torture, retort, extort, distort, contort, torsion, tortuous, torturous
tox	poison	toxic, intoxicate, antitoxin
tract, tra, trai, treat	drag, draw, pull	attract, tractor, traction, extract, retract, protract, detract, subtract, contract, intractable
trans	across, beyond, change	transform, transoceanic, transmit, transportation, transducer
tri	three	tripod, triangle, trinity, trilateral
trib	pay, bestow	tribute, contribute, attribute, retribution, tributary
tribute	give	contribute, distribute, tributary
turbo	disturb	turbulent, disturb, turbid, turmoil
typ	print	type, prototype, typical, typography, typewriter, typology, typify
ultima	last	ultimate, ultimatum
umber, umbraticum	shadow	umbra, penumbra, (take) umbrage, adumbrate
un	not, against, opposite	unceasing, unequal
uni	one	uniform, unilateral, universal, unity, unanimous, unite, unison, unicorn
-ure	Noun: act, condition, process, function	exposure, conjecture, measure
vac	empty	vacate, vacuum, evacuate, vacation, vacant, vacuous
vade	go	evade, invader
vale, vali, valu	strength, worth	equivalent, valiant, validity, evaluate, value, valor
veh, vect	to carry	vector, vehicle, convection, vehement

ven, vent	come	convene, intervene, venue, convenient, avenue, circumvent, invent, convent, venture, event, advent, prevent
ver, veri	true	very, aver, verdict, verity, verify, verisimilitude
verb, verv	word	verify, veracity, verbalize, verve
vert, vers	turn, change	convert, revert, advertise, versatile, vertigo, invert, reversion, extravert, introvert, diversion, introvert, convertible, reverse, controversy
vi	way	viable, vibrate, vibrant
vic, vicis	change, substitute	vicarious, vicar, vicissitude
vict, vinc	conquer	victor, evict, convict, convince, invincible
vid, vis	see	video, evident, provide, providence, visible, revise, supervise, vista, visit, vision, review, indivisible
viv, vita, vivi	alive, life	revive, survive, vivid, vivacious, vitality, vital, vitamins, revitalize
voc, voke	call	vocation, avocation, convocation, invocation, evoke, provoke, revoke, advocate, provocative, vocal
vol	will	malevolent, benevolent, volunteer, volition
volcan	fire	volcano, vulcanize, Vulcan
volv, volt, vol	turn about, roll	revolve, voluble, voluminous, convolution, revolt, evolution
vor	eat greedily	voracious, carnivorous, herbivorous, omnivorous, devour
-ward	Adverb: in a direction or manner	homeward
-wise	Adverb: in the manner of, with regard to	clockwise, bitwise

with	against	withhold, without, withdraw, forthwith
-y	Noun: state, condition, result of an activity	society, victory
-y	Adjective: marked by, having	hungry, angry, smeary, teary
zo	animal	zoo (zoological garden), zoology, zodiac, protozoan

Chapter 7: Paragraph Comprehension

The Paragraph Comprehension test measures your ability to understand, analyze, and evaluate written passages. The passages will contain material from a variety of sources and on a number of different topics, and consists of 15 multiple choice questions to be answered in 13 minutes. This chapter of the book will discuss the various types of questions typically asked.

The Main Idea

Finding and understanding the main idea of a text is an essential reading skill. When you look past the facts and information and get to the heart of what the writer is trying to say, that's the **main idea**.

Imagine that you're at a friend's home for the evening:
> "Here," he says, "Let's watch this movie."
> "Sure," you reply. "What's it about?"

You'd like to know a little about what you'll be watching, but your question may not get you a satisfactory answer, because you've only asked about the subject of the film. The subject—what the movie is about—is only half the story. Think, for example, about all the alien invasion films ever been made. While these films may share the same general subject, what they have to say about the aliens or about humanity's theoretical response to invasion may be very different. Each film has different ideas it wants to convey about a subject, just as writers write because they have something they want to say about a particular subject. When you look beyond the facts and information to what the writer really wants to say about his or her subject, you're looking for the main idea.

One of the most common questions on reading comprehension exams is, "What is the main idea of this passage?" How would you answer this question for the paragraph below?

> "Wilma Rudolph, the crippled child who became an Olympic running champion, is an inspiration for us all. Born prematurely in 1940, Wilma spent her childhood battling illness, including measles, scarlet fever, chicken pox, pneumonia, and polio, a crippling disease which at that time had no cure. At the age of four, she was told she would never walk again. But Wilma and her family refused to give up. After years of special treatment and physical therapy, 12-year-old Wilma was able to walk normally again. But walking wasn't enough for Wilma, who was determined to be an athlete. Before long, her talent earned her a spot in the 1956 Olympics, where she earned a bronze medal. In the 1960 Olympics, the height of her career, she won three gold medals."

What is the main idea of this paragraph? You might be tempted to answer, "Wilma Rudolph" or "Wilma Rudolph's life." Yes, Wilma Rudolph's life is the **subject** of the passage—who or what the passage is about—but the subject is not necessarily the main idea. The **main idea** is what the writer wants to say about this subject. What is the main thing the writer says about Wilma's life?

Which of the following statements is the main idea of the paragraph?
   a) Wilma Rudolph was very sick as a child.
   b) Wilma Rudolph was an Olympic champion.
   c) Wilma Rudolph is someone to admire.

Main idea: The overall fact, feeling, or thought a writer wants to convey about his or her subject.

The best answer is **c)**: Wilma Rudolph is someone to admire. This is the idea the paragraph adds up to; it's what holds all of the information in the paragraph together. This example also shows two important characteristics of a main idea:

- It is **general** enough to encompass all of the ideas in the passage.

- It is an **assertion.** An assertion is a statement made by the writer.

The main idea of a passage must be general enough to encompass all of the ideas in the passage. It should be broad enough for all of the other sentences in that passage to fit underneath it, like people under an umbrella. Notice that the first two options, "Wilma Rudolph was very sick as a child" and "Wilma Rudolph was an Olympic champion", are too specific to be the main idea. They aren't broad enough to cover all of the ideas in the passage, because the passage talks about both her illnesses and her Olympic achievements. Only the third answer is general enough to be the main idea of the paragraph.

A main idea is also some kind of **assertion** about the subject. An assertion is a claim that something is true. Assertions can be facts or opinions, but in either case, an assertion should be supported by specific ideas, facts, and details. In other words, the main idea makes a general assertion that tells readers that something is true. The supporting sentences, on the other hand, show readers that this assertion is true by providing specific facts and details. For example, in the Wilma Rudolph paragraph, the writer makes a general assertion: "Wilma Rudolph, the crippled child who became an Olympic running champion, is an inspiration for us all." The other sentences offer specific facts and details that prove why Wilma Rudolph is an inspirational person.

Writers often state their main ideas in one or two sentences so that readers can have a very clear understanding about the main point of the passage. A sentence that expresses the main idea of a paragraph is called a **topic sentence.**

Notice, for example, how the first sentence in the Wilma Rudolph paragraph states the main idea:

"Wilma Rudolph, the crippled child who became an Olympic running champion, is an inspiration for us all."

This sentence is therefore the topic sentence for the paragraph. Topic sentences are often found at the beginning of paragraphs. Sometimes, though, writers begin with specific supporting ideas and lead up to the main idea, and in this case the topic sentence is often found at the end of the paragraph. Sometimes the topic sentence is even found somewhere in the middle, and other times there isn't a clear topic sentence at all—but that doesn't mean there isn't a main idea; the author has just chosen not to express it in a clear topic sentence. In this last case, you'll have to look carefully at the paragraph for clues about the main idea.

Main Ideas vs. Supporting Ideas

If you're not sure whether something is a main idea or a supporting idea, ask yourself the following question: is the sentence making a **general statement,** or is it providing **specific information?** In the Wilma Rudolph paragraph above, for example, all of the sentences except the first make specific statements. They are not general enough to serve as an umbrella or net for the whole paragraph.

Writers often provide clues that can help you distinguish between main ideas and their supporting ideas. Here are some of the most common words and phrases used to introduce specific examples:

1. **For example...**
2. **Specifically...**
3. **In addition...**
4. **Furthermore...**
5. **For instance...**
6. **Others...**
7. **In particular...**
8. **Some...**

These signal words tell you that a supporting fact or idea will follow. If you're having trouble finding the main idea of a paragraph, try eliminating sentences that begin with these phrases, because they will most likely be too specific to be a main ideas.

Implied Main Idea

When the main idea is implied, there's no topic sentence, which means that finding the main idea requires some detective work. But don't worry! You already know the importance of structure, word choice, style, and tone. Plus, you know how to read carefully to find clues, and you know that these clues will help you figure out the main idea.

For Example:

> "One of my summer reading books was *The Windows of Time*. Though it's more than 100 pages long, I read it in one afternoon. I couldn't wait to see what happened to Evelyn, the main character. But by the time I got to the end, I wondered if I should have spent my afternoon doing something else. The ending was so awful that I completely forgot that I'd enjoyed most of the book."

There's no topic sentence here, but you should still be able to find the main idea. Look carefully at what the writer says and how she says it. What is she suggesting?
  a) *The Windows of Time* is a terrific novel.
  b) *The Windows of Time* is disappointing.
  c) *The Windows of Time* is full of suspense.
  d) *The Windows of Time* is a lousy novel.

The correct answer is **b)** – the novel is disappointing. How can you tell that this is the main idea? First, we can eliminate choice **c)**, because it's too specific to be a main idea. It deals only with one specific aspect of the novel (its suspense).

Sentences **a)**, **b)**, and **d)**, on the other hand, all express a larger idea – a general assertion about the quality of the novel. But only one of these statements can actually serve as a "net" for the whole paragraph. Notice that while the first few sentences praise the novel, the last two criticize it. Clearly, this is a mixed review.

Therefore, the best answer is **b)**. Sentence **a)** is too positive and doesn't account for the "awful" ending. Sentence **d)**, on the other hand, is too negative and doesn't account for the reader's sense of suspense and interest in the main character. But sentence **b)** allows for both positive and negative aspects – when a good thing turns bad, we often feel disappointed.

Now let's look at another example. Here, the word choice will be more important, so read carefully.

> "Fortunately, none of Toby's friends had ever seen the apartment where Toby lived with his mother and sister. Sandwiched between two burnt-out buildings, his two-story apartment building was by far the ugliest one on the block. It was a real eyesore: peeling orange paint (orange!), broken windows, crooked steps, crooked everything. He could just imagine what his friends would say if they ever saw this poor excuse for a building."

Which of the following expresses the main idea of this paragraph?
   a) Toby wishes he could move to a nicer building.
   b) Toby wishes his dad still lived with them.
   c) Toby is glad none of his friends know where he lives.
   d) Toby is sad because he doesn't have any friends.

From the description, we can safely assume that Toby doesn't like his apartment building and wishes he could move to a nicer building **a)**. But that idea isn't general enough to cover the whole paragraph, because it's about his building.

Because the first sentence states that Toby has friends, the answer cannot be **d)**. We know that Toby lives only with his mother and little sister, so we might assume that he wishes his dad still lived with them, **b)**, but there's nothing in the paragraph to support that assumption, and this idea doesn't include the two main topics of the paragraph—Toby's building and Toby's friends.

What the paragraph adds up to is that Toby is terribly embarrassed about his building, and he's glad that none of his friends have seen it **c)**. This is the main idea. The paragraph opens with the word "fortunately," so we know that he thinks it's a good thing none of his friends have been to his house. Plus, notice how the building is described: "by far the ugliest on the block," which says a lot since it's stuck "between two burnt-out buildings." The writer calls it an "eyesore," and repeats "orange" with an exclamation point to emphasize how ugly the color is. Everything is "crooked" in this "poor excuse for a building." Toby is clearly ashamed of where he lives and worries about what his friends would think if they saw it.

Context Clues

Often in your reading you will come across words or phrases that are unfamiliar to you. How can you understand what you're reading if you don't know what all the words mean? You can often use **context** to determine meaning! That is, by looking carefully at the sentences and ideas surrounding an unfamiliar word, you can often figure out exactly what that word means.

For example, read the following paragraph:

> "Andy is the most unreasonable, pigheaded, subhuman life-form in the entire galaxy, and he makes me so angry I could scream! Of course, I love him like a brother. I sort of have to, because he *is* my brother. More than that, he's my twin! That's right. Andy and Amy (that's me) have the same curly hair and dark eyes. Yet though we look alike, we have very different dispositions. You could say that we're opposites. While I'm often quiet and pensive, Andy is loud and doesn't seem to stop to think about anything. Oh, and did I mention that he's the most stubborn person on the planet?"

As you read this passage, you probably came across at least two unfamiliar words: **dispositions** and **pensive**. While a dictionary would be helpful, you don't need to look up these words. The paragraph provides enough clues to help you figure out what these words mean.

Let's begin with **dispositions**. In what context is this word used? Let's take another look at the sentence in which it's used and the two sentences that follow: "Yet though we look alike, we have very different dispositions. You could say that we're opposites. While I'm often quiet and **pensive**, Andy is loud and doesn't seem to stop to think about anything."

The context here offers several important clues:

1. The sentence in which **dispositions** is used tells us something about what dispositions are not.

2. The sentence sets up a contrast between the ways that Amy and Andy look and between their dispositions; this means that dispositions are not something physical.

3. The general content of the paragraph. We can tell from the paragraph that dispositions have something to do with who Andy and Amy are, since the paragraph describes their personalities.

4. Yet another clue is what follows the sentence in which **dispositions** is used. Amy offers two specific examples of their dispositions: She's quiet and pensive, while Andy is loud and doesn't seem to think much.

These are specific examples of personality traits. By now you should have a pretty good idea of what the word dispositions means. A disposition is:
a) A person's physical characteristics.
b) A person's preferences.
c) A person's natural qualities or tendencies.

The best answer, of course, is **c)**, a person's natural qualities or tendencies. While a person's disposition often helps determine his or her preferences, **b)**, this passage doesn't say anything about what Amy and Andy like to do (or not do). Nor are these characteristics physical, **a)**. Amy is talking about their personalities.

Now, let's look at the second vocabulary word: **pensive**. Again, the context provides us with strong clues. Amy states that she and Andy "are opposites" – that though they look alike, they have opposite dispositions; she is quiet, and he is loud. So we can expect that the next pair of descriptions will be opposites, too.

Now we simply have to look at her description of Andy and come up with its opposite. If Andy "doesn't seem to stop to think about anything," then we can assume that Amy spends a lot of time thinking.

We can therefore conclude that *pensive* means:
a) Intelligent, wise.
b) Deep in thought.
c) Considerate of others.

The best answer is **b)**, deep in thought. If you spend a lot of time thinking, that may make you wise. But remember, we're looking for the opposite of Andy's characteristics, so neither **a)** nor **c)** can be the correct answer.

When you're trying to determine meaning from context on an exam, two strategies can help you find the best answer.

1. First, determine whether the vocabulary word is something positive or negative. If the word is something positive, then eliminate the answers that are negative, and vice versa.

2. Replace the vocabulary word with the remaining answers, one at a time. Does the answer make sense when you read the sentence? If not, you can eliminate that answer.

Cause and Effect

Understanding cause and effect is important for reading success. Every event has at least one cause (what made it happen) and at least one effect (the result of what happened). Some events have more than one cause, and some have more than one effect. An event is also often part of a chain of causes and effects. Causes and effects are usually signaled by important transitional words and phrases.

Words Indicating Cause: Because (of); Created (by); Caused (by); and Since.

Words Indicating Effect: As a result; Since; Consequently; So; Hence; and Therefore.

Sometimes, a writer will offer his or her opinion about why an event happened when the facts of the cause(s) aren't clear. Or a writer may predict what he or she thinks will happen because of a certain event (its effects). If this is the case, you need to consider how reasonable those opinions are. Are the writer's ideas logical? Does the writer offer support for the conclusions he or she offers?

Reading Between the Lines

Paying attention to word choice is particularly important when the main idea of a passage isn't clear. A writer's word choice doesn't just affect meaning; it also creates it. For example, look at the following description from a teacher's evaluation of a student applying to a special foreign language summer camp. There's no topic sentence, but if you use your powers of observation, you should be able to tell how the writer feels about her subject.

"As a student, Jane usually completes her work on time and checks it carefully. She speaks French well and is learning to speak with less of an American accent. She has often been a big help to other students who are just beginning to learn the language."

What message does this passage send about Jane? Is she the best French student the writer has ever had? Is she one of the worst, or is she just average? To answer these questions, you have to make an inference, and you must support your inference with specific observations. What makes you come to the conclusion that you come to?

The **diction** of the paragraph above reveals that this is a positive evaluation, but not a glowing recommendation.

Here are some of the specific observations you might have made to support this conclusion:

1. The writer uses the word "usually" in the first sentence. This means that Jane is good about meeting deadlines for work, but not great; she doesn't always hand in her work on time.

2. The first sentence also says that Jane checks her work carefully. While Jane may sometimes hand in work late, at least she always makes sure it's quality work. She's not sloppy.

3. The second sentence tells us she's "learning to speak with less of an American accent." This suggests that she has a strong accent and needs to improve in this area. It also suggests, though, that she is already making progress.

4. The third sentence tells us that she "often" helps "students who are just beginning to learn the language." From this we can conclude that Jane has indeed mastered the basics. Otherwise, how could she be a big help to students who are just starting to learn? By looking at the passage carefully, then, you can see how the writer feels about her subject.

Practice Drill: Paragraph Comprehension

Read each of the following paragraphs carefully and answer the questions that follow.

My "office" measures a whopping 5 x 7 feet. A large desk is squeezed into one corner, leaving just enough room for a rickety chair between the desk and the wall. Yellow paint is peeling off the walls in dirty chunks. The ceiling is barely six feet tall; it's like a hat that I wear all day long. The window, a single 2 x 2 pane, looks out onto a solid brick wall just two feet away.

1. What is the main idea implied by this paragraph?
   a) This office is small but comfortable.
   b) This office is in need of repair.
   c) This office is old and claustrophobic.
   d) None of the above.

There are many things you can do to make tax time easier. The single most important strategy is to keep accurate records. Keep all of your pay stubs, receipts, bank statements, and other relevant financial information in a neat, organized folder so that when you're ready to prepare your form, all of your paperwork is in one place. The second thing you can do is start early. Get your tax forms from the post office as soon as they are available and start calculating. This way, if you run into any problems, you have plenty of time to straighten them out. You can also save time by reading the directions carefully. This will prevent time-consuming errors. Finally, if your taxes are relatively simple (you don't have itemized deductions or special investments), use the shorter tax form. It's only one page, so if your records are in order, it can be completed in less than an hour.

2. How many suggestions for tax time does this passage offer?
   b) One.
   c) Two.
   d) Three.
   e) Four.

271

3. The sentence "It's only one page, so if your records are in order, it can be completed in less than an hour" is:
   a) The main idea of the passage.
   b) A major supporting idea.
   c) A minor supporting idea.
   d) A transitional sentence.

4. A good summary of this passage would be:
   a) Simple strategies can make tax time less taxing.
   b) Don't procrastinate at tax time.
   c) Always keep good records.
   d) Get a tax attorney.

5. According to the passage, who should use the shorter tax form?
   a) Everybody.
   b) People who do not have complicated finances.
   c) People who do have complicated finances.
   d) People who wait until the last minute to file taxes.

6. The sentence, "The single most important strategy is to keep accurate records," is a(n):
   a) Fact.
   b) Opinion.
   c) Both of the above.
   d) Neither of the above.

Being a secretary is a lot like being a parent. After a while, your boss becomes dependent upon you, just as a child is dependent upon his or her parents. Like a child who must ask permission before going out, you'll find your boss coming to you for permission, too. "Can I have a meeting on Tuesday at 3:30?" you might be asked, because you're the one who keeps track of your boss's schedule. You will also find yourself cleaning up after your boss a lot, tidying up papers and files the same way a parent tucks away a child's toys and clothes. And, like a parent protects his or her children from outside dangers, you will find yourself protecting your boss from certain "dangers"—unwanted callers, angry clients, and upset subordinates.

7. The main idea of this passage is:
   a) Secretaries are treated like children.
   b) Bosses treat their secretaries like children.
   c) Secretaries and parents have similar roles.
   d) Bosses depend too much upon their secretaries.

8. Which of the following is the topic sentence of the paragraph?
   a) Being a secretary is a lot like being a parent.
   b) After a while, your boss becomes dependent upon you, just as a child is dependent upon his or her parents.
   c) You will also find yourself cleaning up after your boss a lot, tidying up papers and files the same way a parent tucks away a child's toys and clothes.
   d) None of the above.

9. According to the passage, secretaries are like parents in which of the following ways?
    a) They make their bosses' lives possible.
    b) They keep their bosses from things that might harm or bother them.
    c) They're always cleaning and scrubbing things.
    d) They don't get enough respect.

10. This passage uses which point of view?
    a) First person.
    b) Second person.
    c) Third person.
    d) First and second person.

11. The tone of this passage suggests that:
    a) The writer is angry about how secretaries are treated.
    b) The writer thinks secretaries do too much work.
    c) The writer is slightly amused by how similar the roles of secretaries and parents are.
    d) The writer is both a secretary and a parent.

12. The sentence, "'Can't I have a meeting on Tuesday at 3:30?' you might be asked, because you're the one who keeps track of your boss's schedule," is a:
    a) Main idea.
    b) Major supporting idea.
    c) Minor supporting idea
    d) None of the above.

13. "Being a secretary is a lot like being a parent" is:
    a) A fact.
    b) An opinion.
    c) Neither of the above.
    d) Both of the above.

14. The word "subordinates" probably means:
    a) Employees.
    b) Parents.
    c) Clients.
    d) Secretaries.

Day after day, Johnny chooses to sit at his computer instead of going outside with his friends. A few months ago, he'd get half a dozen phone calls from his friends every night. Now, he might get one or two a week. It used to be that his friends would come over two or three days a week after school. Now, he spends his afternoons alone with his computer.

15. The main idea is:
    a) Johnny and his friends are all spending time with their computers instead of one another.
    b) Johnny's friends aren't very good friends.
    c) Johnny has alienated his friends by spending so much time on the computer.
    d) Johnny and his friends prefer to communicate by computer.

We've had Ginger since I was two years old. Every morning, she wakes me up by licking my cheek. That's her way of telling me she's hungry. When she wants attention, she'll weave in and out of my legs and meow until I pick her up and hold her. And I can always tell when Ginger wants to play. She'll bring me her toys and will keep dropping them (usually right on my homework!) until I stop what I'm doing and play with her for a while.

16. A good topic sentence for this paragraph would be:
    a) I take excellent care of Ginger.
    b) Ginger is a demanding pet.
    c) Ginger and I have grown up together.
    d) Ginger is good at telling me what she wants.

Practice Drill: Paragraph Comprehension – Answers

1. c)
2. d)
3. c)
4. a)
5. b)
6. b)
7. c)
8. a)
9. b)
10. b)
11. c)
12. c)
13. b)
14. a)
15. c)
16. d)

Chapter 8: Arithmetic Reasoning

The Arithmetic reasoning tests your ability to use fundamental math concepts to solve word problems. During the test, you will have 39 minutes to answer 16 problems. The most important step in solving any word problem is to read the entire problem before beginning to solve. You shouldn't skip over words or assume you know what the question is from the first sentence. The following are the general steps used to solve word problems:

General Steps for Word Problem Solving:

Step 1: Read the entire problem and determine what the problem is asking for.

Step 2: List all of the given data.

Step 3: Sketch diagrams with the given data.

Step 4: Determine formula(s) needed.

Step 5: Set up equation(s).

Step 6: Solve.

Step 7: Check your answer. Make sure that your answer makes sense. (Is the amount too large or small; are the answers in the correct unit of measure; etc.)

Note: Not all steps are needed for every problem.

In chapter four, you will be given a list of the most commonly-made mistakes on the mathematics knowledge test – they will apply here as well. Even if an answer you calculated is a given answer choice, that doesn't make it the correct answer. Remember that not all of the information given in a problem is needed to solve it.

For example:

Kathy had $12.45, John had $10.30, and Liz had $6.90. How much money did the girls have combined?

The amount John has is not needed to solve the problem, since the problem is only asking for the combined amounts of Kathy and Liz.

Mistakes most commonly occur when answers for only a part of the problem are given as answer choices. It's very easy to get caught up in thinking, "That's the number I have here! It looks right, so I'll go with that." Trust yourself, and always check your answers. The best way to prepare for the arithmetic section is to practice! At first, don't concern yourself with how long it takes to solve problems; focus on understanding how to solve them, and then time yourself.

This section will go over some of the most common types of word problems found on the Arithmetic Reasoning Section, but keep in mind that any math concept can be turned into a word problem.

Key Words

Word problems generally contain key words that can help you determine what math processes may be required in order to solve them. Here are some commonly-used key words:

- **Addition:** Added, combined, increased by, in all, total, perimeter, sum, and more than.
- **Subtraction:** How much more, less than, fewer than, exceeds, difference, and decreased.
- **Multiplication:** Of, times, area, and product.
- **Division:** Distribute, share, average, per, out of, percent, and quotient.
- **Equals:** Is, was, are, amounts to, and were.

BASIC WORD PROBLEMS

A word problem in algebra is the equivalent of a story problem in math, only word problems are solved by separating information from the problems into two equal groups (one for each side of an equation). Examine this problem:

Sara has 15 apples and 12 oranges. How many pieces of fruit does she have?

We know that the sum of 15 and 12 is equal to the total amount of fruit. An unknown number or value is represented by a letter. The total number of pieces of fruit is unknown, so we will represent that amount with x. When the value that a particular variable will represent is determined, it is defined by writing a statement like this:

Let x = Total Amount of Fruit.

Once again, the sum of 15 apples and 12 oranges is equal to the total amount of fruit. This can be used to translate the problem into an equation:

$15 + 12 = x$
$x = 27$
Sara has 27 pieces of fruit.

Of course, you could probably have solved this problem more quickly without having set up an algebraic equation. But knowing how to use an equation for this kind of problem builds your awareness of which concepts are useful; some of them are even critical to solving much harder problems.

Examples:

1. A salesman bought a case of 48 backpacks for $576. He sold 17 of them for $18 at the swap meet, and the rest were sold to a department store for $25 each. What was the salesman's profit?

    Calculate the total of the 17 backpacks, which you know the cost to be $18:
    17 * $18 = $306.

    Calculate how many backpacks were sold at $25: 48 – 17 = 31.

Calculate the total amount of profit for the backpacks sold at $25: 31 * $25 = $775.

Add the two dollar amounts for backpacks sold: $306 + $775 = $1081.

Subtract the salesman's initial cost: $1081 - $576 = $505.

The answer to the question asked about his profit is: $505.

2. Thirty students in Mr. Joyce's room are working on projects over the duration of two days. The first day, he gave them 3/5 of an hour to work. On the second day, he gave them half as much time as the first day. How much time did the students have altogether?

> 1st day = 3/5 of an hour.
> 2nd day = 1/2 (3/5) = 3/10 of an hour.
> Total = 3/5 + 3/10 = 6/10 + 3/10 = 9/10 of an hour.
>
> An hour has 60 minutes, so set up a ratio:
>
> 9/10 = x/60.
> x = 54.
> So the students had 54 minutes altogether to work on the projects.
>
> Another way to do this problem is to calculate first the amount of time allotted on the first day: 3/5 * 60 minutes = 36 minutes.
>
> Then take half of that to get the time allotted on the second day:
> 36 minutes * 1/2 = 18 minutes.
>
> Add the two together for your total time! 36 + 18 = 54.

CONSECUTIVE NUMBER PROBLEMS

Examples:

1. Two consecutive numbers have a sum of 91. What are the numbers?

To begin solving this problem, define the variable. You do not know what the first consecutive number is, so you can call it x.

The First Consecutive Number = x.

Since the numbers are consecutive, meaning one number comes right after the other, the second number must be one more than the first. So, $x + 1$ equals the second number.

The Second Consecutive Number = $x + 1$.

The problem states that the sum of the two numbers is 91. This can be shown in the equation like the following: $x + (x + 1) = 91$. That equation can be solved as follows:

Initial Equation: $x + (x + 1) = 91$.

Combine Like Terms: $2x + 1 = 91$.

After subtracting 1 from each side: $2x = 90$.

After dividing each side by 2, $x = 45$.

Careful! In a situation like this, it's almost a sure thing that one of the answer choices will be "45" on the test. This is a trap! You aren't done with your problem yet. Remember, x only equals the value of the first consecutive number – you want the sum of *both*.

Since x equals 45, and the Second Consecutive Number equals $x + 1$, you can simply add 1 to 45 to find that Second Consecutive Number. It should be shown like the work below:

Let x = The First Consecutive Number = 45.
Let $x + 1$ = The Second Consecutive Number = 46.

$x + (x + 1) = 91$.

Don't forget to check your work!

$2x + 1 = 91$.

$2x = 90$.

$x = 45$.

Sometimes you will encounter a problem which has more than two consecutive numbers, such as:

2. When added, four consecutive numbers have a sum of 18. What is the largest number?

You can solve this much like the previous problem. The difference is that you will have to define four numbers (instead of two).

Note: Each consecutive number is found by adding 1 to the previous number.

The First Consecutive Number = x.

The Second Consecutive Number = $x + 1$.

The Third Consecutive Number = $x + 2$.

The Fourth Consecutive Number = $x + 3$.

Your equation will look like this: $x + (x + 1) + (x + 2) + (x + 3) = 18$.

$4x + 6 = 18$.

278

$4x = 12.$

$x = 3.$

Remember the problem asked for largest number, x represents the smallest; so you aren't done!

$x + 3 = 3. \; 3 + 3 = 6.$

EVEN or ODD CONSECUTIVE NUMBERS

The only difference between ordinary consecutive numbers and even or odd consecutive numbers is the space between each number. Each consecutive number would add 2 instead of 1. The trick here is to remember that your first consecutive number will determine whether or not the following consecutive numbers will be even or odd. If the problem calls for even consecutive numbers, then your first number must be even; if odd, then the first number must be odd.

Many problems lend themselves to being solved with systems of linear equations.

1. The admission fee at a small fair is $1.50 for children and $4.00 for adults. On a certain day, 2,200 people enter the fair, and $5,050 is collected. How many children and how many adults attended?

   Using a system of equations allows the use of two different variables for the two different unknowns.

   Number of adults: a.
   Number of children: c.
   Total number: $a + c = 2200$.
   Total income: $4a + 1.5c = 5050$.

   Now solve the system for the number of adults and the number of children. Solve the first equation for one of the variables, and then substitute the result into the other equation.

   Because $a + c = 2200$, we know that:

   $$a = 2200 - c$$
   $$4(2200 - c) + 1.5c = 5050$$
   $$8800 - 4c + 1.5c = 5050$$
   $$8800 - 2.5c = 5050$$
   $$-2.5c = -3750$$
   $$c = 1500$$

   Now go back to that first equation: $a = 2200 - (1500) = 700$. There were 1500 children and 700 adults.

2. A landscaping company placed two orders with a nursery. The first order was for 13 bushes and 4 trees, and totaled $487. The second order was for 6 bushes and 2 trees, and totaled $232. The bills do not list the per-item price. What were the costs of one bush and of one tree?

First pick variables ("*b*" for the price of bushes and "*t*" for the price of trees) and set up a system of equations:

First order: $13b + 4t = 487$.

Second order: $6b + 2t = 232$.

Multiply the second row by 2, so when they are subtracted, one variable is eliminated.

To subtract, multiple the second row by negative 1. Then you have: $13b + 4t = 487$.
$-12b - 4t = -464$

This says that $b = 23$. Back-solving, you will find that $t = 47$. Bushes cost $23 each; trees cost $47 each.

PERCENTAGE WORD PROBLEMS

Basic Equations:

Percent Change:
　　　Amount of Change ÷ Original Amount * 100

Percent Increase:
　　　(New Amount – Original Amount) ÷ Original Amount * 100

Percent Decrease:
　　　(Original Amount – New Amount) ÷ Original Amount * 100

Amount Increase (Or Amount Decrease):
　　　Original Price * Percent Markup (Or, for Amount Decrease, Markdown)

Original Price:
　　　New Price ÷ (Whole - Percent Markdown)

Original Price:
　　　New Price ÷ (Whole + Percent Markup)

Many percentage problems consist of markup and markdown. For these, you calculate how much the quantity changed, and then you calculate the percent change relative to the original value.

Examples:

1. A computer software retailer used a markup rate of 40%. Find the selling price of a computer game that cost the retailer $25.

    The markup is 40% of the $25 cost, so the equation to find markup is: $(0.40) * (25) = 10$.

    The selling price is the cost plus markup: $25 + 10 = 35$. The item sold for $35.

2. A golf shop pays its wholesaler $40 for a certain club, and then sells it to a golfer for $75. What is the markup rate?

First calculate the markup: $75 - 40 = 35$.

Then find the markup rate: $35 is (some percent) of $40, or: $35 = (x) * (40)$.

...so the markup over the original price is: $35 \div 40 = x$. $x = 0.875$.

Since the problem asks for a percentage, you need to remember to convert the decimal value.

The markup rate is 87.5%.

3. A shoe store uses a 40% markup on cost. Find the cost of a pair of shoes that sells for $63.

This problem is somewhat backwards. You are given the selling price, which is "cost + markup", and the markup rate. You are not given the actual cost or markup.

Let x be the cost. The markup, being 40% of the cost, is $0.40x$. The selling price of $63 is the sum of the cost and markup, so:

$63 = x + 0.40x$.

$63 = 1x + 0.40x$.

$63 = 1.40x$.

$63 \div 1.40 = x$.

$x = 45$. The shoes cost the store $45.

4. An item originally priced at $55 is marked 25% off. What is the sale price?

First, find the markdown. The markdown is 25% of the original price of $55, so: $x = (0.25) * (55)$. $x = 13.75$.

By subtracting this markdown from the original price, you can find the sale price: $55 - 13.75 = 41.25$. The sale price is $41.25.

5. An item that regularly sells for $425 is marked down to $318.75. What is the discount rate?

First, find the amount of the markdown: $425 - 318.75 = 106.25$. Then calculate "the markdown of the original price", or the markdown rate: $106.25 is (some percent) of $425, so:

$106.25 = (x) * (425)$.

...and the markdown over the original price is: $x = 106.25 \div 425$. $x = 0.25$.

Since the "*x*" stands for a percentage, remember to convert this decimal to percentage form. The markdown rate is 25%.

6. A bike is marked down 15%; the sale price is $127.46. What was the original price?

This problem is backwards. You are given the sale price ($127.46) and the markdown rate (15%), but neither the markdown amount nor the original price.

Let "*x*" stand for the original price. Then the markdown, being 15% of this price, will be $0.15x$. The sale price is the original price, minus the markdown, so: $x - 0.15x = 127.46$.

$1x - 0.15x = 127.46$.

$0.85x = 127.46$.
$x = 127.46 \div 0.85$.

$x = 149.95$. The original price was $149.95.

Note: In this last problem, we ended up – in the third line of calculations – with an equation that said "eighty-five percent of the original price is $127.46". You can save yourself some time if you think of discounts in this way: if the price is 15% off, then you're only actually paying 85%. Similarly, if the price is 25% off, then you're paying 75%, etc.

Note: While the values below do not refer to money, the procedures used to solve these problems are otherwise identical to the markup - markdown examples.

7. Growing up, you lived in a tiny country village. When you left for college, the population was 840. You recently heard that the population has grown by 5%. What is the present population?

First, find the actual amount of the increase. Since the increase is five percent of the original population, then the increase is: $(0.05) * (840) = 42$.

The new population is the old population plus the increase, or: $840 + 42 = 882$.

The population is now 882.

8. You put in an 18 X 51 foot garden along the whole back end of your backyard. It has reduced the backyard lawn area by 24%. What is the area of the remaining lawn area?

The area of the garden is: $(18) * (51) = 918$. This represents 24% of the total yard area, or 24% of the original lawn area. This means that 918 square feet is 24% of the original, so: $918 = 0.24x$.

$918 \div 0.24 = x$.

$3825 = x$.

The total back yard area is 3825 square feet, and we know from the problem that the width is 51 feet. Therefore, to find the length: $3825 \div 51 = 75$. The length then is 75 feet. Since 18 feet are taken up by the garden, then the lawn area is: 75 – 18 = 57 feet deep. The area of the lawn now measures 51' X 57'.

WORK WORD PROBLEMS

"Work" problems involve situations such as: two people working together to paint a house. You are usually told how long each person takes to paint a similarly-sized house, and then you are asked how long it will take the two of them to paint the house when they work together.

There is a "trick" to doing work problems: you have to think of the problem in terms of how much each person/machine/whatever does in a given unit of time.

Example:

Suppose one painter can paint the entire house in twelve hours, and the second painter takes eight hours. How long would it take the two painters together to paint the house?

> If the first painter can do the entire job in twelve hours, and the second painter can do it in eight hours, then (here is the trick!) the first painter can do 1/12 of the job per hour, and the second guy can do 1/8 per hour. How much then can they do per hour if they work together?

> To find out how much they can do together per hour, add together what they can do individually per hour: 1/12 + 1/8 = 5/24. They can do 5/24 of the job per hour.

Now let "*t*" stand for how long they take to do the job together. Then they can do 1/*t* per hour, so 5/24 = 1/*t*. When for *t* = 24/5, *t* = 4.8 hours. That is:

Hours to complete job:

> First painter: 12.
> Second painter: 8.
> Together: *t*.

Work completed per hour:

> First painter: 1/12.
> Second painter: 1/8.
> Together: 1/*t*.

Adding their labor:

> 1/12 + 1/8 = 1/*t*.
> 5/24 = 1/*t*.
> 24/5 = *t*.
> *t* = 4 4/5 hours.

As you can see in the above example, "work" problems commonly create rational equations. But the equations themselves are usually pretty simple.

283

More Examples:

1. One pipe can fill a pool 1.25 times faster than a second pipe. When both pipes are opened, they fill the pool in five hours. How long would it take to fill the pool if only the slower pipe is used?

Convert to rates.

Hours to complete job:

Fast pipe: f.
Slow pipe: $1.25f$.
Together: 5.

Work completed per hour:

Fast pipe: $1/f$.
Slow pipe: $1/1.25f$.
Together: $1/5$.

Adding their labor:

$1/f + 1/1.25f = 1/5$.

Solve for f:

$5 + 5/1.25 = f$.
$5 + 4 = f$.
$f = 9$.

Then $1.25f = 11.25$, so the slower pipe takes 11.25 hours.

If you're not sure how I derived the rate for the slow pipe, think about it this way: if someone goes twice as fast as you, then you take twice as long as he does; if he goes three times as fast, then you take three times as long. In this case, one pipe goes 1.25 times as fast, so the other takes 1.25 times as long.

This next one is a bit different:

2. Ben takes 2 hours to wash 500 dishes, and Frank takes 3 hours to wash 450 dishes. How long will they take, working together, to wash 1000 dishes?

For this exercise, you are given *how many* can be done in one time unit, rather than *how much* of a job can be completed. But the thinking process is otherwise the same.

Ben can do 250 dishes per hour, and Frank can do 150 dishes per hour. Working together, they can do $250 + 150 = 400$ dishes an hour. That is:

Ben: 500 dishes / 2 hours = 250 dishes / hour.

Frank: 450 dishes / 3 hours = 150 dishes / hour.

Together: (250 + 150) dishes / hour = 400 dishes / hour.

Next find the number of hours that it takes to wash 1000 dishes. Set things up so **units cancel** and you're left with "hours":

(1000 dishes) * (1 hour / 400 dishes).

(1000 / 400) hours.

2.5 hours.

It will take two and a half hours for the two of them to wash 1000 dishes.

3. If six men can do a job in fourteen days, how many would it take to do the job in twenty-one days?

Convert this to man-hours, or, in this case, man-days. If it takes six guys fourteen days, then: (6 men) * (14 days) = 84 man-days.

That is, the entire job requires 84 man-days. This exercise asks you to expand the time allowed from fourteen days to twenty-one days. Obviously, if they're giving you more time, then you'll need fewer guys. But how many guys, exactly? (x men) * (21 days) = 84 man-days.

...or, in algebra: $21x = 84$. $x = 4$. So, only four guys are needed to do the job in twenty-one days.

You may have noticed that each of these problems used some form of the "how much can be done per time unit" construction, but aside from that each problem was done differently. That's how "work" problems are; but, as you saw above, if you label things neatly and do your work orderly, you should find your way to the solution.

DISTANCE WORD PROBLEMS

"Distance" word problems, often also called "uniform rate" problems, involve something travelling at a fixed and steady ("uniform") pace ("rate" or "speed"), or else moving at some average speed. Whenever you read a problem that involves "how fast", "how far, or "for how long," you should think of the distance equation, $d = rt$, where d stands for distance, r stands for the (constant or average) rate of speed, and t stands for time. It is easier to solve these types of problems using a grid and filling in the information given in the problem.

Warning: Make sure that the units for time and distance agree with the units for the rate. For instance, if they give you a rate of feet per second, then your time must be in seconds and your distance must be in feet. Sometimes they try to trick you by using two different units, and you have to catch this and convert to the correct units.

1. An executive drove from his home at an average speed of 30 mph to an airport where a helicopter was waiting. The executive boarded the helicopter and flew to the corporate offices at an average speed of 60 mph. The entire distance was 150 miles; the entire trip took three hours. Find the distance from the airport to the corporate offices.

	d	r	t
driving	d	30	t
flying	$150 - d$	60	$3 - t$
total	150	---	3

The first row gives me the equation $d = 30t$.

Since the first part of his trip accounted for d miles of the total 150-mile distance and t hours of the total 3-hour time, you are left with $150 - d$ miles and $3 - t$ hours for the second part. The second row gives the equation: $150 - d$. $d = 60(3 - t)$.

This now becomes a system of equations problem.

Add the two "distance" expressions and setting their sum equal to the given total distance: $150 - d = 60(3 - t)$. $d = 30t$. $150 = 30t + 60(3 - t)$.

Solve for t: $150 = 30t + 180 - 60t$. $150 = 180 - 30t$. $-30 = -30t$. $1 = t$.

It is important to note that you are not finished when you have solved for the first variable. This is where it is important to pay attention to what the problem asked for. It does not ask for time, but the time is needed to solve the problem.

So now insert the value for t into the first equation: $d = 30$.

Subtract from total distance: $150 - 30 = 120$.

The distance to the corporate offices is 120 miles.

2. Two cyclists start at the same time from opposite ends of a course that is 45 miles long. One cyclist is riding at 14 mph and the second cyclist is riding at 16 mph. How long after they begin will they meet?

	d	r	t
slow guy	d	14	t
fast guy	$45 - d$	16	t
total	45	---	---

Why is t the same for both cyclists? Because you are measuring from the time they both started to the time they meet somewhere in the middle.

Why "d" and "$45 - d$" for the distances? Because I assigned the slower cyclist as having covered d miles, which left $45 - d$ miles for the faster cyclist to cover: the two cyclists *together* covered the whole 45 miles.

286

Using "d = rt," you get d = 14t from the first row, and 45 − d = 16t from the second row. Since these distances add up to 45, add the distance expressions and set equal to the given total: 45 = 14t + 16t.

Solve for t, place it back into the equation, to solve for what the question asked. 45 = 30t. t = 45 ÷ 30 = 1 ½. They will meet 1 ½ hours after they begin.

SIMPLE INTEREST

Formula for simple interest: $I = PRT$.

 I represents the interest earned.

 P represents the principal which is the number of dollars invested.

 T represents the time the money is invested; generally stated in years or fractions of a year.

 R represents the rate at which the principal (p) is earned.

Formula for Amount: $A = P + I$.

 A represents what your investment is worth if you consider the total amount of the original investment (P) and the interest earned (I).

Example: If I deposit $500 in an account with an annual rate of 5%, how much will I have after 2 years?

 1st year: $500 + (500 * .05) = $525.

 2nd year: $525 + (525 * .05) = $ 551.25.

RATIO PROBLEMS

To solve a ratio, simply find the equivalent fraction. To distribute a whole across a ratio:

 1. Total all parts.

 2. Divide the whole by the total number of parts.

 3. Multiply quotient by corresponding part of ratio.

Example: There are 81 voters in a room, all either Democrat or Republican. The ratio of Democrats to Republicans is 5:4. How many republicans are there?

 1. 5 + 4 = 9.

 2. 81 ÷ 9 = 9.

 3. 9 * 4 = 36. 36 Republicans.

PROPORTIONS

Direct proportions: Corresponding ratio parts change in the same direction (increase/decrease).

Indirect proportions: Corresponding ratio parts change in opposite directions; as one part increases the other decreases.

Example (Indirect Proportion): A train traveling 120 miles takes 3 hours to get to its destination. How long will it take if the train travels 180 miles?

120 miles : 180 miles
          is to
x hours : 3 hours

Write as a fraction and cross multiply: $3 * 120 = 180x$.

$360 = 180x$. $x = 2$ hours. It will take the train 2 hours to reach its destination.

Chapter 9: Mathematics Knowledge

The Math Knowledge (MK) section tests various concepts in numbers and operations, algebra, geometry, data analysis, statistics, and probability. In this test section, you will be provided with 16 questions to answer within a 20-minutes time limit, which gives you a little over a minute to solve each problem. This seems like less time than it actually is, so don't worry! Before you take the ASVAB, you want to make sure that you have a good understanding of the math areas which will be covered. You will need to sharpen your skills, but don't worry – we'll provide you with the knowledge that you'll need to know for the test.

Math Concepts Tested

You have a much better chance of getting a good Math Knowledge score if you know what to expect. The test covers math up to and including the first semester of Algebra II as well as fundamental geometry. You will not be given any formulas, such as those required for geometry calculations, so you need to make sure that you have studied them so they are fresh in your mind.

Here is a breakdown of areas covered:

Numbers and Operations
Absolute values, inequalities, probabilities, exponents, and radicals.

Algebra and Functions
Basic equation solving, simultaneous equations, binomials & polynomials, and inequalities.

Geometry and Measurement
Angle relationships, area and perimeter of geometric shapes, and volume.

Math skills that you won't need:
- Working with bulky numbers or endless calculations.
- Working with imaginary numbers or the square roots of negative numbers.
- Trigonometry or calculus.

Important Note: You are not allowed to use a calculator for any section of the ASVAB.

The Most Common Mistakes

Here is a list of the four most commonly- made mistakes concerning mathematics, starting with the most common.

1. Answer is the wrong sign (positive / negative).

2. Order of Operations not following when solving.

3. Misplaced decimal.

4. Solution is not what the question asked for.

These are the basics that individuals tend to overlook when they only have a minute or less to do their calculations. This is why it is so important that you pay attention right from the start of the problem. You may be thinking, "But, those are just common sense." Exactly! Remember, even simple mistakes still result in an incorrect answer.

In the computer version of the ASVAB, there is no opportunity to go back and fix your mistakes. Once you make your answer choice and move on to the next question, there is no going back.

Strategies

Review the Basics: First and foremost, practice your basic skills such as sign changes, order of operations, simplifying fractions, and equation manipulation. These are the skills you will use the most on almost every problem on the Math Knowledge and the Arithmetic tests sections. Remember when it comes right down to it, there are still only four math operations used to solve any math problem, which are adding, subtracting, multiplying and dividing; the only thing that changes is the order they are used to solve the problem.

Although accuracy counts more than speed; **Don't Waste Time** stuck on a question! Remember, you only have 24 minutes to answer 25 questions for this section test. This is why your knowledge of the basics is so important. If you have to stop and think about what 9 * 6 equals, or use your fingers to add 13 + 8, then you need to spend time on these fundamentals before going on to the concepts. There are minute tests at the end of this chapter. If you can complete those tests in the time specified, the time required for you to calculate the more complex problems during the test will decrease greatly.

Make an Educated Guess: If necessary, eliminate at least one answer choice as most probably incorrect and guess which one is most likely correct from the remaining choices.

Math Formulas, Facts, and Terms that You Need to Know

The next few pages will cover the various math subjects (starting with the basics, but in no particular order) along with worked examples. Use this guide to determine the areas in which you need more review and work these areas first. You should take your time at first and let your brain recall the math necessary to solve the problems, using the examples given to remember these skills.

Order of Operations

PEMDAS – Parentheses/Exponents/Multiply/Divide/Add/Subtract

Perform the operations within parentheses first, and then any exponents. After those steps, perform all multiplication and division. (These are done from left to right, as they appear in the problem) Finally, do all required addition and subtraction, also from left to right as they appear in the problem.

> **Example**: Solve $(-(2)^2 - (4 + 7))$.
> $(-4 – 11) = – \mathbf{15}$.
>
> **Example**: Solve $((5)^2 ÷ 5 + 4 * 2)$.
> $25 ÷ 5 + 4 * 2$.
>
> $5 + 8 = \mathbf{13}$.

Positive & Negative Number Rules

$(+) + (-)$ = Subtract the two numbers. Solution gets the sign of the larger number.

$(-) + (-)$ = Negative number.

$(-) * (-)$ = Positive number.

$(-) * (+)$ = Negative number.

$(-) / (-)$ = Positive number.

$(-) / (+)$ = Negative number.

Greatest Common Factor (GCF)

The greatest factor that divides two numbers.

> **Example**: The GCF of 24 and 18 is 6. 6 is the largest number, or greatest factor, that can divide both 24 and 18.

Geometric Sequence

Each term is equal to the previous term multiplied by *x*.

> **Example**: 2, 4, 8, 16.
>
> $x = \mathbf{2}$.

Fractions

Adding and subtracting fractions requires a common denominator.

Find a common denominator for:

$$\frac{2}{3} - \frac{1}{5}$$

$$\frac{2}{3} - \frac{1}{5} = \frac{2}{3}\left(\frac{5}{5}\right) - \frac{1}{5}\left(\frac{3}{3}\right) = \frac{10}{15} - \frac{3}{15} = \mathbf{\frac{7}{15}}$$

To add mixed fractions, work first the whole numbers, and then the fractions.

$$2\frac{1}{4} + 1\frac{3}{4} = 3\frac{4}{4} = \mathbf{4}$$

To subtract mixed fractions, convert to single fractions by multiplying the whole number by the denominator and adding the numerator. Then work as above.

$$2\frac{1}{4} - 1\frac{3}{4} = \frac{9}{4} - \frac{7}{4} = \frac{2}{4} = \mathbf{\frac{1}{2}}$$

To multiply fractions, convert any mixed fractions into single fractions and multiply across; reduce to lowest terms if needed.

$$2\frac{1}{4} * 1\frac{3}{4} = \frac{9}{4} * \frac{7}{4} = \frac{63}{16} = \mathbf{3\frac{15}{16}}$$

To divide fractions, convert any mixed fractions into single fractions, flip the second fraction, and then multiply across.

$$2\frac{1}{4} \div 1\frac{3}{4} = \frac{9}{4} \div \frac{7}{4} = \frac{9}{4} * \frac{4}{7} = \frac{36}{28} = 1\frac{8}{28} = \mathbf{1\frac{2}{7}}$$

Probabilities

A probability is found by dividing the number of desired outcomes by the number of possible outcomes. (The piece divided by the whole.)

Example: What is the probability of picking a blue marble if 3 of the 15 marbles are blue?

3/15 = 1/5. The probability is **1 in 5** that a blue marble is picked.

Prime Factorization

Expand to prime number factors.

Example: 104 = 2 * 2 * 2 * 13.

Absolute Value

The absolute value of a number is its distance from zero, not its value.

So in $|x| = a$, "x" will equal "$-a$" as well as "a."

Likewise, $|\,3\,| = 3$, and $|\,-3\,| = 3$.

Equations with absolute values will have two answers. Solve each absolute value possibility separately. All solutions must be checked into the original equation.

> **Example:** Solve for x:
> $|2x - 3| = x + 1$.
>
> Equation One: $2x - 3 = -(x + 1)$.
> $2x - 3 = -x - 1$.
> $3x = 2$.
> $x = 2/3$.
>
> Equation Two: $2x - 3 = x + 1$.
> $x = 4$.

Mean, Median, Mode

Mean is a math term for "average." Total all terms and divide by the number of terms.

Find the mean of 24, 27, and 18.

$24 + 27 + 18 = 69 \div 3 = 23$.

Median is the middle number of a given set, found after the numbers have all been put in numerical order. In the case of a set of even numbers, the middle two numbers are averaged.

What is the median of 24, 27, and 18?

18, **24**, 27.

What is the median of 24, 27, 18, and 19?

18, 19, 24, 27 ($19 + 24 = 43$. $43/2 = 21.5$).

Mode is the number which occurs most frequently within a given set.

What is the mode of 2, 5, 4, 4, 3, 2, 8, 9, 2, 7, 2, and 2?

The mode would be **2** because it appears the most within the set.

Exponent Rules

Rule	Example
$x^0 = 1$	$5^0 = 1$
$x^1 = x$	$5^1 = 5$
$x^a \cdot x^b = x^{a+b}$	$5^2 * 5^3 = 5^5$
$(xy)^a = x^a y^a$	$(5 * 6)^2 = 5^2 * 6^2 = 25 * 36$
$(x^a)^b = x^{ab}$	$(5^2)^3 = 5^6$
$(x/y)^a = x^a/y^a$	$(10/5)^2 = 10^2/5^2 = 100/25$
$x^a/y^b = x^{a-b}$	$5^4/5^3 = 5^1 = 5$ (remember $x \neq 0$)
$x^{1/a} = \sqrt[a]{x}$	$25^{1/2} = \sqrt[2]{25} = 5$
$x^{-a} = \dfrac{1}{x^a}$	$5^{-2} = \dfrac{1}{5^2} = \dfrac{1}{25}$ (remember $x \neq 0$)
$(-x)^a$ = positive number if "a" is even; negative number if "a" is odd.	

Roots

Root of a Product: $\sqrt[n]{a \cdot b} = \sqrt[n]{a} \cdot \sqrt[n]{b}$

Root of a Quotient: $\sqrt[n]{\dfrac{a}{b}} = \dfrac{\sqrt[n]{a}}{\sqrt[n]{b}}$

Fractional Exponent: $\sqrt[n]{a^m} = a^{m/n}$

Literal Equations

Equations with more than one variable. Solve in terms of one variable first.

Example: Solve for y: $4x + 3y = 3x + 2y$.

Step 1 – Combine like terms: $3y - 2y = 4x - 2x$.

Step 2 – Solve for y: $y = 2x$.

Midpoint

To determine the midpoint between two points, simply add the two x coordinates together and divide by 2 (midpoint x). Then add the y coordinates together and divide by 2 (midpoint y).

$$\left(\frac{x_1 + x_2}{2}, \frac{y_1 + y}{2}\right)$$

Slope

The formula used to calculate the slope (m) of a straight line connecting two points is: $m = (y_2 - y_1) / (x_2 - x_1)$ = change in y / change in x.

Example: Calculate slope of the line in the diagram:

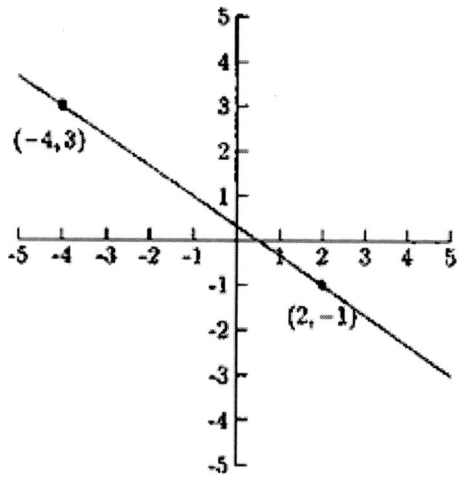

$m = (3 - (-1))/(-4 - 2) = 4/-6 = $ **- 2/3**.

Inequalities

Inequalities are solved like linear and algebraic equations, except the sign must be reversed when dividing by a negative number.

Example: $-7x + 2 < 6 - 5x$.

Step 1 – Combine like terms: $-2x < 4$.

Step 2 – Solve for x. (Reverse the sign): $x > $ **-2.**

Solving compound inequalities will give you two answers.

Example: $-4 \leq 2x - 2 \leq 6$.

Step 1 – Add 2 to each term to isolate x: $-2 \leq 2x \leq 8$.

Step 2: Divide by 2: $-1 \leq x \leq 4$.

Solution set is **[-1, 4]**.

Algebraic Equations

When simplifying or solving algebraic equations, you need to be able to utilize all math rules: exponents, roots, negatives, order of operations, etc.

295

1. Add & Subtract: Only the coefficients of like terms.

   Example: $5xy + 7y + 2yz + 11xy - 5yz = 16xy + 7y - 3yz$.

2. Multiplication: First the coefficients then the variables.

   Example: Monomial * Monomial.

   $(3x^4y^2z)(2y^4z^5) = 6x^4y^6z^6$.

   (A variable with no exponent has an implied exponent of 1.)

   Example: Monomial * Polynomial.

   $(2y^2)(y^3 + 2xy^2z + 4z) = 2y^5 + 4xy^4z + 8y^2z$.

   Example: Binomial * Binomial.

   $(5x + 2)(3x + 3)$.

   First: $5x * 3x = 15x^2$.

   Outer: $5x * 3 = 15x$.

   Inner: $2 * 3x = 6x$.

   Last: $2 * 3 = 6$.

   Combine like terms: $15x^2 + 21x + 6$.

   Example: Binomial * Polynomial.

   $(x + 3)(2x^2 - 5x - 2)$.

   First term: $x(2x^2 - 5x - 2) = 2x^3 - 5x^2 - 2x$.

   Second term: $3(2x^2 - 5x - 2) = 6x^2 - 15x - 6$.

   Added Together: $2x^3 + x^2 - 17x - 6$.

Distributive Property

When a variable is placed outside of a parenthetical set, it is *distributed* to all of the variables within that set.

$5(2y - 3x) = 10y - 15x$ [Can also be written as $(2y - 3x)5$].

$2x(3y + 1) + 6x = 6xy + 2x + 6x = 6xy + 8x$.

Combining Like Terms

This is exactly how it sounds! When a variable (x, y, z, r – anything!) is present in an equation, you can combine those terms with like variables.

$9r + 2r = 11r.$

$4x + 2y + 3 - 2x = 2x + 2y + 3.$

Arithmetic Sequence

Each term is equal to the previous term plus x.

Example: 2, 5, 8, 11.

$2 + 3 = 5; 5 + 3 = 8\ldots$ etc.

$x = 3.$

Fundamental Counting Principle

(The number of possibilities of an event happening) * (the number of possibilities of another event happening) = the total number of possibilities.

Example: If you take a multiple choice test with 5 questions, with 4 answer choices for each question, how many test result possibilities are there?

Solution: Question 1 has 4 choices; question 2 has 4 choices; etc.

4 *4 * 4 * 4 * 4 (one for each question) = **1024 possible test results**.

Linear Systems

There are two different methods can be used to solve multiple equation linear systems:

Substitution Method: This solves for one variable in one equation and substitutes it into the other equation. **Example**: Solve: $3y - 4 + x = 0$ and $5x + 6y = 11.$

1. Step 1: Solve for one variable:
   $3y - 4 = 0.$
   $3y + x = 4.$
   $x = 4 - 3y.$

2. Step 2: Substitute into the second equation and solve:
   $5(4 - 3y) + 6y = 11.$
   $20 - 15y + 6y = 11.$
   $20 - 9y = 11.$
   $-9y = -9.$
   $y = 1.$

3. Step 3: Substitute into the first equation:
   $3(1) - 4 + x = 0$.
   $-1 + x = 0$.
   $x = 1$.

   Solution: **$x = 1$, $y = 1$.**

Addition Method: Manipulate one of the equations so that when it is added to the other, one variable is eliminated. **Example**: Solve: $2x + 4y = 8$ and $4x + 2y = 10$.

1. Step 1: Manipulate one equation to eliminate a variable when added together:
   $-2(2x + 4y = 8)$.
   $-4x - 8y = -16$.
   $(-4x - 8y = -16) + (4x + 2y = 10)$.
   $-6y = -6$.
   $y = 1$.

2. Step 2: Plug into an equation to solve for the other variable:
   $2x + 4(1) = 8$.
   $2x + 4 = 8$.
   $2x = 4$.
   $x = 2$.

   Solution: **$x = 2$, $y = 1$.**

Quadratics

Factoring: Converting $ax^2 + bx + c$ to factored form. Find two numbers that are factors of c and whose sum is b. **Example**: Factor: $2x^2 + 12x + 18 = 0$.

1. Step 1: If possible, factor out a common monomial: $2(x^2 - 6x + 9)$.

2. Step 2: Find two numbers that are factors of 9 and which equal -6 when added:
   $2(x\ \ )(x\ \ )$.
   $-3\ \ , -3$

3. Step 3: Fill in the binomials. Be sure to check your answer signs.
   $2(x - 3)(x - 3)$.

4. Step 4: To solve, set each to equal 0.
   $x - 3 = 0$. So, $x = 3$.

Difference of squares:

$$a^2 - b^2 = (a + b)(a - b).$$

$$a^2 + 2ab + b^2 = (a + b)(a + b).$$

$$a^2 - 2ab + b^2 = (a - b)(a - b).$$

Permutations

The number of ways a set number of items can be arranged. Recognized by the use of a factorial (n!), with n being the number of items.

If n = 3, then 3! = 3 * 2 * 1 = 6. If you need to arrange n number of things but *x* number are alike, then n! is divided by *x*!

Example: How many different ways can the letters in the word **balance** be arranged?

Solution: There are 7 letters so *n!* = 7! and 2 letters are the same so *x!* = 2! Set up the equation:

$$\frac{7 * 6 * 5 * 4 * 3 * 2 * 1}{2 * 1} = \textbf{2540 ways}.$$

Combinations

To calculate total number of possible combinations use the formula:
n!/r! (n-r)!   n = # of objects   r = # of objects selected at a time

Example: If seven people are selected in groups of three, how many different combinations are possible?

Solution:
$$\frac{7 * 6 * 5 * 4 * 3 * 2 * 1}{(3 * 2 * 1)(7 - 3)} = \textbf{210 possible combinations}.$$

Know the Names of Sided Plane Figures:

- **3 Sides** – Triangle (or Trigon)
- **4 Sides** – Quadrilateral (or Tetragon)
- **5 Sides** – Pentagon
- **6 Sides** – Hexagon
- **7 Sides** – Heptagon
- **8 Sides** – Octagon
- **9 Sides** – Nonagon
- **10 Sides** – Decagon

- **11 Sides** – Hendecagon
- **12 Sides** – Dodecagon
- **13 Sides** Tridecagon
- **14 Sides** – Tetradecagon
- **15 Sides** – Pentadecagon
- **16 Sides** – Hexadecagon
- **17 Sides** – Heptadecagon
- **18 Sides** – Octadecagon

Geometry

- **Acute Angle**: Measures less than 90°.

- **Acute Triangle**: Each angle measures less than 90°.

- **Obtuse Angle**: Measures greater than 90°.

- **Obtuse Triangle**: One angle measures greater than 90°.

- **Adjacent Angles**: Share a side and a vertex.

- **Complementary Angles**: Adjacent angles that sum to 90°.

- **Supplementary Angles**: Adjacent angles that sum to 180°.

- **Vertical Angles**: Angles that are opposite of each other. They are always congruent (equal in measure).

- **Equilateral Triangle**: All angles are equal.

- **Isosceles Triangle**: Two sides and two angles are equal.

- **Scalene**: No equal angles.

- **Parallel Lines**: Lines that will never intersect. Y ‖ X means line Y is parallel to line X.

- **Perpendicular lines**: Lines that intersect or cross to form 90° angles.

- **Transversal Line**: A line that crosses parallel lines.

- **Bisector**: Any line that cuts a line segment, angle, or polygon exactly in half.

- **Polygon**: Any enclosed plane shape with three or more connecting sides (ex. a triangle).

- **Regular Polygon**: Has all equal sides and equal angles (ex. square).

- **Arc**: A portion of a circle's edge.

- **Chord**: A line segment that connects two different points on a circle.

- **Tangent**: Something that touches a circle at only one point without crossing through it.

- **Sum of Angles**: The sum of angles of a polygon can be calculated using $(n-1)180°$, when n = the number of sides.

Regular Polygons

Polygon Angle Principle: S = The sum of interior angles of a polygon with n-sides.

$S = (n - 2)180$.

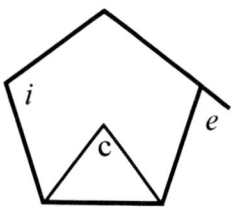

The measure of each central angle (c) is $360°/n$.
The measure of each interior angle (i) is $(n - 2)180°/n$.
The measure of each exterior angle (e) is $360°/n$.

To compare areas of similar polygons: $A_1/A_2 = (\text{side}_1/\text{side}_2)^2$.

Triangles

The angles in a triangle add up to $180°$.

Area of a triangle = ½ * b * h, or ½bh.

Pythagoras' Theorem: $a^2 + b^2 = c^2$.

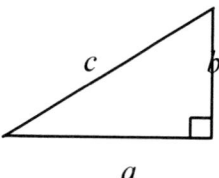

Trapezoids

Four-sided polygon, in which the bases (and only the bases) are parallel.
Isosceles Trapezoid – base angles are congruent.

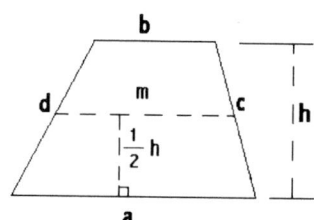

Area and Perimeter of a Trapezoid

$$m = \frac{1}{2}(a + b)$$

$$Area = \frac{1}{2}h * (a + b) = m * h$$

$$Perimeter = a + b + c + d = 2m + c + d$$

If m is the median then: $m \parallel \overline{AB}$ and $m \parallel CD$

Rhombus

Four-sided polygon, in which all four sides are congruent and opposite sides are parallel.

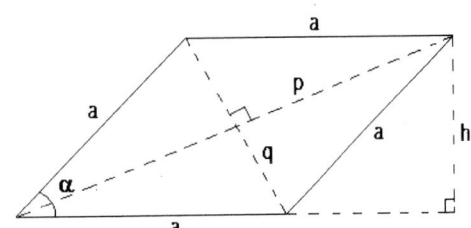

Area and Perimeter of a Rhombus

$Perimeter = 4a$

$Area = a^2 \sin \alpha = a * h = \dfrac{1}{2} pq$

$4a^2 = p^2 + q^2$

Rectangle

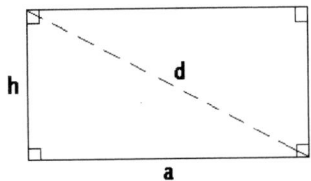

Area and Perimeter of a Rectangle

$d = \sqrt{a^2 + h^2}$

$a = \sqrt{d^2 - h^2}$

$h = \sqrt{d^2 - a^2}$

$Perimeter = 2a + 2h$

$Area = a \cdot h$

Square

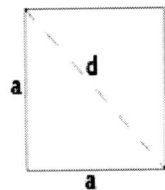

Area and Perimeter of a Square

$d = a\sqrt{2}$

$Perimeter = 4a = 2d\sqrt{2}$

$Area = a^2 = \dfrac{1}{2} d^2$

Circle

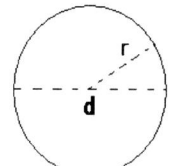

Area and Perimeter of a Circle

$d = 2r$

$Perimeter = 2\pi r = \pi d$

$Area = \pi r^2$

The product length of one chord
equals the product length of the other,
or:
AB=CD

Area and Perimeter of the Sector of a Circle

$\alpha = \dfrac{\theta \pi}{180} \ (rad)$

$s = r\alpha$

$Perimeter = 2r + s$

$Area = \dfrac{1}{2}\theta\, r^2 \ (radians) \ or \ \dfrac{n}{360}\pi r^2$

$length \ (l) \ of \ an \ arc \ \ l = \dfrac{\pi n r}{180} \ or \ \dfrac{n}{360} 2\pi r$

Area and Perimeter of the Segment of a Circle

$\alpha = \dfrac{\theta \pi}{180} \ (rad)$

$a = 2\sqrt{2hr - h^2}$

$a^2 = 2r^2 - 2r^2 cos\theta$

$s = r\alpha$

$h = r - \dfrac{1}{2}\sqrt{4r^2 - a^2}$

$Perimeter = a + s$

$Area = \dfrac{1}{2}[sr - a(r - h)]$

Cube

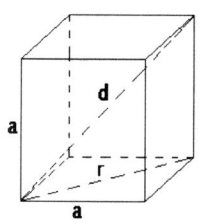

Area and Volume of a Cube

$r = a\sqrt{2}$

$d = a\sqrt{3}$

$Area = 6a^2$

$Volume = a^3$

Cuboid

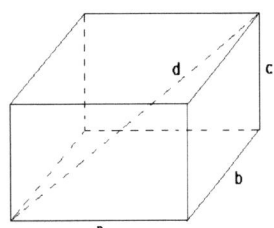

Area and Volume of a Cuboid
$$d = \sqrt{a^2 + b^2 + c^2}$$
$$A = 2(ab + ac + bc)$$
$$V = abc$$

Pyramid

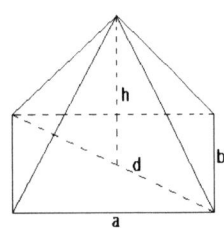

Area and Volume of a Pyramid
$$A_{lateral} = a\sqrt{h^2 + \left(\frac{b}{2}\right)^2} + b\sqrt{h^2 + \left(\frac{a}{2}\right)^2}$$
$$d = \sqrt{a^2 + b^2}$$
$$A_{base} = ab$$
$$A_{total} = A_{lateral} + A_{base}$$
$$V = \frac{1}{3}abh$$

Cylinder

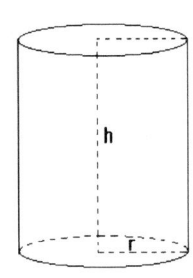

Area and Volume of a Cylinder
$$d = 2r$$
$$A_{surface} = 2\pi rh$$
$$A_{base} = 2\pi r^2$$
$$Area = A_{surface} + A_{base}$$
$$= 2\pi r(h + r)$$
$$Volume = \pi r^2 h$$

Cone

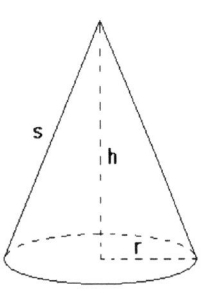

Area and Volume of a Cone
$$d = 2r$$
$$A_{surface} = \pi rs$$
$$A_{base} = \pi r^2$$
$$Area = A_{surface} + A_{base}$$
$$= 2\pi r(h + r)$$
$$Volume = \frac{1}{3}\pi r^2 h$$

Sphere

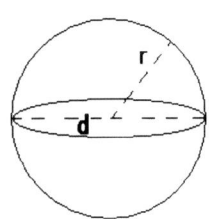

Area and Volume of a Sphere
$$d = 2r$$
$$A_{surface} = 4\pi r^2$$
$$Volume = \frac{4}{3}\pi r^3$$

Practice Drill: Mathematics Knowledge

ORDER OF OPERATIONS

1. $3 * (2 * 4^3) \div 4 = ?$

2. $(4^3 + 2 - 1) = ?$

3. $(5 * 3) * 1 + 5 = ?$

4. $(7^2 - 2^3 - 6) = ?$

5. $(5^3 + 7) * 2 = ?$

ALGEBRA

6. If Lynn can type a page in p minutes, how many pages can she do in 5 minutes?
   a) $5/p$.
   b) $p - 5$.
   c) $p + 5$.
   d) $p/5$.
   e) $1 - p + 5$.

7. If Sally can paint a house in 4 hours, and John can paint the same house in 6 hours, then how long will it take for both of them to paint the house together?
   a) 2 hours and 24 minutes.
   b) 3 hours and 12 minutes.
   c) 3 hours and 44 minutes.
   d) 4 hours and 10 minutes.
   e) 4 hours and 33 minutes.

8. The sales price of a car is $12,590, which is 20% off the original price. What is the original price?
   a) $14,310.40.
   b) $14,990.90.
   c) $15,290.70.
   d) $15,737.50.
   e) $16,935.80.

9. Solve the following equation for a: $2a \div 3 = 8 + 4a$.
   a) -2.4.
   b) 2.4.
   c) 1.3.
   d) -1.3.
   e) 0.

10. If $y = 3$, then what is $y^3(y^3 - y)$?
    a) 300.
    b) 459.
    c) 648.
    d) 999.
    e) 1099.

ALGEBRA 2

11. The average of three numbers is v. If one of the numbers is z and another is y, then what is the remaining number?
  a) $ZY - V$.
  b) $Z/V - 3 - Y$.
  c) $Z/3 - V - Y$.
  d) $3V - Z - Y$.
  e) $V - Z - Y$.

12. Mary is reviewing her algebra quiz. She has determined that one of her solutions is incorrect. Which one is it?
  a) $2x + 5(x - 1) = 9$; $x = 2$.
  b) $p - 3(p - 5) = 10$; $p = 2.5$.
  c) $4y + 3y = 28$; $y = 4$.
  d) $5w + 6w - 3w = 64$; $w = 8$.
  e) $t - 2t - 3t = 32$; $t = 8$.

13. What simple interest rate will Susan need to secure in order to make \$2,500 in interest on a \$10,000 principal over 5 years?
  a) 4%.
  b) 5%.
  c) 6%.
  d) 7%.
  e) 8%.

14. Which of the following is not a rational number?
  a) -4.
  b) 1/5.
  c) 0.8333333...
  d) 0.45.
  e) $\sqrt{2}$.

AVERAGES and ROUNDING

15. Round 907.457 to the nearest tens place.
  a) 908.0.
  b) 910.
  c) 907.5.
  d) 900.
  e) 907.46.

16. What is 1230.932567 rounded to the nearest hundredths place?
  a) 1200.
  b) 1230.9326.
  c) 1230.93.
  d) 1230.
  e) 1230.933.

17. Subtract the following numbers and round to the nearest tenths place:

134.679
− 45.548
− 67.8807

    a) 21.3.
    b) 21.25.
    c) -58.97.
    d) -59.0.
    e) 1.

18. What is the absolute value of −9?
    a) −9.
    b) 9.
    c) 0.
    d) −1.
    e) 1.

19. What is the median of the following list of numbers: 4, 5, 7, 9, 10, and 12?
    a) 6.
    b) 7.5.
    c) 7.8.
    d) 8.
    e) 9.

20. What is the mathematical average of the number of weeks in a year, seasons in a year, and the number of days in January?
    a) 36.
    b) 33.
    c) 32.
    d) 31.
    e) 29.

BASIC OPERATIONS

21. Add 0.98 + 45.102 + 32.3333 + 31 + 0.00009.
    a) 368.573.
    b) 210.536299.
    c) 109.41539.
    d) 99.9975.
    e) 80.8769543.

22. Find 0.12 ÷ 1.
    a) 12.
    b) 1.2.
    c) .12.
    d) .012.
    e) .0012.

23. $(9 \div 3) * (8 \div 4)$ equals:
  a) 1.
  b) 6.
  c) 72.
  d) 576.
  e) 752.

24. $6 * 0 * 5$ equals:
  a) 30.
  b) 11.
  c) 25.
  d) 0.
  e) 27.

25. $7.95 \div 1.5$ equals:
  a) 2.4.
  b) 5.3.
  c) 6.2.
  d) 7.3.
  e) 7.5.

ESTIMATION SEQUENCE

26. Describe the following sequence in mathematical terms: 144, 72, 36, 18, and 9.
  a) Descending arithmetic sequence.
  b) Ascending arithmetic sequence.
  c) Descending geometric sequence.
  d) Ascending geometric sequence.
  e) Miscellaneous sequence.

27. Which of the following is not a whole number followed by its square?
  a) 1, 1.
  b) 6, 36.
  c) 8, 64.
  d) 10, 100.
  e) 11, 144.

28. There are 12 more apples than oranges in a basket of 36 apples and oranges. How many apples are in the basket?
  a) 12.
  b) 15.
  c) 24.
  d) 28.
  e) 36.

29. Which of the following correctly identifies 4 consecutive odd integers, where the sum of the middle two integers is equal to 24?
  a) 5, 7, 9, 11.
  b) 7, 9, 11, 13.
  c) 9, 11, 13, 15.
  d) 11, 13, 15, 17.
  e) 13, 15, 17, 19.

30. What is the next number in the sequence? 6, 12, 24, 48, ___ .
   a) 72.
   b) 96.
   c) 108.
   d) 112.
   e) 124.

MEASUREMENT PRACTICE

31. If a rectangular house has a perimeter of 44 yards, and a length of 36 feet, what is the house's width?
   a) 30 feet.
   b) 18 yards.
   c) 28 feet.
   d) 32 feet.
   e) 36 yards.

32. What is the volume of a cylinder with a diameter of 1 foot and a height of 14 inches?
   a) 2104.91 cubic inches.
   b) 1584 cubic inches.
   c) 528 cubic inches.
   d) 904.32 cubic inches.
   e) 264 cubic inches.

33. What is the volume of a cube whose width is 5 inches?
   a) 15 cubic inches.
   b) 25 cubic inches.
   c) 64 cubic inches.
   d) 100 cubic inches.
   e) 125 cubic inches.

34. A can's diameter is 3 inches, and its height is 8 inches. What is the volume of the can?
   a) 50.30 cubic inches.
   b) 56.57 cubic inches.
   c) 75.68 cubic inches.
   d) 113.04 cubic inches.
   e) 226.08 cubic inches.

35. If the area of a square flowerbed is 16 square feet, then how many feet is the flowerbed's perimeter?
   a) 4.
   b) 12.
   c) 16.
   d) 20.
   e) 24.

PERCENT and RATIO

36. If a discount of 25% off the retail price of a desk saves Mark $45, what was desk's original price?
   a) $135.
   b) $160.
   c) $180.
   d) $210.
   e) $215.

37. A customer pays $1,100 in state taxes on a newly-purchased car. What is the value of the car if state taxes are 8.9% of the value?

    a) $9.765.45.
    b) $10,876.90.
    c) $12,359.55.
    d) $14,345.48.
    e) $15,745.45.

38. How many years does Steven need to invest his $3,000 at 7% to earn $210 in simple interest?

    a) 1 year.
    b) 2 years.
    c) 3 years.
    d) 4 years.
    e) 5 years.

39. 35% of what number is 70?

    a) 100.
    b) 110.
    c) 150.
    d) 175.
    e) 200.

40. What number is 5% of 2000?

    a) 50.
    b) 100.
    c) 150.
    d) 200.
    e) 250.

MATHEMATICS PRACTICE

41. How long will Lucy have to wait before for her $2,500 invested at 6% earns $600 in simple interest?

    a) 2 years.
    b) 3 years.
    c) 4 years.
    d) 5 years.
    e) 6 years.

42. If $r = 5z$ and $15z = 3y$, then r equals:

    a) y.
    b) $2y$.
    c) $5y$.
    d) $10y$.
    e) $15y$.

43. What is 35% of a number if 12 is 15% of a number?

    a) 5.
    b) 12.
    c) 28.
    d) 33.
    e) 62.

44. A computer is on sale for $1,600, which is a 20% discount off the regular price. The regular price is?
   a) $1800.
   b) $1900.
   c) $2000.
   d) $2100.
   e) $2200.

45. A car dealer sells an SUV for $39,000, which represents a 25% profit over the cost. What was the cost of the SUV to the dealer?
   a) $29,250.
   b) $31,200.
   c) $32,500.
   d) $33,800.
   e) $33,999.

46. Employees of a discount appliance store receive an additional 20% off of the lowest price on an item. If an employee purchases a dishwasher during a 15% off sale, how much will he pay if the dishwasher originally cost $450?
   a) $280.90.
   b) $287.
   c) $292.50.
   d) $306.
   e) $333.89.

47. The city council has decided to add a 0.3% tax on motel and hotel rooms. If a traveler spends the night in a motel room that costs $55 before taxes, how much will the city receive in taxes from him?
   a) 10 cents.
   b) 11 cents.
   c) 15 cents.
   d) 17 cents.
   e) 21 cents.

48. Grace has 16 jellybeans in her pocket. She has 8 red ones, 4 green ones, and 4 blue ones. What is the minimum number of jellybeans she must take out of her pocket to ensure that she has one of each color?
   a) 4.
   b) 8.
   c) 12.
   d) 13.
   e) 16.

49. You need to purchase a textbook for nursing school. The book costs $80.00, and the sales tax is 8.25%. You have $100. How much change will you receive back?
   a) $5.20.
   b) $7.35.
   c) $13.40.
   d) $19.95.
   e) $21.25.

50. Your supervisor instructs you to purchase 240 pens and 6 staplers for the nurse's station. Pens are purchased in sets of 6 for $2.35 per pack. Staplers are sold in sets of 2 for $12.95. How much will purchasing these products cost?
    a) $132.85.
    b) $145.75.
    c) $162.90.
    d) $225.25.
    e) $226.75.

51. Two cyclists start biking from a trailhead at different speeds and times. The second cyclist travels at 10 miles per hour and starts 3 hours after the first cyclist, who is traveling at 6 miles per hour. Once the second cyclist starts biking, how much time will pass before he catches up with the first cyclist?
    a) 2 hours.
    b) 4 ½ hours.
    c) 5 ¾ hours.
    d) 6 hours.
    e) 7 ½ hours.

52. Jim can fill a pool with water by the bucket-full in 30 minutes. Sue can do the same job in 45 minutes. Tony can do the same job in 1 ½ hours. How quickly can all three fill the pool together?
    a) 12 minutes.
    b) 15 minutes.
    c) 21 minutes.
    d) 23 minutes.
    e) 28 minutes.

53. A study reported that, in a random sampling of 100 women over the age of 35, 8 of the women had been married 2 or more times. Based on the study results, how many women over the age of 35 in a group of 5,000 would likely have been married 2 or more times?
    a) 55.
    b) 150.
    c) 200.
    d) 400.
    e) 600.

54. John is traveling to a meeting that is 28 miles away. He needs to be there in 30 minutes. How fast does he need to go in order to make it to the meeting on time?
    a) 25 mph.
    b) 37 mph.
    c) 41 mph.
    d) 49 mph.
    e) 56 mph.

55. If Steven can mix 20 drinks in 5 minutes, Sue can mix 20 drinks in 10 minutes, and Jack can mix 20 drinks in 15 minutes, then how much time will it take all 3 of them working together to mix the 20 drinks?
    a) 2 minutes and 44 seconds.
    b) 2 minutes and 58 seconds.
    c) 3 minutes and 10 seconds.
    d) 3 minutes and 26 seconds.
    e) 4 minutes and 15 seconds.

56. Jim's belt broke, and his pants are falling down. He has 5 pieces of string. He needs to choose the piece that will be able to go around his 36-inch waist. The piece must be at least 4 inches longer than his waist so that he can tie a knot in it, but it cannot be more that 6 inches longer so that the ends will not show from under his shirt. Which of the following pieces of string will work the best?
    a) 3 feet.
    b) 3 ¾ feet.
    c) 3 ½ feet.
    d) 3 ¼ feet.
    e) 2 ½ feet.

57. In the final week of January, a car dealership sold 12 cars. A new sales promotion came out the first week of February, and the dealership sold 19 cars that week. What was the percent increase in sales from the last week of January compared to the first week of February?
    a) 58%.
    b) 119%.
    c) 158%.
    d) 175%.
    e) 200%.

58. If two planes leave the same airport at 1:00 PM, how many miles apart will they be at 3:00 PM if one travels directly north at 150 mph and the other travels directly west at 200 mph?
    a) 50 miles.
    b) 100 miles.
    c) 500 miles.
    d) 700 miles.
    e) 1,000 miles.

59. During a 5-day festival, the number of visitors tripled each day. If the festival opened on a Thursday with 345 visitors, what was the attendance on that Sunday?
    a) 345.
    b) 1,035.
    c) 1,725.
    d) 3,105.
    e) 9,315.

60. What will it cost to carpet a room with indoor/outdoor carpet if the room is 10 feet wide and 12 feet long? The carpet costs $12.51 per square yard.
    a) $166.80.
    b) $175.90.
    c) $184.30.
    d) $189.90.
    e) $192.20.

61. Sally has three pieces of material. The first piece is 1 yard, 2 feet, and 6 inches long; the second piece is 2 yard, 1 foot, and 5 inches long; and the third piece is 4 yards, 2 feet, and 8 inches long. How much material does Sally have?
    a) 7 yards, 1 foot, and 8 inches.
    b) 8 yards, 4 feet, and 4 inches.
    c) 8 yards and 11 inches.
    d) 9 yards and 7 inches.
    e) 10 yards.

62. A vitamin's expiration date has passed. It was supposed to contain 500 mg of Calcium, but it has lost 325 mg of Calcium. How many mg of Calcium are left?
    a) 135 mg.
    b) 175 mg.
    c) 185 mg.
    d) 200 mg.
    e) 220 mg.

63. You have orders to give a patient 20 mg of a certain medication. The medication is stored as 4 mg per 5-mL dose. How many milliliters will need to be given?
    a) 15 mL.
    b) 20 mL.
    c) 25 mL.
    d) 30 mL.
    e) 35 mL.

64. You need a 1680 ft^3 aquarium, exactly, for your fish. The pet store has four choices of aquariums. The length, width, and height are listed on the box, but not the volume. Which of the following aquariums would fit your needs?
    a) 12 ft by 12 ft by 12 ft.
    b) 13 ft by 15 ft by 16 ft.
    c) 14 ft by 20 ft by 6 ft.
    d) 15 ft by 16 ft by 12 ft.
    e) 15 ft by 12 ft by 12 ft.

65. Sabrina's boss states that she will increase Sabrina's salary from $12,000 to $14,000 per year if Sabrina enrolls in business courses at a local community college. What percent increase in salary will result from Sabrina taking the business courses?
    a) 15%.
    b) 16.7%.
    c) 17.2%.
    d) 85%.
    e) 117%.

66. Jim works for $15.50 per hour at a health care facility. He is supposed to get a $0.75 per hour raise after one year of service. What will be his percent increase in hourly pay?
    a) 2.7%.
    b) 3.3%.
    c) 133%.
    d) 4.8%.
    e) 105%.

67. Edmond has to sell his BMW. He bought the car for $49,000, but sold it at 20% less. At what price did Edmond sell the car?
    a) $24,200.
    b) $28,900.
    c) $35,600.
    d) $37,300.
    e) $39,200.

68. At a company fish fry, half of those in attendance are employees. Employees' spouses make up a third of the attendance. What is the percentage of the people in attendance who are neither employees nor employees' spouses?

    a) 10.5%.
    b) 16.7%.
    c) 25%.
    d) 32.3%.
    e) 38%.

69. If Sam can do a job in 4 days that Lisa can do in 6 days and Tom can do in 2 days, how long would the job take if Sam, Lisa, and Tom worked together to complete it?

    a) 0.8 days.
    b) 1.09 days.
    c) 1.23 days.
    d) 1.65 days.
    e) 1.97 days.

70. Sarah needs to make a cake and some cookies. The cake requires 3/8 cup of sugar, and the cookies require 3/5 cup of sugar. Sarah has 15/16 cups of sugar. Does she have enough sugar, or how much more does she need?

    a) She has enough sugar.
    b) She needs 1/8 of a cup of sugar.
    c) She needs 3/80 of a cup of sugar.
    d) She needs 4/19 of a cup of sugar.
    e) She needs 1/9 of a cup of sugar.

Practice Drill: Mathematics Knowledge – Answers

1. 96	19. d)	37. c)	55. b)
2. 65	20. e)	38. a)	56. d)
3. 20	21. c)	39. e)	57. a)
4. 35	22. c)	40. b)	58. c)
5. 264	23. b)	41. c)	59. e)
6. a)	24. d)	42. a)	60. a)
7. a)	25. b)	43. c)	61. d)
8. d)	26. c)	44. c)	62. b)
9. a)	27. e)	45. b)	63. c)
10. c)	28. c)	46. d)	64. c)
11. d)	29. c)	47. d)	65. b)
12. e)	30. b)	48. d)	66. d)
13. b)	31. a)	49. c)	67. e)
14. e)	32. b)	50. a)	68. b)
15. b)	33. e)	51. b)	69. b)
16. c)	34. b)	52. d)	70. a)
17. a)	35. c)	53. d)	
18. b)	36. c)	54. e)	

Final Thoughts

In the end, we know that you will be successful in taking the ASVAB. Although the process can be challenging, if you continue with hard work and dedication, you will find that your efforts will pay off.

If you are struggling after reading this book and following our guidelines, we sincerely hope that you will take note of our advice and seek additional help.

Start by asking friends about the resources that they are using. If you are still not reaching the score you want, consider getting the help of a tutor.

We wish you the best of luck and happy studying.

Most importantly, we honor your decision to join the armed forces – you put a lot of work into getting there, and your efforts and drive are more than admirable.

Sincerely,
The Accepted, Inc. Team

CPSIA information can be obtained at www.ICGtesting.com
Printed in the USA
LVOW09s1529210214

374700LV00014B/554/P